Michael Paget Baxter

Louis Napoleon the Destined Monarch of the World

Foreshown in prophecy to confirm a seven years' covenant with the Jews about seven years before the millenium

Michael Paget Baxter

Louis Napoleon the Destined Monarch of the World
Foreshown in prophecy to confirm a seven years' covenant with the Jews about seven years before the millenium

ISBN/EAN: 9783337246068

Printed in Europe, USA, Canada, Australia, Japan

Cover: Foto ©ninafisch / pixelio.de

More available books at **www.hansebooks.com**

LOUIS NAPOLEON
THE
DESTINED MONARCH
OF THE WORLD,

FORESHOWN IN PROPHECY TO CONFIRM A SEVEN YEARS' COVE-
NANT WITH THE JEWS ABOUT SEVEN YEARS BEFORE THE MIL-
LENIUM, AND (AFTER THE RESURRECTION OF SAINTS, AND
ASCENSION OF WATCHFUL CHRISTIANS HAS TAKEN PLACE
TWO YEARS AND FROM THREE TO FIVE WEEKS AFTER THE
COVENANT,) SUBSEQUENTLY TO BECOME COMPLETELY
SUPREME OVER ENGLAND AND MOST OF AMERICA,
AND ALL CHRISTENDOM, AND TO CAUSE A GREAT
PERSECUTION OF CHRISTIANS DURING THE LAT-
TER HALF OF THE SEVEN YEARS, UNTIL HE
FINALLY PERISHES AT THE DESCENT OF
CHRIST, AT THE END OF THE

WAR OF ARMAGEDDON,
ABOUT OR SOON AFTER
1874.

INCLUDING AN EXAMINATION OF THE VIEWS OF BISHOPS IRE-
NÆUS, HIPPOLYTUS, VICTORINUS, PRIMASIUS, REVS. G. S. FA-
BER, EDWARD IRVING, E. BICKERSTETH, T. BIRKS, C. MAIT-
LAND, DR. SEISS, DEBURGH, C. MOLYNEUX, J. KELLY, R.
A. PURDON, D. MCCAUSLAND, J. H. FRERE, SIR E.
DENNY, MAJOR PHILLIPS, JUDGE STRANGE, DR.
TREGELLES, ETC.

WITH NINE DIAGRAMS AND TWO MAPS.

———•———

Nineteenth Thousand.

———•———

BY THE
REV. M. BAXTER.
AUTHOR OF THE "COMING BATTLE," "COMING WONDERS," ETC

PHILADELPHIA:
JAMES S. CLAXTON,
No. 1214 Chestnut Street.
MORGAN & CHASE, 38 LUDGATE HILL.
1867.

THE YEAR-DAY FULFILMENT OF THE APOCALYPSE.

The siege of Jericho by Joshua contains a concentrated bird's-eye view, or type, of the history developed in the Revelation. The character of successive periods of the church is typified by the seven churches of Asia. The prophetic visions are seven.

(This is very nearly a fac-simile of the diagram by the Revs. E. Bickersteth and T. Birks.)

EPISTLES TO THE CHURCHES, CHAPTERS I. II. III.
GENERAL INTRODUCTION, CHAPTER IV.

[1.] THE SEALS.	[2.] THE TRUMPETS.	[3.] THE CHURCH.
THE KINGDOM OF PROVIDENCE, CHRIST THE LAMB OF GOD.	THE KINGDOM OF THE WORLD, CHRIST, THE ANGEL OF THE COVENANT.	KINGDOM OF THE SPIRIT. CHRIST THE SON OF MAN.
Introduction, ch. v. 4 to 14.	Introduction viii. 2 to 6.	The Travail of Church, vii 1 to 4.
Sealed Book, the Secret Councils of the World's Redemption.	*Christ the Priest.* Fire cast on the earth, 70–180, Luke xii. 49. Warning Earthquake, 180 to 250.	Birth of the seed of the woman, ver. 5.
Seal I. vi. 1, 2. Victories of the Church Militant, 33 to 323-4. *Ephesus*		Flight to wilderness begun, ver. 6.
	Trumpet I. viii. 7. Gothic Invasions, 250 to 365.	Tw: witnesses, the two Testaments, their character and office. Ch. xi. 4 to 13. War in heaven, v. 7, 8.
Seal II. vi. 3. 324 to 534. *Smyrna*	Trumpet II. viii. 8, 9. Fall of Rome, 365–412.	Satan cast down, ver. 9 to 12. Paganism overthrown, 323-4. Eagle's wings given to the woman, ver. 14, 395.
Discord of the Church. Sword sent. Mat. x.34. Seal III. vi. 5, 6. Spiritual Famine of the Church, 534 to 803.	Trumpet III. viii. 9, 412–476. Heresies of the East.	Protection of the two empires. Flood from mouth of dragon, ver. 15. 16.
Seal IV. vi. 7, 8. Spiritual Desolation of the Church, 1073 to 1438. *Thyatira* For four first seals, see Zech. vi. 1, 5.	Trumpet IV. viii 12, 476. Extinction of the Western Emperorship. Woe Trumpets 1260 days.	Commencement of their prophesying in sackcloth (a foreign tongue) 534-8 Deluge of Arian nations. Commencement of 1260 days. Rise of Beast from the sea, xiii. 1 to 10, 476. Civil Apostasy of the West.
Seal V. vi. 9 to 11. Cry of the Martyrs, -1658.	Trumpet V. ix. 1 to 12, 609–936. Saracen Woe, 620–936.	Rise of Beast from the earth, xiii. 11 to 18.
Seal VI. vi. 12 to viii. 1793–8. French Revolution. Pause before Judgment, 1815, vii. 1 to 3. The 144,000 sealed. Resurrection of saints and Translation of Wise Virgins. *Sardis*	Trumpet VI. ix. 13, 1063–1843-4. Turkish Woe. *Christ the Prophet,* x. 1 to 4. A time no longer. Prophet risen. Temple measured. Earthquake warning. Remnant affrighted. *Philadelphia* 1793-8 to 1843-8.	Their slaughter and exposure of their dead bodies for 3½ years from 1794 to 1802. Ecclesiastical Empire of the West. First Angel message, xiv. 6, 7. Second Angel message, ver. 8. Third Angel message, ver. 9 to 11.
Seal VII. viii. 1, 1863–8 to 1871-3 Pause at the return of Christ. Events unfolded, xix. xx. Second Translation.	Trumpet VII. xi.15, 1863–8 to 1871-3. Resurrection and first Translation. Napoleonic Woe. *Christ the King.* Second Translation. *Laodicea* 1863-8 to 1871-8	Resurrection and Ascension in 1793-1802. Fourth and Fifth Angels, 14 to 16. The harvest of mercy. Sixth and Seventh Angels, 16 to 20. Vintage of Wrath.

[4.] THE VIALS.
INTRODUCTION, chap. XV.

The Day of Wrath, ver. 1, 7.	The Temple opened, ver. 5, 6.	The Harvest and Vintage. xiv. and xvi. 15, 19.
Vial I. xvi. 1, 2.	A grievous sore.	Eruption of Infidelity and Anarchy, 1792-3.
Vial II. v. 3.	Sea turned to blood.	Bloodshed and massacre in France, 1793-4.
Vial III. ver. 4, 7.	Rivers turned to blood.	Education become murderous, 1795.
Vial IV. ver. 8, 9.	Scorching Heat.	Imperial Despotism of Bonaparte, 1804.
Vial V. ver. 10, 11.	Kingdom of Beast.	Retributive justice on France, 1814.
Vial VI. ver. 12, 16.	Euphrates dried.	Ruin of Turkish Empire, 1821-64-8. Restoration and first translation at the coming of Christ in the air, 1866-8.
Vial VII. ver. 17 to 21.	Fall of Babylon.	Armageddon War 1867 to 1871 & second Translation and Descent of Christ about 1871-8.

[5.] *Vision of first Revealing Angel.* xvii. 1 to xix. THE FALL OF BABYLON.	[6.] *Vision of Christ the Word.* xix. 1 to xxi. 2. THE APPEARING AND KINGDOM OF CHRIST.	[7.] *Vision of last Revealing Angel.* xxi. 9 to xxii. 15. THE HEAVENLY JERUSALEM.

Interpretation of the Seven Heads of the Beast—Rev. xvii. 10, 11 and xiii. 3.—1st. Kings—752 B.C. 2d. Consuls. 3d. Decemvirs. 4th. Dictators. 5th. Tribunes. 6th. The Roman Emperorship. 7th. Napoleonic Dynasty under Napoleon I., 1806 to 1815. 8th, or 7th revived. The Napoleonic Dynasty under Napoleon III., 1852 to 1871-2.

PREFACE TO THE THIRD EDITION.

This prophetical treatise was first published in July, 1861, and is now enlarged to nearly four times its original size. Chapter II was published as an addition to it in August, 1862.

According to the views here presented, and which were briefly stated by the author in "The Coming Battle," printed in 1860, it is considered to be certain that Louis Napoleon will be the Personal Antichrist, and that he will soon make a seven-years' Covenant with the Jews (Dan. ix. 27), seven years and 2½ months before his destruction by the descent of Christ, at Armageddon, at the End of this Dispensation. The Ascension of the 144,000 Wise Virgins is expected to occur two years and from three to five weeks after the date of the Covenant (1 Thess. iv., Rev. xiv., Matt. xxv.).

Opportunity is here taken to mention, that ANY ONE IS AT LIBERTY TO RE-PUBLISH THIS OR ANY OTHER OF THE AUTHOR'S HITHERTO PUBLISHED TREATISES; and it is suggested to those who realize the momentous character of the crisis at which we have arrived, that they can co-operate in the diffusion of these views, and render an important service to ministers and others in their respective neighbourhoods, by sending them a copy of this work.

May the Lord Jesus Christ prosper this publication to the advancement of His glory and the good of His Church, and increasingly guide us into all truth by His Holy Spirit. The prayers of God's people are requested for the bestowment of the Divine blessing upon the circulation of this work, and upon its author.

PREFACE TO THE NINTH THOUSAND.

It is inexpressibly important, during the present postal facilities for spreading information, before they are greatly impeded by approaching wars and revolutions, to send this book, or the abridgement of it, or the author's other pamphlets, such as "The Coming Battle," to ministers, especially in country places and distant colonies, where such information is not easily attainable. With this view any sums of money expressly sent for the Gratis Circulation of these prophetic works, addressed to the Rev. M. BAXTER, Box 1199, Philadelphia, Pa., will be expended in sending these publications by post to ministers, according to the directions of the donors, or according to the printed ministerial lists of the different denominations, as far as such contributions may enable.

Any communications for the Author will reach him by the above address.

March, 1865.

SYNOPSIS.

INTRODUCTORY REMARKS .... 1 to 10

CHAPTER I.

TEN SCRIPTURE PROOFS THAT LOUIS NAPOLEON IS THE DESTINED MONARCH OF THE WORLD AND PERSONAL ANTICHRIST, FORESHOWN IN PROPHECY, TO INSTITUTE AN EXTERMINATING PERSECUTION AGAINST CHRISTIANS DURING THE FINAL $3\frac{1}{2}$ YEARS, AND TO BE ALMOST UNIVERSALLY WORSHIPPED AS GOD, AND THEN TO BE DESTROYED BY CHRIST AT THE BATTLE OF ARMAGEDDON.

Brief Sketch of his past Life............................ 11, 12

I. Because he represents the revived Napoleon dynasty — the Seventh-restored, or Eighth ruling Head of the Beast or Roman Empire—and is thus comprehensively termed the Beast itself, and is foreshown to be the Personal Antichrist, who shall gain "power over all kindreds and tongues and nations," and fiercely persecute Christians, and be almost universally worshipped for $3\frac{1}{2}$ years, and then perish at Christ's descent at Armageddon, (Rev. xiii. 3–8, xvii. 7–14, xix. 20.) .... 13 to 20

II. Because he corresponds with the predicted character of the Personal Antichrist in respect of his warlike prowess, his insatiable ambition, and his vast military power, (Rev. xiii. 3, 4; Is. xiv. 16, 17.)................................... 20 to 22

III. Because he has obtained actual possession of the city of Rome, (Rev. xvii. 7–11.)..................................... 22 to 24

IV. Because he apparently protects and supports the Pope, but yet suffers him to be plundered, and gradually stripped of his temporal power, (Rev. xvii. 1–18.) .... 24 to 28

V. Because the whole extent of the original Roman Empire is becoming subordinated to his control, and is evidently approaching its final division into ten kingdoms, which, according to Rev. xvii. 12—14, are to give their power and strength to the Eighth Head during the closing 3½ years. (The ten toes, Dan. ii. 40—44, and ten horns, Dan. vii. 23—25; Rev. xvii. 12—14) 28 to 34

VI. Because, in respect to his name, he fulfils the prophecy, that the name of the Eighth Head, or Antichrist, should be in the Greek tongue, *Apollyon*, (or *Apoleon*,) and should, numerically, be equal to the number 666, (Rev. ix. 11, xiii. 18.).... 34 to 38

VII. Because his Grecian extraction, his sphinx-like impenetrability of countenance, his addiction to the practice of Spiritualism, and his deceptive professions of a pacific policy, identify him with the description given of the Personal Antichrist in Dan. viii. 9—25.................................... 38 to 45

VII. Because his sudden elevation from obscurity to great power, his obvious determination to sieze Palestine, and also his acquisition of extensive dominions, and of valuable gold fields in the north of Africa, are in accordance with the prophecies in Dan. xi. 21—45, regarding the Personal Antichrist......... 45 to 50

IX. Because the rise of a French Emperor a few years before 1864—68, who should revive the wounded extinct Seventh Head, or Napoleon dynasty, and become the Personal Antichrist, or Eighth Head was foreshown from Rev. xiii. 3, and xvii. 10, 11, by prophetic writers, such as Faber, Frere, Gauntlett, etc., as early as thirty years before Louis Napoleon's accession to the throne of France... 50 to 56

X. Because the End of this Dispensation is shown by ten dates and four septenaries, to be about A. D. 1871-3 and as the Personal Antichrist is to be revealed seven years previously by making a Covenant with the Jews, therefore, at the present time, (1861—62,) he must be approaching the time of his manifestation, and no living person corresponds with his predicted character except Louis Napoleon................................ 56 to 59

Practical exhortation to those who are unready for the impending Advent of Christ, (from McCheyne's Sermons.)........ 60 to 66

Map of Europe.. 67

CHAPTER II.

TWENTY COMING EVENTS, ARRANGED IN THE CONSECUTIVE ORDER IN WHICH THEY ARE FORESHOWN IN PROPHECY TO OCCUR DURING THE FINAL SEVEN YEARS AND $2\frac{1}{2}$ MONTHS OF THIS DISPENSATION, AND WHICH COMMENCE WITH THE DATE OF THE SEVEN-YEARS' COVENANT, AND END WITH ANTICHRIST'S DESTRUCTION AT THE DESCENT OF CHRIST AT ARMAGEDDON.

The relative positions of these twenty events are ascertained, in many cases, by deducing the future literal-day fulfilment of the prophecies from their past year-day fulfilment, as shown in diagram 4. These positions are here shown by giving their distance from the date of the Covenant, as a common standard of reference.

Diagram 2—Chronological Map of these twenty events........ 68

I. The Confirmation of a seven years' Covenant between Napoleon and the Jews, seven years and $2\frac{1}{2}$ months before the End, (Dan. ix. 27,—the $2\frac{1}{2}$ months, or 75 days, being the excess of the 1335 over the 1260 days, or latter half of the seven years, Dan. xii. 7—12.) .... 70 to 72

II. Renewal of the Jewish sacrifices and temple-worship at Jerusalem 2300 days before the cleansing of the Sanctuary, (Dan. viii. 13, 14, Is. lxvi. 8,) that is, about 9 months, or 9 months and 25 days after the Covenant..................... 72 to 74

III. The complete drying up of the Turkish Empire, consisting partly of the separation of Syria from Turkey, within about two years after the Covenant, (year-day, Rev. xvi. 12.)...... 74, 75

IV. The successful invasion of Egypt by Napoleon within about a year or two after the Covenant, (Dan. xi. 25—28.) .... 75 to 77

V. The coming of Christ in the air, the Resurrection of the deceased saints, and Translation or Ascension of the 144,000 Wise Virgins, or Man-child, (Rev. xii. 5, Rev. xiv. 1—5, 1 Thess. iv. 16, 17, Matt. xxv. 10,) two years and from four to six weeks after the Covenant.. 77 to 81

VI. An unprecedented Revival of Religion, and of Missionary effort among the Foolish Virgins, and the Unconverted that are left on the earth after the Translation of the Wise Virgins, (literal-day Rev. vi. 2, xiv. 6—11; the latter passage seems to imply that some angels, or glorified saints will then preach to mankind.).. 81 to 83

The next six events will take place almost entirely within the concluding seven months of the first 3½ years of the 7 years of the Covenant-week.

VII. Commencement of Astounding Physical Phenomena, such as hail and fire falling on the earth, a third part of salt and fresh water becoming blood, and a third part of the luminaries being eclipsed during the first four literal-day trumpets, (Rev. viii.) between the 33d and 42nd month after the Covenant... 83 to 86

VIII. War in Heaven, and Expulsion of Satan and his legions from the air on to the earth about two years and eleven months after the Covenant, (Rev. xii. 7—13.).................. 86, 87

IX. Flight of many of the saints into the wilderness, where they will be fed and preserved during the subsequent 3½ years' persecution, (Rev. xii. 6, 14;) the wilderness, very possibly, being some remote region of the United States. This hegira will be during part of the 3d year, and first half of the 4th year after the Covenant.. 87 to 89

X. The Fall of Babylon, or transformation of Popery, into what may be termed Napoleonism, for the Pope will institute and establish the worship of Napoleon and his image throughout all the earth, principally during the last half of the seven years following the Covenant, (Rev. xiii., xviii. 2.) .... 89 to 97

XI. Complete acquirement by Napoleon of supreme power over Great Britain, and in a less degree over a considerable part of America, within 3½ years after the Covenant, (Rev. xiii. 7, xvii. 12, 13.)..) . 97 to 107

XII. Division of the entire territory of the old Roman Empire into ten kingdoms, Great Britain, France, Spain, Italy, Austria, Greece, Egypt, Syria, the rest of Turkey, and most probably Tripoli with Tunis, and the union of their ten kings in a congressional confederation under Napoleon, within 3½ years after the Covenant, (Rev. xvii. 12, 13, xiii. 1, Dan. vii. 24.) 107 to 116

The next eight events occur almost entirely within the latter half of the Covenant-week of 7 years, that is, the 3½ years of Great Tribulation, or Antichristian persecution, and also the supplementary 2¼ months.

SYNOPSIS.

XIII. Assault upon Jerusalem by Napoleon, the Antichrist, between 3 years and 8½ years after the Covenant, and substitution of the worship of his image in the place of the Jewish sacrifices, after which, during the latter 3½ years of the 7 years, all the ungodly, or non-elect, who dwell upon the prophetic earth, (at least the above-mentioned ten kingdoms, and probably all Christendom,) will worship him, (Rev. xiii. 5—8,) and nearly all within the prophetic earth who refuse to worship him will be killed. (Rev. xiii., xi. 2, 3, xii. 6, 14, vi. 3—11; Dan. vii. 25, xii. 1—7, viii. 24, xi. 31—45, ix. 27; Ezek. xxxviii.; Zech. xiv. 1, 2; Matt. xxiv. 15—28; Mark xiii. 14—23.) ..... 116 to 124

XIV. The prophesying of the two witnesses, (Elijah and another,) during the whole of Napoleon, the Antichrist's, 3½ years' universal reign and persecution, upon the expiration of which they are slain, but after 3½ days raised to life and caught up to heaven. (Rev. xi. 3—12, Mal. iv. 5.)................ 124 to 127

XV. The First Woe during the fifth literal-day trumpet, or the tormenting of the ungodly by supernatural locusts for five months, (Rev. ix. 1-10,) and the hurting of them apparently for five months more, (Rev. ix. 10-12.) This Woe begins three years and 9½ months after the Covenant................. 127 to 131

XVI. The Second Woe during the sixth literal-day trumpet, or the conflicts between countless invading forces from beyond the Euphrates and the armies of Napoleon's ten kingdoms, principally constituting the Armageddon War, and causing the slaughter of the third part of men within the first year and month, (Rev. ix. 13-21, xi. 14.) This Woe continues altogether twice a year and month, as a period of both rise and fall, and begins five years after the Covenant.............................. 131 to 134

XVII. Conversion of upward of from 15 to 50 million persons, chiefly among the heathen, during the five years between the two translations, and especially during the final year. (Literal-day, Rev. vii., x., xiv. 4, 15; Joel ii. 28–32; Is. xxvi. 9.).. 134 to 139

XVIII. Darkening of the constellations and a great earthquake, (Rev. vi. 12, xi. 13,) simultaneously with the commencement of the seven successive literal-day Vials, which during the final 2½ months (1) afflict the Napoleonists with sores, (2) turn all fresh and (3) all salt water into blood, (4) produce intolerable heat, (5) cover Europe with darkness, (6) dry up the literal Euphrates, and (7) cause an unparalleled earthquake and hail-storm, and the Battle of Armageddon. (Rev. xvi.) These final 2½ months commence seven years after the Covenant. .... 140 to 144

XIX. Visible manifestation of Christ coming in the clouds of heaven, and Second Translation of living saints about five days, before this Dispensation ends, and the Millennium begins. (Matt. xxiv. 81; Mark xiii. 26, 27; Luke xxi. 27; Dan. vii. 13; literal-day, Rev. vii. 9–17, xi. 15–19, xvi. 15, xiv. 16.) This occurs seven years, two months, and ten days after the Covenant.. 144 to 150

XX. The Third Woe during the seventh literal-day trumpet, and within the final 3½ days, consisting principally in the transformation of the territory adjoining Rome into a perpetual lake of fire, (Rev. xix. 3,) and the destruction of Napoleon and the Pope and five-sixths of their vast armies at the Battle of Armageddon, when Christ will descend on the earth and slay all incorrigible rejectors of the Gospel. (Isaiah xxxiv., lxvi.; Ezek. xxxix.; Zech. xiv.; Rev. xi. 15, xvi. 17, xix.) This Woe terminates seven years and 2½ months from the date of the Covenant.. 150 to 154

The ensuing Millennial dispensation, or Day of the Lord, or Day of Judgment, lasting for a thousand years, (2 Peter iii. 8, 10, Rev. xx.,) with the burning of the earth partially at its commencement, but chiefly at its close, (Rev. xxi. 1;) BLESSEDNESS of the Millennial earth, (1.) Physically; (Amos ix. 13, Joel iii. 18,) its population probably being 150 times greater than 1300 million, as at present. (2.) Politically and socially: Jesus Christ, (Dan. vii. 14, Zech. xiv. 4, 9,) with his glorified, raised, and translated saints dwelling in the Heavenly Jerusalem, (Rev. xxi.,) and reigning over the earth's unglorified mortal inhabitants who will be the descendants of the ungodly that will be spared and converted at his Second Advent, (Is. lxvi. 19, Zech. xiv. 16, Rev. xx.) (3.) Spiritually: Christianity universally prevalent, (Is. xi. 9, Hab. ii. 14, Rev. xi. 15, xx.) (4.) As regards the Jews: their spiritual and earthly prosperity, (see also Is., iv., xi., xii., xxxv., liv., lx., lxi., lxv., lxvi.; Ezek. xl. to xlviii., Jer. xxxii., xxxi., xxxiii., etc.).......... 154 to 161

Purdon's description of the Millennium; Practical remarks: necessity of becoming born again, or converted, (John iii. 8,) and of constantly praying to Jesus, and studying the Scriptures; Importance of open air preaching .... 161 to 172

CHAPTER III.

EVIDENCE FROM MORE THAN FIFTY EXPOSITORS SHOWING THAT DANIEL'S SEVENTIETH WEEK OF SEVEN YEARS WILL BE FULFILLED WITHIN ALMOST EXACTLY THE FINAL SEVEN YEARS OF THIS GENTILE DISPENSATION, AND WILL COMMENCE WITH A SEVEN YEARS' COVENANT BEING CONFIRMED BETWEEN THE PERSONAL ANTICHRIST AND THE JEWS. THEREFORE LOUIS NAPOLEON, IF HE IS THE PERSONAL ANTICHRIST, WILL CONFIRM A SEVEN YEARS' COVENANT WITH THE JEWS ABOUT SEVEN YEARS BEFORE THE END.

Diagram 3, showing the fulfilment of the 70 weeks.......... 174

Preliminary Observations—Fulfilment of the Seventy Weeks explained—Distinction between the Year-day and Literal-day systems of Interpretation............................ 175 to 183

All the following fifty books or expositors state or imply Daniel's 70th week (Dan. ix. 27) to be the last seven years of this dispensation, closing with the almost immediate destruction of Antichrist by Christ's descent upon the earth; and the greater part of them expressly specify the Personal Antichrist to be the confirmer of the covenant with the Jews for seven years. They also mostly hold that its latter half is the 3½ years of the Great Tribulation, or Antichrist's persecuting reign, as described in Dan. vii. 25, xii. 7; Rev. xi. 2, 3, xii. 6, 14, xiii. 5, and that the Personal or Infidel Antichrist is a single individual, an avowed infidel, (1 John ii. 22,) and the same person as the Little Horn of Dan. vii., and Dan. viii., the Wilful King of Dan. xi., the Eighth Head of the Beast, which is also called the Beast itself, in Rev. xiii., and xvii., and the Man of Sin, (2 Thess. ii.,) who will be worshipped in the Jewish Temple, and whose image, the abomination of desolation, will be set up there, as described in Matt. xxiv., and Mark xiii.; they generally state the Two Witnesses, (Rev. xi.,) to be two literal persons who will prophesy on earth during Antichrist's 3½ years' tyranny. The extracts here quoted from these writers give their statements to this effect at some length.

(1.) Irenæus, Bishop in the Primitive Church, (A. D. 180;) Antichrist to lay waste all the world during his half-week, or 3½ years' tyranny, then to perish at Christ's appearing....... 184

SYNOPSIS.

(2.) Hippolytus, Bishop of Ostia, (A. D. 220;). Antichrist to persecute Christians, and desolate the world during the last halfweek, and to be opposed by the Witnesses, Elias and Enoch, 185

(3) Origen, (225,).. 186, 187

(4.) Victorinus, Bishop of Pettau, (A. D. 290;) 70th week future; Antichrist's image to be set up like Nebuchadnezzar's, and to speak; His mark to be branded upon men.................. 187

(5) and (6.) Apollinarius, Bishop of Laodicea, (380,) and Primasius, Bishop of the Carthagenian Province, (500,)......... 188

(7.) Rev. Dr. Burgh, of the Church of England, author of "Second Advent Lectures," (1832,) "Exposition of Revelation," etc.; The Seventy Weeks Expounded; Bishop Horsley's statement that Antichrist and his image would be worshipped........ 189 to 191

(8) and (9.) Rev. E. Bickersteth, and Rev. T. Birks, of the Church of England: their united statement in Bickersteth's "Guide to the Prophecies," (1839,) as to the futurity of the 70th week, and the Infidel Antichrist's 3½ years' persecution during its last half, before which the Wise Virgins would be removed... 191 to 195

(10.) J. Darby, author of "The Hopes of the Church," (1842,) 194

(11.) Sir Edward Denny, Baronet, author of "Companion to the Chart of Seventy Weeks," (1845;) The Seventy Weeks fully explained; The coming of Elias future.............. 195 to 202

(12.) Dr. S. P. Tregelles, LL.D., author of "Remarks on Daniel;" Complete exposition of the 70 weeks; Jewish sacrifices to recommence 2300 days before the End, (Dan. viii. 14;) Antichrist's literal image to speak and breathe, and fire to be brought down on the earth; his appalling persecution of Christians, 202 to 208

(13.) Henry Kelsall, M. D., author of "The Antichrist," (1846;) 70th week future; Animal magnetism, or Mesmerism, the revival of sorcery and witchcraft which is to co-exist with Antichrist's speaking image; Those killed who will not worship the image; Antichrist to subdue England............ 208 to 211

(14.) Rev. C. Maitland, of the Church of England, author of "the "Apostles' School of Prophetic Interpretation," (1849;) 70th week; Graphic description of Antichrist's delusive miracles, sanguinary persecution, and final overthrow; The tormenting locusts; Slaughter of the Two Witnesses; Battle of Armageddon.. 211 to 219

(15.) B. W. Newton, author of "Prospects of the Ten Kingdoms," (1849;) Detailed exposition of the 70 weeks; Antichrist to abolish the restored Jewish sacrifices; His 3½ years' persecution of those who will not worship him; Five of his ten horn or toe kingdoms to be formed out of the Eastern Roman Empire, and five out of the Western; England, France, Spain, Greece, Egypt, Syria, the rest of Turkey, and Tunis with Tripoli, to be eight of his ten kingdoms; all the ten to have clay-iron, or democratic-monarchic governments, (already verified in Italy;) Impending separation of Ireland from England........ 219 to 228

(16.) R. A. Purdon, the eminent author of "The Last Vials," (published monthly, since 1845.) His remarkable forestatement in May, 1852, that Louis Napoleon, as the Eighth Head of the Beast, must necessarily become Emperor, and regain supremacy over the Empire of Napoleon, revived in its full territorial extent, and over the countries that formed the Babylonian, Medo-Persian, Grecian, and Roman Empires; also, that he would make a seven years' Covenant with the Jews, and in the midst of the seven years, set up his image, the Abomination, in the Jewish Temple, and after fiercely persecuting Christians for 3½ years, would fall and perish; England to be subject to him, (see also page 184)................................ 228 to 232

(17.) Rev. James Kelly, of the Church of England, author of "The Apocalypse Interpreted," "Lectures on Prophecy," (1850;) The 70th week; The majority of mankind literally to worship Antichrist's image, and to receive his mark, (Rev. xiii.).. 232 to 234

(18.) W. Kelly "The Prospect," (1849;) 70th week future... 234

(19.) Judge T. Lumisden Strange, author of "The Light of Prophecy," (1852;) The 70 weeks expounded.......... 235 to 237

(20.) Rev. Capel Molyneux, of the Church of England, author of "Israel's Future," "The World to come," (1852;) 70th week future; Antichrist's 3½ years' murderous persecution of those who refuse to worship him or his image; Simultaneous counter-testimony of the Two Witnesses, Elias and another.. 237 to 239

(21.) An English work, "Armageddon, or a Warning Voice from the Last Battle-field of Nations," by a Cambridge Master of Arts,

SYNOPSIS.

3 vols. octavo, (1857–8.) An exposition of unsurpassed ability and correctness; Napoleon III. shown to be the Personal Antichrist, who will make a Covenant with the Jews for 7 years, and during the latter 3½ years will slaughter those who will not worship him, or his image, or receive his mark: the Two Witnesses, meanwhile, testifying on earth against him, but at last being killed; The Wise Virgins taken to heaven *before* this 3½ years: The surviving Foolish Virgins caught up at Christ's appearing after the same 3½ years; England, with all the territory of the Four Empires, to be subject to Napoleon III........ 239 to 245

(22.) Alexander Porter, author of "The First-Fruits," (1856;) Louis Napoleon, the Antichrist, to make a seven years' Covenant with the Jews, (Dan. ix. 27,) seven years before Christ's descent on the earth; His persecution and the Great Tribulation during the latter 3½ years, before which the Wise Virgins will be caught up.................................. 245 to 247

(23.) E. W. P. Taunton, author of "The Days in which we Live," (1857;) Dan. ix. 27 unfulfilled; Louis Napoleon shown to be the Eighth Head, and future Antichrist; Massacre of Christians by the Romish Church, or two-horned Beast, (Rev. xiii. 11–18,) directed by Napoleon, during the last half of the final seven years following his Covenant with the Jews; Ascension of the Wise Virgins before this 3½ years................. 247 to 252

(24.) Major Scott Phillips, author of "Interpretations," (1859;) The earthquake at Christ's descent, (Zech. xiv. 4,) to open a channel from the Mediterranean to the Dead Sea, flowing from thence to the Red Sea; The Pope the year-day Antichrist of 1260 years; Louis Napoleon the literal-day Antichrist of 1260 days, the latter half of his future seven years' Covenant-week with the Jews; Wise Virgins caught up before this 1260 days.. 252 to 254

(25.) Rev. H. G. Guinness, author of "The Second Coming of Christ," (1861;) The Personal Antichrist to make the seven years' Covenant with the Jews; Its latter 3½ years the time of Great Tribulation and persecution before Christ's descent; Counsel to sinners to come to Jesus................. 254 to 258

(26.) Dominick McCausland, LL.D., author of "The Latter Days of Jerusalem and Rome," (1859;) The 70th week the final seven years of this Dispensation; Its latter part the period of the worship of the Antichrist's image in conjunction with the universal triumph of Romanism; England cannot escape this; Extract from Birk's work... .... 258 to 262

(27.) Rev. W. Marrable, Prebendary of St. John's Episcopal Church, Dublin, author of "What the Lord saith concerning Israel and Jerusalem," (1858;) The Man of Sin, or Antichrist, identical with "the Prince that shall come," (Dan. ix. 26, 27,) who shall confirm a seven years' Covenant with the Jews, seven years before Christ's descent on the earth; the same also as "Gog," in Ezek. xxxviii............................... 262

(28.) An Israelite writer of some articles in the "Quarterly Journal of Prophecy," for 1861; "Gog," of Ezek. xxxviii., the person who is to confirm a seven years' Covenant with the Jews, seven years before the glorious appearing of Messiah...... 263

(29.) Rev. Dr. Seiss, Pastor of St. John's Lutheran Church, Philadelphia, author of "The Day of the Lord," "Last Times," etc.; Antichrist to be a French Emperor, who will make a seven years' Covenant with the Jews, seven years before Christ's descent; Wise Virgins caught up before the last 3½ years; Surviving repentant Foolish Virgins caught up after that 3½ years' Great Tribulation.... .... 263, 264

(30.) E. Guers, author of "Israel aux derniers jours de l'economie actuelle," (Paris, Grassart,) also published in German, as "Israel's Zukunft," (Leipsic, Ernst Bredt,) 1856............... 264

(31) "Temoignage." (32) "The Parousia and Epiphaneia." (33) "The Coming Battle." (34) "The Millenium." (35) Rev. W. G. Barker. (36) Arthur Rees. (37) James Hunter. (38) "Notes on Scripture." (39) "Syllabus of Lectures." (40) The Church and the Kingdom." (41) Rev. F. G. Middleton, "Rapture of the Church." (42) W. C. Baynes. (43) A Writer in the Advent Herald. (44) Rev. G. Brookman. (45) H. P. Sholte. (46) Rev. D. Bosworth. (47) F. W. Grant. (48) A. P. Jolliffe. (49) J. Fondey. (50) W. Trotter. (51) J. Litch. (52) Rev. E. E. Reinke. (53) Dr. Williamson. (54) "The Present Testimony." (55) J. L. Hopkins. (56) Rev. Mr. Thurman. (57) C. Stanley.............................. 265 to 271.

Exhortation; Future glory of the saints; "Believe in the Lord Jesus Christ and thou shalt be saved;" "Pray without ceasing," (Acts xvi. 31, 2 Thess. v. 17)........................ 267 to 273

CHAPTER IV.

TEN REASONS, PROVING THAT THE ADVENT OF CHRIST "IN THE AIR" TO RAISE THE DECEASED SAINTS, AND TO TRANSLATE THE WISE VIRGINS, WILL PRECEDE THE FINAL 3½ YEARS' GREAT TRIBULATION, OR NAPOLEONIC PERSECUTION, AND WILL BE ABOUT FIVE YEARS BEFORE THE END OF THIS DISPENSATION, AND TWO YEARS AND FROM FOUR TO SIX WEEKS AFTER THE DATE OF THE COVENANT; THE SECOND TRANSLATION OF LIVING SAINTS BEING FIVE DAYS BEFORE THE END.

Diagram 4, showing, in two parallel columns, the double fulfilment of Daniel and Revelation within 2520 years, and also within 2595 days, (explained on page 288).................... 274

Preliminary remarks: Time of Christ's Advent not unrevealed; Six proofs of its being premillennial, Rev. xx. 4–6, Zech. xiv. 4, 2 Thess. ii. 8, Matt. xxiv. 29–31, Mark xiii. 24–27; Luke xxi. 27, Dan. xii., Rev. xi. 15–19, etc.................. 275 to 287

I. Two distinct Translations or removals of living saints from the earth at Christ's coming, are plainly described in literal-day, Rev. xiv., the first being an earlier and smaller ingathering than the second, and consisting of 144,000 persons, called the First-Fruits, (ver. 4,) who are caught up *before* the fall of Babylon, and Antichrist's subsequent 3½ years' persecution; the second being composed of all the saints found on the earth *after* Antichrist's 3½ years' persecution, and who are called the Harvest, (Rev. xiv. 15, vii. 9)................................. 289 to 292

II. The general descriptions of Christ's Second Advent intimate that he comes to remove the Wise Virgins at a time of comparative peace and prosperity, (Luke xvii. 28, Matt. xxiv. 37, 1 Thess. v. 2, 3,) and then comes, after a short interval of awful tribulation, to gather up the remnant of saints, and to destroy Antichrist and the unrepentant, (Rev. xvi. 18, Matt. xxiv. 29, Dan. xii., Zech. xiv. 1–4)...................................... 292 to 296

III. Two different Greek words παρουσια and επιφανεια, are used in Scripture to describe the Second coming of Christ,—the one signifying only his actual presence transferred to the vicinity of this earth, the other denoting the subsequent appearing or open manifestation of that presence. There are thus two distinct stages in his Advent.............................. 296 to 298

IV. A distinct promise is given in Luke xxi. 36, and Rev. iii. 10, that those who faithfully watch for Christ's Advent shall *escape*, and be kept altogether OUT OF *the hour of temptation*, that is, the $3\frac{1}{2}$ years' Great Tribulation...................... 298 to 300

V. In the Parables of the Ten Virgins and of the Marriage Supper, and in the Narrative of the Wise and Evil Servants, the Wise Virgins and Wise Servants are an earlier ingathering, and the Foolish Virgins and Evil Servants, being real saints, are a later ingathering, to the Marriage Supper of the Lamb. (Matt. xxv.; Luke xiv. 22, xii. 42; Matt. xxiv. 45).............. 300 to 302

VI. The ultimate literal-day fulfilment of the prophetic visions of Revelation obviously lasts for rather more than $3\frac{1}{2}$ years, (Rev. xi. 2, 3, xii. 6, 14, xiii. 5,) and is shown by the scenery of Rev. v., not to begin until after Christ has come and taken up the raised and translated saints to the heavens......... 302 to 305

VII. In the literal-day fulfilment of Rev. xii., expectant believers in Christ's Advent are represented under the figure of a Manchild, as being caught up into the heavens before the $3\frac{1}{2}$ years' Great Tribulation and Infidel persecution commences. 305 to 311

VIII. There is an ingathering of the saints to heaven at Christ's Advent, at the beginning of the seventh year-day Seal, about five years before the End, and also at the beginning of the seventh literal-day Seal, about five days before the End. (Rev. vii. 9–17, viii. 1)..................................... 311 to 314

IX. There is an ingathering to heaven of raised and translated saints at the beginning of the year-day seventh trumpet, about five years before the End, and again at the beginning of the literal-day seventh trumpet, five days before the End, constituting the two stages in the First Resurrection and Second Advent, (Rev. xi. 15–19, x. 7, xx. 6; 1 Cor. xv. 51, 52)..... 314 to 317

X. The coming of Christ, accompanied necessarily by a translation and resurrection of saints, takes place just before the year-day seventh vial, about five *years* previous to the End, and also just before the literal-day seventh vial, five *days* previous to the End; occurring thus in two stages, (Rev. xvi. 15–17)..... 317 to 321

Concluding observations and appendices............... 321 to 640

LOUIS NAPOLEON
THE DESTINED MONARCH OF THE WORLD.

INTRODUCTION.

"Power was given him (Louis Napoleon, the healed head of the Beast) over all kindreds and tongues and nations."—Rev. xiii. 7.

THE study of prophecy, which during the dark ages of the Christian era, was almost wholly neglected, has for the last half-century, attracted unwonted attention. The French Revolution of 1794, which was shown by many expositors, upward of one hundred years beforehand, to be predicted in the eleventh chapter of Revelation, had the effect of drawing many intelligent minds to the consideration of this subject. In that great political convulsion commentators have universally recognized a most important prophetical landmark, by means of which the slight degree of obscurity in which the year-day fulfilment of the prophecies was previously vailed has been almost entirely removed.

Guided by the light which that momentous epoch shed upon the page of prophecy, standard expositors have completely elucidated the year-day interpretation of the Books of Daniel and Revelation; and the soundness and reliability of their principles of exposition have been fully attested by the identity of the conclusions at which they have independently arrived. Although differing in minor details, they remarkably agree as to the general outlines of prophecy, and a great many of them concur in showing the general period about 1864 to 1872 to be the time of Christ's Coming, the close of the Christian dispensation, and the beginning of the Millennium. More than a hundred able treatises have been published during the last seventy years, in demonstration of this view; and when the scarcity of really profound students of prophecy is considered, it must be admitted that a conclusion reached by so many serious and sober-minded writers, is not very likely to be devoid of foundation.

Ever since the old-established system of things was broken up, at the time of the French Revolution, eminent expositors have persistently asserted that much more extensive and tremendous revolutions were foreshown to happen at the end of this dispensation, about the decade from 1860 to 1870; and in view of the present aspect of the world, it may now be asked, whether their forestatements have not been signally verified? The expectations of the total cessation of war, and of the gradual introduction of a millennium of peace and earthly prosperity, which have been so confidently entertained by those who disregarded prophecy, are now shown to have been vain and delusive. To illustrate the wide prevalence, twenty years ago, of such erroneous expectations, it may be sufficient to quote the sentiments expressed in 1844 by the President of the United States, the Queen of England, and the King of France.

President Tyler, in his Message, on Dec. 2, 1844, to the United States Congress, said: "With all the powers of Europe we continue on the most friendly terms. Indeed, it affords me much satisfaction to state, that at no former period has the peace of that enlightened and important quarter of the globe ever been apparently more firmly established. The conviction that peace is the true policy of nations would seem to be growing and becoming deeper among the enlightened every where. We continue to receive assurances of the most friendly feelings on the part of all the European powers, with whom it is so obviously our interest to cultivate the most amicable relations. Nor can I anticipate the occurrence of any event which would be likely in any degree to disturb those relations." The Queen thus addressed the English Parliament in February, 1844: "I entertain a confident hope that the general peace, so necessary for the happiness and prosperity of all nations, will continue uninterrupted. My friendly relations with the King of the French, and the good understanding happily established between my government and that of his Majesty, with the continued assurances of the peaceful and amicable dispositions of all princes and states, confirm me in this expectation." Louis Philippe, addressing the French Chamber of Deputies in 1843, said, "The world is at peace; France is free, active, and happy. We can enjoy with security these blessings of peace, for it never was better secured;" and on December 26th, 1844, referring to his recent visit to England, he said: "I have gathered, in the sentiments that have been expressed to me, additional guarantees for the long duration of that generous peace, which assures to our country abroad, a dignified and strong position, and at home an eternally increasing prosperity." He also expressed the assured belief, that "if he lived a few years longer, a general war in Europe would become impossible."

Let these fallacious anticipations be contrasted with the far-sighted views expressed at that period by prophetic investigators, such as the eminent Bickersteth, Faber, and Elliott. The Rev. E. Bickersteth, who showed from the prophetic dates that the Great Tribulation would intervene between the first and second Translations, from about 1864 to 1868, said in his *Guide to the Prophecies* and *Divine Warning*, in 1844-6: "The world seems now ripening by its sins for that fearful vintage of divine wrath which is the subject of so many predictions of the word of God. . . . . It is a dangerous delusion for the Church to be anticipating peaceful triumphs, prosperous days of enlarging dominion and uninterrupted successes, when we may be on the verge of increasing trial and conflict, sorrow and suffering. . . . . It is a time of universal peace. . . . . But we have no reason to expect that the present state of peace and prosperity will continue many years. It will rather, we have reason to think from God's word, soon cease, and times of peculiar trial and conflict succeed. . . . . Many who have deeply studied the subject, fully believe, and I can not but concur with them, that we are in the last period of the fourth great empire, just previous to the Lord's return, as revealed to Daniel; that six out of the seven seals of Revelation have been opened, six out of the seven trumpets have sounded, six out of the seven vials have been poured out. The Lord's return is also, as many of us believe, nearly connected with the seventh seal, the seventh trumpet, and the seventh vial. We believe also that the chief prophetical dates that were to intervene have either run their course, or are nearly closing." The Rev. E. B.

Elliott, in his celebrated work, *Horæ Apocalypticæ*, (first published in 1844,) having demonstrated the period 1865 to 1869, to be the time of the Second Advent, said: "The thought of the nearness of the consummation is of itself unspeakably awakening and solemn; and the rather when we consider further that there is to be expected antecedently a time of sifting and trial such as, perhaps, has never yet been experienced. For our Christian poet Cowper's exquisite language does by no means adequately express the probable severity of the coming crisis. Ere the sabbatism of the saints begins, something much more is to be looked for than the mere gusty, closing blasts of a long-tempest or billowy heavings of the sea before a calm, as 'it works itself to rest.' The final conflict between Christ's true Church and antichrist, and their respective chiefs and supporters, both visible and invisible, seems set forth in prophecy as most severe." The Rev. G. S. Faber,* who showed the time of the End to begin in 1864, spoke thus in his *Secessions to Popery*, in 1846: "The Ottoman empire totters to its fall: and the three spirits of Hellish Infidelity, Despotism, springing out of Anarchy, and Jesuitical Popery, are already engaged in their allied predicted vocation (Rev. xvi.) The peace of Europe and of the world apparently rests upon the life of a single wise old man, (Louis Philippe.) When the obstacle presented by this modern Sobrino shall have been removed, the demons of discord, now scarcely repressed, will be let loose. Revolution will elevate the successful soldier, the revived Bonaparte of the day, to the imperial throne of military despotism. Then will follow that fearful material Universal War which is foretold by all the prophets as occurring at the *Time of the End*, and synchronically with the Restoration of Israel. And then Popery, budding as it has ever done into Lawlessness and Infidelity through the loathliness of its own corruptions, and

---

* His *Revival of the French Emperorship*, written in 1853, and republished at Appletons', in New-York, America, under the title of *Napoleon III. the Man of Prophecy*, (37 cents,) demonstrates most convincingly that Louis Napoleon is the Eighth Head of the Beast and Infidel Antichrist. He, as well as Frere and Gauntlett, showed previous to 1820, that a second French Emperor, exactly like Napoleon I. would arise some few years before 1864-7, and would be the last great Antichrist. More than twenty other writers have (up to 1861) shown Napoleon III. to be the eighth head or future personal Antichrist.

allied with the great God-denying Antichrist: the False Romish Prophet, associated with the Apostatic Secular Empire under its last governing Head, will by some extraordinary process of violence come to its end, none helping it."

Many other extracts similar to the foregoing might be quoted from writings that have been published during the last seventy years. In the Appendix to this work a list is given of more than fifty writers such as the Honorable Gerard Noel, Rev. Drs. J. Cumming, J. Seiss, G. S. Faber, S. H. Tyng, G. Duffield, Bickersteth, etc., all of whom have demonstrated the Coming of Christ to be about the period from 1864 to 1872. And some of these writers, as for instance, Frere, Verner, Purdon, Scott Phillips, Shimeall, etc., firmly maintain the view that Louis Napoleon is the Antichrist and Eighth Head of the Beast. Among other expositors who have written more upon the general outlines than the chronology of prophecy, there may be mentioned the Earl of Carlisle, the Duke of Manchester, the late Bishops of Durham and Norwich, Lord Congleton, Sir E. Denny, etc., according to whose views the End of this Dispensation is close at hand. The two last-named writers have specially shown in their works that Christ will come to take away the Wise Virgins *before* Antichrist's three and a half years' persecution, and will remain in the pavilion-cloud during its continuance, and then descend at its termination upon Mt. Olivet at the Battle of Armageddon.

But although there is almost an unanimous belief among those who have honestly and laboriously investigated the prophecies, that desolating judgments are now about to descend upon the world, in connection with Christ's coming; yet among the majority* of professing Christians, there is no such belief, owing to their utter ignorance

---

* This is not so much the case in England, where the study of Prophecy is increasingly pursued, as throughout America, in which country the prophecies of Daniel and Revelation very rarely form the subject of a pulpit discourse, except in the churches of the Second Advent sect, which are only few in number. In consequence of Prophecy being thus universally neglected and ignored, there exists such a general ignorance and disbelief of it, that it is exceedingly difficult to get

and disregard of prophetic truth. As very few were watching for Christ's first Advent, although his appearance, as the Messiah, was distinctly foretold to take place 69 weeks or 483 years after the seventh year of Artaxerxes; so scarcely any are really watching for his second Advent, although it is explicitly predicted to occur during the five years preceding the end of the 6000 2520, 2500, 2300, and 1335 years, and under the seventh year-day vial, trumpet, and seal, and at the time of the eighth Head of the Beast. The text, " *Of that day and that hour knoweth no man, no,* . . . *not the Son,*" (Mark xiii. 32,) which is continually quoted by scoffers, in support of the idea that the time of Christ's Advent can never be discovered, evidently was only spoken in the present tense, to the then existing generation, and can not be true at the present period, for the Son of Man must now be fully aware of the day and hour of his approaching Advent; and moreover, since those words were uttered, our knowledge of the future has been much increased by the gift of the Holy Ghost on the day of Pentecost, and the bestowment of the Book of Revelation. "to show the things which shall be hereafter." Under any circumstances, the concealment of the day and hour could not necessarily prevent the discovery of the month, or even the week, of Christ's Advent.

A leading event, in connection with our Saviour's return, is the manifestation of Antichrist or the Man of Sin, as foretold in 2 Thess. ii. 3: "*That day (the day of Christ) shall not come, except there come* THE (Gr.) *falling away first, and that Man of Sin be revealed, the son of perdition, who opposeth and exalteth himself above all that is called God, or that is worshipped ; so that he, as God, sitteth in the temple of God, showing himself that he is God* . . . *whom the Lord shall consume with the*

---

persons even to listen to the subject. The Author having given lectures upon this subject in upward of a hundred different localities in America, including Washington, Philadelphia, New-York, Boston, Toronto, Detroit, etc., can testify to the contempt and hostility which in most cases these views have to encounter. A better hearing is given to the subject in the Protestant part of Canada than any where else, owing probably to the absence of Spiritualism, Universalism, and Unitarianism.

spirit of his mouth, and destroy with the brightness of his coming; also in 1 John ii. 18, 22: *"As ye have heard that* THE (Gr.) *Antichrist shall come, even now are there many Antichrists, whereby we know that it is the last time.* . . . *He is* THE (Gr.) *Antichrist that denieth the Father and the Son."* From these and other passages, it has long been concluded, that although many Antichrists have arisen, such as the Pope and Mahomet, yet there is a particular and individual Antichrist to arise, just before Christ's Advent, who is generally called the Personal or Infidel Antichrist, and who is to be worshipped as God in the temple at Jerusalem, and is utterly to deny the existence of Jehovah and of Christ. His exploits are fully described in Daniel xi. and Revelation xvii. and also in the literal-day fulfilment of Daniel vii. viii. xii., and Revelation ix. xi. xiii., although the year-day fulfilment of these chapters relates to Popery and Mahometanism.

This great Personal Antichrist is distinctly foreshown to be none other than Louis Napoleon, who is consequently very soon to acquire supreme ascendency over the whole of Christendom, and for three and a half years is ruthlessly to slay nearly every one who will not acknowledge him to be God. Christendom will then become a slaughter-house or shambles, in which tens of thousands of Christ's sheep will be butchered, and scarcely any one will escape the awful ordeal of being put to the test, whether they will confess Christ and be killed, perhaps with dreadful tortures; or whether they will acknowledge Napoleon to be God, and thus purchase temporary safety at the cost of eternal damnation. Those who choose the latter alternative will be branded in their forehead or hand with Napoleon's name, or the number 666, or some particular mark, just as cattle have stamped upon them the name of their owner, (Rev. xiii.) This exterminating persecution is the leading feature in the three and a half years Great Tribulation; there will, however, be superadded unparalleled wars, earthquakes, pestilences, and famines.

Such is *"the temptation which shall come upon* ALL *the world, to try them that dwell upon the earth."* Its universal prevalence, at least throughout Christendom, is declared in the most emphatic terms. The Personal Antichrist is to obtain "*power over* ALL *kindreds, and tongues, and nations;*" "*to make war with the saints, and to overcome them,*" (Rev. xiii.;) "*to make war with the saints and prevail against them until the Ancient of Days comes,*" (Dan. vii. 21;) "*to be worshipped by* ALL THAT DWELL UPON THE * EARTH," except the saints; "*to make the world a wilderness,*" (Isaiah xiv. 17.) It would evidently be impossible for him "to overcome the saints," unless his persecution extended to every place where they could be found; nor would the company of saints, that is to be specially hid in the wilderness, be particularly mentioned, unless to show that they alone are to be exempted from the persecution.

In view of the nearness of these overwhelmingly crushing judgments, how criminal is the conduct of those whose duty it is to admonish persons of approaching calamities, but who are giving no real attention to Prophecy, and even smiting those of their fellow-servants who do proclaim these truths. How many there are, who in the excitement and agitation of having to choose between worshipping Antichrist or being put to death, will choose the former, and receive the fatal mark; whereas, had they been forewarned of the great trial coming upon them, they would have prepared to witness a bold confession, even unto death. A terrible day of reckoning is close at hand, when the treacherous and blind leaders of the blind, who make a mock at Prophecy and prophetic expositors, will be confronted by the bitter reproaches of those whom they have lulled into false security, by crying Peace and safety, when sudden destruction is about to descend with the fury of an avalanche.

The mistaken idea that if we are born again and prepared for death, we are also prepared for the Second Advent, leads many to neglect prophecy; for they naturally think that the study of it is not at all necessary to salva-

---

* The expression "upon the earth," (επι της γης,) can not, in its literal fulfilment, be merely limited to Europe, for the very same Greek words are used in the Lord's prayer in the sentence, *Thy will be done upon the earth as it is in heaven,* (Matt. vi. 10, Luke xi. 2.) Although inaccurately translated *in earth* in Matthew and Luke, yet the Greek words are precisely the same as in Rev. xiii. 8.

spirit of his mouth, and destroy with the brightness of his coming;" also in 1 John ii. 18, 22 : "As ye have heard that THE (Gr.) Antichrist shall come, even now are there many Antichrists, whereby we know that it is the last time.... He is THE (Gr.) Antichrist that denieth the Father and the Son." From these and other passages, it has long been concluded, that although many Antichrists have arisen, such as the Pope and Mahomet, yet there is a particular and individual Antichrist to arise, just before Christ's Advent, who is generally called the Personal or Infidel Antichrist, and who is to be worshipped as God in the temple at Jerusalem, and is utterly to deny the existence of Jehovah and of Christ. His exploits are fully described in Daniel xi. and Revelation xvii. and also in the literal-day fulfilment of Daniel vii. viii. xii., and Revelation ix. xi. xiii., although the year-day fulfilment of these chapters relates to Popery and Mahometanism.

This great Personal Antichrist is distinctly foreshown to be none other than Louis Napoleon, who is consequently very soon to acquire supreme ascendency over the whole of Christendom, and for three and a half years is ruthlessly to slay nearly every one who will not acknowledge him to be God. Christendom will then become a slaughter-house or shambles, in which tens of thousands of Christ's sheep will be butchered, and scarcely any one will escape the awful ordeal of being put to the test, whether they will confess Christ and be killed, perhaps with dreadful tortures; or whether they will acknowledge Napoleon to be God, and thus purchase temporary safety at the cost of eternal damnation. Those who choose the latter alternative will be branded in their forehead or hand with Napoleon's name, or the number 666, or some particular mark, just as cattle have stamped upon them the name of their owner, (Rev. xiii.) This exterminating persecution is the leading feature in the three and a half years Great Tribulation; there will, however, be superadded unparalleled wars, earthquakes, pestilences, and famines.

Such is "*the temptation which shall come upon* ALL *the world, to try them that dwell upon the earth.*" Its universal prevalence, at least throughout Christendom, is declared in the most emphatic terms. The Persona Antichrist is to obtain "*power over* ALL *kindreds, and tongues, and nations;*" "*to make war with the saints, and to overcome them,*" (Rev. xiii.;) "*to make war with the saints and prevail against them until the Ancient of Days comes,*" (Dan. vii. 21;) "*to be worshipped by* ALL THAT DWELL UPON THE * EARTH," except the saints; "*to make the world a wilderness,*" (Isaiah xiv. 17.) It would evidently be impossible for him "to overcome the saints," unless his persecution extended to every place where they could be found; nor would the company of saints, that is to be specially hid in the wilderness, be particularly mentioned, unless to show that they alone are to be exempted from the persecution.

In view of the nearness of these overwhelmingly crushing judgments, how criminal is the conduct of those whose duty it is to admonish persons of approaching calamities, but who are giving no real attention to Prophecy, and even smiting those of their fellow-servants who do proclaim these truths. How many there are, who in the excitement and agitation of having to choose between worshipping Antichrist or being put to death, will choose the former, and receive the fatal mark; whereas, had they been forewarned of the great trial coming upon them, they would have prepared to witness a bold confession, even unto death. A terrible day of reckoning is close at hand, when the treacherous and blind leaders of the blind, who make a mock at Prophecy and prophetic expositors, will be confronted by the bitter reproaches of those whom they have lulled into false security, by crying Peace and safety, when sudden destruction is about to descend with the fury of an avalanche.

The mistaken idea that if we are born again and prepared for death, we are also prepared for the Second Advent, leads many to neglect prophecy; for they naturally think that the study of it is not at all necessary to salva-

---

* The expression "upon the earth," ($\epsilon\pi\iota$ $\tau\eta\varsigma$ $\gamma\eta\varsigma$,) can not, in its literal fulfilment, be merely limited to Europe, for the very same Greek words are used in the Lord's prayer in the sentence, *Thy will be done upon the earth as it is in heaven*, (Matt. vi. 10, Luke xi. 2.) Although inaccurately translated *in earth* in Matthew and Luke, yet the Greek words are precisely the same as in Rev. xiii. 8.

INTRODUCTORY REMARKS.

tion. But although salvation from hell-fire may be obtained by the new birth and true faith in Christ's atonement, yet salvation from the shame and misery of being left on the earth at Christ's coming can only be obtained by real belief in the immediate nearness of his Advent, and by faithful confession of that belief. The distinction drawn between the wise and foolish virgins, and between the faithful and evil servant, who is cut *off* (Gr.) and left to endure the Great Tribulation, (Matt. xxiv. 45–51,) as well as other Scripture statements, such as in Heb. ix. 28, 2 Tim. iv. 8, Rev. xvi. 15, etc., plainly shows that many who are true children of God, but unbelievers in the nearness of the Advent, and in a backsliding and lukewarm state, will not be caught up to meet Christ (Rev. xiv. 1–5) at his coming in the air, *before* the $3\frac{1}{2}$ years Great Tribulation; but will be left to endure the awful woe of the Tribulation, and if they survive, will be caught up in the Second Translation, *after* the $3\frac{1}{2}$ years, (Matt. xxiv. 31.) It is a painful but undeniable fact, that a great many pious persons are exceedingly prejudiced and hostile against the view of Christ's Advent being close at hand: they assert that it is sufficient if we prepare for death, and that death is the Coming of Christ; but they will soon discover to their sorrow that the prophecies can not be neglected with impunity, and that READINESS FOR DEATH IS NOT NECESSARILY READINESS FOR THE SECOND ADVENT.

THE SUBJECT OF THIS TREATISE may be divided into four chapters: I. Ten Proofs that Louis Napoleon is THE Antichrist, and Destined Monarch of the World, and Eighth or Last Head of the Roman Empire. II. Twenty Coming Events, that are foreshown to occur during the final seven years and $2\frac{1}{2}$ months of this Gentile Dispensation. III. Evidence that THE Antichrist (Napoleon) is to make a seven-years' Covenant with the Jews, seven years and $2\frac{1}{2}$ months before the End of the Dispensation, as shown by above fifty writers. IV. Ten Reasons proving that the Advent of Christ in the air, and the resurrection of the righteous, and ascension of the Wise Virgins, PRECEDES the final $3\frac{1}{2}$ years' Great Tribulation or Napoleonic persecution, and is about five years before the End.

1806 to 1815.—The Roman Empire under Napoleon I.,

Who represented the Napoleon dynasty—the seventh governing Head of the seven-headed and ten-horned Wild-Beast.—(Dan. vii. 7; Rev. xiii., xvii.)

1815 to 1852.—The Roman Empire Headless.

1852 to 1871-73.—The Roman Empire under Napoleon III.,

Who represents the Napoleon dynasty—the seventh revived, or eighth Head of the Wild-Beast healed of the deadly wound it received at Waterloo in 1815. He is comprehensively termed the Wild-Beast itself, and is also called *the Assyrian*, (Is. x., xlv., xxx.,) *the Little Horn*, (Dan. vii., viii.,) *the Wilful King*, (Dan. xi. 21-45,) *the Antichrist*, (1 Jn. ii. 22,) *the Man of Sin*, destined to perish at the personal descent of Christ, (2 Thess. ii. 3, 8.)

And I saw one of his heads, as it had been wounded to death, and his deadly wound was healed, and all the world wondered after the Wild-Beast, and power was given him over all kindreds, and tongues, and nations, (Rev. xiii.)

CHAPTER I.

TEN REASONS IN SUPPORT OF THE VIEW THAT LOUIS NAPOLEON IS THE INDIVIDUAL WHO IS SHORTLY TO BE REVEALED AS THE PERSONAL ANTICHRIST (THAT IS, THE ANTICHRIST) WHO IS FORESHOWN IN SCRIPTURE TO OBTAIN ALMOST A UNIVERSAL EMPIRE, AND FOR $3\frac{1}{2}$ YEARS TO HAVE HIMSELF WORSHIPPED AS GOD, AND THEN TO PERISH AT THE DESCENT OF CHRIST AT THE BATTLE OF ARMAGEDDON, ABOUT OR SOON AFTER 1871-2.

BEFORE adducing the evidence in support of this view, it may be well to glance briefly at the past history of this remarkable person. Louis Napoleon (or Napoleon III.) was born on April 24th, 1808, at the Tuileries; and his birth, like that of Bonaparte's only son the King of Rome, was announced by the firing of cannon, a mark of honor only conferred upon those who were of the Imperial family. His father, Louis, brother to Napoleon I., was formerly King of Holland; and his mother, Hortense Beauharnais, was the daughter of the Empress Josephine. Napoleon Bonaparte is reported to have been much attached to him, and on more than one occasion to have expressed a presentiment that he would be the ultimate representative of the Napoleon dynasty. At the age of twenty he united for a short time with his brother in an Italian rebellion against the Pope. His conduct in the dangers to which he was thus exposed was marked by great self-possession and courage. From an early period in life he was profoundly impressed with the conviction that he had a great mission and destiny to fulfil in relation to France. In accordance with this belief he landed at Strasbourg on December 17th, 1836, with a few associates, and endeavored to excite the garrison and inhabitants of that city to revolt against the government of Louis Philippe. A portion of the military forces stationed there ranged themselves under his banner, but from a want of compliance on the part of other regiments, the attempt proved abortive, and he was apprehended, and upon trial banished to the United States, where he did not remain more than two or three months. A second expedition for the same purpose, and with a like result, was undertaken by him on August 6th, 1840. Embarking from the English coast in company with a band of devoted adherents, he landed at Boulogne, and marched with his followers into the town, hoping to cause an uprising of the people in favor of his movement. They failed, however, to respond as he had anticipated, and upon his consequent arrest and trial he was sentenced to incarceration for the term of his natural life in the fortress of Ham. He effected his escape from this place of confinement on May 25th, 1846. Assuming the disguise of a workman with a plank upon his shoulder, he contrived to pass all the sentinels who guarded the gates of the castle. In order to gain time before his flight was discovered, as it was the duty of the commandant of the fortress to see him every few hours, his physician reported him to be ill, and placing a stuffed figure in his bed, by this stratagem succeeded in allaying all suspicion as to his absence, until it was too late to recapture him. The Revolution in France in 1848 opened the way for his return to his native land, and on the 8th of June he was chosen Deputy of one of the provinces, and admitted to his seat in the National Assembly. On December 30th, in the same year, he was elected by more than five million votes of the people to be their President for three years. When the three years of his Presidency were drawing to a close, in 1851, he dissolved the National Assembly, because of its refusal to listen to proposals for the extension of his term of office; and on December 4th he consummated the famous *coup d'etat*, arresting in the dead of night all the principal men in military and political circles who stood in the way of his being permanently invested with the supreme power. At a Court-ball given by him on this eventful evening, he displayed his characteristic imperturbability and self-possession, by appearing to enter heartily into the enjoyment of the festivities of the hour, although the blow was at that moment being struck which was to decide whether he was to overcome or be supplanted by his political rivals. The plot of the *coup d'etat* was contrived with consummate skill and secresy; all those whom he feared were seized and either imprisoned or sent into exile.

Having thus fairly settled himself in the seat of supreme authority, he submitted a proposal to the French people that he should be re-elected President of the Republic for ten years; and partly through the influence of the Catholic priests, who were strongly enlisted on his side, he obtained, on December 24th, seven millions of votes in ratification of this measure. His ambition, however, had always aimed at the acquirement of the Imperial dignity, and the reëstablishment of the Napoleon dynasty; consequently, on December 2d, 1852, the anniversary of the battle of Austerlitz, and also of the coronation of Napoleon I., he assumed the title of Emperor, giving utterance at the same time to his famous declaration: "The Empire is peace." In this manner the French Emperorship became resuscitated in 1852, after an extinction of 37 years since A.D. 1815. During that 37 years' interval the Bourbon family had reigned over France in the persons, successively, of Louis XVIII., Charles X., and Louis Philippe. The following are the ten reasons advanced in proof of Napoleon III. being the individual who is soon to be fully manifested as the Personal or Infidel Antichrist, (that is, THE Antichrist, in contradistinction to the Papal and Mahomedan Antichrist.)

I. BECAUSE HE IS THE BEAST'S Seventh revived or Eighth Head, which is predicted in Rev. xiii., xvii., and xix. to wage an exterminating war against the saints for 3½ years, and to be almost universally worshipped by the ungodly, and then with his ten kings to perish at Christ's descent at Armageddon.

This is the main and principal argument by which it is demonstrated with mathematical certainty that Louis Napoleon is THE Antichrist. First, in proof of the fact that the last great Antichrist is identical with the Eighth Head of the Beast, it is only necessary to compare the various passages in which he is described.* The following are some of the different names given to him:

1 John ii. 18, 22. THE Antichrist that denieth the
    Father and the Son.
2 Thess. ii. 3. The Man of Sin or Son of Perdition.
Dan. vii. A Little Horn, (in relation to the Gentiles.)
Dan. viii. A Little Horn or King of fierce countenance.

Dan. ix. 26. The Prince that shall come.
Dan. xi. 25. A vile person or King who shall do according to his own will, (the Wilful King.)
Rev. xiii., xvii., etc. The Beast, or Eighth Head of the Beast, or Beast whose deadly wound was healed.

The subjoined comparison of the passages in which these names occur shows the resemblance between them.

1 John ii. 18, 22.	Dan. xi. 36, 37.
Ye have heard that ⸺ (Gr.) Antichrist shall come. . . . He is TUE (Gr.) Antichrist that denieth the Father and the Son.	And *the king shall do according to his will;* and he shall exalt himself and magnify himself above every god, and shall speak marvellous things against the God of gods. . . . Neither shall he regard the God of his fathers, nor the desire of women, (the Seed of the woman, Christ,) nor regard any God, for he shall magnify himself above all.
2 Thess. ii. 3, 4, 9. The day of Christ . . . shall not come except there come THE apostasy (ἡ αποστασια) first, and that *Man of sin* be revealed the *son of perdition*, who opposeth and exalteth himself above all that is called God or that is worshipped; so that he, as God, sitteth in the temple of God, showing himself that he is God . . . whose coming is after the power of Satan, with all power, and signs, and lying wonders.	Rev. xvii. 11, 14. The Beast, that was and is not, even he is of the Eighth and is of the seven, and goeth *into perdition* . . . and shall make war with the Lamb, and the Lamb shall overcome them.
Dan. vii. 25. And he (the little horn) shall speak great words against the Most High, and shall wear out the saints of the Most High; and they shall be given into his hand until a time and times and the dividing of time.	Rev. xiii. 6, 7. And he (the Beast) opened his mouth in blasphemy against God. . . . And it was given unto him to make war with the saints, and to overcome them, and power was given him over all kindreds, and tongues, and nations; and all that dwell upon the earth shall worship him, (except the righteous.)
Dan. viii. 24, 25. He (*the king of fierce countenance*) shall destroy the mighty and the holy people . . . he shall also stand up against the Prince of Princes, but he shall be broken without hand.	Rev. xix. 19. I saw the Beast and the kings of the earth gathered together, to make war against him (Christ) that sat on the horse, and the Beast was taken.

It is evident from the above passages (see also Chapter I., Event XIII.) that THE Antichrist will be an avowed and barefaced infidel, totally rejecting the Christian religion, and not, like the Pope, professedly upholding it. The atheism of France in 1792–6 somewhat resembled Antichrist's approaching apostasy, and Spiritualism, which denies the cardinal doctrines of Christianity, is its incipient manifestation. A considerable part of Daniel and Revelation, having had a year-day typical precursive fulfilment in the apostasy of Popery, has led many persons mistakenly to suppose that the Pope is the Man of Sin and the Antichrist. But although he has had great power for 1260 years, as the mystical Man of Sin and the Papal Antichrist, there is yet to arise, at the time of Christ's Advent, a Personal Man of Sin and Infidel Antichrist, who will have great power for 1260 days, and will literally sit in *the temple of God*, which is expressly shown in lit. day Rev. xi. 1 to be the rebuilt Jewish temple.

Secondly, the Eighth Head being unquestionably identical with the Antichrist, it has to be shown that Louis Napoleon is the Eighth or Seventh revived Head. This is proved from Rev. xiii. and xvii. 10, 11, where the Seven Heads of the Beast, which represents the Roman Empire, were explained by the interpreting angel in these words: "*There are seven kings; five are fallen, and one is, and the other is not yet come, and when he cometh he must continue a short space. And the Beast that was and is not, even he is the Eighth and is of the seven, and goeth into perdition.*" It has been the generally received interpretation, among Protestant commentators, that the term *seven kings** signifies seven successive modes of political administration, or forms of government, over the Roman Empire. Dr. H. More and R. Fleming, about the year 1710, spoke of this interpretation as generally prevalent in their day; and the latter said: "Seeing that five of the forms of the Roman government were fallen in John's time, (when the angel spoke to him,) namely: Kings, Consuls, Dictators, Decemvirs, and Military Tribunes, and seeing the Imperial form of government (the Roman Emperorship) was that which was in being then, we have no reason to quit so plain and exact an interpretation, until more be said against it than has ever yet been produced

---

* The word *kings* bears in prophecy three slightly different meanings. In Dan. vii. 17 it signifies *kingdoms*, (see Dan. vii. 23;) in Rev. xvii. 10, *lines or classes of rulers, or forms of governments;* in Rev. xvii. 12, *kingdoms or the individual kings that govern them.*

to the world." Livy, Tacitus, (Annal. lib. i. sect. 2,) Cassiodorus, Panvicinus, etc., also mention these as the first six forms of the Roman government. Moreover, the plain statement of the angel, that the sixth Head was the Head then (in A.D. 96) in actual existence, coupled with the fact that the Roman Emperorship was the then existing Head, conclusively proves that the Roman Emperorship was the sixth Head. The seventh Head would of course not arise until the fall of the sixth Head, which took place in 1806, as is shown by the following brief outline of history.

The Roman Emperorship had an unbroken series of representatives at Rome until A.D. 476, when Augustulus, Emperor of the Western Roman Empire, was deposed by the barbarian Odoacer. But in accordance with the Roman Laws, which allowed several Roman Emperors to exist at the same time in different parts of the Roman Empire, there was another Roman Emperor, named Zeno, reigning in Constantinople, in 476, over the Eastern Roman Empire. To him, therefore, the Senate at Rome sent deputies, acknowledging him to be the sole remaining Emperor, and recognizing his authority as now extending over the Western as well as the Eastern part of the Empire, (Gibbon's Rome, chap. xxxvi.) After this, the Roman Emperorship had a continued succession of representatives at Constantinople until the taking of Constantinople by the Turks, in 1453. It had, however, obtained another representative in the Western Roman Empire in A.D. 800, in the person of Charlemagne, who was crowned by the Pope *Emperor of the Romans*, and whose successors kept up the title until, in A.D. 962, it vested in the Emperor of Germany, whose chief title became EMPEROR OF THE ROMANS, and who was considered the official successor of Augustus Cæsar. Germany, with its feudatory Italian appendages, was also thenceforth designated the Holy Roman Empire. Thus, when the line of Roman Emperors in Constantinople came to an end, in 1458, the Roman Emperorship still had a representative in the Emperor of Germany. In 1806 a number of German Princes transferred their allegiance from Francis, Emperor of Germany, to Napoleon Bonaparte, Emperor of France, under whose protection they united themselves into the Confederation of the Rhine. This, in conjunction with his defeat at Austerlitz, induced the German Emperor to adopt the sole title of "Emperor of Austria," and to renounce the title of "Emperor of Germany and of the Holy Roman Empire,"* in these words: "Considering the bonds which unite us to the Empire as dissolved by the Confederation of the Rhine, we renounce the Imperial Crown," etc. Thus ended the sixth Head or Roman Emperorship; and the title of "Emperor of the Romans," which from B.C. 28 to A.D. 1806 had never failed to have some representative within the Roman Empire, now at last became altogether extinct.

The seventh Head, which must immediately succeed the sixth Head, was foreshown in Rev. xiii. and xvii. to be distinguished by five leading marks. (1) It would be the dynasty of that Sovereign who, at the fall of the sixth Head, should be Master of Rome and of a considerable part of the Roman Empire. (2) Although possessing much the same power as the preceding six Heads, yet it must be distinguished from them by a different *official title*. (3) It must only *continue a short space*, and (4) must be violently slain, instead of being voluntarily resigned. (5) It must be healed and reëxist some few years before the Advent of Christ.—These five characteristics are all found in the Napoleon dynasty or French Emperorship, as existing under Napoleon Bonaparte from 1806 to 1815. (1) Bonaparte was the actual Sovereign of Rome, and virtually the supreme Head of most of the

* Sir A. Alison, in his History of Europe, Chapter xlii., gives this extract at full length, and states that in 1806 the Emperor of Germany thus ceased to be the representative of the Empire of the Cæsars. Historians generally take the same view, as may be seen in C. Butler's Revolutions of Germany, p. 208; Baronius' Annal. Eccles. in A.D. 800; Gibbon, vol. ix. p. 171; Mod. Univ. Hist. vol. xxx., in Golden Bull in 1356; Sir G. Mackenzie's work on Precedency, etc. Although historians show so clearly that the Roman Emperorship continued till 1806, yet not a few expositors have fallen into the glaring error of supposing that it terminated in 476, when its seat was transferred to Constantinople. The idea that it fell in 813, because its representative was converted from Paganism to Christianity, is also utterly groundless. It is lamentable to see that certain writers have not the candor to relinquish such obviously erroneous interpretations, when the interpretation of Faber, Frere, Gauntlett, etc., which is here given, has been proved by its fulfilment to be correct.

European monarchs when the sixth Head fell. The Emperor of Austria, the Kings of Wirtemberg, Westphalia, Bavaria, Saxony, Naples, Spain, and Prussia were all more or less subject to him; even Egypt and Palestine had been previously invaded by his victorious armies. He had been crowned Emperor of France by the Pope, in Paris, on Dec. 2, 1804; and was again crowned King of Italy and Rome, with the iron crown of Charlemagne, at Milan, on May 26, 1805, at which time the Roman States were formally annexed to France, and Rome was made the second city in his dominions, the title of King of Rome being given to his heir-apparent.

(2) His dynasty was an entirely new Head of the Beast, being altogether different from any of the six preceding Heads, in respect of its *official title*, for though in reality he occupied the position of Emperor of the Roman Empire, yet he did not, like the former German Emperors, adopt that title, but was crowned only as *Emperor of France and King of Italy*. If, for example, the King of Spain, instead of Bonaparte, had been supreme over Rome and a great part of the Roman Empire, when the sixth Head fell, then the Kingship of Spain would have become the seventh Head.

(3) The seventh Head was expressly predicted only to *continue a short space*, (Rev. xvii. 10,) and accordingly the Napoleon dynasty, after existing for nine years as the seventh Head, came to an end at Bonaparte's overthrow at Waterloo, in 1815.

(4) The Napoleon dynasty did not fall like the preceding six Heads, or, as it were, die a natural death, but it was politically slain by the sword of military violence at Waterloo. This accorded with the statement in Rev. xiii. and xvii., that the seventh Head should be wounded to death by the sword.

Rev. xiii. 3, 14.	Rev. xvii. 10, 11
And I saw one of his heads that had been, (Gr.) as it were, wounded to death; and his deadly wound was healed, and all the world wondered after the Beast . . . the Beast which had the wound by a sword and did live.	Five are fallen, (A.D. 96,) and one is, and the other is not yet come; and when he cometh he must continue a short space. And the Beast that was and is not, even he is the eighth, and is of the seven, and goeth into perdition.

As the first six Heads *fell* or were voluntarily abdicated, therefore it must be the seventh Head that was *wounded to death by a sword*, and which was afterward to revive and to appear as an eighth Head, although in reality only the seventh Head, raised to life again. On this account the Beast is pictured with only seven Heads, and yet is spoken of as having an Eighth Head.

(5) The Beast or Roman Empire remained headless from 1815 to 1852, as there was not among its various monarchs any great leader or political chief, who was in possession of Rome and acknowledged to be the Supreme Head preëminent over the rest, like the German Emperors or Bonaparte, who had towered so majestically over Europe. But its recovery from its non-existent headless state was effected in 1852, by Louis Napoleon assuming the title of French Emperor, and thus restoring the seventh Head or Napoleon dynasty. It appears that the complete restoration of this Head to the same position that it held in Bonaparte's days will probably be effected by Louis Napoleon being crowned a short time before the 3½ years' Tribulation.

Thus the Napoleon dynasty is clearly shown to be the seventh Head from 1806 to 1815, and also the seventh revived or Eighth Head reëxistent since 1852. In the universal amazement excited by its reäppearance, we see the fulfilment of the prophecy: *They that dwell on the earth shall wonder when they behold the Beast that was and is not and yet is,* (Rev. xvii. 8.) It *was* until it received its deadly wound under Napoleon I., in 1815; it *is not* from 1815 to 1852, under Napoleon II., who never reigned and died prematurely; and it *yet is* since 1852, under Napoleon III. The Napoleon dynasty is thus a resurrection dynasty, for it has passed through the three stages of life, death, and resurrection — existence, non-existence, and reëxistence. The fatal accuracy with which Louis Napoleon fulfils this prophecy is strikingly shown in his determination to be called Napoleon III., although Napoleon II. never reigned. Almost the very words used in Rev. xvii. 8 have been unwittingly applied to him by the French people. On an arch erected in his honor this expression was inscribed: "The Uncle that was; the Nephew that is." It is noticeable that England, Russia, Prussia, and Austria, which have all recognized Louis Napoleon as French Emperor, were the four allied Powers which, at the Vienna Congress, in November, 1814, agreed that no member of Napoleon Bonaparte's family should ever be permitted to hold sovereign power in France. It might perhaps be thought that although the Personal Antichrist must be a representative of the Napoleon dynasty, yet that he might be another French Emperor standing in the place of Louis Napoleon, if the latter were to die. But this can not be the case, because as the seventh Head was a *personal* dynasty, summed up and comprehended in the life of a single individual, Napoleon I., so also the Eighth Head, which is exactly to resemble the seventh Head, must be a personal dynasty, entirely comprehended in the life of a single individual, Napoleon III. The seventh Head had altogether only one representative, therefore the Eighth Head has only one representative. Moreover, as the person who represents the Eighth Head is to center in himself all the power of the Roman Empire, therefore he is comprehensively called the Beast itself—a term which thus is used in Rev. xiii. and xvii. as a synonym for Louis Napoleon.

II. BECAUSE HE ANSWERS to the description of the Antichrist in Rev. xiii. in respect of his warlike prowess, insatiable ambition, great military and naval strength, and growing "power over all kindreds, and tongues and nations."

In Rev. xiii. 3, 4, as soon as the Beast's wounded head is healed, all the world is described as being filled with unspeakable amazement, and giving utterance to their astonishment in the exclamation: "*Who is like unto the Beast? who is able to make war with him?*" Louis Napoleon has been clearly demonstrated to be the person by whom the wounded head was healed, inasmuch as the French Emperorship, which had been extinguished in 1815, was revived by him in 1852. It is in reference to him, therefore, that the above exclamation is predicted to be made; and when we consider the unrivalled boldness, matchless skill, and unscrupulous determination with which he has carved his way to his present commanding position, and moreover, the tact, astuteness, and subtle policy with which he maintains and strengthens that position, we recognize the appropriateness of the interrogation: "Who is like unto him?" Nor is there less fitness in the application to Louis Napoleon of the inquiry: "Who is able to make war with him?" The great increase in the numbers and effectiveness of the French army since his accession to power is too well known to require comment. Notwithstanding his reiterated assertions that "the Empire is peace," the apprehensions of neighboring countries are naturally excited by the continuous augmentation of his military forces, and the active preparations that are unceasingly carried forward in the French dockyards and arsenals. He does not fail to secure for his troops the advantage of every modern improvement in the construction of warlike implements, and thus they are rendered unapproachably formidable, not only by their masterly skill in the management of their weapons, but by the inconceivably deadly nature of their engines of destruction. At the head of nearly 750,000 admirably trained and disciplined soldiers, furnished with Minié rifles and cannon of unprecedented efficiency, and with a fleet of war-steamers not even inferior to that of Great Britain, Louis Napoleon stands forth as one of whom it may well be asked: "Who is able to make war with him?" The surprising skill in generalship he displayed on the plains of Lombardy during the war waged by the Austrians against the French and Sardinians in 1859, has demonstrated his military talents and strategical ability in the disposition and manœuvring of troops upon the battle-field to be of the highest order. The singular expedient he adopted in that campaign of sending up a man in a balloon to ascertain the precise position of the Austrian forces, marks a mind peculiarly inventive and fertile in resources. He seems to be convinced that the bullet is not yet cast which can be the messenger of death to him; for with regard to his fearlessness under the hot fire of the enemy, at the battle of Solferino, it was stated "that the Emperor's courage amounted to the verge of rashness, electrifying the soldiers by the coolness he always displayed, engaged in the thick of the contest, and merely walking his horse when he shifted his position, in the midst of a shower of balls and bullets."

There will soon be stronger reason than ever for the

question to be raised: "Who is able to make war with him?" The inquiry implies that his power will reach such a point of culmination that the whole world will be challenged in vain to produce any one capable of staying his victorious progress or successfully withstanding him in the battle-field. In the fact that all the world is represented as raising this inquiry, we discover how universal will be the acknowledgment of the power, which he is to possess as a mighty conqueror, in the exercise of which he is further stated, in Rev. xiii. 7, to bring into subjection "all kindreds, and tongues, and nations." His policy and actions hitherto plainly indicate that he is hastening to fulfil this his appointed destiny. He pants for a universal empire, and is inflamed with the ardent ambition of eclipsing the victorious achievements of Cæsar, Alexander, and Napoleon Bonaparte. There will doubtless be a period in his career when he will very nearly approximate to the possession of the sovereignty of the whole earth. Some have considered that the Roman earth alone will be the scene of his victorious exploits, but it is at least not unlikely that some French troops may soon be landed on the American continent, in consequence of the war of which it is unhappily the scene. Some of the extreme Southern States—Florida, Louisiana, and Mississippi—were once French possessions, as was likewise the greater part of St. Domingo; and it is not improbable that Napoleon's restless ambition would lead him to make any practicable endeavor to restore them to their former position, French colonies. The annexation of part of Lower Canada to France is also not unlikely to be attempted in event of war between France and England. There is a growing disaffection of the French Canadians to the British Government, and it is believed that a friendly understanding is being established by their leaders between them and Napoleon. This Man of War is extending his conquests in Europe, Asia, and Africa, three of the four great continents of the earth, and he cannot long be expected to leave the fourth, the American continent, unvisited.*

* Since the above was printed, in July, 1861, Napoleon landed some forces in Mexico, in Dec., 1861, and is rapidly progressing toward its complete conquest. He will, doubtless, soon form an alliance with the Southern States, and not long afterwards invade and overcome the Northern States, and, eventually, also Canada.— (4th Edition, Nov. 1863.)

III. BECAUSE HE has obtained actual possession of Rome. The seven Heads are explained in Rev. xvii. 9, 10, to be a double type: first, of the Seven Hills of Rome, and secondly, of the Seven Dynasties which have successively ruled over the Roman Empire. On this account, as well as because Rome was the ancient Capital of the Roman Empire, it is essential to the character of each of the Seven Heads or Forms of Government, that during at least some period of its continuance its representative should have possession of the City of Rome. If Louis Napoleon were lacking in this grand prerequisite, he could not be the Personal Antichrist, or septimo-octave Head of the Beast. But ever since 1849 he has maintained military occupation of Rome; and although this is not essential to a character of a Head of the Beast for more than part of its existence, yet it is not likely that he will relinquish that city, (except perhaps temporarily,) as it seems to be indicated in Prophecy to be possessed by the last Antichrist until it is destroyed by a volcanic eruption. There is scarcely any circumstance in Louis Napoleon's career more remarkable than that events should so have fallen out, as to enable him to make Rome virtually an appendage of the French Empire at the very period at which it was demanded by the necessity of Prophecy.

It was held by some of the Fathers that the Roman Empire, after remaining torpid for some centuries, would be revived at the End of the World, in all its laws and forms. Hippolytus (A.D. 200) said: "The system of Augustus Cæsar, who was founder of the Roman Empire, shall be adopted and established by him (Antichrist) in order to his own aggrandisement and glory." In accordance with this view, Rome will doubtless be possessed by Napoleon as one of his principal cities during his 3½ years' reign as Antichrist, although it appears that Jerusalem will be his ecclesiastical metropolis, and in its temple divine worship will be offered to him, (2 Thess. ii. 4,) and to his image, which is the abomination of desolation, (Matt. xxiv. 15, Mark xiii. 14, Dan. ix. 27, xi. 31, xii. 11.) As the Pope is foreshown to cause Louis Napoleon's image to be worshipped, (Rev. xiii. 11–18,) and as the image is particularly to be set up in the Jewish temple at the beginning of the 3½ years, (Dan. xii. 11,) therefore it is highly probable that the Pope will then be at Jerusalem, especially as he is to be the almost inseparable companion of Napoleon, exercising all his power in his presence. He is also foreshown in Rev. xix. 20, xvi. 16, to be destroyed at Armageddon, near Jerusalem, shortly after the end of the 3½ years; but whether he will at any time permanently transfer the Pontifical seat from Rome to Jerusalem, does not clearly appear. It seems 'that the Burning of Rome (Is. xxxiv., Rev. xviii., xix. 3) will not occur until the overthrow of Napoleon and the Roman Pontiff at Armageddon; and then the full restoration of the Jews will take place, as Kimchi in 1660 expressed it: "This is the hope of the nation¹—when Rome shall be desolated, then there shall be the redemption of Israel."*

IV. BECAUSE HE APPARENTLY protects and supports the Pope, but yet suffers him to be plundered, and gradually stripped of his temporal power. (Rev. xvii.)

It was distinctly foretold in Rev. xvii. that the Eighth Head of the Beast should for a time sustain the Papacy, and then, in conjunction with his ten vassal kings, consummate its ruin. The ten-horned Beast is represented in that chapter as carrying upon its shoulders the scarlet-clad unchaste woman, who symbolizes the Romish Church. The exact period in the history of the Beast to which this representation applies is clearly stated by the interpreting angel in verse 8: "The beast that thou sawest was, and is not, and shall (is just about to) ascend out of the abyss, and go into perdition." The point of time, then, at which the Beast was seen carrying the woman, was precisely at the period when it could be said of it, "It was and is not;" that is, during its headless, non-existent state, from 1815 to 1852, and also just before it ascended out of the abyss to go into perdition—in other

* The partial restoration of the Jews, when Antichrist makes the covenant with them, and which occurs about seven years before their complete restoration at the commencement of the Millennium, was apparently referred to by Isaac Peyreyra, in 1643, in his "Recall of the Jews," where he said: "This recall and establishment of the Jews in land that is promised them shall be effected by a temporal prince. . . This temporal king shall be the universal king foretold by the holy prophets, and to whom all the rest of the kings of the earth shall do homage. And this king will be a king of France."

words, just previous to its emergence in 1852 from that headless, non-existent state. Turning to the page of history, we find that this hieroglyphical picture exactly corresponds with the position of the secular beast in 1849, when Napoleon, as President of France, sent French troops to support the Pope in Rome; thus, in accordance with the vision exhibited by the angel in Rev. xvii., the Beast recommenced carrying the woman just before its ascent out of the abyss of political non-existence. This ascent was effected on the 2d December, 1852, when Louis Napoleon assumed the old Roman title of Emperor, restoring the Empire and Monarchy as in the time of Bonaparte.

But although Napoleon has maintained the Pope in the Vatican of Rome ever since July 15th, 1849, he has remorselessly permitted him to be despoiled of his most valuable temporalities. In 1859–60, Victor Emmanuel, the present King of United Italy, reduced the Pope's Italian provinces to one quarter of their former dimensions. Whereas there were previously two millions inhabitants in the Papal dominions, there are now left only half a million, since the three provinces of the Marshes, Umbra, and Viterbo were annexed to Victor Emmanuel's kingdom. In a protest addressed from the Vatican on September 18th, 1860, to the members of the diplomatic corps in Rome, the Pope complains that he has seen nearly all the States, which are the patrimony of the Church, torn away from him bit by bit. The papal bull, which as a last resort was fulminated against Victor Emmanuel, was utterly disregarded by the object of its anathemas, and has only served to demonstrate more clearly the unpopularity and impotence of the Pope. The interference of Napoleon, to stay the victorious progress of Garibaldi, was anxiously desired by the Romish Church, but "the eldest son of the Pope" complied no further than by preserving the city of Rome itself from actual invasion. In this his selfish indifference to the interests of the Pope, and concern only for his own aggrandizement, are apparent, as it is believed that he chiefly continues the occupation of Rome because he deems its possession, as the capital of the old Roman Empire, to be indispensable to his intended position of King over the subordinate kings of the Roman earth.

Had Napoleon been a real defender of the Pope, he would have opposed the onward march of Garibaldi, who has publicly avowed his hatred of Popery in such terms as these: "I tell you that your chief enemy is the Pope. The Pope is no Christian; he denies the very principle of Christianity." It is evident, however, that the general spoliation of the Papal Hierarchy, foretold in Rev. xvii. to take place under the eighth Head, has already begun, and will progress until the Pope and Romish priests, denuded of their wealth and power, will become pliant tools in the hand of Napoleon to cause the idolatrous worship of him to be universally instituted. It was declared in Rev. xvii. that under the eighth Head, the ten Horn kingdoms should "hate the harlot and make her desolate and naked, and eat her flesh and burn her with fire." This general confiscation of the wealth and temporalities of the Papal Church will take place at the time of the establishment of Napoleon's $3\frac{1}{2}$ years' infidel apostacy, which will arise Phœnix-like out of the smoking ruins of fallen Babylon. The Papal Hierarchy will then FALL. From being a professedly Christian Church, it will become a system of downright infidelity, commanding men to worship Napoleon and his image. In this new form it will attain almost universal predominance. Bigoted Papists will then boast of the universal supremacy of their Church, but in reality the Roman Catholic Church will then no longer exist, for its priests will have become converted to a new religion — a system of pagan heathenism, having for its chief object of worship not God or Christ, but a man — even Napoleon, the Man of Sin. Thus a brief but terrible period of $3\frac{1}{2}$ years will succeed the fall of Babylon, during which Napoleon will install himself in the place of Deity itself, and will claim and receive the adoration of a great portion of mankind.* All (the ungodly) *that dwell*

---

* A suspicion of this appalling fact is beginning to find expression in many quarters. In the London *Christian World* of November, 1860, in an article on the Papacy, it is said: "A dark cloud hangs over Europe; we cannot conceal the settled conviction that the fall of Popery is the signal for the appearance of something immeasurably more terrible than itself. That the continuance of the tremendous visitation will be brief, it is consolatory to believe; but during its short period of existence, its work in the world will be very awful. Nor do we say that Louis Napoleon is the Personal Antichrist, so distinctly set before us *upon the earth* (at least nearly all Christendom and some parts of Heathendom) *shall worship him*, (Rev. xiii. 8,) either by worshipping his image or by having stamped upon their foreheads or right hands his mark or name, or 666, the number of his name, (Rev. xiii. 11–18.) Hundreds of thousands of persons will be martyred *by flame and by the sword*, (Dan. xi. 33, Rev. vi. 9, xv. 2, xx. 4,) for refusing thus to worship him, and scenes similar to those witnessed at the setting up of Nebuchadnezzar's golden image (Dan. iii.) will again be enacted. Those who do thus worship* him, in order to escape being put to death, will be hereafter ETERNALLY DAMNED IN HELL-FIRE, (Rev. xiv. 9–12.)

In several instances lately, the French Emperor, in his predicted character of a Wild Beast rending and devouring the Papal harlot, has begun to show his teeth and to unsheath his claws. He is reported to have declared to the Bishop of Versailles, that the temporal power of the Pope was incompatible with the advance of civilization, and must be put down. A pamphlet called "The Pope and the Emperor," which is suspected to shadow forth Napoleon's intentions, has also appeared recently in Paris,

by the prophets of both Testaments; but every thing in his history—his connection with France, the resurrection of the Empire by his skill, his nominal protection of the Pope, while he allows his temporal authority to pass from his hands, his extraordinary reserve, and his insatiable ambition to become the greatest monarch in the world—fixes our thoughts upon him as possibly the Pope Emperor, whose character, career, and destiny are stated with such terrible fidelity in the book of truth."

* While literal-day futurist expositors have always held the *image of the Beast* to be the literal image of the Personal Antichrist, year-day expositors for the most part have supposed it to be the image-worship of the Papists. They might, however, consistently admit that there would yet be a more complete and literal accomplishment of it; for it is clear that the Romish priests have never, even in a single recorded instance, caused any man to have the number 666 marked on his forehead or right hand, (Rev. xiii. 17.) The fulfilment that the prophecies have undergone on the year-day scale, with regard to Popery and Mahommedanism, is only a typical, accommodated, and precursive one. The *image of the Beast* (Rev. xvi. 2) could not have been set up before 1852, for it is made to the Beast *which had the wound by a sword and did live*, (Rev. xiii. 14,) that is, subsequent to 1852, when the Beast's wounded seventh Head was healed. Bengelius and Smucker are year-day expositors who believe it to be a literal image, not yet set up.

and gravely proposes that the Emperor shall himself become Pope, and unite the political and religious sovereignties in his own person. A serious disagreement has likewise arisen between the Roman Pontiff and Napoleon, owing to the refusal of the former to appoint some nominees of Napoleon to the vacant bishoprics; the Pope's objection to them arising from their not being upholders of the Ultramontane policy of the Vatican. The opposition, however, of the Pope and Cardinals cannot avail to shake the foundations of Napoleon's throne, and perhaps will not last long, as the present Pope is old and feeble, and another may soon succeed him, whom the Emperor may find more compliant and manageable.

V. BECAUSE THE WHOLE EXTENT of the original Roman Empire is becoming subordinated to his control, and is evidently approaching its final division into ten kingdoms, whose ten kings united a European Congress are to give their power and strength to the Eighth Head during the closing $3\frac{1}{2}$ years. Rev. xvii. 13. (See also ch. ii., events xi. xii.)

The Lion, the Bear, the Leopard, and the nondescript ten-horned Beast mentioned in Dan. vii., are universally allowed to symbolize the four successive Gentile Monarchies, the Babylonian, Medo-Persian, Grecian and Roman, to which kingly power has been temporarily transferred from the Jews (in consequence of the unfaithfulness of the latter) for 2520 years, (*seven times*, Dan. iv. 16,) from 649 B.C. to 1871-2. A.D. The ten horns on the fourth Beast, in common with the ten toes of the Metallic Image, (Dan. ii. 41,) are foreshown (Rev. xvii. 12) to be ten kings, among whom the *whole* Roman Empire is during the existence of its Eighth Head, to be subdivided for *one hour*, (which always in year-day Revelation means $3\frac{1}{2}$ years, Rev. iii. 10, xi. 11, 13.) This is further represented in literal-day Rev. xiii., where Satan having been cast to the earth (Rev. xii. 17) persecutes the Church by causing the Roman Wild-Beast under its Eighth Head, Napoleon, to arise with its ten horns crowned, (showing that the ten kings have now received power for *one hour*:) and the Antichristian career of the Beast in this form, with its ten kings crowned, (Rev. xiii.,) is limited to 42 months, or $3\frac{1}{2}$ years, being the same period as the one hour of Rev. xvii. 12. It thus appears that Napoleon's

NAPOLEON III. KING OF THE TEN KINGS. 23

ten vassal kings will not be elected and crowned over the ten Horn-kingdoms of the Roman earth until just before the final 3½ years, which begin 3½ years after the Covenant.

The present rulers within the Roman Empire will have been displaced or deposed by that time. As Napoleon I. made his brothers Jerome, Louis, and Joseph (to whom the crown of Mexico was afterwards offered) respectively the kings of Westphalia, Holland, and Spain, and his brother-in-law, Murat, king of Naples: so Napoleon III., the modern "Augustus, nephew and heir of Cæsar," as the Paris *Constitutionnel* has termed him, will doubtless cause some if not all of his ten vassal kings to be members of the Bonaparte family; and it seems that one of them will be King or Viceroy over France, while Napoleon will act exclusively as King over the ten Kings, and Supreme Head of the European Congress.

It is nearly certain that the ten Toe or Horn kingdoms will in the main be Great Britain, France, Spain, Italy, Austria, Tripoli, (with contiguous territory annexed to them,) together with the four Macedonian Horn-kingdoms, namely: Greece, Egypt, Syria, and the rest of Turkey. Louis Napoleon is increasingly shown to be the Eighth Head or last Antichrist by the fact that the Roman Empire is gradually being moulded into this decem-regal form, and he is rapidly progressing in the acquirement of greater ascendency over these countries, so that the time when ten kings shall be elected over these ten kingdoms, and shall unanimously give their power and strength to him, (Rev. xvii. 12,) is manifestly not far distant. Although at the outset of his reign, he was regarded as a *parvenu* and an upstart by the European governments, which at the Congress of the Holy Alliance in 1815 had decreed that no Bonaparte should ever sit upon the throne of France, yet he now has nearly all the European nations at his nod, and soon they will be compelled to bow in yet more complete submission to his will. The Crimean war in 1855 served to display the efficiency and strength of the French army, and contributed in no slight degree to make France increasingly feared and respected. It greatly advanced her influence both with the Turkish Sultan and the Czar of Russia, and is believed to have resulted in the conclusion of a secret treaty on the part of France with the latter. In this treaty an understanding was doubtless established between Napoleon and the Czar for the future promotion of their mutual interests by seizing possession of the Turkish dominions. Another proof of the commanding position which he has attained in Europe, was exhibited in his interposition in 1859 in the war between Austria and Sardinia, which humbled the power of Austria and greatly strengthened the alliance between France and Italy. The subsequent annexation of Savoy and Nice to France in 1860, although viewed with jealousy and suspicion by the other powers, was an act to which none of them dare offer any effectual opposition. This event, as well as the separation of Belgium from Holland on Nov. 2, 1830, and of Hanover from England in 1837, and the severance from Turkey of Greece in 1822, of Algiers in 1830, of Egypt in 1840, and of Moldavia and Wallachia in 1857, and also the fusion of the different Italian States into one United Kingdom under Victor Emmanuel in 1860, are preparatory steps toward the moulding of the original Roman earth into exactly ten kingdoms, which shall own Napoleon as their Supreme Head. He now possesses almost paramount influence over Spain and Italy, and appears to be succeeding in the effort to persuade the sovereigns of Prussia and Russia that it is for their interest to act in the strictest concert and union with him. His energy in extending his power in Algiers and elsewhere on the northern coast of Africa, and his evident determination to obtain possession of Palestine,* additionally indicate his design to become supreme over the Roman earth.

* The restoration of the Jews to Palestine was meditated by Napoleon I.; he convoked a great sanhedrim of Jewish Rabbins at Paris in 1807, who requested of him the admission of their nation to a free participation in civil and religious rights. Madame D'Abrantes (ch. 18) remarks upon this: "The Emperor knew that in Poland, Russia, Hungary, and Bohemia, troops of this race were congregated whose hearts, oppressed by persecution and misfortune, would open with ecstacy to an honorable futurity, and would salute with the name of Messiah the man who would offer it to them." Bicheno, who wrote in 1790, and predicted the coming of Christ to occur about 1864, said: "If the French should get possession of Syria, nothing is more probable than that they will invite the Jews to join them, and to take possession of their own country." There are now about five million Jews, if not more, estimated to be scattered throughout the world, and 11,000 of them in Palestine, of

The power of Great Britain offers the principal impediment to Napoleon's attainment of uncontrolled dominion over the Roman world, but Prophecy most clearly shows that England is soon to *give its power and strength* to him, and to be included among the ten Horn-kingdoms that are to *agree and give their kingdom* to him, (Rev. xvii. 12-17.) These ten kingdoms are to be formed *out of* the whole Roman earth, which will thus undergo a tenfold division, (Dan. ii. 41, vii. 24.) England was undeniably part of the Roman Empire, being occupied by a Roman garrison for about 400 years at the beginning of the Christian era; there is therefore NOT THE SLIGHTEST DOUBT but that it will be comprehended among Napoleon's ten vassal kingdoms. Although it separated from the Papal kingdoms at the Reformation, and being made whole, like the tenth leper, turned back and with a loud voice of Antipapal protestation glorified God, yet it only thereby severed its connection with the territory of Babylon, which is to be burnt with fire, (Rev. xviii.) And this cannot in the least alter the naked historical fact of its being part of the Roman earth,*

whom 7000 are settled in Jerusalem, (at the date of the third edition of this book in 1862.) Perhaps Louis Napoleon will convoke a general assembly of the leading Jews, like that of 1807, when he makes the Covenant with them.

* Sismondi in his Fall of the Roman Empire (ch. l.) says: "From the time of Augustus to that of Constantine the world of Rome was bounded by nearly the same frontiers. ... On the north the Empire was bounded by the wall of the Caledonians or Picts, the Rhine, the Danube, and the Black Sea, (Dacia, north of the Danube, was also included for 150 years.) The Picts' wall, which transected Scotland at its narrowest point, left the Romans in possession of the Lowlands of that country and of the whole of England." Tacitus in his "Life of Agricola," translated by Murphy, gives a detailed account of the subjugation of England partially by Plautius and then fully by Agricola: he says (sec. xiv.): "Under the auspices of Aulus Plautius and Ostorius Scapula the southern part of Britain took the form of a Roman province, (A.U.C. 799 and A.D. 48, in the reign of the Emperor Claudius.) Gibbon in his Decline and Fall of Rome (ch. i.) also narrates how Agricola (who lived from A.D. 40 to 93) completed the conquest of all Britain as far as the Friths of Scotland. David Hume in his History of England, (ch. i.) writes: "The general, who finally established the dominion of the Romans in this island (Britain) was Julius Agricola, who governed it in the reigns of Vespasian, Titus and Domitian, (A.D. 70 to 85.) Thus also Lingard. And John Wade, in his British History (at Bohn's, London) dates the Roman rule over England from A.D. 49 to 428.

which from the Euphrates to the Atlantic, and from northern Africa to the Clyde, the Rhine, and Upper Danube, is to fall under the power of Louis Napoleon, the Eighth Head, (Rev. xvii. 13.) Either by internal revolution or diplomacy or foreign invasion, or all three influences combined, the sovereign of England will be induced to become the vassal of Napoleon within about 3 or 3½ years after the date of the Jewish covenant: and tens of thousands of persons in Great Britain will be slain for refusing to worship Napoleon's image during the subsequent 3½ years' infidel persecution. Ireland will doubtless be the scene of the same persecution of Christians; and as it never was part of the old Roman Empire, it will within about 5 or 6 years secede from England and be placed under a separate government.* It is not unlikely that Great Britain is one of the three among the ten horns that are to be violently subdued by Napoleon, (literal-day Dan. vii. 24, *after them*, is literally οπως, behind them;) the other two being probably Syria and Egypt, (Dan. xi. 40.) England's naval superiority, which prevented Napoleon I. successfully invading her, now no longer exists. It cannot now be said that Britannia rules the waves: for her wooden walls are rendered useless by the recent invention of iron-clad men-of-war, with which France is as well, if not better, supplied than Great Britain. The French army is also much larger than the British army, for it is stated by the *London Times* to have 2¼ times more infantry and ten times more cavalry; and to cost annually for its maintenance twenty-four million pounds sterling, (one hundred and twenty million dollars.) Although it is more than questionable whether Christians are justified in resisting evil by taking up arms, yet there is at least real ground for the apprehensions which have led England to vote ten million

* Nearly one-third of the 220,000 British soldiers are Irish Romanists, who, Sepoy-like, will be led by the Jesuits to help Napoleon to revolutionize Ireland, and overmaster the British Empire. Well-nigh half of the 220,000 are now garrisoning distant colonies, leaving England, even with her 200,000 volunteers, but feebly armed against 650,000 French soldiers. That all the Roman Empire, including England, will become subject to the Last Antichrist, is distinctly held by Sir E. Denny, Dr. Tregelles, B. W. Newton, Kelsall, Taunton, etc.

pounds sterling for additional fortifications, and to arm and equip two hundred thousand volunteers. It is a significant fact that Napoleon on his trial after the Boulogne expedition said to his judges: "I represent before you a principle, a cause and a defeat. The principle is the sovreignty of the people: the cause is that of the Empire: the defeat is that of Waterloo. The principle—you have recognized it; the cause—you have served in it; the defeat—you would avenge it." He also addressed his army after the "coup d'etat" in 1851: "Soldiers, I have given you now two revenges, one for 1830 and one for 1840. The third I now promise you is for Waterloo." He is likewise reported to have said during his residence in England: "I shall be Emperor of France one of these days, and I shall then invade England. I like you very well as a people, but I must wipe out Waterloo and St. Helena."*

It is foretold in year-day (Rev. xvi. 14) that all nations will be gathered to the Armageddon War by the spirits of Spiritualism and Popery. This War will be at its height during a year and a month, (literal-day Rev. ix. 15,) beginning 5 years after the Jewish Covenant, and will consist in Crusades of all the nations of Christendom under Napoleon's leadership against countless hosts from Asia that will invade Palestine. The next few years will therefore witness a wide diffusion of the influence of these spirits, preparing men to submit to Napo-

* Prophecy distinctly shows that all the ten kingdoms in the Roman earth will have become republican before the final 8½ years; in short, England, Spain, Austria, Greece, Egypt, Turkey, Syria, Tripoli, will have elected their kings by universal suffrage, (see ch. ii. event xii.) The "Last Vials" for August, 1858, gives extracts from pamphlets published in France foreshadowing Napoleon's designs against England. One called "Cherbourg and England" says: "Let the English upper classes reflect on what support they would obtain from the English people, when a French General should present himself with universal suffrage in one hand and the Code Napoleon in the other." "From the present day amidst all his misery, the English workman will keep his eyes fixed upon CHERBOURG and seek to discover the approach of the fleet of deliverance." It is easy to foresee that amid coming troubles a strong Chartist party will be formed in England that will hail Napoleon's advent to their shores, as the great champion of universal suffrage and the people's rights. Thus will England "give (spontaneously yield) its power and strength" to Napoleon, (Rev. xvii. 13.)

leon as their Supreme Head. Indeed Spiritualism has already *gone forth to the kings of the earth,* for several of them practise it, and it is rapidly spreading throughout Europe. Although no such idea seems hitherto to have occurred to Spiritualists, yet it is certain that the miracle-working spirits will soon instruct them to accept Napoleon as their political and ecclesiastical Head, and ultimately to worship him as their god, (II. Thess. ii.) During the same 3½ years' worship of Napoleon, the Roman Pontiff will be "the constituted vice-president of the inquisitorial tribunals of this Antichristian Reign of Terror over all kindreds and tongues and nations, and the ecclesiastical vicegerent of that undivided sovereignty in Church and State which the Septimo-octave Head will assume as the pro-Christ and long promised Regenerator of a fallen world."

VI. BECAUSE IN RESPECT OF HIS NAME he fulfils the prophecy, that the name of the Eighth Head or Antichrist should be in the Greek tongue *Apollyon* (or *Apoleon*) and should numerically be equal to the number 666, (Rev. ix. and xiii.)

As Josiah's name was foretold 300 years before he was born, (1 Kings xiii. 2, 2 Kings xxiii. 16,) and Cyrus's name 150 years prior to his birth, (Is. xliv. 28, Ez. i. 2,) so the very name of Napoleon the Antichrist has been foretold 1750 years before his existence, for we read in Rev. ix. 11, *They* (that is, the locusts, unless the men whom they torment are spoken of) *had a king over them which is the angel of the bottomless pit, whose name in the Hebrew tongue is Abaddon, but in the Greek tongue hath his name Apollyon.* The majority of expositors nave understood this to be a description of the human deputy and chief envoy of Satan; and it is generally interpreted in the year-day fulfilment to refer to Mahomed, who typified the Antichrist; but in the principal and literal-day fulfilment it signifies that Antichrist's name in Greek must literally be *Apollyon.* Every sensible person can see that *Napoleon* and *Apollyon* are substantially the same words and resemble each other quite as much as Hezekiah and Ezekias, (Matt. i. 10,) or Uzziah (2 Kings xv. 32) and Ozias, (Matt. i. 9,) which are instances of the dissimilar ways in which the same name is spelt in different portions of Scripture. *Apollyon* in the original Greek is Απολλυων, the present participle of the verb απολλυμι, *I destroy;* but another form in which this Greek verb is sometimes written is απολεω, (as in lexicon to Bohn's Greek Testament,) with its participle απολεων, which in English is *Apoleon*—a word precisely identical with *Napoleon*, excepting the first letter *N*, nor can this trivial difference (as is the opinion of the Rev. Dr. Croly, who maintains the identity of the two words) be deemed of the slightest importance. Bengel and other expositors who hold Apollyon to be identical with Antichrist, have remarked that as the word *Antichrist* is exactly the reverse of *Christ*, so *Apollyon*, signifying a Destroyer, is precisely the opposite of *Jesus*, which means a Saviour, (Matt. i. 21.) Thus Louis Napoleon's predestined name, (*N*)*apollyon the Antichrist* is diametrically antagonistic in its signification to our Lord's name *Jesus the Christ*. The one comes to destroy men's lives, the other to save them, (Luke ix. 56.) Apollyon is likewise called *the angel of the bottomless pit*, which is clearly parallel with the prediction that Antichrist or the Eighth Head *ascends out of the bottomless pit*, (Rev. xvii. 8, xi. 7.). Hengstenberg, who speaks of the *striking resemblance* between the words *Napoleon* and *Apollyon*, justly remarks that Satan cannot be denoted by *Apollyon*, for although he is spoken of as having his angels, (Matt. xxv. 41, Rev. xii. 9,) yet he is never himself called an angel. The circumstance of Louis Napoleon determining to be designated by his present name, remarkably shows the overruling hand of Providence, because if out of his original name of Charles Louis Napoleon Bonaparte he had selected the words Charles Bonaparte to be his usual designation he would not so completely have fulfilled the prophecy.

We also read in Rev. xiii. 18: "*Here is wisdom. Let him that hath understanding count the number of the Beast*, (θηριον, properly the Wild-Beast:) *for it is the number of a man; and his number is six hundred threescore and six.*" The Wild-Beast here referred to is evidently from the context *the Wild-Beast which had the wound by a sword and did live*, (verse 14,) and whose *deadly wound was healed*, (verse 12,) that is, the Wild-Beast since 1852 under Napoleon III.,* its seventh-revived or resurrected Head, the career of which is specially described in Rev. xiii. Although the Wild-Beast primarily signifies the Roman Empire, yet Louis Napoleon, its Eighth Head, as its personal representative, is himself comprehensively denominated the Wild-Beast; and in Rev. xiii., it is stated that during his 3½ years' persecution of the saints, (verse 5,) a second Wild-Beast, the Roman Pontiff, will cause people to make an idol or image (εικων, as in Rom. i. 23) to him and worship it, and have imprinted on their right hands or foreheads his mark or his name, (one of the words *Louis Napoleon*,) or 666, the number of his name, (Rev. iii. 17, xv. 2.) This will be a revival of the custom, that formerly obtained among the Greeks, of putting upon their hands or foreheads the hieroglyphic name or mark of the heathen deity they worshipped. In the Latin, Greek, and Hebrew languages, the letters of the alphabet were used as numerals instead of the Arabic figures, and therefore when Antichrist's name is translated into those languages, the letters composing it will necessarily amount to a certain number, which is called the number of his name. *Louis* is essentially a word of Latin origin, and becomes in Latin *Ludovicus;* thus the Roman Catholic priests, in their Latin prayers for Napoleon, say *Fac salvum Ludovicum.* This word was long since thought of by many expositors as likely to be the name of the Antichrist or Wild-Beast, because of the exactness with which it con-

---

* Even secular writers use the prophetic imagery in describing the resurrection in 1852 of the Napoleon dynasty *that was and is not and yet is.* Mr. St. John, in his Biography of Napoleon III., p. 273, says: "They elected him as one of their representatives in that Legislative Babel, the National Assembly. From that moment the fate of the Republic was sealed. *The skeleton of Napoleon*, already brought from St. Helena, *rose from its grave* to crush the fragile form of Liberty to death. *The old man stood in the young one*, whom he had invested with artificial interest, and enabled him to stifle the voice of freedom." Napoleon III. is moreover better prepared than his uncle for the position of universal monarch, from having resided in the United States, England, Italy, Switzerland, Germany, etc., and being in fact a cosmopolite, or citizen of the world. He may almost be regarded as a naturalized Englishman, having lived so long in England, and even acted as special constable to suppress apprehended riots in London in April, 1848.

NAPOLEON'S NAME EQUAL TO 666.

tains the number 666. The Rev. J. Brooks, in his "Elements of Prophecy," in 1836, said:—"Seebachius was, I believe, the first that fixed upon *Ludovicus* as the name of the Beast, on account of France being considered the principal of the kingdoms of the Beast; but many others have adopted the name." The Rev. David Simpson and the Rev. Joseph Sutcliffe, in their writings more than half a century since, and Bengel, a German writer more than a century ago, in his "Gnomon," also considered it to be the word foresignified, as containing 666. But still (*N*)*apoleon* must be Antichrist's chief name. (Rev. ix. 11.)

In the Latin tongue only seven letters of the alphabet possess any numerical value: I=1, V (or U)=5, X=10, L=50, C=100, D=500, M=1000; the remaining letters are ciphers. *Ludovicus*, when reduced to figures according to the respective values of these Roman letters, amounts precisely to 666: as is shown thus: L 50+U 5 +D 500+O 0+V 5+I 1+C 100+U 5+S 0=666. In the Greek language every letter represents a numeral, according to the following scale: α=1, β=2, γ=3, δ=4, ε=5, ς (stigma)=6, ζ=7, η=8, θ=9, ι=10, κ=20, λ=30, μ=40, ν=50, ξ=60, ο=70, π=80, (koppa) =90, ρ=100, σ=200, τ=300, υ=400, φ=500, χ=600, ψ=700, ω=800. When the word *Napoleon*, which is of Greek origin, is written in the dative case in Greek—the usual Greek form of dedicatory inscriptions upon the foreheads of devotees, or temples (e. g. Acts xvii. 23)*—it becomes Ναπολεοντι, which contains the fatal number 666, as is thus shown: N 50+α 1+π 80+ο 70+λ 30+ ε 5+ο 70+ν 50+τ 300+ι 10=666. For the Revelation being written in Greek, the number 666 must be contained in Antichrist's name in Greek, and in the

---

* There appears to be an allusion to Napoleon's name in Jer. iv. 7, where the desolation of Palestine by the last great Antichrist is thus described: "The lion is come up from his thicket and the destroyer of the Gentiles is on his way: he is gone forth from his place to make thy land desolate." In Greek, ναπος (*napos*) means a *thicket*, and λεος (*leos*) means a *lion*; these two words combined, almost exactly form the word Ναπολεον, *Napoleon*.

If the Personal Antichrist is denoted by the "Idol Shepherd" in Zech. xi. 17, then it would seem that before leaving this earth, he will become blind in his right eye and paralysed in his arm by the stroke of a sword.

inscriptive form of the dative case. This number 666 is contained not only in each of the words *Louis Napoleon*, separately, in the manner just mentioned, but also in both of them written in Greek, Λοις Ναπολεον, and added together thus: Λ 30+ο 70+ι 10+ς 200+Ν 50+ α 1+π 80+ο 70+λ 30+ε 5+ο 70+ν 50=666.

The statement that *the number of the Wild-Beast is the number of a man*, clearly implies that the term, *the Wild-Beast*, is used as a synonym for its Eighth Head, the Man of Sin, the number of whose name must be 666. This principal fulfilment does not, however, exclude additional fulfilments in other designations of the ten-horned Wild-Beast, as well as in regard to the two-horned Wild-Beast, (Rev. xiii.,) or Roman Pontiff, (whose two horns probably point to his becoming the Head of two hitherto separate Hierarchies, the Romish and Greek Church, or perhaps the Mahomedan Church.) For thus the number 666 is contained in a Latin title of the Pope, *Vicarius filii Dei*, and again in the Greek words αποςατης, *an apostate*, λατεινος, (all the letters of which, except the last, are found in Ναπολεοντι,) a Latin man, and ή λατινη βασιλεια, the Latin kingdom. As the number 7 is a symbol of the most perfect excellence, so the number 6 is a symbol of the most complete depravity; and 8 is a resurrection number; the Greek letters of the name of Jesus, (Ιησους,) who is the first-fruits of the Resurrection, numerically amount to 888; also the 8th Head of the Roman Empire is, as it were, a resurrection man, who has raised the Napoleon dynasty from its grave, and who will leave this earth without himself undergoing death, (Rev. xix. 20.)

VII. BECAUSE HIS GRECIAN EXTRACTION, his sphinx-like impenetrability of countenance, his addiction to the practice of Spiritualism, and his deceptive professions of a pacific policy, identify him with the description given of the Personal Antichrist in Dan. viii.

In the prophetic vision recorded in Dan. viii., a two-horned ram, representing the Medo-Persian kingdom, was exhibited as being assaulted and trampled under foot by a goat symbolizing the Grecian kingdom. Between the goat's eyes was a notable horn, which was explained

to signify Alexander the Great, (verse 21.) When by
Alexander's death the notable horn was broken, four
great horns came up in its place, denoting Egypt, Greece,
Thrace, and Syria, the four kingdoms respectively of
Ptolemy, Cassander, Lysimachus, and Seleucus, Alexander's generals, among whom the Grecian kingdom thus
became subdivided. Out of one of these four horns or
kingdoms there afterwards came *forth a little horn which
waxed exceeding great toward the south and toward the
east and toward the pleasant land*, (verse 9.) This little
horn, which is typically the Mahomedan Antichrist, but
antitypically the Personal Antichrist, Louis Napoleon, is
further described in verses 23, 24, 25:

" When the transgressors are come to the full, a king of fierce countenance, and understanding dark sentences, (*of obdurate countenance
and penetrating with mysterious craft*—Wintle's translation,) shall stand
up. And his power shall be mighty, but not by his own power: and
he shall destroy wonderfully and shall prosper, and practise, and shall
destroy the mighty and the holy people. And through his policy also
he shall cause craft to prosper in his hand ; and he shall magnify himself in his heart and by peace shall destroy many: he shall also stand
up against the Prince of Princes, but he shall be broken without hand."

Louis Napoleon has *come forth out of* Greece, one of
the four horn-kingdoms, because he derives his origin and
is lineally descended from a Grecian family of high rank.
One of his ancestors, David II., Emperor of Trebisonde,
was the rightful heir to the throne of Constantinople, but
was put to death by Mahomed II.; his only surviving
son, George Nicephor Comnène, fled to Mania in Peloponesus in 1476, and was made Protogeras over the community that was settled there. This official dignity was
held by ten members of the Comnène family in succession,
until 1675, when Constantine Comnène, the tenth protogeras, was induced from fear of being subjugated by the
Turks, to emigrate from Mania to Italy with 3000 of his
fellow-countrymen. Arriving in Genoa on Jan. 1, 1676,
he obtained from the Genoese Senate a grant of some
tracts of land in Corsica, which were thenceforth colonized by him and his descendants. One of his sons, Calomeros Comnène, subsequently settled in Florence in
Tuscany, and as the Greek word *Calomeros* ($καλχ ὑιρος$)
signifies in Italian *buona parte*, he therefore adopted the
name of Buonaparte. In 1719 Antonio Buonaparte, a

member of this Buonaparte branch of the Comnéne family, emigrated from Tuscany to Corsica: and Napoleon Buonaparte, who was born at Ajaccio in Corsica on Aug. 15, 1769, was his grandson. Corsica was ceded by the Genoese to France in 1768. The descent of the Comnène family from David II., last Emperor of Trebisonde, was attested by letters patent of Louis XVI., issued on Sept. 1, 1783. This account of Napoleon's family is given in the Memoirs of the Duchess D'Abrantes, published at Paris in 1835.

The characteristics of the *little horn* of Dan. viii. also apply to Louis Napoleon in respect of his being *a king of fierce countenance*, taking this Hebrew phrase to signify (as in Deut. viii. 50) the possession of iron strength and indomitable determination. Or if we translate the adjective *fierce* from the Greek of the Septuagint, where it is rendered αναιδης, it will signify a brazen-faced, imperturbable, immovable, unreadable visage. Napoleon's countenance has long been noticed to be of this character: it expresses no emotion either of joy or grief, of affection or hatred, of exultation or disappointment. Being thus, no index whatever to his mind, it assists him in concealing his dark schemes, and cloaking his deep designs.*

The expression *understanding dark sentences* indicates in a general sense Napoleon's sagacity and great intelligence, but seems to refer more specially to his skill in the practice of that dark and mysterious development of Satanic power — Spiritualism. One of the most noted American mediums, named Hume, has frequently practised his magic art in presence of the Emperor: the spirits of deceased persons are supposed to enter into and possess these mediums whose faculties of articulation

---

* "Another peculiarity in his character is his unequalled power of *unfolding himself* according to the circumstances of the case. In this respect, he bears a formidable resemblance to the typical enemy of mankind—the serpent. He lay for years, coiled together in a lethargy until aroused by the occasion, he displayed his fangs, uncoiled his folds, and shot forth his icy frame just far enough to seize his prey, but no further. With impenetrable secrecy he forms his plans, and carries them out when formed with invincible determination. But he never wastes a word and seldom an action. He thinks more than he says, and says less than he does."—*Purdon's Last Vials.*

they then make use of to speak to their earthly acquaintances: the spirit of Napoleon I. is reported to have often communicated in this manner with his Imperial nephew; and it was probably in direct allusion to this, that Louis Napoleon once said to the French Senate: "What most affects my heart is the thought that the spirit of the Emperor is with me, that his mind guides me, and his shade protects me." It is evident, that the spirits which speak through mediums and which claim to be the spirits of deceased persons, are in reality demons possessing great powers of impersonation. They enable the medium to imitate the voice, accent, gestures, and handwriting of the deceased with such accuracy, as completely to deceive those who have not learned from Scripture that this is entirely the work of the Devil. Spiritualism is the most Antichristian system that has ever yet arisen, and its most ardent followers do not disguise their desire to see Christianity and all its institutions, such as marriage and the observance of the Sabbath, swept out of existence. It is by the supernatural art of Spiritualism that the False Prophet will make fire come down out of heaven on the earth to induce men to worship Napoleon's image, (Rev. xiii.) Gigantic prodigies will be wrought very soon by this latter-day manifestation of necromancy and witchcraft; and those will be entrapped who have not learned from Prophecy that the infidel man of sin is to arise accredited by such miracles. Already there are speaking, writing, painting, music-performing, healing, and physical manifestation mediums, by whose diabolical sorceries more than two million persons in America have become more or less confirmed in infidelity. Those who deride the marvels of spiritualism, and regard them only as displays of legerdemain or sleight-of-hand, manifest exceeding blindness and ignorance. Its miraculous operations were plainly predicted to characterize the period immediately preceding the Second Advent, (II. Thess. ii. 9–12, Rev. xvi. 13, 14.)

The statement respecting this king of fierce countenance, "*his power shall be mighty, but not by his own power,*" is explained by his being the delegated representative of Satan: "*The Dragon gave him his power, and his seat, and great authority.*" (Rev. xiii. 2.) Also the prediction, "*He shall destroy wonderfully,*" refers to his approaching persecution of the saints, (from 1868 to 1872.) We are further told that "*by peace he shall destroy many;*" this has been remarkably fulfilled by his assertion from the moment of ascending the Imperial throne, "The Empire is peace;" but in the face of this assurance his actions make it plain that his policy is a warlike and aggressive one, so that whenever he now speaks of peace, apprehensions are excited that he meditates fresh conquests. Never was there a monarch that professed greater anxiety to avoid war, and yet made greater preparations for engaging in it., *He shall stand up against the Prince of Princes, but shall be broken without hand;* his heaven-defying audacity shall reach such a height, that he will determine to fight neither with small nor great, save only with the King of Israel, and will thus gather his forces to contend with Christ in the valley of Megiddo, (Rev. xix. 19,) but he shall be destroyed without human interposition by the personal descent of Christ, "*the stone cut out without hands,*" (Dan. ii. 15.

The subjoined descriptions of Louis Napoleon by literary writers strikingly illustrate his identity with *the king of inscrutable countenance, and understanding dark sentences,* (that is, of exceeding wisdom and subtlety.) C. Phillips, in his "Life of Napoleon III.," says: "I was introduced to the present Emperor by his uncle Joseph, the ex-King of Naples and of Spain. With such an introduction opportunities were not wanting for studying the character of Louis Napoleon, a species of study to which much of my time has been necessarily devoted. The problem was difficult, and for a long time its solution seemed impossible. Frigidly affable and repulsively polite, he avoided either offence or familiarity, but seemed instinctively to coil up his nature from observation. In phrase and demeanor all that became his birth, still the man was perfectly inaccessible. It was scarcely to be wondered at. Even from his boyhood beset by espionage, reserve became an armor. Scarcely at home in the household of his uncle, the object of homage as much as of respect, he stood isolated and original. None presumed to interrupt his reveries, and to few, if indeed to any, did he accord his confidence. Yet even through that habitual reserve there would at times gleam forth indications of a character replete with kindness, and of a disposition generous and noble. There was much of peculiarity, much of contrast, abstracted yet vigilant, inquisitive in everything, but studiously uncommunicative, diligent in acquiring all men's knowledge, retentive of his own, cold and impassive, but full of latent energy, cautious in decision, but having decided, prompt, rapid and impetuous. Almost intuitive in grasping opportunity, or detecting weakness; improved by study, steeled by adversity, disciplined for every vicissitude of fortune, he has inestimable qualifications for his own position. Nor in private life is he deficient in commanding respect, or captivating sympathy: of the most winning manners when minded to assume them; perfectly munificent by nature and by habit; chivalrous, sincere, constant: of him it will never be said that he forgot a kindness or abandoned a friend. Marvellous as his character appears at present, it in my judgment is as yet very partially developed. The reserve, however, in which he habitually shrouds himself may not now be violated, though that very reserve has made him the victim of the grossest misconception. Few can see in the taciturn recluse, the talents, attainments and accomplishments, which he undoubtedly possesses. They are only revealed by some unlooked for accident."

The editor of one of the Paris journals thus sketches his character: "Louis Napoleon is a superior man, but with that superiority which conceals itself under a doubtful exterior. His life is altogether internal: his words do not indicate his inspiration: his gesture does not show his audacity; his glance does not intimate his ardor; his demeanor does not reveal his resolutions. All his moral nature is in a certain manner kept under by his physical nature. He thinks and does not discuss: he decides and does not deliberate; he acts and does not make much movement; he pronounces and does not assign his reasons. His best friends do not know him: he commands confidence and never seeks it. Every day he presides in silence at his council of ministers; he listens to everything that is said, speaks but little, and never yields; with a phrase brief and clear as an order of the day, he decides the most disputed questions. But with that inflexibility of will there is nothing abrupt or absolute in the form. Queen Hortense used to call him mildly obstinate, and that judgment of the matter is completely true. The somewhat English stiffness of his person, manners, and even language, disappears under an affability, which with him is only the grace of sentiment. Many are deceived by that appearance, and take his goodness for weakness and his affability for insincerity. At bottom he is completely master of himself; and his kindest movements enter into his actions only according to the exact measure he has determined on. Easily roused, he cannot soon be led away; he calculates everything, even his enthusiasm and acts of audacity; his heart is only the vassal of his head."

Another portraiture of Napoleon III. is given by Mr. Madden, in his "Life of Lady Blessington," Vol. I., p. 470, from which the above extract is taken: "This man-mystery, the depths of whose duplicity no Œdipus has yet sounded, is a problem even to those who surround him. I watched his pale, corpse-like, imperturbable features, not many months since, for a period of three hours. I saw 80,000 men in arms pass before him, and I never observed a change in his countenance or an expression in his look, which would enable the bystander to say whether he was pleased or otherwise at the stirring scene that was passing before him, on the very spot where Louis XVI. was put to death. He did not speak to those around him except at very long intervals, and then with an air of nonchalance, of ennui, and of eternal occupation with self. He rarely spoke a syllable to his uncle Jerome Bonaparte, who was on horseback somewhat behind him. It was the same with his brilliant staff. All orders came from him. All seemed centred in him. He gave me the idea of a man who had a perfect reliance on himself, and a feeling of complete control over those around him. I should be disposed to regard him as a man originally well intentioned and well disposed, of good qualities wrongly directed in his studies, strongly imbued with feelings of veneration for his imperial uncle, taught to conceal them in the times of the reverses of his family; in his tender years trained to dissimulation, who had grown up to manhood accustomed to silence, secresy and self-communion, an ambitious, moody young man, with a dash of genius in the composition of his mind, and a tinge of superstition in his credence in the connection of his fortune with the dispensations of Divine Providence, that give a permanent color of fatalism to his opinions, in keeping with the impulses of an immoderate ambition which may have perturbed to some extent his imagination."

"A man whose life is all interior, (not spiritually so, but wholly worldly-minded,) who lives for himself, in himself, and by himself, whether in a state prison or on a throne, cannot long remain in a state of mind either safe for himself or the confidence that others may place in his stability of purpose, policy, or promises. He is a man of considerable talent, of measureless ambition, and of no moral principles: of one fixed idea, a belief in the destiny of his elevation to supreme power, and the sufficiency of his own abilities to maintain it: a fatalist working out a destiny that is desired by him: a projector on a grand scale of plans for the promotion of selfish objects; wrapt up in the traditions of the Empire and its glory: without sympathies with other men, without confidence in any man, a speculator on the meanness, the imbecility and sordid dispositions of all around him: silent, self-sufficient, self-confident, self-opinionated, self-willed: in the words to me of one of the deepest thinkers and closest observers of France, 'a man of no convictions of good or evil, all wrapt up in self.'"

VIII. BECAUSE HIS SUDDEN RISE FROM OBSCURITY to great power, his obvious determination to seize Palestine, and also his acquisition of extensive dominions and of valuable gold fields in the north of Africa, are in accordance with the prophecies in Dan. xi. regarding the Personal Antichrist.

Dan. xi. 21: "And in his estate (on his own basis) shall stand up a vile person, to whom they shall not give the honor of the kingdom: but he shall come in peaceably, and obtain the kingdom by flatteries. ... 41: He shall enter also into the glorious land." ... 43: But he shall have power over the treasures of gold and of silver, and over all the precious things of Egypt: and the Libyans and the Ethiopians shall be at his steps."—(See Chap. H. Event IV.)

It is generally admitted by the most discriminating expositors, that in the literal-day fulfilment of Dan. xi. 21 to the end of Dan. xii., we have a continuous narrative of the actings of the *vile person* or Man of Sin, who is plainly cotemporary with the time of the Resurrection of the righteous, (Dan. xii. 2.)* The first two verses of Dan. xi. refer to the four Persian kings, Cambyses, Smerdis, (called Ahasuerus and Artaxerxes, Ez. iv. 6, 7,) Darius, and Xerxes, who followed in succession after Cyrus' death; then Alexander the Great, (verses 3, 4,) having conquered Xerxes, ultimately left his vast kingdom to be divided among his four generals, Lysimachus, Cassander, Ptolemy, and Seleucus. The two latter, ruling over Egypt and Syria, are called the kings of the South and the North, because Egypt is south, and Syria north of the Holy Land. Expositors generally understand verses 5 to 20 to contain the history of the Ptolemies and Seleucidæ, who subsequently governed Egypt and Syria. Between verses 20 and 21 there is a break and a transition to the time of the Personal Antichrist.

Louis Napoleon was originally regarded as a *vile person*, (verse 21,) that is, an ignoble, obscure, despised, and uninfluential person. Before he became French Emperor, the most opprobrious epithets and terms of contempt used to be heaped upon him by various public journals; he was nicknamed "Napoleon the Little;" his Strasbourg and Boulogne expeditions were referred to as indicating an utter lack of understanding: and scarcely any one gave him credit for the possession of those extraordinary powers of mind which he has since displayed. It was from the lowest depths of adversity that he was elevated to the dizzy heights of absolute power. As Joseph in olden time was transferred from the dungeon to the seat of chief ruler over Egypt, so Napoleon passed almost instantly from being a prisoner in the fortress of Ham to be an absolute monarch upon the throne of France.

* It is noticeable that Dan. xii. 2, if correctly translated, reads thus: "And many of them which sleep in the dust of the earth shall awake: these to everlasting life; but those (the rest of the sleepers) to shame and everlasting contempt." The resurrection of the last-named wicked does not take place until 1000 years after the resurrection of the righteous, (Rev. xx. 5.)

He also *came in peaceably,* dissembling his ambitious schemes, and professing to desire the uninterrupted maintenance of peace. At first the French would not give him the honor of the kingdom by permitting him to assume the Imperial dignity, but only made him President for 3 years, yet he *obtained the kingdom by flatteries:* he gradually contrived by his subtle policy, and by the *coup d'etat* in 1851, to become permanently invested with supreme authority as Emperor.

It is remarkable that in the days of his comparative obscurity, he had the fullest confidence in the greatness of his future destiny. Alison the historian, vol. v., says: "The idea of a destiny and his having a mission to perform was throughout a fixed one in Louis Napoleon's mind. No disasters shook his confidence in his star or the belief in the ultimate fulfilment of his destiny. This is well known to all who were intimate with him in this country after he returned from America in 1837. Among other noble houses, the hospitality of which he shared, was that of the Duke of Montrose, at Buchanan near Lochlomond, and the Duke of Hamilton, at Broderick Castle in the Island of Arran. His manner in both was in general grave and taciturn; he was wrapt in the contemplation of the future, and indifferent to the present. In 1839, the present Earl of W——, then Lord B——, came to visit the author after having been some days at Buchanan House. One of the first things he said was: 'Only think of that young man, Louis Napoleon, nothing can persuade him that he is not to be Emperor of France; the Strasbourg affair has not in the least shaken him; he is constantly thinking of what he is to do when on the throne.' The Duke of N—— also said to the author in 1854: 'Several years ago, before the Revolution of 1848, I met Louis Napoleon often at Broderick Castle in Arran. We frequently went out to shoot together; neither cared much for the sport, and we soon sat down upon a heathery brow of Goatfell and began to speak seriously. He always opened these conferences by discoursing of what he would do when he was Emperor of France. Amongst other things he said he would obtain a grant from the Chambers to drain the marshes of the Bries, which, you know, once fully cultivated, became flooded when the inhabitants, who were chiefly Protestants, left the country on the Revocation of the Edict of Nantes; and what is very curious, I see by the newspapers of the day, that he has got a grant of two millions of francs from the Chambers to begin the drainage of these very marshes,' (Alison's Europe, vol. v.)

The last twenty-four verses of Dan. xi. will be fulfilled by Louis Napoleon during the 7 years and 2½ months between the confirmation of his seven-years' Covenant or league with the Jews (verses 22, 23, Dan. ix. 27) and his final overthrow. They show that he will come in peaceably and by his subtle manœuvres obtain supreme power over Palestine and gradually get the fortified places, probably such as Gaza, Jaffa, and Acre, into his possession. His three expeditions against Egypt (verses 25, 29, 40) take place before his image* is set up in the Jewish Temple in the midst of the 7 years, (verse 31, Dan. ix. 27;) for the narrative is retrogressive at verse 40, and *the time of the end* is clearly the period of about 5 years between the first Translation and the descent of Christ upon Mount Olivet. It is observable that Napoleon's military occupation of Palestine during part of the years 1860 and 1861, and the reluctance with which he with-

* The willingness of Napoleon III. to receive divine honors is foreshadowed by his reception of addresses in his journeys through the French provinces, styling him "their Saviour, Regenerator, the Elect of God, the Messiah of the French nation" and in parody of the Lord's Prayer: "Our prince who art in power, thy kingdom come, thy will be done at home as it is abroad," etc. He is reported to have rewarded with a gold snuff-box a preacher who described him as equal to if not greater than Christ himself. In like manner Napoleon I., intoxicated with breathing the incense of constant adulation, desired to be addressed by the title of "Votre Providence," (Frere on Prophecy:) also in March 1807, when he convoked the Jews at Paris, he was styled by them *the Lord's anointed Cyrus, the living image of the Divinity*, etc., and the ciphers of his name and that of Josephine's were blended with the name of God and inscribed over the ark of the Covenant, which was farther surmounted with the Imperial eagle. A prefect addressing him once said: "God created Bonaparte and rested from his labors." On another occasion Bonaparte asked one of his courtiers what people thought of him; the reply was: "Some think you an angel, Sire: some a devil: but all agree you are more than a man." This kind of flattery naturally leads great conquerors to aspire after divine honors, as was the case with Nebuchadnezzar, Cyrus, Alexander, Romulus, Augustus Cæsar, Herod, Antiochus, etc.

drew his forces from it, plainly evince his determination ultimately to enter upon the possession of that *glorious holy land*, (verses 41, 45.) Nor should it be forgotten that in 1852-3 he took the title of "Defender of the Faith and Protector of the Holy Places," and constituted himself the special guardian of the interests of the Roman Catholics in Palestine. The recent extension of his power in Algiers and elsewhere in Africa is evidently preparing the way for the fulfilment of the prophecy that *the Libyans and the Ethiopians shall be at his steps.* Also the statement in regard to his connection with Africa that *he shall have power over the treasures of gold and of silver* (verse 43) seems from the following facts to be already receiving an incipient fulfilment. According to the *New-York Herald* of September 29, 1860, it appears that a Mr. R. A. Parrish, of Philadelphia, has applied to the United States Government to assist him in recovering three million dollars to which he claims to be entitled under a contract with the French Emperor. In 1853, having discovered from geological researches the existence of a valuable gold-mine in Senegal, Africa, he communicated information respecting it to Napoleon, and was promised a share in the proceeds, which in consequence of the abundant yield has amounted to the above sum. In December, 1853, the Emperor sent out thirteen ships and upwards of three thousand men to work this mine, and has ever since been obtaining from it, principally by slave-labor, enormous supplies of the auriferous metal. So rich and inexhaustible is this gold-field, that Mr. Parrish states that the only fear is that the value of the metal will soon be depreciated by the vast amount brought into circulation. According to the official statements of the amount of gold coined by the three leading nations in 1855 and the two following years, we learn that the amount coined in France was about sixty-one million pounds sterling, ($306,000,000,) in England twenty million pounds sterling, ($100,000,000,) and in the United States twenty-nine and a half million pounds sterling, ($148,000,000;) thus the coinage of France considerably exceeded the conjoint amounts of both England and the United States, and possibly the published statistics rather understated its real sum. The mines of Senegal seem in fact to have yielded more than both California and Australia added together. It was probably this that caused the Bank of France to remain unshaken in the commercial crisis of 1857, and that has enabled Napoleon to bear the otherwise ruinous expense of maintaining a standing army of nearly three quarters of a million of men, of providing them with the most costly munitions of war, and also of fitting out a steam navy not inferior in strength to that of England.*

IX. BECAUSE THE RISE OF A FRENCH EMPEROR a few years before 1864-8, who should revive the Napoleon dynasty, and become the Personal Antichrist, was predicted by prophetic writers as early as thirty-five years before Louis Napoleon's accession to the throne of France.

The following seven writers, Faber, Frere, Ganntlett, Jackson, Irving, Jones and another, may be mentioned as having all distinctly predicted from the same prophetic interpretation of the seven Heads of the Roman Wild-Beast, that a second French Emperor, like the first Napoleon, would arise a few years before 1864-8, and then

---

* The following paragraph from the Bankers' Reporter (1861) additionally testifies to the existence of some mysterious source from which Napoleon obtains "*treasures of gold and of silver :*"

"It has been a great mystery to English bankers and to the Directors of the Bank of England, how the bullion of the Bank of France could be so greatly increased within the last three years, while the institution has been constantly sending gold to England, to Germany, and to America. Not long since the Bank of France drew some fifteen million francs in silver from the Bank of England, which it paid for in gold bars with the French mint stamp on them. At its last report it showed a balance of one hundred and seventeen million francs in gold, while the amount one year ago was under eighty million—nearly one third increase. It is whispered that this abundance of gold is the result of a scientific discovery, which the Emperor Napoleon has secured the monopoly of. Gold is at the present moment manufactured at Paris in a secret manner. Though it is not known how extensively the precious metal is produced, yet several hundred-weight of the material are taken to a certain place on the first of each month. Everything is conducted with the utmost secrecy. None of the workmen are allowed to leave, and nothing definite can be known; but the fact that gold is produced is beyond peradventure. How long Napoleon III. will be able to keep this wonderful secret remains to be seen."

at this last-named period would perish at Armageddon antecedently to the commencement of the Millennium.* In 1818 the Rev. G. S. Faber, Prebendary of Salisbury, and an expositor of great celebrity, showed in his *Supplemental Third Volume to a Dissertation on the Prophecies* that the French Emperorship or Napoleon dynasty from 1806 to 1815 was the seventh Head of the Roman Empire, and that although "wounded to death" at Waterloo in 1815, it must according to Rev. xiii. and xvii. be revived a few years before 1864–6: and shortly after that date its representative having become manifested as THE Antichrist, would perish at Armageddon in Palestine. The same statement was reiterated by him in 1828 in his *Sacred Calendar of Prophecy;* and in 1852 he issued a little work called *Revival of the French Emperorship* (republished at Appletons', New-York, and entitled *Napoleon III. the Man of Prophecy*) directing attention to the fact that his forestatement in 1818 had been verified by Louis Napoleon's investiture with the Imperial dignity in 1852. He also expressed his increased conviction that the French Emperor would perish soon after 1864 in the Armageddon War introductorily to the inauguration of the Millennium.

In 1815 J. H. Frere published his Combined View of the Prophecies, in which he advanced the same prediction as to the Napoleon dynasty being revived some few years before 1867, which he considered to be the probable period of Christ's descent at Armageddon to destroy this seventh-revived or eighth Head of the Roman Empire. He also expressed himself to this effect: "There will be a resemblance between Napoleon I. the seventh Head, and the yet future eighth Head, short only of actual identity."

* It is sometimes said that the restoration of the Napoleon dynasty might easily have been anticipated. The real fact, however, is, that scarcely any one ever expected such an event. In the "Napoleon Dynasty" (Sheldon, New-York) it is truly remarked: "More than half a century had swept by since the brilliant vision of Napoleon's star burst upon the world. Men had nearly forgotten that a Napoleon dynasty ever existed. That it would ever be restored, few believed even in moments of inspired hope." The same writer says: "The further the scholar extends his researches, the more he will be inclined to concede an originally Greek origin to the Bonaparte family."

Another able expositor, the Rev. H. Gauntlett, who held that Antichrist would be destroyed at Armageddon about 1866, likewise predicted that the Napoleon dynasty would be revived a few years before that period. He said: "It appears that within the first twenty years of the nineteenth century the *sixth* and *seventh* heads of the Apocalyptic Beast (the Roman Emperorship and the French Emperorship) have fallen. Plain facts demonstrate the fulfilment of this part of the prophecy. Let a head of the secular Roman Empire now (1820) be sought, and it can nowhere be found. But not a day can be mentioned for more than 752 years before the birth of Christ, to the 18th of June, 1815, on which a head of the Roman Empire did not exist under one of the forms symbolized by the seven-headed Apocalyptic Beast described in this chapter.... The Apostle asserts that he saw one of the heads of the beast 'as it were wounded unto death, and his deadly wound was healed;' and he afterwards speaks of the 'beast, which had the wound by a sword, and did live.' It is evident, therefore, that the head which he saw thus wounded, was not the *sixth*, but the *seventh* head of the Roman beast. Historical facts will demonstrate this position; for it is certain that the sixth head did not receive a mortal wound by the stroke of a sword, but rather died a kind of natural death, by the Austrian Emperor abdicating the title of Emperor of the Romans. The head, therefore, that was wounded unto death by the stroke of the sword, was the seventh, and the deadly blow was given it on the field of Waterloo. This point, therefore, is rendered certain by a plain matter of fact. It seems equally certain that the revival of the beast, under his eighth head or form of government, which was to be the same as one of the preceding seven, can be no other than a revival or restoration of the seventh head. In the hieroglyphical emblem which was exhibited to St. John, the wild beast appeared to revive in consequence of his deadly wound being healed. The identical wound, therefore, which occasioned the death of the beast, was again healed. But the wound which the Apostle saw thus healed, was inflicted on the short-lived *seventh* head. This head has been shown to be the FRANCIC EMPERORSHIP. Therefore the FRANCIC EMPERORSHIP is the head whose deadly wound is destined to be healed. It is evident, therefore, that the head which was slain by the sword is to be the revived eighth head, which will nevertheless be one of the seven. In fact, it will be the seventh healed and restored."

An anonymous Exposition of the Apocalypse was published in 1829, predicting from the same interpretation of the seven Heads that a French Emperor like the first Napoleon would arise a few years before 1867 and would perish at Christ's Advent at the Battle of Armageddon, and that during his career he would most assuredly gain supremacy over Great Britain,* (ch. xvii.)

The Wild-Beast's seven Heads were similarly explained by the Rev. J. S. Jackson in his *Millennial Church* in 1831. He said: "The sixth Head (the Roman Emperorship) continued till the subversion of the Germanic empire in the year 1806; and the seventh Head which was

* This writer's expectation that the seventh-revived or eighth Head would be Bonaparte's son has virtually been fulfilled, inasmuch as Louis Napoleon is the lineal heir of Napoleon I. He thus expressed his expectation: "Who is this fiery flying serpent that is to bring such destruction upon the earth? Doubtless the same mystery as that contained in the text, the beast that 'was and is not, and yet is the eighth head of the beast, though of the seven,' who is to lead up the confederation of the kings of the earth, to make war with the Lamb, and whom 'Christ will destroy with the breath of his mouth, and consume with the brightness of his coming.' Does the reader ask, When are we to look for a development of this new character who is thus predicted to appear in such fearful terms, who is 'to ascend out of the bottomless pit, and go into perdition;' and at whose sudden reappearance, 'they that dwell on the earth shall wonder, whose names were not written in the Book of Life'? We answer: Await a few short years, and thou shalt be at no pains in answering the question. God will reveal him in his own time; but in the interval, we will throw out for thy meditation, that Napoleon left a son, who was ushered into being with the ominous title of King of Rome."

This writer correctly designates the Personal Antichrist as "the fiery flying serpent," (Is. xvi. 29;) for whereas Isaiah xiv. 3–27 typically alludes to the overthrow of the literal Babylon, which oppressed Israel; yet it also predicts the future rise of a fiery flying serpent—the Antichrist, the mystical King of Babylon, or Assyrian — who shall more grievously afflict Palestine (verse 31) and to whom the description in Isaiah xiv. 3–27 antitypically applies. Some have also typically applied it to Napoleon I.; its ultimate application, however, undoubtedly relates to Napoleon III., the last great Antichrist. The destruction of the Napoleons I., II. and III.—the uncle, "son, and nephew," seems to be referred to in verse 22.

only to 'continue a short space,' (Rev. xvii. 10,) arose immediately in the Franco-Italian Emperorship founded by Napoleon Bonaparte. It 'was' from 1806 to the Battle of Waterloo in June, 1815. And it then received a deadly wound, and now 'is not,' (A.D. 1831:) but 'yet is,' or more properly 'yet shall be,' (Rev. xvii. 8;) it shall again spring up in the revival of the seventh Head of the Roman Beast, in its eighth form, which 'is of the seven and goeth into perdition,' (Rev. xvii. 11.) Nor can there be any reasonable doubt but that the seventh Head revived is the mystic Assyrian (Is. xxx. xxxi., Micah v. 5) and corresponds with the wilful king of Daniel 'who shall come to his end and none shall help him,' (Dan. xi. 45:) no less also than with 'that wicked whom the Lord shall destroy with the brightness of his coming,' (2 Thess. ii. 8,) A few short years may now suffice to prove who this portentous being, the revived seventh Head of the Roman Empire, shall be.... The career of Napoleon Bonaparte, the seventh Head of the Roman Beast, was a kind of type or representation of the time of greater shaking and more intense convulsions, which await a guilty and suffering world under the despotism of the seventh revived Head and last form of the infidel power." This writer also showed that the coming of Christ would be before or about 1868.

The Rev. Edward Irving, in his published discourses upon Revelation, (Part V.,) delivered about 1825-30, speaks as follows regarding the future appearance of a French Emperor who should be the seventh-eighth, or last Head of the Beast; he also held that 1867-8, as the end of the 1335 years, (Dan. xii.,) is the time of Christ's descent on the earth to destroy Antichrist. "To the seven sovereignties of Rome, Livy, Tacitus, and the other classical historians do help us in the enumeration of the first five, as is well proved in the *Synopsis Prophetica* or Henry More: Kings, Consuls, Consular Tribunes, Decemviri, Dictators. After these, for the sixth form of sovereignty we have Emperors.... *Five are fallen—* these are the five enumerated from the Latin historians; *one is*—that is, the Head of Emperors, then in being and which continued in being until our times; *the other is not* *yet come, and when he cometh he must continue a short space.* This seventh hath come in the late Emperor of the French, who having deposed the Emperor of Germany from the sovereignty of Rome, took that city into the bounds of the French Empire, and ruled over it and in it, as the Emperor of France, making it the second city of his dominions. So that with what truth the King of Great Britain is sovereign over the capital of Scotland or Ireland, with that same truth was Napoleon sovereign in Rome. And he abode a short time compared with the others; for lo! he is already gone: and Rome is actually at present (1829) without a temporal head; for the Prophet doth never contemplate the Pope as such. The Pope is but as an assessor to the Imperial Head. . . . Rome, since the abdication of Napoleon, hath therefore been without a Head: but is not long so to continue, for it is said 'the beast that was, and is not, he is the eighth, and is of the seven, and goeth into perdition,' (Rev. xvii.) Here for the first time mention is made of an eighth Head upon the Beast, but to account for the novelty, it is added *it is of the seven:* apparently an eighth, yet in some way included in the seven. . . . Now if it should be the purpose of the Eternal and Almighty Governor of the Universe to bring Napoleon Bonaparte's son* forth in the footsteps of his father, so that in the revolution that is impending he should start into being as the Sovereign of Rome, the prophecy would have its exact fulfilment; for while he was the eighth Head, he would also be of the seven, . . . both together constituting the Personal An-

* This has been completely fulfilled by Bonaparte's nephew, Napoleon III., whose continued occupation of Rome is the stepping-stone to his elevation over all the Roman Empire. Auberlen on Daniel, p. 221, justly says: "The Germanic Empire knew no greater honor than to be a Holy Roman Empire of German nationality. And even before it was dissolved, Bonaparte had taken up the idea of the Roman Empire. His universal monarchy was essentially and avowedly Roman: his son was called King of Rome: his nephew, (Napoleon III.,) in order to found his power, distributed among the French army Roman eagles. The Roman Empire is the ideal, which exerts fascinating power on the rulers of the world, which they are ever striving to realize and will doubtless succeed in realizing. Of all phenomena of history none bears more essential resemblance to Antichrist than this demoniac Napoleonism which from the outset identified itself with the idea of the Roman Empire."

tichrist of the last days, who is to bring the judgments upon the Papacy to an end, and then to pass into perdition. His second title, 'that ascendeth out of the bottomless pit and goeth into perdition,' denotes the brief stay he is to be permitted to make upon this earth. We have already seen that he is to appear in the person of some one who is destined to exercise sway and authority in Rome, and to become the eighth Head, while he is also of the seven. And to his standard all the kingdoms of the Papacy are to join themselves, and while at the head of this confederacy, he is to execute signal vengeance upon Babylon."

A seventh expositor, the Rev. T. Jones, of Creaton, in 1830 gave the same explanation of the Wild-Beast's seven Heads, in his treatise, "The Interpreter," and considered that the seventh-revived or eighth Head would be destroyed at Armageddon about or soon after 1866. He said: "The woman (Rev. xvii. 3) is the Church of Rome, and the beast on which she rides is the Roman Empire. The seven heads are seven mountains, and signify also seven forms of government. Five heads of the beast had fallen, when John had the vision. The sixth head also fell at the time that the Austrian Emperor relinquished the title of Emperor of the Romans, (in 1806.) The seventh head is evidently Napoleon Bonaparte, 'who continued but a short time, and received the deadly wound by the sword.' And now (1836) 'he is not.' The Roman Empire has no head at present, but his 'deadly wound shall be healed' in the eighth head which is yet to come This will be 'of the seven,' probably of the seventh, that is of the same form of government with Bonaparte's."

Another expositor, M. Habershon, in his Dissertation on the Prophetic Scriptures in 1840, likewise predicted on the same grounds the resuscitation of the Napoleon dynasty, or septimo-octave Head, although he did not distinctly, like the others, refer to 1864–7 as the time of the end.

X. BECAUSE THE END OF THIS DISPENSATION is shown by ten dates and four septenaries to be about A.D. 1871–72: and as the Personal Antichrist is to be revealed seven years previously by making a Covenant with the Jews, therefore he will soon have arrived at the time of his manifestation; and no living person corresponds with his predicted character except Louis Napoleon.

Not only has a man arisen who exactly answers to the description of the Personal Antichrist, but also the time has come when the rise of that Antichrist must necessarily be looked for. The Scriptures have foretold not less the *circumstances* than the *time* of Antichrist's, as well as of Christ's presentation to Israel. It was prophesied of Christ that he should be born of a virgin (Is. vii. 14) of the family of Jesse (Is. xi. 1) at Bethlehem, (Micah v. 2,) and should temporarily reside in Egypt and Galilee, (Matt. ii. 15, iv. 15,) and should be a man of sorrows, (Is. liii.,) and that the *time* of his presentation to the Jews should be 69 weeks, or 483 years after the 7th year of Artaxerxes, (Dan. ix. 25.) It is predicted concerning Antichrist, that he shall be the Eighth Head of the Roman Empire, have 666 contained in his name, possess Rome, be a mighty man of war, support the Papacy, become supreme over the Roman earth, (Rev. xiii., xvii.,) destroy many by peace, emerge from opprobrium to great fame, (Dan. viii., xi.,) and also make a seven-years' Covenant with the Jews, seven years before the Consummation, (Dan. ix. 27.) Thus as Jesus could be recognized as the Christ, by Anna and Simeon (Luke ii.) and others who took *heed to the sure word of Prophecy*, so Napoleon III. can be recognised as the Personal Antichrist, by those who vigilantly watch and *discern the signs of the times.* The fact of the End or Consummation being about or soon after 1871-72, requires Antichrist to make the Jewish Covenant about or soon after 1864, and Louis Napoleon is the only prophetic character in existence by whom such Covenant could properly be made.

The ten dates,* which combine in showing the End to

* The following is a brief explanation of the dates: (1) The 6000 years from the Creation end about A.D. 1872-3. The computations of those who have most thoroughly studied the chronology of this date, such as Fynes Clinton, Sylvester Bliss, Revs. J. Scott, R. C. Shimeall, B. Saville, C. Bowen, all terminate it between 1862 and 1881. The Nativity of Christ was about the year 4128, anno mundi, which, added to 1872, makes up the 6000 years. Usher, according to whose chronology the Nativity was in 4004, omitted to reckon nearly 130 years in the time of the Judges, on which account his chronology is fundamentally erroneous.

be about 1871-72, are the 6000, 2520, (seven times, Dan. iv.,) 2500, 2300, (Dan. viii. 14,) and 1335 years, (Dan. xii, 12,) which all terminate in 1871-2: also the 1290, 1260, (Dan. xii.;) 666, 390, and 360 years, (Rev. xiii., ix. 15, x. 6,) which ending respectively in 1824-7, 1794-7,

It was a general belief among the Jews and the Fathers that the millennium would commence with the personal coming of Christ, 6000 years after the creation. (2) The 2520 years is "*the seven times*" mentioned in Dan. iv. 16, and Lev. xxvi. 18, during which the Jews were to have the pride of their power broken and be chastised for their unfaithfulness, and have their kingly power transferred to the four Gentile Monarchies. A *time* means a Jewish year of 360 days, which, by taking a day for a year, as in Numb. xiv. 34, Ezek. iv. 6, represent 360 years. The 2520 years commencing in 648-9 B.C., at the captivity under Manasseh, and at the time of Nebuchadnezzar's birth, will terminate in 1871-2, as the period of the full restoration to Palestine of the Jews that are spared at Christ's Advent. (3) The 2500 years is a period of 50 times 50 years, ending with a Jubilee of Jubilees. It commences about 628-9 B.C., at the time of the great passover in Josiah's 18th year, (2 Chron. xxxv.,) when the last Jubilee seems to have been kept, and ends in 1871-2, when the next Jubilee will be celebrated at Christ's Coming. (4) The 2300 years in Dan. viii. 13, 14, commence primarily in 456-7 B.C., at Ezra's restoration of the sacrifices, (Ez. vii.,) and secondarily in 428-9 B.C., at Nehemiah's completed renewal of the sacrifices, (Neh. xiii.,) and thus bring us to 1843-4 as the commencement, and to 1871-2, as the completion of the cleansing of the sanctuary of the Holy Land by the destruction of Mohammedanism and the full restoration of Israel. (5,) (6,) and (7,) The 1335, 1290, and 1260 years in Dan. xii. 7, 11, 12, have a common commencement in A.D. 534-7, when the temporal power of Popery was first established by Justinian's Code. They end respectively in 1794-7; 1824-7, and 1872. The temporal power of the Pope was broken at the French Revolution, 1794-7; in 1824-7 the mystic Euphrates or Turkish Empire began to dry up under the 6th Vial, precursory to Babylon's overthrow; and in 1871-2, the time of millennial blessedness will arrive. There is also a secondary fulfilment of the 1269 years from 606-12 to 1866-72. (8) The 666 years in Rev. xiii. 18, taken as a date and commencing 534-7, end in 1202 A.D., when the papal power reached its height. Carried on again from 1202, it ends in 1868, the beginning of the 3½ years' Tribulation. (9) The 390 years in Rev. ix. 15, carried on twice from 1063, measures the duration of the Turkish Woe, and ends in 1843-4. (10) The 360 years in Rev. x. 6 is denoted by the phrase *a time*, which literally means a Jewish year, or 360 days, but prophetically 360 years. *There shall be a time no longer*, means, "*There shall be 360 years no longer*," from the Reformation in 1517, which Rev. x. describes, until the End. The dates and septenaries are also explained in diagrams I. and III., and more fully in the Author's work: "The coming Battle." It should be remembered that the year 1871, according to Jewish reckoning, ends about April or September, in 1872.

1868, 1844, and 1872, form additional links in the chronological chain of evidence. As regards the four septenaries—the 7 Heads of the Beast, the 7 Seals, 7 Trumpets, and 7 Vials—we are living under the seventh-revived or last Head of the Beast, and just before the fulfilment of the year-day 7th Seal, 7th Trumpet, and 7th Vial, which will last for about 5 years, from 1866-7 to 1871-73. (Rev. vii. xi. 18. xvi. 15). As soon as they commence the first stage in Christ's Advent, His Coming in the air to translate the 144,000 Wise Virgins, takes place, at the distance of about two years, and five or six weeks after the date of the seven-years' Covenant, (see Chap. II., Event 5.) During the succeeding five years, the seals, trumpets, vials, and nearly all the dates in Daniel and Revelation have their future recapitulated literal-day fulfilment. Their past year-day fulfilment has been interpreted by more than a hundred expositors to show that the coming of Christ and end of this Dispensation would occur between 1864 and 1869-73. It is at this last-named year probably that the second translation and descent of Christ upon Mt. Olivet, at the Battle of Armageddon, will take place, and Antichrist and his followers being slain, the Millennium will be fully inaugurated.

FROM ALL THESE CONSIDERATIONS it appears that whereas Napoleon Bonaparte slew his thousands, Louis Napoleon will slay his hundreds of thousands: the former scourged men with whips, but the latter will chastise them with scorpions. The one only required homage to be offered to him as a King, but the other will demand worship to be rendered him as a god. The Uncle made Europe the principal theatre of his desolations: but the Nephew will fill the four Continents of Europe, Africa, Asia, and America, with destruction and slaughter. The former unsuccessfully meditated, but the latter will triumphantly achieve, the humiliation and conquest of England, Russia, and Turkey. Satan was but experimenting when he raised up the first Napoleon as a Great Destroyer, but he has taxed his powers to the utmost to produce his most finished masterpiece, the Third Napoleon, who will be unapproachably the Greatest of all Destroyers,

This chapter may be suitably concluded by the following practical address to the unconverted, from McCheyne's sermons (published at Carter's, New York; and in Edinburgh).

"There is a great day coming, often spoken of in the Bible—the Day of Judgment—the day when God shall judge the secrets of men's hearts by Christ Jesus. The Christless will not be able to stand in that day: The ungodly shall not stand in the judgment. At present, sinners have much boldness; their neck is an iron sinew, and their brow brass. Many of them cannot blush when they are caught in sin. Is it not amazing how bold sinners are in forsaking ordinances? With what a brazen face will some men swear! But it will not be so in a little while. When Christ shall appear—the holy Jesus, in all his glory, then brazen-faced sinners will begin to blush. Those that never prayed will begin to wail. Sinners, whose limbs carried them stoutly to sin and to the Lord's Table, will find their knees knocking against one another. Who shall abide the day of his coming, and who shall stand when he appears? When the books are opened—the one the book of God's remembrance, the other the Bible—then the dead will be judged out of those things written in the books. Then the heart of the ungodly will die within them; then will begin 'their shame and everlasting contempt.' Many wicked persons comfort themselves with this, that their sin is not known, that no eye sees them; but in that day the most secret sins will be all brought out to the light. 'Every idle word that men shall speak they shall give an account thereof in the Day of Judgment.' How would you tremble and blush, oh wicked man, if the secret sins you have committed during your past life were known to your acquaintances; all your secret fraud and cheating; your secret uncleanness; your secret malice and envy; how you would blush and be confounded! How much more in that day, when the secrets of your whole life shall be made manifest before an assembled world! What eternal confusion will sink down your soul in that day! You will be quite chop-fallen; all your pride and blustering will be gone.

"From the day you were born you who are unconverted have gone astray from the path of God's commandments.

Every year, month, week, day, hour, minute, has been filled up with sin. Every day has seen you go further from holiness, further from God, nearer to hell. You are treasuring up wrath against the day of wrath. Oh! what a treasure; keeping up fuel to burn you through eternity. If any of you live in drinking or swearing, or any one sin, you are heaping up fuel for your eternal hell. You are getting further on in your sin. You are wreathing your chains more and more round you. By a law of human nature, every time you sin, the habit becomes stronger, so-that you are every day becoming more completely like the devil. It is every day more hard to turn. Experience shows that most people are converted when young. 'They that seek me early shall find me.'

"The natural man is ignorant of God from the very womb. God is a stranger to him, so that he does not know him. He has no true discovery of God's infinite purity, of his immutable justice, and of the strictness of his law. He does not know the love of God, nor how freely he has provided a Saviour. He is mainly ignorant of God. Psalm x. 4. 'God is not in all his thoughts.' Either he does not turn his mind upon God at all, or else he thinks him altogether such an one as himself. 'There is none that understandeth.' Psalm xiv. 2.

"A new born child will naturally feel after its mother's breast: it naturally sucks the breast. But it does not in the same manner seek after God. 'There is none that seeketh after God.' From the very first we dislike God. A child soon comes to relish the presence of its earthly parents, and of other children. But it does not relish the *presence* of God. The natural tendency of the heart is to go away from God, and to remain out of his sight. A natural man does not like the presence of a very eminent saint. If he has full liberty, he will leave the room, and seek other company more suited to his taste. This is the very way he treats God. God is too holy for him; he is too pure, and, therefore, he does all he can to leave his company. This is the reason you cannot get unconverted men to pray in secret. They would rather spend half an hour in the tread-mill every morning than go to meet God. This is the true condition of every one of you who is now unconverted; indeed it was the condition of us all, but some of you have been brought out of it. From the time you were in the womb, till now, your whole head and heart have been turned away from God. Gen. viii. 21. 'The imagination of man's heart is evil from his youth,' &c. Job xiv. 4. 'Who can bring a clean thing out of an unclean, not one?' Your *whole nature* is totally depraved. You are accustomed to think that you have some parts good; that a great part of your life has been innocent. You admit that some pages of your life are stained with crimson and scarlet sins; some pages you blush to look back upon; but surely you have some fair leaves also. Learn that you are 'estranged from the womb.' Every moment you have spent without God, and turning away from God; every page has got this written at the top of it, This day God was not in all his thoughts, he did not like to retain God in his knowledge. Genesis vi. 5. 'Every imagination of the thoughts of his heart was only evil continually.'

"The place in hell is quite ready for every unconverted soul. When Judas died, the Scriptures say, 'he went to his own place.' It was his own place before he went there, being quite prepared and ready for him. As when a man retires at night to his sleeping room, it is said he is gone to his own room, so a place in hell is quite ready for every Christless person. It his own place. When the rich man died and was buried, he was immediately in his own place. He found every thing ready. He lifted up his eyes in hell, being in torments. So hell is quite ready for every Christless person. It was prepared, long ago, for the devil and his angels. The fires are all quite ready, and fully lighted and burning.

"Ah! should Christless souls then make mirth! A malefactor might, perhaps, say that he would be merry as long as the scaffold was not erected on which he was to die. But if he were told that the scaffold was quite ready, that the sword was sharpened, and the executioners standing ready, oh! would it not be madness to make mirth? Alas! this is your madness, poor Christless soul. You are not only condemned, but the sword is sharpened and ready, that is to smite your soul; and yet you can be happy, and dream away your days and nights in pleasures that perish in the using. The disease is ready, the arrow is on the string, the grave is ready, yea, hell itself is ready, your own place is made ready; and yet you can make mirth ! You can play games and enjoy company. How truly is your laughter like the crackling of thorns under a pot : a flashy blaze, and then the blackness of darkness forever !

"You are not only condemned, and not only is the sword ready, but it may fall on you at any one moment. Your head is, as it were, on the block. Your neck is bared before God, and the whetted sword is held over you; and yet can you make mirth ? Can you take up your mind with business and worldly things, and getting rich, building and planting, and this night your soul may be required of you ? Can you fill up your time with games and amusements, and foolish books and entertaining companions ? Can you fill up your hours after work with loose talk and wanton behaviour, adding sin to sin, treasuring up wrath against the day of wrath, when you know not what hour the wrath of God may come upon you to the uttermost ? Can you go prayerless to your bed at night, your mind filled with dark and horrid imaginations not fit to be named, and yet you may be in hell before the morning ?

"When the day of grace is done, when the sinner sinks into hell, the Spirit will strive no more. There will be no family worship in hell, no Bible read, no Psalms sung. There will be no Sabbath in hell, no preached gospel, no watchman to warn you of your sin and danger. The voice of the watchman will be silent, the danger has come, your doom will be past, and no room for repentance. There will be no more convictions by the Spirit. Conscience will condemn, but it will not restrain. Your hearts will then break out. All your hatred to God, the fountains of contempt and blasphemy in your heart will be all broken up. You will blaspheme the God of Heaven. All your lusts and impurities that have been pent up and repressed by restraining grace and the fear of man, will burst forth with amazing impetuosity. You will be wicked and blasphemous as the devils around you. Oh the misery of this ! it is an evil thing and bitter. The way of transgressors is hard. Ah ! sinners, you will yet find sin the hardest of all masters; you will yet find your grovelling lusts to be worse than the worm that neve dies. 'He that is unjust, let him be unjust still. Rev. xxii. 11.

"When the day of grace is past, all holy creatures will cast you away. Reprobate silver shall men call them, for the Lord hath rejected them. The angels will no longer take any interest in you. They will know that it is not fit they should pity you any more. You will be tormented in the presence of the holy angels, and in the presence of the Lamb. (Rev. xiv. 10). The redeemed will no longer pray for you, nor shed another tear for you. They will see you condemned in the judgment, and not put in one word for you. They will see you depart into everlasting fire, and yet not pray for you. They will see the smoke of your torments going up forever and ever, and yet cry, Alleluiah! Ministers will no more desire your salvation. It will no more be their work. The number of the saved will be complete without you; the table will be full. Ministers will bear witness against you in that day. Even devils will cast you off. As long as you remain on earth, the devil keeps you in his train; he flatters you, and gives you many tokens of his friendship and esteem; but soon he will cast you off. You will be no longer pleasant to him; you will be a part of his torment; and he will hate you and torment you, because you deceived him, and he deceived you.

"At present, unconverted men are often very self-complacent. They love to employ their faculties; the wheels of their life go smoothly; their affections are pleasant. Memory has many pleasant green spots to look back upon. How different when the day of grace is done! 1. *The understanding* will be clear and able to apprehend the real nature of your misery. Your mind will then see the holiness of God, his almightiness, his majesty. You will see your own condemned condition, and the depth of your hell. 2. *The will* in you will be all contrary to God's will, even though you see it add to your hell; yet you will hate all that God loves, and love all that God hates. 3. *Your conscience* is God's vicegerent in the soul. It will accuse you of all your sins. It will set them in order and condemn you. 4. *Your affections* will still love your kindred. (Luke xvi. 28.) Earthly fathers who are evil know how to give good gifts to their children. Even in hell you will love your own kindred; but oh! what misery it will cost you, when you hear them sentenced along with you. 5. *Your memory* will be very clear. You will remember all your misspent Sabbaths, your sermons heard, as if you did not hear; your place in the house of God, your minister's face and voice, the bell: through millions of ages after this, you will remember these, as if yesterday. 6. *Your anticipations.* Everlasting despair. Oh how you will wish that you had never been! How you will wish to tear out your memory, these tender affections, this accusing conscience! You will seek death, and it will flee from you. This, this it is, to be lost! This is everlasting destruction!

"Oh do not keep away from Christ now. Now he says, Come; soon, soon he will say, Depart. Oh do not resist the Holy Spirit now. Now he strives, but he will not always strive with you. Soon, soon he will leave you. Oh do not despise the word of ministers and godly friends. Now they plead with you, weep for you, pray for you. Soon they will be silent as the grave, or sing hallelujah to see you lost. Oh do not be proud and self-admiring. Soon you will loathe the very sight of yourself, and wish you had never been.

"When a poor sinner cleaves to Jesus, and finds the forgiving love of God, he cannot but love God back again. When the prodigal returned home and felt his father's arms around his neck, then did he feel the gushings of affection toward his father. When the summer sun shines full down upon the sea, it draws the vapors upward to the sky. So when the sunbeams of the Son of Righteousness fall upon the soul, they draw forth the constant risings of love to him in return.

"If you love an absent person you will love their picture. What is that the sailor's wife keeps so closely wrapped in a napkin, laid up in her best drawer among sweet smelling flowers? She takes it out morning and evening, and gazes at it through her tears. It is the picture of her absent husband. She loves it because it is like him. It has many imperfections, but still it is like. Believers are the pictures of God in this world. The spirit of Christ dwells in them. They walk as he walked. True, they are full of imperfections; still they are real copies. If you love him, you will love them. You will make them your bosom friends.

"Learn the amazing love of Christ. He was the only one that knew the wickedness of the beings for whom he died. He that searches the hearts of sinners died for them. His eye alone had searched their hearts; aye, was searching at the time he came. He knew what was in men; yet he did not abhor them on that account—he died for them. It was not for any goodness in man that he died for man. He saw none. It was not that he saw little sin in the heart of man, that he pitied him and died for him. He is the only being in the universe that saw all the sin that is in the unfathomable heart of man. He saw to the bottom of the volcano, and yet he came and died for man. Herein is love! When publicans and sinners came to him on earth, he knew what was in their hearts. His eye had rested on their bosoms all their life, he had seen all the lusts and passions that had ever rankled there; yet in no wise did he cast them out. So with you. His eye hath seen all your sins; the vilest, darkest, blackest hours you have lived, his pure eye was resting on you; yet he died for such, and invites you to come to him; and will in no wise cast you out. 'God so loved the world, that he gave his only begotten Son, that whosoever believeth in Him should not perish, but have everlasting life.' (John iii.)

"Look to the cross. Behold the amazing gift of love. Salvation is promised to a look. Sit down like Mary and gaze upon a crucified Jesus. So will the world become a dim and dying thing. When you gaze upon the sun, it makes every thing else dark; when you taste honey, it makes every thing else tasteless; so when your soul feeds on Jesus, it takes away the sweetness of all earthly things; praise, pleasure, fleshly lusts, all lose their sweetness. Keep a continued gaze. Run, looking unto Jesus. Look, till the way of salvation by Jesus fills up the whole horizon, so glorious and peace-speaking. So will the world be crucified to you, and you unto the world."

Convergent Ending of the Principal Prophetic Periods.

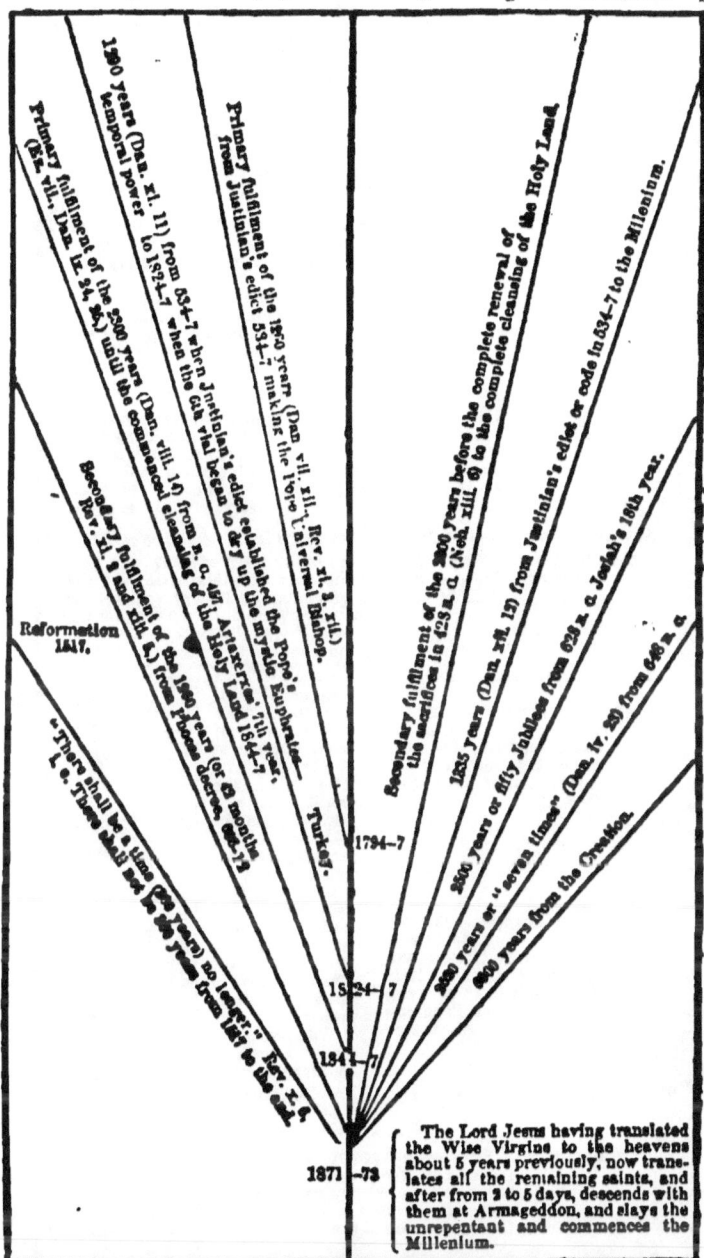

The chronological position of twenty leading events of the final 7 years and 2½ months of the Christian Dispensation, which commence with Louis Napoleon's Covenant with the Jews, and end with his destruction.

First Event.—Confirmation of a seven-years Covenant between Napoleon and the Jews, exactly 7 years and 2½ months before the End.—Dan. ix 27.

In prophetic calculations, a year is always reckoned as containing 360 days, or 12 months of 30 days each.

In this diagram, Daniel and Revelation, unless otherwise stated, are taken only in their literal day fulfilment, wherever they have any.

Second Event.—Renewal of the Jewish sacrifices at Jerusalem, 9 months, or 9 months and 25 days after the Covenant.—Dan. viii. 14.

Third Event.—The complete overthrow of the Turkish Empire, at some period during the first two of the seven years—Yearday Rev. xvi. 12.

Fourth Event.—The three expeditions of Napoleon against Egypt, will occur during the first 3 years—probably the first in the 1st or 2d year, and the second & third in the 2d or 3d year—Dan. xi. 25 to 42.

Fifth Event.—The coming of Christ in the air, resurrection of the Saints and translation of the 144,000 Wise Virgins about the 5th or 6th week of 3d year. Rev. xiv. 1-5 & xii. 5.

Sixth Event.—Great revival of religion among the foolish virgins and the unconverted that are left on the earth. Rev. vi. 2 & xiv. 6.

Seventh Event.—The first four trumpets in this & next 8 months. Rv. 12. 9

Eighth Event.—War in Heaven & casting down of Satan. Rv. 12. 9

Ninth Event.—Flight of many Saints into the wilderness. Rv. xii 14

Tenth Event.—Fall of Babylon, or change of Popery (as well as spiritualism) into Napoleonism. Rev. xiii-xvii.

11th Event.—Napoleon supreme over England & part of America

Twelfth Event.—The ten kingdoms submit to Napoleon. Rv. 17

Thirteenth and Fourteenth Events.—These both begin with the 7th month of the 4th year, in the midst of the seven years. The 13th is the institution and continuance for 3½ years of the worship of Napoleon, after he has assaulted Jerusalem, and had his image placed in the temple. Rv. xiii. The 14th event is the 3½ years testimony of the 2 Witnesses and their slaughter and resurrection Rev. xi. The 1290 & 1335 days begin with these events.

Fifteenth Event.—The 1st Woe of supernatural locusts, for twice five mos. from the 12th day of mouth 10 of year 4.—Rev. IX.

Sixteenth Event.—The 2d Woe, or conflicts of the horsemen for twice a year and month from the 19th day of month 12 of year 5.—Rev. xi. This mainly constitutes the Armageddon War.

THE GREAT TRIBULATION, OR ANTICHRIST'S REIGN OF 3½ YEARS.

The worship of Napoleon and his image, together with the slaughter of those who refuse to bow before it; also the preaching of Elijah and the other Witness, continue during the whole of this 3½ years.

Seventeenth Event.—Conversion of millions of persons chiefly among the heathen, between the two translations, and especially from the 3d month of the 7th year until the End. Rev. x.

End of the 3½ years of Napoleon's universal power

18th Event.—Total darkness & literal fulfilment of 7 Vials begins.

19th Event.—Second translation, 4 days before the end (1335th dy.)

20th Event.—Third Woe—Battle of Armageddon, & descent of Christ

CHAPTER II.

THE ARRANGEMENT IN CONSECUTIVE ORDER OF TWENTY LEADING EVENTS THAT MAY BE EXPECTED TO OCCUR DURING THE CLOSING SEVEN YEARS AND $2\frac{1}{2}$ MONTHS OF THE CHRISTIAN DISPENSATION.

THE seven years' Covenant, which is to be made between Louis Napoleon and the Jews, exactly seven years and $2\frac{1}{2}$ months before the end of this Dispensation, constitutes the starting-point for these twenty events.

During the first $3\frac{1}{2}$ years of the seven years, twelve out of these twenty events occur; and during the second $3\frac{1}{2}$ years of the seven years, together with the additional $2\frac{1}{2}$ months, (Dan. xii. 12,) the remaining eight of the twenty events take place. A list of them, enumerated seriatim, is given in the preliminary table of contents.

If the Covenant is made before October, in 1865, then the seven years and $2\frac{1}{2}$ months will of course extend from 1865 to 1872, and the first $3\frac{1}{2}$ years, including the twelve events, will be from 1865 to 1868–9; and the second $3\frac{1}{2}$ years, with the $2\frac{1}{2}$ months, including the remaining eight events, will be from 1868–9 to 1872. But if the Covenant should be made between October 16, 1865, and October 16, 1866, then the seven years and $2\frac{1}{2}$ months would extend from 1865–6 to 1872–73. The fact of 1871–2 seeming, from the prophetic dates, to be the End of this Dispensation, makes it exceedingly probable that the Covenant will be made in 1864–5; but still, if it is made a year or two later, the difference will be comparatively small. The evidence of the prophetic dates, as well as the circumstance that Louis Napoleon will be 64 years old in 1872, shows that the destruction of Antichrist at the End of this Dispensation cannot be much later than 1872, and consequently the Covenant cannot be made much later than 1864–5. As it is absolutely certain, beyond all possibility of doubt, that Antichrist will be destroyed by the descent of Christ at Armageddon, exactly seven years and $2\frac{1}{2}$ months after the date of the Covenant, we only have to wait until the date of the

Covenant is ascertained, and shall then know almost to a day the precise time of the Consummation.

EVENT I. — THE CONFIRMATION OF A SEVEN YEARS' COVENANT between Napoleon and the Jews, (Dan. ix. 27.)
It is universally admitted that 69 of Daniel's 70 weeks (Dan. ix. 25, 26) terminated just before Christ began his public ministry, and that they signified 69 weeks of years, or 483 years, which commenced about 457 B.C. The remaining 70th week, or seven years, is considered by many expositors to be unfulfilled until the closing period of the Gentile economy, when *He* (the Antichrist) *shall confirm the covenant with many for one week*, (7 years,) *and in the midst of the week he shall cause the sacrifice and oblation to cease, and . . . shall make it desolate, even until the consummation*, (Dan. ix. 27.) The conclusion of a seven years' league between the Jews and some earthly potentate, which shall speedily lead to the restoration of their sacrifices at Jerusalem, will therefore be a clearly defined landmark, showing that in seven years' time the epoch of the consummation will be reached. An additional 75 days, (1335-1260,) or 2½ months, is mentioned in Dan. xii. 12, which makes 7 years and 2½ months to be the exact interval between the date of the Covenant and *the time of blessedness*, when Christ will commence the Millenium by descending on Mount Olivet. Daniel's 70th week is explained at greater length in Chapter III. of this treatise.

The recent French expedition to Syria shows Napoleon's intention to obtain possession of Jerusalem; and in taking this step he is only carrying out the plans of the first Napoleon, who convened an assembly of the Jews at Paris, and meditated their restoration to Palestine under his protectorship. It is natural to suppose, that in case of the Jews being guaranteed secure possession of the Holy Land, the other European Powers would be consenting parties to the compact as well as France; but the exclusive mention of Antichrist as the maker of the Covenant implies that he will be the prime mover in the transaction, and he alone is specified, as all the other European Powers will soon be subordinate to him.

As soon as the seven-years' compact between Napoleon

and the Jews is made, there will be a great stir and movement among those Christians who are "discerning the signs of the times," and "giving heed to the sure word of Prophecy." They will accept it as a positive proof and unmistakable signal that, in two or three years' time, Christ will come into the air, to take away from the earth the 144,000 wise virgins; and they will forthwith proceed to raise a loud and continuous proclamation of these heart-thrilling and momentous truths. When the midnight cry, "Behold the Bridegroom cometh," is thus made, ALL the virgins, foolish as well as wise, will awake; and those that are foolish will begin too late to endeavor to obtain the oil of prophetic knowledge, and will find themselves incapable of acquiring sufficient understanding of the prophecies to enable them fully to confess Christ's impending Advent, so as to be included among the wise virgins. Many professing Christians, and even some who are truly converted, will undoubtedly join with the ungodly world in bitterly opposing and persecuting those who boldly testify to these truths. So strong and deeply rooted is the general prejudice against the Second Advent, that it is not likely that any fulfillment of prophecy, however startling and extraordinary, will really convince the generality of nominal Christians, although it may make them less unwilling to listen to these views than heretofore. Nothing less than the disappearance of the Wise Virgins, and the terrors of the subsequent 3¼ years' great tribulation, will produce a general belief in Churches that the Day of Judgment has indeed commenced. Ministers who at the present time will venture to disturb the false peace of their hearers, by faithfully and emphatically declaring these things, must inevitably expect to see a considerable part of their congregation, especially the wealthier members, withdraw to some other church, where the preacher will "speak smooth things, and prophesy deceits." It is morally impossible that those whose hearts are fixed upon the treasures of this world will submit to be continually told that, in two or three years' time, Christ will personally come to remove his waiting people, and to pour out desolating judgments over the whole earth; they will rather prefer, like the ostrich, to bury their head in the sand of temporary forgetfulness of such an alarming prospect, and to continue, like the antediluvians, immersed in the business and pleasures of this life, until the Wise Virgins are caught up into the ark of the Heavenly Jerusalem, and the flood of the 3½ years' *great tribulation* sweeps away the unrepentant into perdition. It must be expected that many ministers of eminence, and even of piety, will come forward with an imposing array of arguments, to prove that, notwithstanding all the startling signs of the times, the Advent of Christ is yet many years distant. Great divisions will arise in churches, and probably not a few preachers will be ejected from their pulpits, for daring to confess these truths; but the "wise virgins, who understand," will possess the sustaining assurance, in the midst of opposition, that in about two years, and from four to six weeks, from the date of the Covenant, (as shown in diagram 4, by the position of the Manchild's rapture,) Christ will take them up from among unbelieving scoffers, to meet him in the air; and "*when he shall appear, we shall be like him; for we shall see him as he is.*"

EVENT II. RENEWAL OF THE JEWISH SACRIFICES and temple-worship at Jerusalem 9 months, or 9 months and 25 days after the Covenant, (Dan. viii. 13, 14.)

One of the first objects to which the Jews, who are induced by the seven-years' treaty to migrate to Jerusalem, and those who are already settled there, will naturally turn their attention, will be the reëstablishment of their temple-worship and the restoration of the ceremonies of the Mosaic ritual. In Dan. viii. 13, this is foretold to happen 2300 days before the sanctuary is cleansed, (by Antichrist's destruction at Armageddon,) and as the last-mentioned event takes place exactly 7 years and 2½ months after the date of the Covenant, it results that the sacrifices will be commenced just 295 days or 9 months and 25 days after the date of the Covenant, and at the distance of 2300 days before the end of the 7 years and 2½ months, (or 2595 days.) The passage in Dan. viii. 13, 14, reads thus, "*How long shall be the vision concerning the daily sacrifice and the transgression of desolation, to give both the sanctuary and the host to be trodden underfoot?*" that is to say: How long will the period be, during which the sacrifices will first be restored, and then after their removal the desolation of the sanctuary will continue? The answer is, *Unto 2300 days then shall the sanctuary be cleansed.* It is manifest that the sacrifices beginning 9 months and 25 days after the Covenant will only continue for 965 days, or 2 years 8 months and 5 days, until the end of the first 3½ years, because *in the midst of the week* of 7 years Antichrist *will cause the sacrifice to cease . . . and make it desolate until the consummation*, (Dan. ix. 27.) The period of the subsequent desolation of the temple by the setting up of Napoleon's image there, extends over the latter 3½ years of the 7 years, and the supplementary 2½ months (Dan. xii. 7-12, Rev. xi. 2, lit. ful.) Thus 965 of the 2300 days constitute the period of the daily sacrifice; and the remaining 1335 of the 2300 days constitute the period of the desolation of the sanctuary by the substitution of the worship of Napoleon's image, instead of the sacrifices. The analogy of the yearday fulfilment of the 2300 days shows that there will probably be a partial renewal of the sacrifices 9 months after the Covenant, and a partial cleansing of the sanctuary 25 days before the Consummation.

It is said that the Jews consider Mt Moriah upon which the Mahomedan Mosque of Omar is now standing, to be the only proper place for the offering of their sacrifices, in virtue of its having been the consecrated site of Solomon's Temple; and the fact of its being in the hands of the uncircumcised, constitutes the main impediment to the reinstitution of their sacrificial rites. Louis Napoleon's approaching Covenant with them will probably permit the conversion of this Mosque of Omar into a Jewish temple: it will then be appropriately fitted up with altars and sacrificial tables and vessels; and the daily temple-services will be strictly observed, accompanied with the burning of incense, and the slaying of oxen and lambs, (Is. lxvi. 3.) It is within their Temple that Napoleon is to be worshipped as God (II. Thess. ii.) 3½ years after the date of the Covenant.

The great amelioration in the condition of the Jews throughout the world, and the improvement in the aspect of Jerusalem itself during the last few years, unequivocally indicate the partial restoration of Israel under the Antichrist to be close at hand. A resident comparing Jerusalem with what it was seventeen years ago, says: "The city was poor and miserable in its appearance, the houses mean and dirty, the streets narrow and crooked. Now the streets are wide and straight, and alive with the busy hum of traffic. Many handsome dwellings have been erected, with beautiful gardens attached, in which flourish all the luscious fruits of this favored clime. Fine churches, synagogues, hospitals, dispensaries, hotels, and stores are everywhere met with; and rich men from Constantinople Babylon, Bagdad, Damascus, Egypt, England, France, and other places, have contributed to improve and beautify Jerusalem. The British Consul at Jerusalem, in an official communication in 1861, stated that ever since 1844 many Jews have returned to Palestine, and the ill-treatment they formerly met with from Mahomedans has to a great extent ceased. A most noticeable symptom of their preparing for some concerted movement is the formation in Paris in 1860 of a "Universal Israelite Alliance" to facilitate communication among themselves in every quarter of the globe.

EVENT III. THE COMPLETE DRYING-UP of the Turkish Empire, consisting partly of the separation of Syria from Turkey, within 2 or 3 years after the Covenant.

There is no sign of the times that testifies more clearly to the nearness of Christ's coming than the decay of the Turkish power. Several hundred expositors who have written during the last 300 years agree that the drying-up of the river Euphrates in its yearday fulfilment must denote the overthrow of the Ottoman Empire, as we read in Rev. xvi. 12: *"And the sixth angel poured out his vial upon the great river Euphrates, and the water thereof was dried up that the way of the kings of the East* (the Jews) *might be prepared. . . . Behold, I come as a thief."* The Advent of Christ is here stated to happen immediately after the drying-up of the Turkish Empire, and therefore cannot take place until the Empire is dissolved. As long as the integrity of Turkey is maintained, Christ will delay his coming; but almost directly it is overthrown, the Saviour's Advent will occur. The prophecy is as plain as if these very words had been written in the Bible: AS SOON AS THE TURKISH EMPIRE IS DISSOLVED, THE SECOND ADVENT WILL TAKE PLACE.

It is evident from Dan. viii. 9, 23, that the four kingdoms of Greece, Egypt, Syria, and what is now nearly all the rest of Turkey, are distinctly to reäppear just before Christ's Advent, and this constitutes another remarkable sign of the times, inasmuch as both Greece and Egypt have been dissevered from Turkey since 1822, and it only remains for Syria to be divided off from Turkey, and then the four kingdoms will reëxist. These will be four of the ten kingdoms that are to be ranged under the military feoffship of Napoleon during his 3½ years' reign as Antichrist, and therefore there is no ground for the apprehension that they will ever be permanently absorbed into Russian territory. It is, however, a question whether the Czar might not assume the title of king over one of them, and thus become one of Napoleon's ten vassal kings. But it seems rather to be intimated that Russia may soon assist to break up the Turkish Empire, and perhaps even seize Constantinople, and then be driven back by Napoleon and the other European powers. The seizure of Constantinople and overthrow of the Turkish government will probably constitute the complete drying-up of the mystic Euphrates.

EVENT IV. THE SUCCESSFUL INVASION of Egypt by Napoleon within 2 or 3 years after the Covenant.

In Dan. xi. 21 to 31 * (where *"the vile person,"* or

* 21 And in his estate shall stand up a vile person, to whom they shall not give the honor of the kingdom: but he shall come in peaceably, and obtain the kingdom by flatteries.
22 And with the arms of a flood shall they be overflown from before him, and shall be broken; yea, also the prince of the covenant.
23 And after the league made with him he shall work deceitfully: for he shall come up, and shall become strong with a small people.
25 And he shall stir up his power and his courage against the king of the south with a great army; and the king of the south shall be stirred up to battle with a very great and mighty army; but he shall not stand: for they shall forecast devices against him.
26 Yea, they that feed of the portion of his meat shall destroy him, and his army shall overflow: and many shall fall down slain.
28 Then shall he return into his land with great riches; and his

"*king that shall do according to his will,*" (verse 36,) is generally admitted to mean the Antichrist, and the kings of the North and the South to signify the sovereigns of Syria and Egypt) it is clearly predicted that after the Antichrist has made the seven-years' league with the Jews, he will successfully invade Egypt, and defeat the army of the Sovereign of Egypt with great slaughter, and then return to his own land with exceedingly valuable spoil. The time of this event is distinctly mentioned as being between the making of the Covenant (ver. 23) and the setting up of the Abomination 3½ years subsequently, (ver. 31,) and is most probably from 6 months to 2 years after the date of the Covenant, in which case it will take place before the Translation of the Wise Virgins. But still it may possibly occur just after the First Translation.

The Antichrist is further represented as remaining for an interval in his own land, and then again returning toward Egypt, (about 2 or 3 years after the Covenant,) but is opposed by the "*ships of Chittim,*" which most probably mean the English navy, since there is no other fleet that would be likely to offer any effectual resistance to his progress. Being caused by this opposition to return back to his land, he determines in his indignation to break the Covenant which he had entered into with the Jews. To this end he returns for the third time toward Egypt and Palestine, and holds communication with some apostate Jews in Jerusalem who are willing to have the provisions in the Covenant regarding Divine worship violated. By force of arms the daily sacrifice is then taken away and the abomination of desolation, which is the

heart shall be against the holy covenant; and he shall do exploits, and return to his own land.

29 At the time appointed he shall return, and come toward the south; but it shall not be as the former, er as the latter.

30 For the ships of Chittim shall come against him: therefore he shall be grieved, and return, and have indignation against the holy covenant: so shall he do; he shall even return, and have intelligence with them that forsake the holy covenant.

31 And arms shall stand on his part, and they shall pollute the sanctuary of strength, and shall take away the daily sacrifice, and they shall place the abomination that maketh desolate.

image of Napoleon himself, is set up in the Jewish temple.

This third expedition of Napoleon against Egypt and Palestine is apparently described at fuller length in verses 40, 41, which are retrospective and which chronologically precede verse 31, because *the time of the end*, at which they are stated to commence, is spoken of in Dan. xii. 1 as *that time when Michael shall stand up*, which is evidently Michael's war with Satan (Rev. xii. 7) seven months before Napoleon's 3½ years' persecution. The King of Egypt, assisted by the King of Syria with *many ships*, which he will probably obtain from some friendly maritime power, is represented as coming against Napoleon, who nevertheless overflows and passes over and enters into the glorious land, (Palestine,) and this is doubtless the period when he encompasses Jerusalem with his armies and sets up his image in the Temple. The commencement of the conflict between Napoleon and the confederate kings of Syria and Egypt is additionally indicated to be about 6 or 7 months before the 3½ years' persecution, by the fact that there could not be *many ships* in the vicinity of Europe at a later period, because the ships in the third part of the sea (the part nearest Europe) will be destroyed under the second trumpet (Rev. viii.) 4 or 5 months before the 3½ years begin. The subjugation of England by Napoleon does not take place until about the beginning of this 3½ years, and therefore there is no reason why the *ships of Chittim* and the *many ships* may not be identical with the British navy. The remaining 4 years of Napoleon's career after his victory over the kings of Egypt and Syria, are described in verses 41 to 45. It seems that he will have possession of Jerusalem during the 3½ years' Tribulation, and then, while elsewhere, will receive unpleasant tidings, which will cause him to lead up a vast army to exterminate the Jews. Having encamped with his hosts *upon the glorious holy mountain between the seas*, (the Mediterranean and Dead Sea,) he will suddenly *come to his end, and none shall help him.*

EVENT V. THE COMING OF CHRIST IN THE AIR, the Resurrection of the sleeping saints, and Translation of the 144,000 Wise Virgins (or Manchild Rev. xii. 5) about two years and from four to six weeks after the Covenant. (Rev. xiv. 1–5. Thess. iv, 16)

This event is shown in many passages of Scripture to take place *before* the 3½ years' Great Tribulation, (see Chapter iv.,) and the precise time of its occurrence is discovered by the chronological pósition of the Rapture of the Manchild (Rev. xii. 5) in the literal-day fulfilment, being ascertained from its chronological position in the year-day fulfilment. The different visions of the Seals, Trumpets, Vials, etc., in Revelation, are fulfilled first on the year-day scale within about 1872 years, and secondly on the literal-day scale within about 1872 days, and the second fulfilment is a miniature fac-simile of the first; the relative order of events in each fulfilment being almost exactly the same. Thus as the year-day Rapture of the Manchild is evidently the Ascension of Christ in A.D. 29– 33, at the distance of from 1838 to 1843 *years* before the End of this Dispensation in 1871–2; therefore the literal-day Rapture of the Manchild, which incontestably denotes the Ascension of the Wise Virgins, will be at the distance of from 1838 to 1843 *days*, that is rather more than five years, *before* the End ; and as the End of this Dispensation will be seven years and 2½ months, or 2595 days after the date of the Covenant, therefore the ascension of the Wise Virgins will thus be from 752 to 757 days, in other words, (allowing an ample margin to avoid particularity as to a precise day,) two years and from four to six weeks *after* the date of the Covenant.*

* The advent of Christ and Resurrection and Translation of the saints are also further shown to happen in their first stage rather more than five years before the End, by the fact of their being distinctly described in Rev. vii. 9–17, viii. 1, xi. 15–19, xvi. 15–17, as taking place just before or at the commencement of the 7th seal, 7th trumpet, and 7th vial, which, in their year-day fulfilment, begin nearly simultaneously about five years before the End.

It is, moreover, manifest from Rev. xiv. 4, 15, that there is a *Firstfruits* or smaller and earlier ingathering and ascension of 144,000 living saints a short time BEFORE—and also a *Harvest* or much larger and later ingathering of living saints AFTER—the fall of Babylon and 3½ years persecution by the Beast and worship of his image. And that Christ will come to translate the watchful saints before this awful 3½ years, is obvious from Rev. iii. 10, Luke xxi. 36, xvii. 28.

Ignorant persons who might think that the texts, "*it is not for you to know the times or the seasons,*" or, "*of that day and hour knoweth no man,*" prohibit such accurate knowledge of the time of the Second Advent, should remember that those words were spoken in the present tense to the then existing generation, and before the gift of the Book of Revelation.

As soon as we arrive at the period of two years and from four to six weeks after the date of the Covenant, we shall enter upon a season of solemn expectation, when those of us who are the Wise Virgins may be translated at any moment. The instant Christ descends into the air, (1 Thess. iv. 16; Rev. xiv. 1–5,)* we shall be changed into the likeness of his glorified body, and caught up, like Elijah in the whirlwind—with chariots and horses of fire, until after ascending to a great height above the earth, we shall be ushered into the presence of the Lord Jesus, surrounded by his saints and angels in the New Jerusalem or Heavenly Zion, where we shall remain about five years, until the end of the Great Tribulation, and then

---

* 1 Thess. iv. 16, 17: "16 For the Lord himself shall descend from heaven with a shout, with the voice of the archangel, and with the trump of God: and the dead in Christ shall rise first:

"17 Then we which are alive and remain shall be caught up together with them in the clouds, to meet the Lord in the air: and so shall we ever be with the Lord."

The Apostle here includes both the Translations in the general statement: "Then we which are alive and remain shall be caught up."

Rev. xiv. 1–5: "1 And I looked, and, lo, a Lamb stood on the mount Sion, and with him an hundred forty and four thousand, having his Father's name written in their foreheads.

"2 And I heard a voice from heaven, as the voice of many waters, and as the voice of a great thunder: and I heard the voice of harpers harping with their harps:

"3 And they sung as it were a new song before the throne, and before the four beasts, and the elders: and no man could learn that song but the hundred and forty and four thousand, which were redeemed from the earth.

"4 These are they which were not defiled with women; for they are virgins. These are they which follow the Lamb whithersoever he goeth. These were redeemed from among men, being the firstfruits unto God and to the Lamb.

"5 And in their mouth was found no guile: for they are without fault before the throne of God."

The following passages also refer to this First Translation: 1 Cor. xv. 52; Dan. xii. 1–3; Matt. xxiv. 28, 37–42; xxv. 10; Luke xiv 22; Rev. iii. 10; vii. 1–8; xii. 5, 6; xi. 18; xvi. 15.

descend to the earth, mounted upon white horses, (Rev xix.,) and execute the final judgment upon the ungodly. After this, the Lord, with his glorified saints, will reign over the earth for 1000 years.

It is not at all certain that Christ will be visibly manifested to the world at this stage in his Advent about two years, and from 4 to 6 weeks after the Covenant. It is doubtful whether there will even be any appearances in the skies to indicate the solemn transaction that is being accomplished: "the voice of the archangel and the trump of God" may be only audible to those who are to rise heavenward in obedience to the divine summons; and the foolish virgins and the ungodly that are left behind may, perhaps, only discover, from the unaccountable disappearance of the Wise Virgins, that Christ has indeed come "as a thief." It is not precisely revealed whether the upward ascent of the raised and translated saints to meet Christ in the air will be conducted visibly, so as to be distinctly witnessed by those remaining on the earth, or whether it will be effected imperceptibly by their suddenly vanishing, like a vapor that exhales from the surface of the sea. It is evident that the fact of this momentous event having occurred, will be very widely recognized; for an unprecedented revival of religion is represented as immediately taking place among the foolish virgins and the unconverted, against whom the door of the first translation will have been shut. It is, therefore, to be inferred that some very convincing evidence will have been afforded in order to overcome the deep prejudice and blindness universally prevalent respecting the Second Advent, and this consideration favors the view that possibly the voice of the archangel may be a sound that will audibly reverberate throughout the globe like the crash of ten thousand thunders or the explosion of innumerable parks of artillery, startling the infidel and ungodly world from its slumber of carnal security and unbelief. The exact number of the Wise Virgins is stated in Rev. vii. and xiv. to be 144,000, and there is no valid reason for understanding the number otherwise than literally. The total sum of those who are the subjects of this first translation is intimated to be so small in comparison with the far more abundant ingathering that will be caught up in the second translation 5 years later, that even if the number were not stated to be 144,000, we should be led to form very nearly the same estimate from all the other passages that refer to the point. If that proportion of the earth's population which has any acquaintance with Gospel truth be considered to amount to about 150 millions, then the removal from among them of 144,000 persons would be an average of about one out of every thousand, and in America and England the average would probably be as high as one out of every seven hundred and fifty. And if we compute about ten millions of all the nominal Christians to be truly converted, then the 144,000 wise virgins, as compared with the remainder of the ten millions converted persons, will be in the proportion of one to seventy: in other words, there will be about seventy foolish virgins to one wise virgin. It must be remembered that the foolish virgins are not unconverted, but are converted persons in an unwatchful, backsliding state, who are left behind at the first translation, but are finally saved, either at their death or at the second translation.

EVENT VI. AN UNPRECEDENTED REVIVAL OF RELIGION and of Missionary effort among the foolish virgins and the unconverted that are left on the earth, will follow the Translation of the Wise Virgins. (Rev. xiv. 6.)

It is obvious that the translation of one out of about every 750 persons will produce a great sensation. Lists of the missing, and copious reports of the circumstances under which they have disappeared, will fill the journals of the day; but as very few are aware that this is the manner in which the Second Advent is to commence, it is likely that many will account for the mysterious event by every explanation except the right one. Especially as the ordinary course of nature will continue undisturbed for several months subsequently, the ungodly will soon recover from their temporary alarm and become more hardened, like Pharaoh and the Egyptians of old. But the brief period of respite afforded by these few months will be diligently employed by the pious persons then on the earth in preaching the Gospel and warning men not to worship Napoleon or his image, which is about to be set up. It is during this lull before the coming storm, and just after the translation of the 144,000 Wise Virgins to the Heavenly Zion, that the first seal in Rev. vii., and the three angel messages in Rev. xiv., have their ultimate literal-day fulfilment, in which the saints remaining on the earth are represented as being filled with an extraordinary fervor and zeal, and proclaiming on every side: "*Fear God and give glory to him, for the hour of his judgment is come.*" As the Pentecostal Revival was under the first year-day seal, so a Revival even greater will occur under the first literal-day seal. The prophecy of the angel carrying the everlasting Gospel to every nation, kindred, tongue, and people, will then be accomplished by innumerable copies of the Bible being circulated through every country, especially in heathen lands, to an extent never before known, and the seed thus sown will by harrowed in during the subsequent 3½ years' Great Tribulation, when events will furnish so striking a commentary on Revelation, that none who read it can fail to be warned against worshipping the Antichrist. Many Scripture types and predictions show that there will be an outpouring of the Holy Spirit far more abundant than at the day of Pentecost, and that it will be characterized by the same features, such as believers having all things in common, and being empowered to work miracles and speak with tongues. It is by this means that so many missionaries will be raised up who are represented in Rev. xiv. 6, 7, as then going forth to preach Second Advent truth to the heathen. The interval during which this great diffusion of the Gospel, consequent upon the translation of the Wise Virgins, will continue, appears to be about ten months,* at

* There is strong ground for believing with divers expositors that some of the 144,000 wise virgins, or else literal angels, will then come from the heavens to assist in proclaiming the Gospel everywhere.

Not only is open confession of a belief in the immediate and definite nearness of Christ's *personal* Advent necessary to constitute any one a wise virgin, but also a high degree of actual as well as imputed sanctification, (Rev. xiv. 4, 5.) It is evidently possible, even in this life, to become, by increased faith in Jesus and prayer, *wholly sanctified* and be preserved *blameless* unto the coming of Christ, (1 Thess. v. 23,) and cleansed from *all* sin and unrighteousness, (1 John i. 7, 9, iii. 3,) and redeemed from *all* iniquity, (Titus ii. 14, John xvii. 17, Ps. li. 7, Eph. i. 4, etc.) See Wesley on Christian Perfection, Foster on Christian Purity, Mrs. Palmer's Way of Holiness and other works; Boardman's Higher Christian Life; also the Guide to Holiness, and Beauty of Holiness, published monthly at Beekman St., New York.

the end of which peace will be taken from the earth at the literal-day opening of the second seal. There will yet, however, be an additional seven months to elapse before the 3½ years' Great Tribulation begins with the placing of the image of Louis Napoleon in the Jewish temple, and although universal warfare will prevail during this seven months, much will be done by "the people that do know their God," in forewarning mankind of the dreadful persecution about to arise, and reminding them that it is emphatically with reference to this crisis that the promise is made: "*Whosoever shall call upon the name of the Lord shall be saved.*"—Joel ii. 32.

THE NEXT SIX EVENTS will take place almost entirely within the concluding seven months of the first 3½ years of the 7 years of the Covenant-week.

EVENT VII. COMMENCEMENT OF ASTOUNDING PHYSICAL PHENOMENA, such as hail and fire falling on the earth, a third part of salt and fresh water becoming blood, and a third part of the luminaries being eclipsed. (Rev. viii.)

This series of marvellous phenomena continues throughout the last nine months of the primary 3½ years, and is caused by the first four Trumpets. As the first Trumpet is believed to have been accomplished in the year-day fulfilment from about A.D. 250 to A.D. 365, its corresponding position in the literal-day fulfilment will be from about the 10th day of the 9th month of the 3d year to the 11th day of the 1st month of the 4th year, (reckoning from the date of the Covenant;) and during part or the whole of this period of nearly four months, *literal hail and fire mingled with blood* will be *cast on the earth, and the third part of trees burnt up, and all green grass burnt up.* This plague, as well as those caused by the other trumpets and by the vials has had its counterpart in the plagues inflicted by Moses upon the Egyptians, which were evidently intended as types of these yet unfulfilled plagues; and a decisive and unanswerable argument is thus afforded against the objections of the unbelieving skeptic, who denies the probability of this literal fulfilment of Revelation; for it is obvious that the deliverance of the Israelites out of the hand of Pharaoh was, in all its circumstances, preëminently a type of the far greater deliverance of the Christian and Jewish Church from the tyranny of the last great Antichrist at the time of the Final Crisis. The extent of the calamity caused by the first trumpet cannot be accurately estimated unless we know the period of the year at which it will occur. Such a hailstorm between October and April would cause far less damage than at any other season, when it would destroy all the crops and the harvest. The statement that all green grass will be burnt up seems to imply that it will happen in the spring or summer. Its precise time will, however, be ascertainable as soon as the seven-years' Covenant is made.

"*And the second angel sounded, and as it were, a great mountain burning with fire was cast into the sea, and the third part of the sea became blood; and the third part of the creatures that were in the sea, and had life, died; and the third part of the ships were destroyed.*" The judgment inflicted under this second trumpet will continue nearly two months after the close of the first trumpet, and culminate in the destruction of the ships, three or four months before the $3\frac{1}{2}$ years' Tribulation. Some brilliantly luminous object, *as it were* a burning mountain or pillar of fire, will be cast into the sea, a third part of which (that part which is adjacent to Europe) will become blood; and as a natural consequence, every living creature in the third part which is thus affected will die, and their carcases, floating upon the surface of the crimson, blood-dyed waters, and breeding pestilence by their insufferable odor, will present a spectacle of unequalled horror. All the ships likewise that are in that same third part of the sea will be destroyed, being doubtless consumed by the devouring flames that will be kindled by the fiery cloud which, like a burning mountain, had previously fallen upon the ocean. Subsequent intercommunication between different countries by sea will be greatly impeded by this unexampled destruction of vessels. Not a few of the gigantic iron-plated men-of-war which are now being constructed by France and England will probably be among the ships that are thus destroyed. A larger proportion of French war-vessels may escape, because many of them, being engaged in different quarters of the globe, in carrying out Napoleon's schemes of universal conquest, may be outside the third part of the sea which is the scene of this visitation. "*And the third angel sounded, and there fell a great star from heaven burning, as it were a lamp, and it fell upon the third part of the rivers, and upon the fountains of waters. And the name of the star is called Wormwood: and the third part of the waters became Wormwood; and many men died of the waters, because they were made bitter.*" (Rev. viii. 10, 11.)

"The great star" here spoken of need not necessarily mean a firmamental star, as the word is frequently used to signify an angel or any person of distinction, as in Job xxxviii. 7, Dan. viii. 10, Rev. xii. 4, Isaiah xiv. 12. But whether we understand it to be an animate agent, such as a fallen angel, or an inanimate agent, like a flaming meteor, (in which case, not merely one, but probably showers of falling stars would descend on the rivers,) it is evident that by its means the nauseous flavor of wormwood will be supernaturally imparted to all fresh water in the third part of the earth, within which all salt water had previously been turned into blood; and the infusion of this bitter ingredient will even poison many men, and result in their death. This judgment of the third trumpet will continue, in a greater or less degree, about 64 days, because in the year-day fulfilment it continued about 64 years, from 412 to 476.

At the 4th trumpet, the third part of the sun, moon, and stars will be darkened. The prophecy further states, "*the day shone not for a third part of it, and the night likewise;*" and if this is accepted as the correct rendering of the Greek, then it would imply that the usual amount of light which is given during the day and at night-time will be withheld every day and night for one third of the time of its ordinary continuance. This will diminish the light of each twenty-four hours in *duration*, and will not be at all the result of the first-mentioned darkening of one third of the luminaries, which would only diminish the light in *strength and lustre*. The date of this phenomenon, which probably will last a few days, will be about 58 days before the 1260 days of infidel persecution, just as the year-date of this trumpet in 476 was 58 years before the 1260 years of papal dominancy.

Thus the first four trumpets are foreshown to conmence respectively about nine, five, three, and two months before Napoleon's 3½ years' reign as Antichrist; and the fearful sights and great signs introduced by them in the heavens above and in the earth beneath, and in the waters under the earth, will give ample warning to mankind of the awful woes that are about to follow.

EVENT VIII.—WAR IN HEAVEN, and Expulsion of Satan and his legions from the air on to the earth.

A great battle is about to be fought in the heavens, (Rev. xii. 7–12, Dan. xii. 1,) in which Satan and his hosts will be attacked by Michael and his angels, and cast out of the heavenly places or regions of the atmosphere into the earth, whereupon a song of victory will be raised in heaven, and an admonitory voice exclaim: "*Woe to the inhabitants of the earth and of the sea, for the devil is come down to you, having great wrath, because he knoweth that he hath but a short time.*" This occurrence furnishes a solution to the otherwise inexplicable mystery of Antichrist's unprecedented power. Satan, who is at present "the Prince of the power of the air," and leader of the "wicked spirits in heavenly places," (Eph. ii. 2, vi. 12,) having even access to the presence of God, (1 Kings xxii., Job ii., Rev. xii. 10,) is to be expelled from the aërial regions, and restricted to this earth as the sphere of his operations. The time when this is to happen is clearly revealed in Rev. xii. to be shortly after the Wise Virgins or Manchild have been caught up into the air to meet Christ, previously to the 3½ years' Tribulation. The presence of Christ with his raised and translated saints "in the air" (1 Thess. iv. 17) necessitates the dejection of Satan from that region, and therefore the 7th year-day Vial is at that very juncture poured "into the air," in order to dislodge him. Being cast to the earth, and gnashing his teeth with the wildness of despair, "knowing that his time is short," and that his doom is sealed, he summons up all his strength to make a last expiring effort to exterminate the Church Militant. The plan he adopts is described at full length in Rev. xiii., which is a narrative of the actions of Napoleon and the Pope (the two-horned Beast) during the final 3½ years.

He gives his power and seat and great authority "to the Beast which had the wound by a sword and did live." This is none other than Louis Napoleon, the last representative of the Roman Empire, who, by his restoration of the Napoleonic dynasty in 1852, healed the seventh head or form of government, which was "wounded to death" at Waterloo in 1815. Having thus invested Napoleon with universal power, Satan will energize and incite him "to make war with the saints for forty-two months, and overcome them," and to slay all who will not worship his image, until he is at last destroyed with the brightness of Christ's appearing. The grand secret of the superhuman power which Napoleon will acquire is thus explained by the fact that the Dragon, after being cast to the earth, will, through his special instrumentality, conduct the last desperate assault against the Christian Church. Legions of devils being also cast down with Satan, will enter into the ungodly, and cause them to become like raging demons and incarnate fiends. Demoniacal possession, which has recently been revived by spiritualism, will then become exceedingly prevalent, and great signs and wonders will be shown by the mediums, so as to *deceive, if it were possible, the very elect.* The time of Satan's expulsion from "the air" will be about 210 days, or seven months, before Napoleon's 1260 days' persecution, just as its year-day fulfilment by the overthrow of Paganism was 210 years before the 1260 years of Papal supremacy.

EVENT IX.— FLIGHT OF MANY OF THE SAINTS into the wilderness, most probably some remote region of the United States. (Rev. xii. 6, 14.)

In Rev. xii. 13, 14, we read : "*And when the Dragon saw that he was cast into the earth, he persecuted the woman which brought forth the Manchild. And to the woman were given two wings of a great eagle, that she might fly into the wilderness, into her place, where she is nourished for a time, and times, and half a time, from the face of the serpent.*" The Devil and his hosts being driven from the heavens, will instigate the wicked bitterly to persecute that portion of Christ's Church which is remaining on the earth, and from the midst of which the Wise Virgins had previously been caught up. But the persecution will not be so severe before as after the beginning of the 3½ years' Tribulation. England and the European Continent will doubtless be the scene of its commencement, and a great number of Christians who understand from Prophecy what Napoleon is about to do, will naturally desire to escape to a remote and secluded region, where they may be beyond his reach. For this purpose no place could be suggested as more appropriate than some unexplored region in America. And this seems to be the very locality designated in Prophecy. For as in the year-day fulfilment the great eagle with two wings represented the Roman Empire, which had an eagle for its heraldic symbol, so in the literal fulfilment it must necessarily denote a country that has a great eagle as its national emblem; and no nation corresponds with this prefiguration so completely as the United States. France could not be signified, for it will be the persecuting power at that time. It has long been the opinion of some expositors, that the United States is represented by this eagle; and it is highly improbable that Prophecy which especially traces the history of the Christian Church would make no direct mention of a country that occupies so conspicuous and important a position among the nations of Christendom. The heraldic emblems of England and France are referred to in Prophecy as being respectively a lion (Ezek. xxxviii. 18) and three frogs, (Rev. xvi. 13,) which were the ancient arms of France. And it is therefore not unreasonable to suppose that the national arms of the United States would also be mentioned. Although it seems that the United States will help Christians to escape into the wilderness, by permitting them to pass through its territory unmolested, in order to seek a distant retreat before the 3½ years' persecution begins; yet as soon as that awful persecution commences, America, as well as every other part of Christendom, will be the scene of an unparalleled slaughter of the saints and temporary triumph of infidelity.

Only a portion of the saints will be able to flee into the wilderness, for we read in Rev. xii. 17 of the *remnant of the woman's seed* who were unable thus to escape from the Dragon's assaults. The flight will partially commence as soon as the Wise Virgins are caught up, (Rev. xii. 6;) but will principally take place about two months after the casting down of Satan, just as its year-day fulfilment consisted in the protection granted to the Church from 379 to 395 by Theodosius the Great, 55 years after the overthrow of Paganism in 323–4. The two wings of the eagle signified, with regard to the Roman Empire, the Eastern and Western divisions into which it was bisected, and in like manner they appear to denote, with reference to the United States, that it will have undergone a corresponding bipartition into two sections, by the time that the woman's flight into the wilderness takes place. The statement that the saints who are hid in the wilderness during the 3½ years will be *fed* and *nourished* there, (Rev. xii. 6, 14,) viewed in connection with the types of the miraculous sustenance of the Israelites for 40 years in the desert, and of Elijah during the 3½ years' famine, (1 Kings xvii. 6, 16,) seems to intimate that they will be fed by angels, or some other miraculous means. It is obvious that no food could be obtained in the wilderness otherwise, because not a drop of rain will fall during the 3½ years, (Rev. xi. 6,) and the third and fourth literal-day seals, which are comprehended in the same period, are specially characterized by dreadful famines. The place into which the company of saints, symbolized by *the woman*, will retreat, is manifestly some one particular locality specially appointed by God for that purpose, for it is called "*her place*," "*a place prepared of God that they should feed her there*," (Rev. xii. 6, 14.) The saints who are to be hid there will perhaps be miraculously guided to the spot after the manner of the Israelites who were led by the pillar of cloud and pillar of fire, or of the wise men who were conducted to Bethlehem by the star which went before them. The fact of the woman's flight being twice mentioned in the same chapter, shows it to be an event of special importance.

EVENT X. THE FALL OF BABYLON, or transformation of Popery into what may be termed Napoleonism, for the Pope will institute and establish the worship of Napoleon and his image throughout all the earth. (Rev. xiii.)

The Harlot, or Babylon, (Rev. xvii. and xviii.,) is universally allowed to denote the Papal Hierarchy: the true Church being represented by a chaste and faithful bride, it is appropriate that the false Popish Church should be depicted as an unchaste and adulterous woman. She is exhibited in Rev. xvii., in her last stage of existence, sitting upon the ten-horned Beast, which is then under its eighth Head, (Louis Napoleon,) and just about to be destroyed; and the statement is made: *The ten horns which thou sawest upon the Beast, these shall hate the whore and shall make her desolate and naked, and eat her flesh, and burn her with fire.* This shows that the Papal Church, after being supported and upheld by Napoleon for some time, will be stripped bare and plundered of all its wealth by the governments of the Ten Kingdoms, which are denoted by ten horns. But it is stated in a previous verse of Rev. xvii. that these Ten Kingdoms will not be all formed until the closing *hour* or final $3\frac{1}{2}$ years of this Dispensation, and, therefore, the complete spoliation of the Church of Rome will not take place until then. The Pope's temporal power is already being regarded with increased disfavor through out Europe, and just as in the Revolutions of 1794 the temporal possessions of the Papacy were confiscated, so will it be in the far greater Revolutions which are now approaching. Under the name of Babylon, the Papacy is three times declared, in Rev. xviii. 10, 17, 19, to be finally consumed during the closing *hour* of $3\frac{1}{2}$ years; and in Rev. xiv., after the Translation of the Wise Virgins, the first angel who announces that the *hour* of God's judgment is come, is followed by a second angel, who cries out, *Babylon is fallen, is fallen ;* again showing that the final *hour* of $3\frac{1}{2}$ years is the time of Popery's destruction. But the fact must not be overlooked that after the fall of Popery a third angel (Rev. xiv.) proclaims: *If any man worship the Beast and his image and receive his mark in his forehead or in his hand, he shall be tormented . . . . forever and ever.* This clearly proves that the worship of the Beast's image is something quite distinct from Popery, because it arises subsequently to Popery's downfall, and is denounced in terms that appear to signify that all who worship the image must inevitably be damned. Such a denunciation could not apply to Popery, for it must be admitted that some Papists have been converted and saved.

Further explanations are given in regard to the image of the Beast in Rev xiii., where it is declared that all the wicked shall worship the Beast shortly after the deadly wound of its seventh head (the Napoleonic dynasty) is healed, and this came to pass in 1852, when the Napoleonic dynasty revived and recovered from the wound received at Waterloo. The universal worship of the Beast is predicted to be brought about through the agency of another two-horned Beast, which is understood by all able expositors to signify the Pope and Romish priests. It is said of this second Beast that *he exerciseth all the power of the first Beast before him,* (ενωπιον in his presence,) *and causeth the earth and them which dwell therein to worship the first Beast, whose deadly wound was healed. And he doeth great wonders, so that he maketh fire come down from heaven on the earth in the sight of men. And deceiveth them that dwell on the earth by the means of those miracles which he had power to do in the sight of* (ενωπιον) *the Beast; saying to them that dwell on the earth, that they should make an image to the Beast which had the wound by the sword, and did live,* (Rev. xiii. 12-14.) Here again the fact is twice stated that the image is made to the Beast after it has recovered from its deadly wound, which is unquestionably the restoration of the Napoleonic dynasty in 1852, (see chapter ii. sec. 1,) and therefore the image of the Beast cannot be made until after 1852.* This alone proves the untenableness of expositions which

---

* The *image of the Beast*, mentioned under the first vial, (Rev. xvi. 2,) never having been yet set up, shows that the vials cannot have had their complete antetypical literal-day fulfilment, although undoubtedly may have an accommodated typical year-day fulfilment from 1789 to 1872. Year-day interpreters have held that the image is a literal one. For instance, the Rev. Mr. Shimeall, of the New-York Presbytery, whose *Bible Chronology* is highly commended by Dr. Cumming in his *Great Preparation,* showed in his discourses in 1842 that the Infidel Antichrist, the Eighth Head, would arise a few years before 1868, and would ultimately have a literal image of himself worshipped throughout the earth. He is also fully of opinion that Louis Napoleon is the Antichrist that is to be so worshipped.

would fritter away the particular meaning of this passage by explaining it to signify in a general sense the image-worship of the Papists. Popery, as well as Mahomedanism, has in many respects remarkably typified and foreshadowed the great infidel apostasy of Napoleonism that is about to arise, but it cannot be said with truth that the Pope has ever yet made fire come down from heaven in the sight of men, nor has he hitherto done great miracles, for comparatively few have been really imposed upon by such transparent deceptions as the liquefaction of St. Januarius' blood or the winking of Madonnas. The second or two-horned Beast is especially to work his miracles in the sight of the first or ten-horned Beast, who is spoken of as being a man: for although the ten-horned Beast originally means the whole Roman Empire, yet Louis Napoleon, as the last head and representative of that Empire, thereby himself becomes the Beast, according to his own saying: "L'Empire c'est moi." The personality of these two Beasts (Napoleon and the Pope) is additionally stated in Rev. xix., where their destruction at Armageddon is described. *The Beast* (Napoleon) *was taken, and with him the False Prophet* (the Pope) *that wrought miracles before him,* (ενωπιον,) *with which he deceived them that had received the mark of the Beast, and them that worshipped his image. These both were cast alive into a lake of fire burning with brimstone.* Here, as in Rev. xvi. 13, the second Beast, or the Pope, is called the False Prophet, and is referred to in the same terms as in Rev. xiii. Both these Beasts are cast ALIVE into the lake of fire, which proves that they cannot be mere empires or systems, but must be actual living, moving, breathing persons. And when the lake of fire is described a thousand years afterward, (Rev. xx. 10,) it is said *where the Beast and False Prophet are*, establishing the fact that they are yet alive, 1000 years after being cast into hell, and, therefore, must be persons, and not mere systems. It is also manifest that as Napoleon is the Beast to be destroyed at Armageddon, and as that Beast is stated in the above passage to be the one whose image is to be worshipped and whose mark men are to receive, therefore it is Napoleon's image that is to be worshipped, and the mark of Napoleon that men will receive.

The narrative in Rev. xiii. declares very plainly that the person (Napoleon III.) by whose rise the last head of the Beast (the Napoleonic dynasty) should be healed of its deadly wound, (inflicted at Waterloo,) is to be worshipped by all the earth for 42 months, or 3½ years, and that the worship of him is to be brought about by the Pope and Romish priests becoming endowed with Satanic power to do great miracles, so as to induce people to make an image to him. It is also said of the Pope: "*And he had power to give life ($\pi\nu\epsilon\nu\mu a$, breath) unto the image of the Beast, that the image of the Beast should both speak, and cause that as many as would not worship the image of the Beast should be killed. And he caused all, both small and great, rich and poor, free and bond, to receive a mark in their right hand, or in their foreheads. And that no man might buy or sell, save he that had the mark or the name of the Beast, or the number of his name. . . . . And his number is six hundred threescore and six,*" (Rev. xiii.) Sundry ingenious attempts have been made to explain away this prophecy, as having been fulfilled by the persecuting edicts of Popery, which in some cases anathematized those who traded with heretics, but not a single instance has ever yet been shown in which the Romish priests have imprinted on any man's forehead or hand either the name of the Beast or the number 666: and as we are told that ALL, both small and great, are to receive a mark of this kind, it is clear that this part of the prophecy has never yet been accomplished. The real fact is that the Pope will cause a literal image or statue of Napoleon to be made, and although constructed of wood or metal, it will be made to breathe and also speak, and some of the words that it will utter will be to the effect that every one who will not worship it shall be killed. This, as well as the bringing fire down from heaven, will be a genuine miracle permitted by God to be performed through Satanic agency, in order that the Scripture may be fulfilled. Acute and intellectual persons, who would laugh to scorn all the miracles that have hitherto been worked by Papists, will be completely ensnared by the startling signs and wonders that will then be manifested by Antichrist's adherents. Not simply one image, but a great many, will be fabricated and worshipped all throughout Christendom, and the most relentless persecution, causing the slaughter of several million persons, will be carried on against all who will not worship the image, or have imprinted on their forehead or hand either the number 666 or one of words, *Louis Napoleon*, or some other appointed mark. The image appears to be specially referred to in Isaiah xli. 5, 6, 7, xliv., and also in Rev. ix., (literal fulfil.:) *The rest of the men . . . repented not of the works of their hands, that they should not worship devils, and idols of gold, and silver, and brass, and stone, and of wood: which neither can see nor hear nor walk.* It is not said of these idols or images that they cannot *speak*, for the reason that in many cases the gift of vocal articulation will be miraculously imparted to them by the False Prophet.

Popery will in one sense be completely destroyed at that time, because Napoleon and his ten kings will confiscate all its temporal possessions, and totally abolish the Christian religion, which professedly constitutes the foundation of the Popish creed. But, in another aspect, it will be more powerful and universally prevalent than ever, for although it will no longer exist in its old form, yet in its new form, as a religion enjoining the worship of Napoleon, it will succeed in the conversion of nearly the whole world. The means by which this will be accomplished will be three-fold: first by the unparalleled corruption and demoralization of all who are not true Christians, owing to the removal of the restraints of God's Spirit and to the energy with which Satan will work when he is cast to the earth; secondly, by the stupendous miracles which will be performed by Antichrist's emissaries; and thirdly, by the most convincing of all arguments, the unsparing use of the sword. It will soon be seen that the great majority of professing Christians, who *have the form of godliness, but deny the power thereof*, will at once abjure Christianity when they find themselves exposed to the awful alternative of either taking that step or else being killed, perhaps with dreadful tortures. The false and unscriptural teachings of the present day, such as Universalism and Unitarianism and Materialism, which deny the literality and eternity of the punishment

of the wicked in hell-fire, necessarily prepare men for the
ready commission of any crime, however great; for they
are thus taught to believe that they may be as wicked
as they like, and yet receive hereafter very little punishment, or none at all, and then be ultimately made happy,
or else annihilated. Such a belief will lead persons unhesitatingly to worship Napoleon and be branded with
his mark, rather than be killed, for they will have very
little dread of future retribution. But God, foreseeing
the infidel doubts that would be injected into men's
minds, tending to blind them to the awful consequences
of worshipping the Beast, has pronounced against that
crime the most distinct and solemn anathema that the
Bible contains: "*If any man worship the Beast and his
image, and receive his mark in his forehead, or in his
hand . . . he shall be tormented with fire and brimstone
in the presence of the holy angels, and in the presence of
the Lamb: and the smoke of their torment ascendeth
up forever and ever,*" (Rev. xiv. 9-11.) This language
certainly appears to signify that the sin here denounced
is an unpardonable one, like that of blasphemy against
the Holy Ghost, (Matt. xii. 31,) and the declaration
that all shall worship the Beast *whose names are not
written in the book of life*, (Rev. xiii. 8,) also appears to
imply that only the non-elect, and none of those who are
to be saved, will be guilty of so great a sin. The torments of those who commit it are unequivocally declared
to be of unending duration: the Greek words εις αιωνας
αιωνων, translated *forever and ever*, are never used in
any limited sense, and are applied to describe the eternal
existence of God himself, *who liveth forever and ever*,
(Rev. iv. 9, 10.) The cognate word αιωνιος, used in
Matt. xxv. 41, 46, in speaking of the *everlasting* fire of
hell and the *eternal* life of the righteous, likewise never in
a single instance in the Bible denotes a period less than
eternity.

It is remarkable that some of the spiritualist mediums have already been induced by the unclean spirits
with which they are demoniacally possessed, to make
an image of a man, and endeavor to give life to it.*

---

* About the year 1852, J. Spear, a quondam Universalist minister,
and more recently the Boston Spiritualist seer, in obedience to a com-

They aspire to imitate the acts of God's creative power so as to succeed in breathing the breath of life into, in animate substance, and almost appearing to create a human being. This is the very miracle which, according to the predictions of Prophecy, they are repeatedly to perform during Antichrist's 3½ years. It is also noticeable that in Europe, about ten years ago, a person named Andrew Towianski, a native of Æsel-Berg in Switzerland, founded a sect which has for its chief object the worship of Napoleon I. The number of its adherents has greatly increased throughout all Europe: their proceedings are conducted with the profoundest secrecy: each member of their society has a picture representing Napoleon I. rising from the grave, with a halo of glory around his head: and their expectation of his resurrection, combined with their strong belief in metempsychosis, is quite likely to end in Napoleon III. being worshipped by them as the living personification of his deceased Uncle.

Bunyan's representation of Popery as a giant that has grown old and feeble, and incapable of persecuting the saints with the same violence as in past times, is not altogether correct. The giant is to be galvanized into fresh activity, and THE ROMAN CATHOLIC CHURCH IS YET TO BECOME ALMOST UNIVERSALLY DOMINANT. As Samson slew more at his death than in his life, so the Romish Church during its last 3½ years will slaughter more saints than at any period of equal length during its whole career. The fall of Babylon, (the Romish Church,) which takes place before that 3½ years,

---

munication from the spirits, persuaded a number of other Spiritualists in Boston to join him in constructing *a large image in the shape of a man*, which cost 2000 dollars, (£400,) and was erected on the High Rock, Lynn, Massachusetts. It was intended as the grand apparatus for spirit communication, and was to be animated by a soul miraculously born of a Medium. Great enthusiasm was manifested by many persons of reputed intelligence and position, who believed in the revelation. Various names were given to the image, such as The New Motive Power, Heaven's Last Best Gift to Man, Physical Saviour, New Creation, The Great Spiritual Revelation of the Age, The Philosopher's Stone, The Art of all Arts, etc. It did not, however, answer their expectations. The incident is mentioned in Gordon's Threefold Test, an excellent exposé of Spiritualism.

does not denote the complete destruction of the ecclesiastical organization of Popery, but only signifies that Babylon will then be plundered of its wealth, and will sink into a state of deeper corruption and more avowed infidelity, and *become the habitation of devils and the hold of every foul spirit*, (Rev. xviii. 2.) Popery will *in reality* then be destroyed, for it will be changed into a new religion enforcing the worship of Napoleon, but *apparently* it will still exist, for its priests will be more active than ever, and its churches will be crowded with the worshippers of their new deity Napoleon. Before this hour of darkness arrives, may God enable all true Christians who are members of the Papal Church to obey the command: *Come out of her, my people, that ye be not partakers of her sins and that ye receive not of her plagues*, (Rev. xviii. 4.)

EVENT XI. ACQUIREMENT BY NAPOLEON of supreme power over Great Britain and in a less degree over America, (Rev. xiii. and xvii.)

The 3½ years' universal empire of this great Antetypical, Papistico-Infidel, Democratico-Despotic, Personal Antichrist is to be a mimicry of the fifth universal monarchy and millennial kingdom of the Lord Jesus Christ, (Dan. ii. 44, vii. 27.) As during the millennial 1000 years, when the earth will be almost a heaven, the Divine King of the Jews and true Messiah will be specially worshipped in the Jewish temple, and will be a king of the subordinate kings who will reign over the various nations: so during the 3½ years' GREAT TRIBULATION, when the earth will be almost a hell, Napoleon the Antichristian King of the Jews and false Messiah will be worshipped, as God, in the Jewish temple, (2 Thess. ii. 4,) and will be a king over the other kings of the earth. Nearly all the governments of the world will at that time be democratic-despotic monarchies, and it is evident that in America the present political convulsion is tending to that result. Regarding the predicted subjection of England to Napoleon, the eight following considerations are worthy of attention. (1.) England was unquestionably part of the Roman Empire, (Gibbon ch. i.,) being occupied by a Roman military garrison from A.D. 45 until the Romans finally withdrew from it in A.D. 436: and it is manifest, from Dan ii. vii. and Rev. xiii. xvii., that the whole territory of the old Roman Empire, including its Eastern as well as its Western Half, is to be divided into ten kingdoms, represented by the ten toes and ten horns, shortly before *the hour of temptation* or final 3½ years, (Rev. iii. 10, xvii. 12, xiii. 5,) and that the ten kings of these ten kingdoms are then to *give their power and strength* to the Eighth Head of the Beast, (Rev. xvii. 13, 17.) (See Event XII.) As Louis Napoleon is the Eighth Head of the Beast, (see ch. ii.,) and as England must be included among these ten kingdoms, therefore England must *give its power and strength* to Louis Napoleon. This is the main and principal argument which decisively shows that IT IS ABSOLUTELY CERTAIN THAT ENGLAND WILL FALL UNDER THE POWER OF LOUIS NAPOLEON. The ten kingdoms have not yet been completely formed, because we have not arrived at the final 3½ years of this dispensation, but their formation is rapidly progressing and will manifestly soon be completed. The division of Belgium from Holland, the separation of Egypt and Greece from Turkey, and of Bessarabia from Russia, the consolidation of Italy into a United Kingdom, the annexation of Savoy and Nice to France, are important steps toward the accomplishment of the tenfold partition of the Roman Empire. Even those expositors who erroneously look for the ten kingdoms in the Western Roman Empire alone, cannot avoid including England, since it was undoubtedly part of the Western Roman Empire. Nor has the separation of England from Papal Christendom at the Reformation any thing whatever to do with the question; for the ten toe and horn kingdoms are to be formed not out of the territory of Papal Christendom, but out of the territory of the original undivided Roman Empire, of which England was undoubtedly a part. This tenfold division, as mentioned in Rev. xvii. 12, is understood by Bickersteth, Cuninghame, and many other year-day interpreters, not to occur until the close of this dispensation.

(2.) England possesses one of the most marked characteristics of the future ten kingdoms, in the fact that there by a considerable admixture of the *clay* of democratic power with the *iron* of monarchic authority in her government. In Dan. ii. 42 the ten toes of the Image are depicted as being part of clay and part of iron, which unmistakably denotes that the government of each of the ten kingdoms will be of the clay-iron or democratic-monarchic form, being neither a pure republic like that of Switzerland, nor a hereditary despotism like that of Russia. The ruling power is not yet so completely in the hands of the people as, according to Rev. xvii., it will be in about three years after the Jewish Covenant, at which time the present government will be overthrown, and a king elected by universal suffrage, who will in reality be the mere vassal and deputy of Louis Napoleon. The government of Louis Napoleon as administered through his ten kings will practically be a despotism, for he *shall do according to his will*, (Dan. xi. 36,) without being controlled by the will of the people: still it is a question whether he may not give the ten kingdoms the appearance of being limited or constitutional monarchies, by permitting legislative assemblies of the people to be held. The partially clay-iron character of England's present government is of itself a strong, presumptive proof of her being one of the ten kingdoms.

(3.) England was one of the kingdoms of the Western Roman Empire, about ten in number, which became subject to the Papal Antichrist at the commencement of his 1260 years; and was thus foreshadowed to be included amongst the ten kingdoms that will become subject to the Personal Antichrist at the beginning of his 1260 days. The division of the Western half of the Roman Empire in the sixth century into about ten kingdoms, and their submission to the authority of the Papal Antichrist, was eminently a *type* of the yet future division of the whole Roman Empire, Eastern as well as Western, into precisely ten kingdoms, which are unanimously to submit to Napoleon, the great antitypical Antichrist. But *the type* must not be mistaken for *the antitype*, otherwise men will be diverted from watching for the final manifestation of Antichrist; which is to be the most terrible. England's separation from Papal Christendom at the Reformation can only have the effect of exempting it from those special judgments which are to descend on the territory of Babylon or Papal Christendom; and cannot in the least alter the fact that it must be among the ten kingdoms into which the whole area of the Roman Empire is to be divided for the first time during the Personal Antichrist's brief *hour* of supremacy. It appears that the resemblance between the literal-day and year-day fulfilment will be so exact that there will be some great movement toward the close of Napoleon's 1260 days analogous to the Reformation in the latter part of the Pope's 1260 years.

(4.) The independence of England during Napoleon's 8½ years' universal supremacy would be incompatible with the world-wide dominion which he is then to possess, (Rev. xiii. 7.) Even if any one could so completely shut their eyes to the plain statements of Prophecy (Rev. xvii. 12) as to fancy that England is not to form part of the Personal Antichrist's ten kingdoms, it would yet be impossible to deny that it must fall under his power to a very great extent, in accordance with the prediction: "*Power was given him* (that is, Napoleon III., the Wild Beast after its 7th Head was healed) *over all kindreds and tongues and nations*," (Rev. xiii. 7.) There is evidently a distinction between the absolute and despotic sway with which Napoleon will govern the ten kingdoms that will be welded into a compact confederation under his Headship, and the less absolute authority which he will exercise over all the communities of Christendom, (with very slight exceptions.) The Ten Kingdoms will constitute the chief seat of his dominion, and (excepting the Asiatic nations that rebel against his authority and assault him during the Armageddon war) the other nations of the world will be all more or less subordinate to him: if England could possibly be excluded from the first, it must fall within the second category; moreover, it is utterly improbable that Napoleon at the Head of Ten Kingdoms, even supposing England was not one of the ten, would be either unable or unwilling to reduce England to submission. At the present time his effective army is two or three times as large as that of Great Britain, and his Iron Fleet is at least equal if not superior to the English Iron-clad Navy. His ambition will not suffer him to brook a rival, and with the auxiliary forces which he will soon be able to draw from his allies in Europe, he will occupy a position which will render it useless for England to offer resistance to his overwhelming hosts.*

(5.) The ominous silence observed in Ezek. xxxviii. 13, as to the consequences of the interference of England (the merchants of Tarshish) with Napoleon when he goes up against the Jews shortly before the midst of the final seven years, seems to indicate that England's opposition is effectually overcome by her being subjugated, especially as Napoleon continues his expedition unhinderedly. The great Antichristian leader spoken of as Gog in Ezek. xxxviii., has long been understood by many Jewish and Christian interpreters to be the Antichrist or Eighth Head: the narrative obviously describes the Armageddon war and Antichristian invasion and desolation of Palestine during the last 3½ years; and it is clearly parallel with the narratives in Dan. xi. Zech. xiv., and Rev. xix: in which the titles of the great leader of the armies that invade Palestine are respectively *the king that shall do according to his own will,* (generally called the Wilful King,) *the idol shepherd,* and *the Wild-Beast,* (or Eighth Head of the Beast;) these titles are admitted by the best interpreters to designate the Personal or Infidel Antichrist, and therefore it must be inferred that Gog of Ezek. xxxviii. is the same person as the Antichrist. Gog's identity with the Wilful King is placed beyond a doubt by the statement that each of them is followed by the Ethiopians and Libyans; it is also said of Gog that he goes up *to take a spoil and to take a prey,* (ver. 12,) which is the very act attributed to the Antichrist, who is termed the Assyrian in Isaiah x. 6, "I will give him a charge *to take the spoil and to take the prey;*" and Gog is again shown to be the great Antichrist who is the universal subject of all the prophecies, by the statement, (ver. 17:) "*Art thou he of whom I have spoken in old*

* The latest statistics of the available military forces of the European nations are as follows: Great Britain, 200,000 volunteers and militia, and 220,000 regulars, of which 60,000 are in India. France, 650,000. Austria, 650,000. Italy, 300,000. Spain, 230,000 Portugal, 24,000, Turkey, 200,000. Belgium, 73,600. Bavaria, 70,000. Outside the Roman Empire, Prussia has 600,000, and Russia 800,000.

time by my servants the prophets of Israel which prophesied in those days many years that I would bring thee against them?" These words fully demonstrate the utter fallacy of the view by which Gog is taken to signify the Czar of Russia, for whereas the whole Bible is full of types and direct predictions concerning the last Antichrist, there is scarcely a single allusion in all prophecy to the Emperor of Russia. Understanding Napoleon, then, to be the Gog of Ezek. xxxviii., we find that his expedition against the Jews, after their return to Palestine, as described in verse 12, takes place while "*they are at rest and dwelling safely*," (ver. 11,) and must therefore be previous to the final $3\frac{1}{2}$ years, during which they are to be "*trodden under foot*," (Luke xxi. 24, Rev. xi. 2,) and cruelly persecuted, and many of them "*led away into captivity*," (Zech. xiv. 2, Luke xxi. 24.) All the parallel prophecies seem to show that this expedition will be during the six months which precede the closing $3\frac{1}{2}$ years, and will either be a little after, or at the same time as, the coming of "*the ships of Chittim*" against the Antichrist. When this vast Antichristian host sets out to invade the Holy Land, "*Sheba and Dedan and the merchants of Tarshish, with all the young lions thereof*," by which the generality of reliable expositors understand England to be denoted, will say to Gog, that is, Napoleon: "*Art thou come to take a spoil? Hast thou gathered thy company to take a prey?*" etc., (ver. 13.) The expostulation is evidently unavailing, as Gog pursues his onward march to Palestine, and is ultimately destroyed there about $3\frac{1}{2}$ years after his first invasion of the land. It might appear, from a superficial perusal of Ezek. xxxviii., that Gog's overthrow immediately follows his irruption into Palestine; other prophecies, however, plainly show that he first invades Palestine, and continues his military occupation of it for about $3\frac{1}{2}$ years, at the end of which he assembles a countless host upon the plains of Megiddo to fight with the Lamb, but "comes to his end, none helping him." The circumstance of England (the merchants of Tarshish) opposing Gog (Napoleon) when he first marches against the Jews, just before the last $3\frac{1}{2}$ years, shows that she will have retained her independence up to that time, while the fact of her opposition proving unsuccessful, viewed in connection with the portentous silence maintained in Ezek. xxxviii. as to her subsequent fate, leads to the conclusion that it is at that very point of time that Napoleon vanquishes and subjugates her; and this conclusion is fully confirmed by other parallel prophecies.

(6.) England is implied to be the scene of Napoleon's 3½ years' relentless warfare with the saints, (Rev. xiii.,) because a wilderness, apparently in America, is represented in Rev. xii. 14 as the only spot where a hiding-place from the murderous assaults of Antichrist will be found. Napoleon, as the Antichrist, is "to make war with the saints and to overcome them" (Rev. xiii.) throughout the whole world, with the exception of those who have escaped before the 3½ years into the wilderness. Christianity is outwardly to be almost extirpated by him through all Christendom. This could never be the case unless he subdued England, which contains a very large proportion of those in Europe who are true Christians. In fact, the predicted universality of Antichrist's military, civil, and ecclesiastical power during the final 3½ years, is such as to preclude all possibility of England remaining unsubdued by him. It must be remembered that the ungodly, who constitute nine tenths of the population even in England and America, will be dazzled by the attractiveness and glory of Antichrist, and will spontaneously cluster around him as their Head, for *God shall send them strong delusion*, and thus the submission of England to Napoleon, the Antichrist, may take place without much opposition on the part of many of its inhabitants.

(7.) Retribution for national sins must be meted out to England as well as to every other country at the time of THE GREAT TRIBULATION, when all the nations of the earth are to be chastised ; and the Antichrist is specially appointed by Providence as a scourge to inflict the chastisement; therefore on this ground alone it must be expected that England will fall under Napoleon's power. Among her national sins may be mentioned the patronage of Paganism, by giving annual contributions to the maintenance of heathen temples in India, and of Popery, by making annual grants to Maynooth College and to Roman Catholic schools and chaplains : also the acquirement of a revenue of five million pounds sterling from the opium traffic with China, by which half a million Chinese are annually poisoned. It must likewise be borne in mind that the fearful prevalence in England of Sabbath-breaking, drunkenness, and immorality will be visited with much severer vengeance than in the case of countries that have not enjoyed such abundant religious privileges.

(8.) The first six Vials of Wrath, in their year-day fulfilment from 1789 to 1866-7, are only poured out on special localities exterior to England, but the seventh Vial (from 1866-7 to 1872) is poured into "the air," whereby its universality is denoted, "*A great and mighty earthquake*"—that is, a terrible world-wide Revolution will be caused by it. From its tremendous effects it is hopeless for England to expect to escape: her fall under the Antichrist will be brought about at that time as much by internal convulsion as by foreign invasion, but as the last Vial will not be poured out until Christ comes into the air, (Rev. xvi. 15,) and as the four angels are to hold back the four winds of desolation until then, (Rev. vii.,) we may expect that the most calamitous of the approaching wars and revolutions will be to a great extent averted during the next two or three years.

HAVING BRIEFLY CONSIDERED eight reasons which show England's submission to Napoleon to be inevitable, we may next notice four considerations from which it appears that the American Continent, although not comprised among the horns, will nevertheless, like Prussia, Holland, and other countries outside the Roman earth, be brought in a great measure under the political and ecclesiastical supremacy of Napoleon. First, Napoleon's power is to extend over *all kindreds and tongues and nations, and all that dwell on the earth shall worship him*, except the righteous, (Rev. xiii. 7, 8:) a few remote heathen nations will also escape, (Isaiah lxvi. 19:) he is likewise to *make war with and overcome the saints*, and as most of the saints are to be found among the Protestants, either in America or England, he must necessarily gain great power in those countries, or else his persecution could not reach them. The 3½ years' *hour of temptation* and of Antichrist's persecution is to come upon

ALL the world, and, except it should be shortened, *no flesh should be saved*, not a single human being would be left alive, (Rev. iii. 10, Matt. xxiv. 22.) Satan, who is declared in the Bible to be *the Prince of this world*, (John xiv. 30,) is to bestow on Antichrist that which was in vain offered by him to Christ, namely, *all the kingdoms of the world and the glory of them;* in other words, *his power and his seat and great authority*, (Rev. xiii. 2.) Thus the universality of Antichrist's predicted dominion forbids the supposition that England or America can escape being included within it.

Secondly, the designated agencies by which Antichrist is to be placed upon the throne of universal dominion, are specially at work in America. During the latter part of the year-day sixth vial, from 1826 to 1866, three unclean spirits of devils, performing miracles, are foreshown, in Rev. xvi. 14, 16, to go forth from the mouths of the Dragon, Beast, and False Prophet, *to the kings of the earth and of the whole world, to gather them to the Battle of that great day of God Almighty . . . toward* (εις) *a place called in the Hebrew tongue Armageddon.* Now it is manifest that these three spirits of Infidelity, Lawlessness, and Popery, (which the three spirits are generally interpreted to signify,) are actively operating in America, and ripening it for the last Antichristian apostasy. Infidelity is being widely diffused through the joint efforts of Universalism, Unitarianism, and especially Spiritualism, which has infected two or three millions out of the thirty million inhabitants of the United States. Lawlessness and insubordination have reared their serpent-heads in an unprecedented manner recently in parts of America, and Popery is dominant in South-America, and Mexico, and Lower Canada, and numbers one fourth of the population of the United States among its adherents. When the appointed time arrives, the Pope and Romish priests will strenuously urge men to make Napoleon their king, as well as acknowledge him as their god: the devils, speaking through the Spiritualist mediums, will unceasingly reiterate the same exhortation: their persuasions will be seconded by the marvellous miracles which they will work: and speedily throughout the greater part of the world will be heard the universal shout: There is no god like unto Napoleon, (2 Thess. ii. 4.) And then during his 3½ years' supremacy he will gather nearly all the armies of Christendom to contend against the hosts from Asia that will invade the Roman Empire for 13 months, (Rev. ix. 15,) and also to fight at the battle of Armageddon, where they will be crushed in the wine-press of God's wrath. The preliminary step toward the consummation of this tragedy is the conversion of every nation into a nation of soldiers, so that the whole earth may become like one vast military camp: and when the cry, To arms, To arms, has resounded from North to South, and from East to West, and when even the implements of husbandry have been beaten into weapons of war, (Joel iii. 10,) the next step will be the subordination of all these countless military hosts to the supreme authority of one great Commander-in-chief, Napoleon, the Apocalyptic Beast and Apostatic Man of Sin: and thus when at last he assembles all his allies to Palestine to engage in the wars that will be waged there during the last 3½ years, thousands of soldiers will go from America to take part in those conflicts, and will perish in the scene of slaughter that will ensue, in which the blood will come up *even unto the horses' bridles by the space of a thousand and six hundred furlongs*, (Rev. xiv. xix.; Zech. xiv.)

Thirdly, America contains a population that has principally been created during the last hundred years, by the influx of emigrants from the Ten-Horn Kingdoms, and may therefore be regarded as to a great extent identical with those kingdoms and involved in nearly the same destiny. Western Europe is more closely connected with America in respect of the language, religion, and habits of its people, than even with the countries geographically nearer to it, such as Russia. On this account the approaching convulsions in Europe cannot but extend to America and produce corresponding effects there. The unequaled skill with which Napoleon will make those convulsions subservient to the increase of his own power, will greatly predispose the Americans to look to him in the hour of general revolution and anarchy, as the only man competent to take the helm of state, and to unite the discordant factions under one government. And this introduces the consideration that, Fourthly, there is to be *a great Revolution, such as was not since men were upon the earth, so mighty a Revolution and so great,* (earthquake meaning Revolution,) under the 7th year-day vial, (Rev. xvi. 18,) shortly before the last 3½ years, from which France alone is to escape; and the result of this overthrow of nearly all existing governments will be the complete establishment of Napoleon in the coveted position of arbiter of the world's destinies and supreme dictator over the rulers of the nations. Although he will probably soon acquire political power over Mexico and the Southern States especially as many of the inhabitants of Louisiana, Florida, and Mississippi are French in origin, and Roman Catholic in creed, yet it seems that he will not gain his predestined supremacy (Rev. xiii. 7) over the Northern States until a later period. For the great Revolution adverted to will not take place until two or three years after the Jewish Covenant, and as the four winds of anarchy and desolation are to be held back until then, the complete break-up of existing governments will apparently not happen before that time.

EVENT XII. DIVISION OF THE ENTIRE TERRITORY of the old Roman Empire into ten kingdoms, Great Britain, France, Spain, Italy, Austria, Greece, Egypt, Syria, the rest of Turkey, and most probably Tripoli with Tunis, and the union of their ten kings in a congress or confederation under Napoleon's headship. Rev. xvii. 12.

Four points may be specially adverted to in connection with this event. First, that the tenfold or decuple partition of the ancient Roman Empire has never yet been fully effected; and the fact of its occurrence being evidently close at hand is a very clear indication of the nearness of the End. The time when it is to happen is predicted to be the closing *hour* or final 3½ years of the Christian dispensation, and also after the rise of the Eighth Head of the Beast—that is, subsequently to 1852: the interpreting angel, in Rev. xvii. 12, having explained the seven heads of the seven-headed and ten-horned Beast to signify seven successive forms of government over the Roman Empire, stated further: "*The ten horns*

*which thou sawest are ten kings which have received no
kingdom as yet, but receive power as kings one hour with
the Beast,* (*i. e.*, Napoleon III., the Eighth Head of the
Beast.) *These have one mind, and shall give their power
and strength unto the Beast.* The one *hour* here mentioned is identical with the *hour* which is spoken of in
five other passages of Revelation, (Rev. iii. 10, xiv. 7,
xviii. 10, 17, 19,) and which in each case represents the
final 3½ years of Antichrist's persecution and of Babylon's
overthrow. The ten horns of the Beast, like the ten
toes of the Image, (Dan. ii. 41,) denote a tenfold division
of the *whole* Roman Empire, Eastern as well as Western;
just as the four horns of the Grecian goat (Dan. viii. 8)
represented the fourfold partition of the *whole* Grecian
Empire into the four kingdoms of Greece, Egypt, Syria,
and Thrace. A fundamental error into which many expositors have fallen is that of considering the tenfold division
of the Roman Empire to have been made in the sixth century, when the Western Roman Empire was partitioned
into about ten kingdoms; but it is obvious that the predicted ten kingdoms must be formed out of and include
all the Eastern as well as all the Western Roman Empire: and this has never yet taken place, and is moreover
distinctly predicted in the above-quoted passage, in Rev.
xvii. 12, not to occur until the concluding *hour* or 3½
years of this Dispensation. The division of the Western
Roman Empire into about ten kingdoms in the sixth
century was, like many other circumstances in connection with the Papal Antichrist, only a type and figure of
the yet future tenfold partition of the whole Roman
Empire at the time of the Infidel Antichrist.

The countries that are to be formed into ten distinct
kingdoms may be thus enumerated. In EUROPE the Roman Empire included England and most of Scotland,
and all that part of Europe that lies west of the Rhine,
or south of the Danube and Vallum Romanum, which
was a stone wall, 200 miles long, stretching from Bingen
on the Rhine to Ratisbon on the Danube, (Gibbon, ch.
xii,) and skirting the north of Baden and Bavaria. The
countries that at present are situated within this portion
of Europe are France, Belgium, Luxembourg, Rhenish
Prussia west of the Rhine, Baden, Wirtemberg, part of

Bavaria, Switzerland, Spain, Portugal, Italy, Austria south of the Danube, Turkey, Greece, and all the islands of the Mediterranean. To this must be added the territory of ancient Dacia above the Danube, that would lie south of a line drawn from Vienna to the most northerly part of the Black Sea, and which would include part of Austria, Wallachia, Moldavia, and Bessarabia. In Asia the boundaries of the Roman Empire may be defined in general terms to be nearly the same as the limits of Asiatic Turkey, which comprehend Asia Minor, Armenia, Mesopotamia, Assyria, and Syria. In Africa the Roman Empire comprised Egypt and all the northern coast corresponding with Barca, Tripoli, Tunis, Algeria, and Fez. The shaded part of the accompanying map shows very nearly the extent of the Roman Empire.*

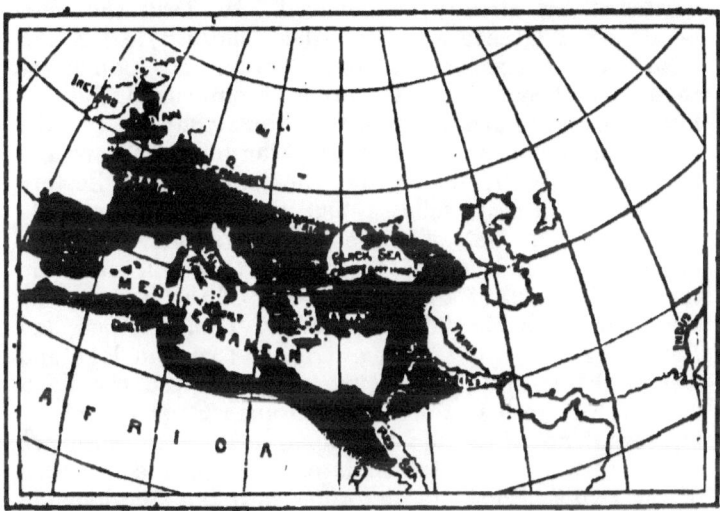

Everywhere within its limits it will be the law of the land, during the last 3½ years, that all shall be killed who will not worship Napoleon's image or receive his mark.

* The life of Julius Cæsar, which Napoleon is said to be preparing, will perhaps contain some intimations of his future plans. The maps with which it will doubtless be furnished will show exactly the geographical area which will be formed into the ten kingdoms. It is noticeable that Hippolytus in the third century explained the clay-iron toes of the Image to signify that the ten kingdoms would at some time be democracies.

Secondly, it is clear that four out of the ten kingdoms will be the four kingdoms into which the Grecian Empire of Alexander the Great was divided at his death, namely, Greece, Egypt, Syria, and what is equivalent to nearly all the rest of Turkey. In Dan. viii. 9, 22, 23, (literal fulfil.,) these four kingdoms are spoken of as being existent at the time of Antichrist's manifestation, for it is said regarding them: *In the latter time of their kingdom when the transgressors are come to the full, a king of fierce countenance* (Antichrist) *shall stand up.* As these kingdoms have long since disappeared and been absorbed into the territory of Turkey, it is evident that they must reappear just before the revelation of Antichrist, since he is to *stand up in the latter time of their kingdom.* It is one the most remarkable signs of the times that their re-existence has already commenced. In 1822 the independence of Greece was established, and Egypt has likewise altogether separated from Turkey. As soon as the severance of Syria from Turkey is accomplished, the four kingdoms will have reappeared. Since they are to exist contemporaneously with the ten kingdoms, and are also geographically included within the limits of the Eastern Roman Empire, it follows that they must necessarily constitute four out of those ten kingdoms. The fifth kingdom, in addition to these four, that will make up the five divisions of the Eastern half of the Roman Empire, will probably be composed of Tunis, Tripoli, and Barca in the north of Africa. As the two iron legs and feet of the Image (Dan. ii. 33, 40) symbolized the Eastern and Western sections of the Roman Empire, and the ten toes denoted the ten kingdoms into which those two sections are to be subdivided, it may be expected that each of the two sections will be formed into five kingdoms, in accordance with the symbol of five toes on each foot. The error of those expositors who have found all the ten kingdoms in the Western section alone, is the same as if they should represent all the ten toes as growing out of one foot. As regards the five kingdoms that will be formed out of the Western Roman Empire there can be scarcely any question but that Great Britain, France, Spain, and Italy will constitute four of them, and probably the fifth will mainly consist of that part of Austria which falls within the Roman Empire. As the line of division between the Eastern and Western Empires was nearly the same as that which now separates Turkey from Austria, and Tunis from Algiers, it follows that in the Western Empire there will remain Belgium, Luxembourg, Baden, Bavaria, Wirtemberg, Rhenish Prussia, west of the Rhine, Switzerland, Portugal, Fez, and Algiers, which will have to be absorbed into the five Western divisions above mentioned. Portugal may be annexed to Spain, and probably France will make the Rhine its eastern boundary, and convert Belgium, Rhenish Prussia, Luxembourg, Baden, Wirtemberg, and part or the whole of Switzerland into French territory: in which case Bavaria would be joined either to France or Austria. It is a question whether Moldavia, Wallachia, and Bessarabia will be joined with Austria or with the kingdom having Constantinople for its capital. Fez and Algiers will probably be annexed to Spain or France. Prussia and the German States lying east of the Rhine, as well as Holland and Hanover, will not be comprehended within the ten kingdoms, because they never constituted part of the Roman earth. This will also be the case with Bohemia, Moravia, and Gallicia, the separation of which from the rest of Austria may be consequently expected. If the view that Ireland was never part of the Roman earth be a correct one, its severance from Great Britain will speedily take place.*

Thirdly, each of the Ten Kingdoms will be a demo-

---

* In 1859 the population of the countries lying within the original Roman Empire (as given in the New Américan Cyclopædia) was nearly as follows: Great Britain, (without the six millions of Ireland,) 23 millions; France, 36 millions; Spain, 16 millions; Portugal, 3½ millions; United Kingdom of Italy under Victor Emmanuel, 23 millions; Austria, excluding the five millions of Gallicia and seven millions of Bohemia and Moravia, 27 millions; Belgium, 4½ millions; Rhenish Prussia, west of the Rhine, 3 millions; Luxembourg, ¼ million; Baden, 1¼ million; Wirtemberg, 2 millions; Southwest Bavaria, 2 millions; Greece, 1 million; Turkey in Europe, 17 millions; Turkey in Asia, including Syria, 16 millions; Egypt, 2¼ millions; Tripoli, ¼ million; Tunis, 2 millions; Algiers, 2 millions; Fez, 1 million. The total amount gives one hundred and eighty-four million (184,000,000) persons as the entire population of the ten Latin kingdoms, over which Napoleon will exercise absolute political, and ecclesiastical supremacy through the administration of his ten vassal kings.

cratic-despotic monarchy, and therefore democratic monarchic principles of government will soon be introduced into those parts of the Roman earth which have not yet received them, such as Great Britain, Spain, Austria, Turkey, etc. There are three reasons for expecting this. (1.) The ten toes of the Iron Legs, which are universally admitted to signify the Eastern and Western Roman Empires, (Dan. ii. 42,) are compounded of iron and clay, whereby it is foresignified that each of the ten kingdoms will be characterized by an admixture of the iron of monarchic authority with the clay of democratic power. It was represented in the vision of the Metallic Image, (Dan. ii.,) which admittedly symbolizes the four great Empires of Babylon, Medo-Persia, Greece, and Rome, that there should be a gradual deterioration and debasement of the governmental power of these four great Empires. They were respectively denoted by the Head of gold, the Breast of silver, the Thighs of brass, and the Legs of iron: and thus there was a progressive descent from one metal to another less precious. The adulteration of the iron with intermingled clay takes place in the last stage of the Roman Empire at a period chronologically coinciding with the feet and toes of the Image, and in accordance with this prefiguration, it was not until the French Revolution of 1793-4 that the clay of popular power began to be mixed to any great extent with the iron of monarchical and oligarchical supremacy throughout the Roman earth. It is true that the Roman Empire was professedly a Republic for nearly five centuries before it became a Monarchy under Julius Cæsar, in 46 B.C., but it did not take its place in sacred history as THE FOURTH PROPHETIC EMPIRE until 32 B.C., when it conquered Egypt, the last remaining portion of the Grecian Empire; and the governments under which it has existed, in its undivided and divided form, since that time until the period of the French Revolution, have been for the most part absolute monarchies, which are fitly symbolized by the unadulterated iron of the Legs of the Image. Previously to the French Revolution there was scarcely any part of the Roman earth, except Switzerland, in which the governmental power had really been possessed by the people. The supreme authority was almost universally vested in the monarch and the aristocracy, but recently in France and Italy the people have been allowed to choose their own ruler, and this principle of a monarchy based on the will of the people is the true form of the clay-iron government. (2.) The entire body of the seven-headed and ten horned Beast, which represents the Roman Empire, is depicted in Rev. xvii. in its last stage, just before the full development of its eighth and last Head, as being *scarlet-colored:* and this indicates that the sovereign power is at that time vested in the people who inhabit the countries composing the body of the Beast. Scarlet is the emblem of sovereignty, and the Greek word κοκκινος, which is rendered *scarlet-colored*, is the same word which is used in Matt. xxvii. 28 in reference to the royal robe of *scarlet* that was put on our Saviour in mockery. This color has not yet spread itself over the whole body of the Beast, for France, Switzerland, and Italy are the only countries on the Roman earth in which the sovereign power has been vested in all the people, and Louis Napoleon and Victor Emmanuel are the only monarchs that have been elected by universal suffrage. But as ALL the Beast's body was scarlet-colored, therefore ALL the previously mentioned nations within the Roman Empire, such as England, Spain, Austria, Turkey, Egypt, etc., will, by internal revolutions or otherwise, soon have the sovereign power placed in the hands of the people, and they by their votes will choose a king, just as Louis Napoleon has been chosen by the ballot in France. The ten horns of the Beast remain uncrowned, in Rev. xvii, until just before the final *hour* of $3\frac{1}{2}$ years, and then they become crowned by the election of ten kings over the ten kingdoms by universal suffrage. This is further represented in the literal-day fulfilment of Rev. xiii. by the Beast rising out of the sea of revolutionary tumult with its ten horns crowned just previous to its 42 months' universal supremacy. Election by the voice of the people is to be the only title by which the ten kings will reign and the democratic-monarchic governmental principles upon which Louis Napoleon's throne is established, are to be universally adopted throughout the Roman earth. (3.) The Beast itself is predicted to become its own Eighth Head, (Rev. xvii. 11,) that is, *the peoples and multitudes and nations* (v. 15) represented by the Beast, are virtually to become the Eighth Head, which is stated to be a man, (Rev. xiii. 18.) The only way in which the Beast can thus be its own Head is by all the people which it symbolizes choosing one individual as their representative, and this will be effected by the population of each of the ten kingdoms, into which the ancient Roman Empire will be divided, electing a king by their votes, and then these ten kings will, in a European Congress, choose Napoleon as their Head and Protector, constituting him in this manner a King of kings. Louis Napoleon will then be the apex of the political pyramid, being elected over the ten kings, who in their turn will have been elected over the people. Although by his restoration of the Napoleonic dynasty in 1852 he has very nearly healed its deadly wound, and almost become the Eighth Head, yet he is at present the Eighth Head only in embryo, and not in its full development, for the ceremony of being crowned, which he will probably not undergo until a short time before the final 3½ years, is the act by which the Eighth Head will arrive at its full maturity. In Rev. xvii. the scarlet-colored Beast remains in its non-existent state *as the Beast that was and is not*, (since the death of its 7th Head in 1815,) and does not completely reëxist and become *the Beast that was and is not and yet is*, until just before the final *hour* of 3½ years: although it has been beginning to reëxist ever since 1852.

There are thus three prefigurations by which it is foreshown that all the nations within the Roman earth are to become republican introductorily to the formation of the ten kingdoms. (1.) Because the ten toes of the Great Image (Dan. ii.) are compounded of the clay of republicanism mingled with the iron of monarchic absolutism. (2.) Because the body of the Beast, (or Roman Empire,) in its last stage, is scarlet-colored, showing the sovereignty to be in the people, (Rev. xvii.) (3.) Because the Beast is to become its own Head, by the people themselves electing their own kings, who in their turn will elect Napoleon to be their Supreme Head, and thus Napoleon will virtually become the Beast, (Rev. xvii.)

Fourthly, it appears that Louis Napoleon will appoint a king over France, as his viceroy, and will assume the position of king over the ten kings who *will give their power and strength unto him* and *agree and give their kingdom unto him until the words of God shall be fulfilled*, (Rev. xvii. 13, 17.) The Antichrist Napoleon is depicted in Dan. vii. as a Little Horn coming up behind the Ten Horns, and in Rev. xvii. as the Eighth Head to whom the Ten Horns give their power, and must therefore be a distinct and separate person from the Ten Kings among whom the Roman Empire will be divided. There is scarcely any doubt but that Great Britain, France, Spain, Italy, Austria, Greece, Egypt, Syria, the rest of Turkey, and Tripoli, with adjacent territories, will in the main (whether or not under different names) constitute the ten divisions: and the remaining parts of the Roman Empire will be annexed to them. Throughout all the Roman earth there will be great revolutions during the six months or year preceding the second half-week of $3\frac{1}{2}$ years, and, as the result of these revolutions, the ten kingdoms will be completely formed and the Ten Kings appointed over them. And then, according to the prediction that the Little Horn will arise *after* the Ten Kings, (Dan. vii. 24,) Louis Napoleon having virtually abdicated the throne of France in favor of his viceroy, will arise in the new character of King of kings and Antichrist, and thenceforth during his predicted $3\frac{1}{2}$ years' *hour* of supremacy he will rule over all the ten kingdoms through the ten kings, who in reality will merely be his deputies. There is reason for supposing, according to the idea of some of the Fathers, that he will perhaps make Rome or Jerusalem the capital and metropolis of his Universal Empire. It is very evident from Prophecy that Louis Napoleon is to be animated with the determination to revive the Roman Empire in more than its pristine splendor and greatness, and to become invested with the titles and dignities of the Cæsars, for otherwise he would not be likely to form ten kingdoms so exactly within the boundaries of the Roman earth. Nor is it surprising that he should then cause himself to be deified, for this will only be following the example of Romulus, Julius Cæsar, and Augustus Cæsar, who were worshipped as gods. This Congressional Confederation of Ten Kings under Napoleon, will somewhat resemble the Confederation of the Rhine, in which sixteen German Princes were united under the protectorship of Napoleon I.; and it will very likely be the policy of Napoleon to establish not only the same religion of Napoleonism, but also the same code of laws and a uniform system of currency throughout all the ten kingdoms. The aspiring ambition which will impel him to stamp his name or mark upon the foreheads or hands of every man, woman, and child, will doubtless lead him to have his name and likeness imprinted upon that which is more imperishable, namely, all the gold, silver, and other coinage that is current. The letters which are likely to be stamped on every coin as the initial letters of the title which he will assume, are exactly equivalent to 666; for his title will probably be: *Louis Napoleon, Cæsar, Divus universi orbis, Rex x regum Romani imperii*, (in English: *Louis Napoleon, Cæsar, God of the whole earth, King of the ten kings of the Roman Empire;*) the initials of which are: L-50, N-0, C-100, D-500, U-5, O-0, R-0, X-10, R-0, I-1, and the total numerical value of these letters is 666, Antichrist's predestined number, (Rev. xiii. 18.)

EVENT XIII. ASSAULT UPON JERUSALEM by Napoleon the Antichrist, and substitution of the worship of his image in the place of the Jewish sacrifices, after which, for $3\frac{1}{2}$ years, *all* (the ungodly) *who dwell upon the earth will worship him*, or else be killed, (Rev. xiii.)

The Antichrist will allow the Jews at Jerusalem to continue their daily sacrifices and oblations until the end of the first $3\frac{1}{2}$ years, or half of the seven years, for which he had made the seven years' Covenant. But as soon as that point of time is reached, (Dan. ix. 27,) he will march against Jerusalem and abolish their sacrificial rites, and cause an image or an idol of himself to be placed in the Jewish temple, which every one will be commanded to worship, under the penalty of death in case of refusal. And thus the second $3\frac{1}{2}$ years, or latter half of the seven years, which is the period of **THE GREAT TRIBULATION** and of Antichrist's unparalleled persecution of the saints, will then commence. It is mentioned in the following eight different parts of the Bible:

Dan. ix. 27.
(1) In the midst of the week he shall cause the sacrifice and the oblation to cease, and for the overspreading of abominations he shall make it desolate, even until the consummation. (*The above-mentioned week is the 70th week of 7 years.*)

Dan. vii. 25.
(3) He shall wear out the saints of the Most High, and think to change times and laws: and they shall be given into his hand, until *a time and times and the dividing of time.*

Rev. xi. 2.
(5) But the court which is without the temple leave out, and measure it not; for it is given unto the Gentiles: and the holy city shall they tread under foot *forty and two months..*

Rev. xii. 5, 6.
(7) And she brought forth a man child. . . . And the woman fled into the wilderness, where she hath a place prepared of God, that they should feed her there *a thousand two hundred and threescore days.*

Dan xii. 7.
(2) It shall be for *a time, times, and an half;* and when he shall have accomplished to scatter the power of the holy people, all these things shall be finished.

Rev. xiii. 5, 7.
(4) There was given unto him a mouth speaking great things and blasphemies; and power was given unto him to continue (or make war) *forty and two months.* And it was given unto him to make war with the saints, etc.

Rev. xi. 3.
(6) And I will give power unto my two witnesses, and they shall prophesy *a thousand two hundred and threescore days.* . . . And when they shall have finished their testimony, the Beast . . . shall kill them.

Rev. xii. 14.
(8) And to the woman were given two wings of a great eagle, that she might fly into the wilderness, into her place, where she is nourished for *a time, and times, and half a time,* from the face of the serpent.

The first four of these eight texts speak directly of Antichrist, and describe his persecution of the Jews at Jerusalem and of the Gentile saints throughout the world: the fifth text depicts the pollution of the temple and the treading-down of Jerusalem by the Gentile power under Antichrist: the sixth speaks of the appearance and ministry of Elias and the other prophet at the same period: and the seventh and eighth texts twice mention the hiding of many saints in a particular place in the wilderness during the same 3½ years.

It is almost needless to say that these eight passages all describe one and the same period of 3½ years. Expositors have nearly all agreed that especially the last seven of them describe the same period, whether in its future literal-day fulfilment as the 1260 days of the Infidel Antichrist, or in its year-day fulfilment as the 1260 years of the Papal Antichrist. Daniel's 70 weeks have of course only one fulfilment as weeks of years, because in the original Greek they do not mean weeks of days, but weeks of years, as in Genesis xxix. 27, and would have been more correctly translated *seventy sevens of years.* The identity of *the time, times, and half time* with the 1260 days, is evident from Rev. xii. 6, 14 : and the meaning of the word *time* is given in Dan. ii. 25, 32, where the *seven times* of Nebuchadnezzar's madness has always been understood to signify seven years ; *a time, times, and half time* signifies one time, two times, and half a time, or 3½ times, which is the half of seven times and denotes 3½ years. A Jewish year or *time* was uniformly reckoned to contain 360 days, or twelve months of 30 days each, and therefore in prophetic calculations the ordinary year must be computed to be of the same length.

When Antichrist goes up to Jerusalem to abolish the Jewish sacrifices, and have his image placed in the temple, he will be accompanied by a great army, and will make an assault upon the holy city, which will thenceforth be trodden under foot by his Antichristian hosts during the succeeding 3½ years' unprecedented persecution ; but it appears that at the end of that time, and in the course of the supplementary final 2¼ months, the Jews will revolt against the garrison which Antichrist will have left in their city ; and when this intelligence reaches him, he will gather together *the kings of the earth and their armies* (Rev. xix. 19 ; xvi. 14) to go up to Palestine to exterminate the Jews, and likewise to fight against the Divine King of the Jews, (Dan. viii. 25 ; Rev. xvii. 14,) of whose expected advent at Jerusalem, to take possession of the kingdoms of this world, he will have been informed. Having arrived at Armageddon in the Holy Land, this vast host will suddenly be destroyed. There are thus two great expeditions of Antichrist against Jerusalem : the first, when he encompasses the city and has his image placed in the temple at the beginning of the final 3½ years and 2¼ months ; and the second, after the 3½ years and during the remaining 2½ months, when he hears of the revolt of the Jews against his army of occupation in Palestine, and leads up an overwhelming force to crush them, but perishes at Armageddon. It does not clearly appear whether in this last expedition Antichrist will succeed in taking vengeance on Jerusalem for having revolted against him, or whether he will be destroyed before carrying his vindictive determinations into effect. The latter view seems on the whole to be the best supported. But if Zech. xiv. 1, 2, describes the second instead of the first expedition, then Jerusalem would appear to be sacked by Antichrist just before his destruction.

The first four of the following five passages clearly describe the first expedition of Antichrist, when he will lead his armies against Jerusalem at the beginning of the 3½ years, and *cause the sacrifice and oblation to cease in the midst of the week*, (Dan. ix. 27,) and then be destroyed 3½ years and 2½ months afterward. The fifth passage most probably delineates the first expedition, but may possibly only refer to the second.

Luke xxi. 20: When ye shall see Jerusalem compassed with armies, then know that the desolation thereof is nigh. Then let them which are in Judæa flee to the mountains. . . . For these be the days of vengeance, that all things which are written may be fulfilled. . . . And they shall fall by the edge of the sword, and shall be led away captive into all nations, (*interval of 3½ years*, Rev. xi. 2:) and Jerusalem shall be trodden down of the Gentiles, until the times of the Gentiles be fulfilled. . . . And then shall they see the Son of man coming in a cloud with power and great glory. (*This prophecy was fulfilled primarily and typically at the destruction of Jerusalem in* A.D. 70 *by the Roman armies under Titus, but it also has a secondary and antetypical fulfilment at Antichrist's future desolation of Jerusalem.*)

Rev. xi. 2: But the court which is without the temple leave out, and measure it not; for it is given unto the Gentiles: and the holy city shall they tread under foot forty and two months.

Dan. xi. 40, 41, 45: And at the time of the end shall the king of the south push at him, (Antichrist:) and the king of the north shall come against him like a whirlwind, with chariots, and with horsemen, and with many ships; and he (Antichrist) shall enter into the countries, and hall overflow and pass over. He shall enter also into the glorious land, (Palestine,) . . . (*interval of 3½ years*,) yet he shall come to his end, and none shall help him. (*It is a question for consideration whether verses* 42, 43, 44 *describe Antichrist's first or last expedition against Palestine.*)

Ezek. xxxviii.: Thus saith the Lord God: Behold, I am against thee, O Gog, (Antichrist,) the chief prince of Meshech and Tubal: . . .

thou shalt say, I will go up to the land of unwalled villages; I will go to them that are at rest, that dwell safely, . . to take a spoil, and to take a prey; to turn thine hand upon the desolate places that are now inhabited, and upon the people that are gathered out of the nations, which have gotten cattle and goods. . . . And thou shalt come from thy place out of the north parts, thou, and many people with thee, all of them riding upon horses, a great company, and a mighty army: And thou shalt come up against my people of Israel, as a cloud to cover the land; it shall be in the latter days, . . . (*interval of* 3½ *years*.) Thou shalt fall upon the mountains of Israel, thou, and all thy bands, and the people that is with thee.

Zech. xiv. 1–4: Behold, the day of the Lord cometh, and thy spoil shall be divided in the midst of thee. For I will gather all nations against Jerusalem to battle; and the city shall be taken, and the houses rifled, and the women ravished; and half of the city shall go forth into captivity, and the residue of the people shall not be cut off from the city. (*Here the* 3½ *years probably intervene*.) Then shall the Lord go forth, and fight against those nations, as when he fought in the day of battle. And his feet shall stand in that day upon the mount of Olives.

The literal image of the Personal Antichrist, which is at this juncture to be placed in the Jewish temple, and made to speak and breathe, (Rev. xiii.,) is three times referred to in Daniel as THE ABOMINATION OF DESOLATION. Our Saviour also alluded to it in Matthew and Mark.

Matt. xxiv. 15–30.	Mark xiii. 14–26.
When ye therefore shall see the abomination of desolation, spoken of by Daniel the prophet, stand in the holy place, (whoso readeth, let him understand:) Then let them which be in Judæa flee into the mountains, etc. . . . For then shall be great tribulation, such as was not since the beginning of the world to this time, no, nor ever shall be. And except those days should be shortened, there should no flesh be saved. . . . Immediately after the tribulation of those days . . they shall see the Son of man coming in the clouds of heaven.	But when ye shall see the abomination of desolation, spoken of by Daniel the prophet, standing where it ought not, (let him that readeth understand,) then let them that be in Judæa flee to the mountains. . . . For in those days shall be affliction, such as was not from the beginning of the creation which God created unto this time, neither shall be. And except that the Lord had shortened those days, no flesh should be saved. . . . But in those days, after that tribulation . . shall they see the Son of man coming in the clouds with great power an glory.

This prophecy of our Lord could not have been fulfilled at the destruction of Jerusalem by Titus in A.D. 70, for three reasons: First, there was no abomination of desolation set up by the Romans in the Jewish temple at that time, for the temple was burned while they were entering the city. Moreover the standards or eagles could not have been considered *an abomination*, which is an expression almost invariably meaning "an idol," (II Chron xv. 8.) Secondly, there was then no universal tribulation such that scarcely any flesh was saved, for the affliction did not extend beyond Palestine. Thirdly, it is stated that the Son of man will come in the clouds IMMEDIATELY after the great tribulation consequent upon the abomination being set up: and this must therefore be something that happens just before the Second Advent. There can only be *one* such unequalled tribulation, and it is clear from the parallel passage in Dan. xii. 1, that this is to be at the time of the End and of the Resurrection. *At that time*, (the time of the End, Dan. xi. 40,) *there shall be a time of trouble, such as never was since there was a nation, even to that same time, . . . and many of them that sleep in the dust of the earth shall awake, some to everlasting life,* etc.

The abomination of desolation is spoken of in the four following prophecies of Daniel, and is distinctly stated in the first two of them to be set up in the midst of the seven years of Antichrist's Covenant with the Jews, and 1335 days (or 3½ years and 2¼ months) before the time of blessedness which must be the time of Christ's descent on the earth.

Dan. ix. 27.
(1) He (Antichrist) shall confirm the covenant with many for one week (of seven years): and in the midst of the week he shall cause *the sacrifice* and the oblation to cease, and for the overspreading of *abominations* he shall make it *desolate*, even until the consummation.

Dan. xii. 11, 12.
(2) From the time that *the daily sacrifice shall be taken away, and the abomination that maketh desolate* set up, there shall be a thousand two hundred and ninety days, (some great event to happen then.) Blessed is he that waiteth, and cometh to the thousand three hundred and five and thirty days.

Dan. xi. 31.
(3) And arms shall stand on his (Antichrist's) part, and they shall pollute the sanctuary of strength, and shall *take away the daily sacrifice, and they shall place the abomination that maketh desolate.*

Dan. viii. 11, 12.
(4) By him (Antichrist) *the daily sacrifice was taken away*, and the place of his sanctuary was cast down. And an host was given him against *the daily sacrifice* by reason of transgression.

It is fully admitted that Dan. vii. and xii. have been

typically fulfilled on the year-day scale by Popery, and Dan. viii. by Mahomedanism, *the daily sacrifice* of the pure worship of God having been taken away wherever *the abomination* of such heresies was set up. But those fulfilments have only foreshadowed the final and yet future literal fulfilment. The characteristics that have been exhibited separately in the Pagan, Papal, and Mahomedan Antichrists will all be combined in Napoleon, the last great Antichrist. Thus as the Pagans frequently bore on their forehead or hand the mark of the heathen deity they worshipped, and were forbidden by one of their Emperors to engage in any commercial transactions with Christians: so in like manner during Napoleon's 3½ years' dominancy, as the Antichrist, his False Prophet (the Pope) will cause " all, both small and great, rich and poor, free and bond, to receive a mark on their right hands or in their foreheads: and that no man may buy or sell, save he that has the mark or the name of the Wild Beast (Napoleon) or the number of his name. . . . and his number is six hundred threescore and six, (Rev. xiii. 16–18.) And as the Papal Antichrist is particularly distinguished by three features, (1) of having himself worshipped by being called " Our Lord God the Pope," and having his toe kissed, (2) of " forbidding to marry," (I Tim. iv. 3,) as in the case of priests and nuns, and (3) of having had about ten kingdoms for 1260 years, as the chief seat of his apostacy; so in like manner Napoleon will (1) arrogate to himself the titles and the worship due only to God; and will (2) forbid the celebration of the ordinance of marriage, (in common with all other Christian rites;) and will (3) have exactly ten kingdoms (Rev. xvii. 13) for 1260 days as the chief seat of his God-denying apostacy, (although it will extend in a less degree to other places.) Also as the Mahomedan Antichrist has abolished the observance of the Sabbath, and substituted for the Christian Calendar one that dates from his flight from Mecca, and has given his followers the Koran instead of the Bible; so in a similar manner Napoleon is to " think to change times and laws,".(Dan. vii. 25,) and will abolish the Sabbath, and probably substitute for the Christian Calendar one dating from some epoch in his own career, and most likely compose for his worshippers some book which shall be to them what the Koran is to the Mahomedans.

The heaven-defying self-exaltation of this Man of Sin during his 3½ years' universal supremacy, is specially described in Is. xiv.; Dan. vii., viii., xi. Nearly ALL* the ungodly throughout Christendom and in some parts of Heathendom will worship him, or receive his mark, (Rev. xiii.:) Pagans, Papists, Mahomedans, Jews, Pantheists, Socialists, Rationalists, Spiritualists, Universalists, Unitarians, Infidels, and in short nearly ALL except those who are truly born again, will either spontaneously or compulsorily, render homage to him as their God. The corrupt passions of mankind being unchained, society will fall into a state of moral putrefaction, and the whole earth resemble a hell or Pandemonium. The wicked becoming possessed with devils, will act more like wild beasts than human beings, and scenes of violence and licentiousness, of bloodshed, carnage, and massacre, and of audacious blasphemy against Jehovah, will be witnessed on every side. Millions of persons will be martyred for refusing to worship the Antichrist, *they shall fall by the sword and by flame many days*, and their number is represented as so great as to call for special notice three times in the Apocalypse, (Rev. vi. 9, xv. 2, xx. 4.) The guillotine is indicated by the Greek word πεπελεκισμενων in Rev. xx. 4, to be the principal means by which these martyrs will be put to death. But they will enjoy the peculiar privilege of being raised up almost directly they are killed, and of being a supplementary addition to the saints of the first resurrection. This honor does not appear to be bestowed upon the saints who die a natural death subsequent to the Resurrection and first Translation, which occurs a little more than 2 years after the Covenant.

* The latest calculations compute the population of the world to be composed of about 90 million Protestants, 170 million Roman Catholics, 75 million of the Greek Church, (principally in Russia,) 5 million Jews, 160 million Mahomedans, 800 million Heathen—total, 1300 million. What criminal illiberality in not adequately supporting Foreign Missionary Societies professing Christians are guilty of; seeing that 1800 years after the Lord Jesus has commanded men to preach the Gospel to every creature, three fourths of the earth's inhabitants have never had it proclaimed to them, and are consequently sinking into hell-fire.

EVENT XIV. THE PROPHESYING OF THE TWO WITNESSES (Elijah and another) during the whole of Antichrist's 3½ years, upon the expiration of which they are slain, but after 3½ days raised to life and caught up to heaven. (Rev. xi. 3-12.)

3. And I will give power unto my two witnesses, and they shall prophesy a thousand two hundred and threescore days, clothed in sackcloth. 4. These are the two olive-trees, and the two candlesticks standing before the God of the earth. 5. And if any man will hurt them, fire proceedeth out of their mouth, and devoureth their enemies: and if any man will hurt them, he must in this manner be killed. 6. These have power to shut heaven, that it rain not in the days of their prophecy: and have power over waters to turn them to blood, and to smite the earth with all plagues, as often as they will. 7. And when they shall have finished their testimony, the beast that ascendeth out of the bottomless pit shall make war against them, and shall overcome them, and kill them. 8. And their dead bodies shall lie in the street of the great city, which spiritually is called Sodom and Egypt, where also our Lord was crucified. 9. And they of the people and kindreds and tongues and nations shall see their dead bodies three days and an half, and shall not suffer their dead bodies to be put in graves. 10. And they that dwell upon the earth shall rejoice over them, and make merry, and shall send gifts one to another; because these two prophets tormented them that dwelt on the earth. 11. And after three days and an half the Spirit of life from God entered into them, and they stood upon their feet; and great fear fell upon them which saw them. 12. And they heard a great voice from heaven saying unto them, Come up hither. And they ascended up to heaven in a cloud; and their enemies beheld them. (Literal-day, Rev. xi. 3-12.)

It was almost the universal belief among the Fathers of the Primitive Church, some of whom had conversed with the Apostles themselves, that Elijah would be the herald of Christ at his Second Advent, as stated in Mal. iv. 5, 6, and would also be one of the two Witnesses. Either Enoch, Moses, or St. John was thought to be the other Witness. The mysterious way in which Moses was taken up to heaven, as well as the fact of his being with Elias at the Transfiguration, and also his having performed actions similar to those ascribed to the Witnesses, point him out as the person who will most probably be Elijah's fellow-prophet. It is noticeable that the Greek word for Witnesses, μαρτυρες, is used about forty times in the Bible, and invariably signifies *living personal* witnesses, which is also the case with the word "Prophets;" therefore this prophecy cannot be completely fulfilled except by real persons, although it has had a mystical accomplishment in the 1260 years' sackcloth testimony of the two Testaments, and their destruction during the $3\frac{1}{2}$ years of the French Revolution. The appearance and ministry of these two supernatural Witnesses will be necessitated by the severity of Napoleon's persecution, against the violence of which no mere mortal can contend. Therefore a testimony in opposition to his Anti-christian apostasy will be maintained by Elias and the other prophet, who from the moment of his image being placed in the Jewish temple, will thenceforth for 1260 days continue to preach the Gospel and warn mankind not to worship the Antichrist or his image, or receive his mark in their forehead or in their hand. It is through their instrumentality in a great degree that the innumerable company of persons (Rev. vii. 9) who are to be converted during the great tribulation will be brought to repentance. In the absence of any definition of the localities where they will prophesy, we may conclude that if they visit every place in which the infidel persecution rages, they will deliver their testimony throughout nearly the whole of Christendom and even in some parts of Heathendom. Their supernatural powers will probably enable them to traverse long distances with the swiftness of angels. Clothed in sackcloth from head to foot, they will suddenly alight in places where many people are congregated together, and proceed to proclaim the truth as it is in Jesus, and show from the prophecies that Napoleon is the Antichrist, and that all the marvellous events of that period have been predicted to accompany Christ's advent. If any person attempts to injure them, they will breathe forth fire, a jet of flame will issue from their mouth, and their assailant will instantaneously fall dead, pierced through as by a flash of lightning. As Jannes and Jambres withstood Moses and Aaron, and counterfeited their miracles, so will the False Prophet (the Pope) and Romish Priests withstand the Two Witnesses and imitate their wondrous deeds. Whereas the Witnesses will breathe forth fire against those who attempt to injure them, the False Prophet will mimic them by making fire come down from heaven on the earth. Thus it will be a contest of fire against fire. And as Moses and Aaron stood before Pharaoh, and remonstrated with him regarding his cruel oppression of Israel, and punished his obduracy by the infliction of grievous plagues, so most probably the Witnesses will enter into the presence of Napoleon, the great antitypical Pharaoh, and expostulate with him respecting his ruthless persecution of the saints, and punish his obduracy by "*smiting the earth with all plagues as often as they will.*" The sore judgments or famine, pestilence, and ravages of wild beasts, that are foreshown under the third and fourth literal-day seals to occur during the 3½ years of Antichrist, will be specially caused by the Witnesses, for they have power to shut heaven that it rain not during the 1260 days of their prophecy, and the appalling scarcity of food that will result from the total absence of rain for 3½ years, will necessarily bring in its train wide-spread disease, and give rise to the predatory incursions of wild beasts, which will overrun many parts of the earth in search of food to satisfy their raging hunger. The two Prophets will also exercise power "over waters to turn them to blood," by converting all salt and fresh water into blood, under the second and third literal-day Vials, at the time of their slaughter and resurrection.

At the termination of their 1260 days' testimony, their invulnerability will cease, and Antichrist will succeed in putting them to death. Great and universal will be the exultation among "the peoples and kindreds and tongues and nations," when the welcome news* is transmitted to them over the electric wires; they will rejoice, and make merry, and send gifts one to another, because these two prophets tormented them by their infliction of plagues for worshipping Napoleon. But their joy will soon be turned into grief. For after the Witnesses' dead bodies have been exposed for 3½ days, they will suddenly stand upon their feet and ascend up to heaven in a cloud. About the same time there will be a

---

* It was once objected to the literal fulfilment of this prophecy, that the intelligence of the slaughter of the Witnesses could not be circulated even through Europe within 3½ days. The invention of the telegraph, however, furnishes a triumphant answer to such an objection, and if the transatlantic cable should be laid down by that time, the death of the two Prophets might be made known in America within a few hours of its occurrence.

great earthquake, and the tenth part of the city (apparently Jerusalem) will fall, and 7000 men be slain, and the remnant will be affrighted and give glory to the God of heaven. The remnant that are constrained by these sights to give glory to God, may be identical with the 144,000 Jews whose conversion and sealing (Rev. vii.) takes place principally during the ensuing $2\frac{1}{2}$ months, and it may be the intelligence of their consequent defection from Antichrist's cause that constitutes "the tidings out of the East," (Dan. xi. 44,) which lead to his last exterminating assault upon them at the time of the Battle of Armageddon.

EVENT XV. THE FIRST WOE, or the tormenting of men by supernatural locusts for ten months, which begins about $3\frac{1}{2}$ months after the midst of the seven years.

And the fifth angel sounded, and I saw a star fall from heaven unto the earth: and to him was given the key of the bottomless pit. And he opened the bottomless pit; and there arose a smoke out of the pit, as the smoke of a great furnace; and the sun and the air were darkened by reason of the smoke of the pit. And there came out of the smoke locusts upon the earth: and unto them was given power, as the scorpions of the earth have power. And it was commanded them that they should not hurt the grass of the earth, neither any green thing, neither any tree; but only those men which have not the seal of God in their foreheads. And to them it was given that they should not kill them, but that they should be tormented five months: and their torment was as the torment of a scorpion, when he striketh a man. And in those days shall men seek death, and shall not find it; and shall desire to die, and death shall flee from them . . . And they had tails like unto scorpions, and there were stings in their tails: and their power was to hurt men five months. And they had a king over them, which is the angel of the bottomless pit, whose name in the Hebrew tongue is Abaddon, but in the Greek tongue hath his name Apollyon. One woe is past; and, behold, there come two woes more hereafter. (Rev. ix.)

The seven judgments introduced by the seven trumpets, successively increase in destructiveness and severity. The first four, which altogether continue only for seven or eight months, are inflicted upon inanimate nature, and consecutively affect the earth, sea, fountains of water, and the luminaries; the last three, which continue for $3\frac{1}{2}$ years, are inflicted upon the animate creation, principally upon *those men which have not the seal of God in their foreheads;* and as an omen of the fearful calamities to be occasioned by them, they are preceded by the thrice-repeated cry of Woe, from which circumstance they derive the name of Woe-trumpets. The year-day fulfilment of the first and second of these three Woe-trumpets is interpreted by several hundred expositors to relate to the invasion of Europe by the Saracens and Turks: Bickersteth, in his Signs of the Times, gives the names of hundred of these expositors. The first year-day Woe trumpet began in 609 A.D., twenty-seven years before the commencement of the Saracen Woe which it introduced, and which consisted in the incursions of the Saracens (symbolized by the locusts) into the Roman Empire for twice 150 years, (twice five year-day months, ver. 5, 10,) from 636 to 936: and therefore this Woe-trumpet, in its literal-day accomplishment, will begin about three years, nine months, and twelve days after the Covenant, twenty-seven days before the commencement of the Woe of literal locusts, which follow it, and which will last for twice five literal months. As soon as the trumpet is sounded, an angel, which had previously fallen ($\pi\epsilon\pi\tau\omega\kappa\sigma\tau\alpha$) from heaven, will open the bottomless pit, which, there is every reason to believe, is the interior of this earth; it is probably called *bottomless* because a continually revolving globular body cannot be said to have either a top or a bottom. Out of the opened pit, a lurid black smoke will ascend in dense volumes, temporarily darkening the firmament, and swarms of locusts will then come forth upon the earth, appearing to be engendered in the smoke, like insects which are generated in the atmosphere of blight. The description given of their outward appearance (ver. 7, 8, 9) will be recognized by every zoölogist as an accurate picture of the ordinary locust, but whereas the instinct of natural locusts leads them voraciously to devour every green thing, these monstrous unnatural locusts will not eat a single green leaf or blade of grass, but will occupy themselves exclusively in stinging the ungodly with the stings which they will have in their scorpion-like tails. So grievously agonizing will be the pain produced by their stings, that men shall *seek for death* and *desire to die*, but by a special restraining power they will be prevented carrying their suicidal designs into successful execution; *death shall flee from them*, and they shall be kept alive against their will, to endure the most excruciating torments. Millions of persons will suffer the intensest anguish from this plague, but scarcely one individual will be killed by it, (ver. 5.) It will commence about 3¼ months after Napoleon's image has been set up in the Jewish temple, and continue twice five months. Whether it will extend only to part or the whole of the Roman Empire, or to America and other places as well, is not stated. But whatever localities are visited by the hail and fire under the first trumpet, nine months previously, may be expected to be likewise the scene of this woe. No objection can be rationally urged against the possibility of such monstrous locusts being created, for we are expressly told that there are then to be fearful sights and great and marvellous signs, and a series of calamitous events *such as was not from the beginning of the world up, nor ever shall be.* The mysterious and supernatural character of those events can alone enable us to understand how it is that these locusts (unlike natural locusts, which have no king,—Prov. xxx. 27) will be under the controlling influence of Napoleon as their king, according to the statement: *They had a king over them which is the angel of the bottomless pit, . . . but in the Greek tongue hath his name Apollyon.* As they come from the bottomless pit, and are of Satanic and diabolical origin, having no instinct but to torment men, it is to be expected that Napoleon, to whom Satan is to give *his seat and his power and great authority,* and who is called *the angel of the bottomless pit,* that is, the minister and vicegerent of Satan, will exercise over the locusts the same authority which Satan otherwise would exercise over them. In fact, so extensive and universal will be Napoleon's supreme power, that even these locusts will be subject to it, apparently somewhat in the same manner that the frogs were subject to the magic power of the Egyptian sorcerers. (Ex. viii. 7.) Some have thought that they will be evil spirits, permitted to assume this form, in which case it is obvious that their subjection to Napoleon will necessarily result from Satan's kingdom having been given to him. As Satan could assume the shape of a serpent in the garden of Eden, and as devils can enter into swine, (Luke viii. 32,) there is no greater improbability in their entering into or taking the form of locusts. No employment is more congenial to evil spirits than that of afflicting and torturing mankind; and it is shown in Rev. xii. 12, that they are to do this to an unprecedented extent during the final 3½ years. The sealed ones who are to remain untouched by them (ver. 4) are probably the 144,000 Jews, whose sealing appears even then to be commenced, although it is not finished until the end of the *literal-day* sixth seal, (Rev. vii.) The *year-day* sixth seal represents the sealing of 144,000 wise virgins out of the different denominations typified by the Jewish tribes, and there are thus two entirely distinct companies of 144,000.

The conventional application of the word *Apollyon* to signify Satan is utterly unwarranted by this passage of Scripture in which it is found. Nearly all expositors, from Bishop Newton to our own day, admit that it denotes the human being who is to be used by Satan at the time of the Woe-trumpets as a great Destroyer. In the year-day typical fulfilment, it symbolized Mahomet, who scourged but did not inflict political death upon the Eastern Roman Empire, and who was an eminent type of Napoleon. In the literal-day antetypical fulfilment, it is evidently the literal name of the last great Antichrist, and it is a lamentable proof of *the spirit of deep sleep* that has fallen upon the minds of men, that although God has graciously condescended to reveal in his Word the name of the Personal Antichrist, and although that name almost exactly corresponds with the name *Napoleon*, yet the significant fact of such correspondence is almost entirely unheeded. It is surprising that Napoleon's name, as thus foretold 1800 years ago, should, with the exception of the first letter N, have been transmitted to us with so much accuracy: some other names are not quoted in the New Testament with even so much precision: for instance, Elijah, Jeremiah, Rehoboam, Abijah, Jehoshaphat, and Hezekiah are called in St. Matthew: Elias, Jeremy, Roboam, Abia, Josaphat, Ezekias, (Matt. i.) The Rev. Dr. Croly in his "Apocalypse" considers the word *Napoleon* to be unquestionably signified by *Apollyon*. However mysterious the whole narrative of this Locust-Woe may at first sight appear, we should remember that it is scarcely more marvellous than many other wonderful events described in Scripture, such, for instance, as took place at the Exodus from Egypt.

EVENT XVI. THE SECOND WOE or the conflicts for 1 year and 1 month between Napoleon's armies and countless invading forces from Asia, resulting in the slaughter of the third part of men, and constituting the principal part of the Armageddon War. (Rev. ix. 13.)

The literal-day sixth trumpet or second Woe-trumpet begins about a year and six months after the commencement of Napoleon's 3¼ years' persecution, and continues for twice a year and month,* as a period of both rise and fall: the slaughter of the *third part of men* taking place principally during the first year and month. The preceding Woe only *tormented* and *hurt* men, but this Woe will *kill* the third part of them; and then the third Woe will kill all the rest of the incorrigibly wicked during the last 3¼ days. This Woe commences with the loosing of four angels, *which are bound in the great river Euphrates,* and *prepared against the hour* of temptation *and against the day* of judgment (εις την ωραν και εις την ημεραν, Matthæus) *for a month and a year, for to slay the third part of men. And the number of the army of the horsemen was two myriads of myriads,* (δυο μυριαδες μυριαδων.) It appears that the restraints which had previously prevented the incursions of the horsemen will be removed by the loosing of four spirits of evil, and the contest will then commence near the river Euphrates, which is the boundary line between the Roman Empire and nearly all Asia. Just as in the year-day fulfilment of this Woe, the Turks made an irruption, in 1063, from beyond the Euphrates into the Roman Empire, and caused the war of the Crusades, in which the Europeans and Asiatics west of the Euphrates engaged in the most sanguinary struggles with the invading hosts of the Asiatics from the east of the Euphrates, so will it be in

* Although the double reckoning of *the year and month* is not explicitly enjoined in the prophecy, yet it is correctly considered by Bickersteth and others to be required by the analogy of the period of the previous Trampet, which is distinctly specified to be counted twice, (v. 5, 10:) also by the fact that the year-day fulfilment unquestionably lasted exactly twice a mystical year and month from 1903 to 1813; and likewise because there is thus a corresponding growth and arithmetical progression in the length of the three year-day Woes (the Saracen, Turkish, and Napoleonic) of 300 years, 780 years, and 1260 days, for 780 is the point of bisection between 300 and 1260.

the approaching literal-day fulfilment. The same desperate conflict is once more to be renewed on a scale of such unexampled magnitude that almost all the armies from the four quarters of the earth will become involved in it. The number of the horsemen is stated to be *two myriads of myriads*, which may either mean an indefinitely great multitude, or else exactly *two hundred thousand thousand*, if the word *myriad* be taken in its original sense to mean *ten thousand*; but this latter view is much less probable than the former, as it would make the number of horsemen to be a sixth part of all the inhabitants of the globe. There may, however, be a larger population than is generally imagined in Asia, from whence the invading forces are to come.

The awful and terrific character of their ravages is not only indicated by their vast numbers, but likewise by the circumstance that *the third part of men* is to be slain in the conflicts that will then ensue. As the Roman Empire is the principal locality of this Woe, it may only be a number equivalent to the third part of its inhabitants that will be slain; but even this would amount to about 60 million persons, the slaughter of whom during the first *year and month* will be an average of about 150,000 every day during that period. The number would be seven times greater if the third part of the population of the entire globe is meant by *the third part of men*. Just as the whole civilized world engaged in the war of the Crusades, so will it be in the approaching repetition of those wars; for Antichrist having made Jerusalem the ecclesiastical metropolis of his universal empire, will summon his adherents from every part of Christendom to prevent that city falling into the hands of the invaders. There will probably be a flux and reflux in the tide of warfare, the Asiatic invaders at first penetrating far into the interior of Europe, and then being driven back by the hosts of Antichrist. The symbolical hail-storm of the 7th year-day Vial also falls at the same time; and, like the hail-storm of the first year-day Trumpet, must signify an invasion of the Roman Empire from the North, and is generally understood to denote an irruption into Europe from Russia. The struggles between these invading forces from Asia and Russia, and the ar-

SECOND WOE, OR CONFLICTS OF THE HORSEMEN. 133

armies of Napoleon and his auxiliaries from America and elsewhere, will constitute the principal part of the 3¼ years' WAR OF ARMAGEDDON, toward which the three unclean spirits are now gathering the nations; according to the prediction that the spirits of devils working miracles should go *forth unto the kings of the earth and of the whole world, to gather them to the war (πολε μον) of that great day of God Almighty . . . (towards, εις) a place called in the Hebrew tongue Armageddon,* (Rev. xvi. 14.) Religious fanaticism will be the main principle by which the contending hosts will be animated, and Antichrist's worshippers will doubtless be assured by the Romish priests that the contest being maintained by them in defence of the holy city and for the extermination of heretics, is preëminently a Holy War. From all parts of Christendom, including America, tens of thousands of soldiers will hasten to the scene of combat, to fight under the banner of Napoleon against the Asiatics who dare to set themselves in battle array against him. These crusades will be at their height during the first year and month, and will decline during the second year and month, until they cease altogether.

The *breastplates of fire and jacinth and brimstone* with which the horsemen appeared in the vision to be equipped, apparently represent, as in the year-day fulfilment, defensive armor decorated with the colors of red and blue and yellow, to which many of the Asiatic nations are extremely partial. The additional statement regarding the horses, that *out of their mouths issued fire and smoke and brimstone . . . for their power is in their mouth and in their tails; for their tails were like unto serpents, and had heads, and with them they do hurt,* very accurately describes the appearance which horsemen armed with carbines and companies of artillery would present to a distant spectator, who might never before have heard of or seen such instruments of destruction as firearms. The Apostle John expressly says that *he saw the horses in the vision:* he beheld afar off in a vision a panoramic representation of the fearful battles in which they engaged, and as he had no conception of such weapons as muskets and cannon, it would necessarily seem to him when the horsemen fired pistols over the heads of their horses that the horses themselves were breathing forth fire and brimstone: and also the serpent shaped cannon dragged at the heels of the artillery horses, and shooting out of their mouths forked tongues of flame, would naturally give those horses the appearance of *having tails like unto serpents which had heads and with them they do hurt.* Almost all expositors agree that in the year-day fulfilment *the fire and smoke and brimstone* denote the gunpowder which was first used at the taking of Constantinople in 1453, and it is very remarkable that 14 centuries before the invention of gunpowder the Bible should have so exactly predicted the period when it first came into use.

This Woe is clearly shown to begin about 4 years 11 months and 19 days after the Jewish Covenant—that is, about 806 *days* before the End; just as in its year-day fulfilment as the Turkish Woe it commenced in 1063, 806 *years* before the End. The Turkish Woe, consisting in the conquest of the Eastern Roman Empire by the Turks (the political death of the third part of the Roman Empire) and their persecution of Christians, continued for twice a year-day *year and month,* as a period of both rise and fall, from 1063 to 1453, the height of their power, and from 1453 to 1843-4. On March 21, 1844, Turkey ceased nationally to persecute Christians.

EVENT XVII. CONVERSION OF UPWARD of from 15 to 50 million persons, chiefly among the heathen, during the five years between the two translations, and especially during the final year. (Lit-day, Rev. vii. x. xiv.)

The number of foolish virgins, or Laodicean converted persons, that will be left behind at the first translation, may be approximately estimated at about ten millions. As Antichrist during his 3½ years' persecution will slay at least several millions of the saints, it is obvious that only three or four millions of them would be left on the earth by the time of the Second Translation, unless their numbers had been augmented by additional converts. It is, however, clearly foreshown that a countless multitude will be caught up in the Second Translation, and most of them will be converted, first, during the Revival of religion (lasting, most probably, about 17 months) between the Translation of the Wise Virgins and the beginning of the Tribulation, and, secondly, during a subsequent Revival which is foreshown in Rev. x. to continue during the final year. The first Revival will occur immediately after the literal-day Rapture of the Manchild and during the literal-day first Seal, and will be the antitype of the Pentecostal Revival which took place after the year-day Rapture of the Manchild and during the year-day first Seal from A.D. 33 to 323-4. The same miraculous gifts that were bestowed at Pentecost may be expected to be again imparted at the approaching repetition of the Pentecostal awakening. The Second Revival will occur during the final year, almost synchronically with the latter *year and month* of the literal-day sixth Trumpet, as described in Rev. x., and will be the antitype of the Revival which has continued from the Reformation to the present day.

All expositors of judgment and reliability admit that Rev. x. describes a great Revival of religion at the period to which it applies. The Angel of the Covenant appeared in the vision to descend to the earth with his face shining as the sun, and with a little book (the Bible) open in his hand. This signifies the diffusion of the illuminating rays of Divine truth and the consequent dissipation of the dark mists of superstition and ignorance. The little book was then delivered to St. John, as a symbolic and representative man, with the declaration, *Thou must prophesy again before many peoples and nations and tongues and kings*, and the Angel likewise announced, *That there should be a time* (χρονος, 360 days, whether literal or year-days) *no longer*. This shows that fresh witnesses were then to be raised up to proclaim the testimony of Jesus, and that the period was little less than *a time* before the End, which was likewise indicated by the fact of the vision being about the midst of the sixth Trumpet. In the year-day fulfilment these prefigurations are universally allowed to refer to the Reformation, which commenced in 1517, about 352 years before the End, and in the literal-day fulfilment they will, of course, describe an analogous Revival, commencing 352 days before the End,—that is, about 6 years, 2 months, and 23 days after the Covenant. It may be that England will then revolt against the Personal Antichrist's supremacy, as it revolted at the Reformation against the Papal Antichrist's dominancy.

The following portions of Scripture refer directly or indirectly to the unprecedented number of conversions that will take place about the time of the Great Tribulation between the Two Translations. In Rev. vii. 9–17, at the end of the literal-day sixth Seal, *a great multitude which no man could number* is exhibited as *coming out of the great tribulation* (ἐκ τῆς θλίψεως τῆς μεγάλης) and standing before the throne of God in heaven. This unexampled tribulation is the same as that which is mentioned in Matt. xxiv. 21 and Mark xiii. 19, as just preceding Christ's descent at Armageddon, and is foreshown in Dan. xii. (lit. ful.) to continue for 3½ years. The *great multitude* being spoken of as coming OUT OF the great tribulation, are evidently living saints who have been on the earth during the persecution, and, having become converted, are caught up to heaven at its termination. The sealed 144,000 Wise Virgins who are caught up *before* the great tribulation, are necessarily quite distinct from this *great multitude* which is translated just *after it*. The palms in the hands of the *great multitude* show that this is the antitype of the Feast of Tabernacles, which was always observed at Harvest-time.

Again, in Rev. xiv., after the 144,000 Wise Virgins are caught up to the Heavenly Zion, (ver. 1 to 5,) there elapses the 3½ years' hour of judgment, (ver. 6 to 14;) and then *the Harvest* is reaped, which is generally hallowed to signify the ingathering of the saints at Christ's descent on the earth, and is identical with "the great multitude" in Rev. vii. Now both the *first fruits* and *Harvest* must necessarily be of the same sort or nature; and each of them consists entirely of translated living saints, neither of them including the raised sleeping saints. But the *first-fruits*, which is the earlier and much smaller ingathering, is declared to consist of 144,000 persons; therefore the *Harvest*, which must be at least two or three hundred times larger than its *first fruits*, will necessarily amount to upward of from 25 to 50 million persons, most of whom will be converted between the two translations.

The parable of the Marriage Supper (Luke xiv. 16) also shows the vast number that will be converted during the tribulation between the two translations. The lord sent his servants to bring in guests from the streets and lanes of the city, and they returned, saying: "*It is done as thou hast commanded, and yet there is room.*" This typifies the first ingathering or translation of the saints to the marriage of the Lamb, (1 Thess. iv. 16, 17.) The lord then sent out his servants to bring in a second company of guests, saying: "*Go out into the highways and hedges and compel them to come in, that my house may be filled.*" This represents the second translation or ingathering of saints, 7 years later, which will be much more numerous than the first, and will be chiefly gathered from the most unpromising and neglected parts of the earth, which are there denoted as the "highways and hedges." So also it was said by our Saviour, in speaking of the Kingdom of Heaven, that there is first the blade, then the ear, and after that the full corn in the ear. But when the fruit is brought forth, immediately he putteth in the sickle, because the harvest is come. (Mark iv. 28.) This harvest evidently refers to the conversion and translation of an immense multitude at Christ's coming, and is the harvest that is spoken of in Rev. xiv. 14. "*And I looked, and behold a white cloud, and upon the cloud one sat like unto the Son of man, having on his head a golden crown, and in his hand a sharp sickle. And another angel came out of the temple, crying with a loud voice to him that sat on the cloud, Thrust in thy sickle, and reap; for the time is come for thee to reap; for the harvest of the earth is ripe. And he that sat on the cloud thrust in his sickle on the earth; and the earth was reaped.*"

The prophet Joel, (chap. ii.,) in describing the awful judgments of fire and the sword that will accompany the Day of the Lord, declares as the Divine promise: *I will pour out my spirit upon all flesh; and your sons and your daughters shall prophesy, your old men shall dream dreams, your young men shall see visions. And I will show wonders in the heavens and in the earth, blood, and fire, and pillars of smoke. The sun shall be turned into darkness, and the moon into blood, before the great and the terrible day of the Lord come. And it shall come to pass, that whosoever shall call on the name of the Lord shall be saved.* The first part of this prediction received a partial and inchoate accomplishment at the day of Pentecost, (Acts ii.,) but its principal fulfilment will be after the first translation, at the time of the great and terrible day of the Lord, which will also be the period of the outpouring of *the latter rain*, (Joel ii. 23, Zech. x. 1, James v. 7,) the former rain having been given on the day of Pentecost. It appears very clearly that the power of working miracles, and the gift of tongues, and of prophecy, and other spiritual gifts, will be bestowed at the same time; and it is doubtless by such means that the Gospel will then have its most extensive diffusion. These gifts may even be expected to be bestowed partially between the present time and the first translation; but they must not be mistaken for the Satanic imitation of them, which is already produced by spiritualism.

It was said to Noah, with typical reference to the 3½ years' Great Tribulation, *"It shall come to pass, when I bring a cloud over the earth, that the bow shall be seen in the cloud,"* (Gen. ix. 14;) and Isaiah, speaking of the same period, says, (Isa. xxvi. 9,) *"When thy judgments are in the earth, the inhabitants of the world will learn righteousness."* The most glowing promises to those who *convert the sinner from the error of his way, and turn many to righteousness*, (James v. 20, Dan. xii. 3,) are given in passages directly referring to the judgments at Christ's Advent. The Psalms of David, many of which are prophetical, and all the Old Testament Prophecies, abound with intimations that Christ will be mighty to save at the very time when he treads down his enemies in his fury, and that in wrath he will remember mercy. As after Christ's ascension the Pentecostal effusion descended on his disciples, and after Elijah's translation a double portion of the Spirit rested on Elisha; so after the Wise Virgins are caught up to meet Christ, the Holy Spirit will be abundantly poured out on the foolish virgins during the yearday Seventh vial (the final five years) which was further prefigured to be the time of the descent of the latter rain of the Spirit by the type of Elijah, who, after the 1260 days of drought, did not obtain rain in answer to his prayers until the seventh time of sending to look for its appearance. The Christian dispensation may also be expected, like the Jewish dispensation, to be characterized by a far greater prevalence of religion at its termination than at any other period during its continuance.* This prospect should lead Christians at the present time to distribute Bibles and tracts as widely as possible throughout the world, for they will be eagerly sought for, but not so easily obtained during the Great Tribulation.

The current belief among the majority of Christians is, that at Christ's Advent all probation will cease, and that the righteous will be glorified and the wicked perish, and the earth be burnt with fire. This notion, however, like most other popular traditions, is fundamentally erroneous. It is altogether unscriptural to suppose that Christ's mediatorial office ends when he leaves the Father's right hand to come to the earth, for, in fact, that is the very time when it begins to be most fully exercised. There will be innumerably more sinners saved by his intercession and advocacy during the 1000 years that succeed his descent from Jehovah's right hand to the earth, than were ever saved during his previous occupation of that position; and just as the elect were converted during the 4164 years before the Lord Jesus sat down at God's right hand, so can they be converted during the millennial 1000 years after he has relinquished that seat, and come to the earth to sit upon the throne of David, and to establish the fifth universal monarchy, (Dan. vii.)

---

* The first sprinklings of the latter-day outpouring of the Holy Spirit are perceptible in the unexampled religious Revivals in America in 1857, in Ireland in 1859, and in England, Scotland, Wales, Sweden, Jamaica, etc., during the last few years. There has never been a time when there were so many revival preachers, such as Spurgeon, Guinness, Reginald Radcliffe, Richard Weaver, Brownlow North, Caughey, E. P. Hammond, Dr. Finney, Dr. and Mrs. Palmer, etc. There can be no doubt but that the visits of revival preachers to different places for a short time, constitute an important adjunct to the efforts of the settled ministry. It is surprising that there are scarcely any ladies at the present day who imitate the example of Mrs. Fry by speaking in public on religious subjects, although there are now in the United States more than a hundred lady-lecturers on secular subjects, especially on Spiritualism, which they have greatly contributed to disseminate.

EVENT XVIII. DARKENING OF THE CONSTELLATIONS and a great earthquake. (Rev. vi. 12, xi, 13,) simultaneously with the commencement of the seven successive literal-day Vials, which, during the final 2½ months (1) afflict the Napoleonists with sores; (2) turn all fresh and (3) all salt water into blood, (4) produce intolerable heat, (5) cover Europe with darkness, (6) dry up the literal Euphrates, and (7) cause an unparalleled earthquake and hail-storm, and the Battle of Armageddon. (Rev. xvi.)

(Lit-day) Rev. xvi. 2. The first poured out his vial upon the earth; and there fell a noisome and grievous sore upon the men which had the mark of the beast, and upon them which worshipped his image. 3 And the second angel poured out his vial upon the sea; and it became as the blood of a dead man: and every living soul died in the sea. 4. And the third angel poured out his vial upon the rivers and fountains of waters; and they became blood. . . . 8. And the fourth angel poured out his vial upon the sun; and power was given unto him to scorch men with fire. . . . 10. And the fifth angel poured out his vial upon the seat of the beast; and his kingdom was full of darkness; and they gnawed their tongues for pain. . . . 12. And the sixth angel poured out his vial upon the great river Euphrates; and the water thereof was dried up, that the way of the kings of the east might be prepared. 13. And I saw three unclean spirits, like frogs . . . go forth unto the kings of the earth and of the whole world, to gather them to the battle of that great day of God Almighty. 15. Behold, I come as a thief. . . . 16. And he gathered them together into a place called in the Hebrew tongue Armageddon. 17. And the seventh angel poured out his vial into the air; and there came a great voice out of the temple of heaven, from the throne, saying, It is done. 18. And there were voices, and thunders, and lightnings; and there was a great earthquake, such as was not since men were upon the earth, so mighty an earthquake, and so great. 19. And the great city was divided into three parts, and the cities of the nations fell: and great Babylon came in remembrance before God, to give unto her the cup of the wine of the fierceness of his wrath. 20. And every island fled away, and the mountains were not found. 21. And there fell upon men a great hail out of heaven, every stone about the weight of a talent; and men blasphemed God because of the plague of the hail; for the plague thereof was exceeding great.

The usual objection as to the alleged diversity of opinion among expositors, which is continually urged by infidel scoffers as a reason for abstaining from the study of Prophecy, is entirely inapplicable in the case of the seven Vials; for there is scarcely a single year-day interpreter within the last sixty years that has not considered them to have commenced with the French Revolution, about

1792-94, at which time the 1260 years of the principal power of Popery terminated. Moreover, the position of the Vials in the Apocalypse, as well as their introduction, (Rev. xv.,) in which all those martyred by Antichrist during his 1260 days' persecution are exhibited singing a song of triumph in heaven, clearly indicate that they are not poured out until just at the close of the 1260 days; and the year-day accomplishment which they have already received fully confirms this view, and shows that the period of their duration is the supplementary 75 days which constitute the difference between the 1260 and the 1335 days mentioned in Dan. xii. 12. The respective dates of commencement of the first six *year-day* Vials are generally held to be about 1792, 1793-4, 1705, 1802, 1815, and 1823-4, which were respectively 1259, 1261, 1262, 1269, 1282, and 1291 *years* after the commencement of the 1260 *years* of the Papal Antichrist's supremacy in 538-7. Therefore the dates of the first six *literal-day* Vials will be respectively 1259, 1261, 1262, 1269, 1282, and 1291 *days* after the commencement of the 1260 *days* of the Personal Antichrist's supremacy. The Vials commence almost simultaneously with the sixth Seal, which opens with a great earthquake and total darkness, that are additionally described in Rev. xi, 13, Matt. xxiv. 29, etc. The slaughter and resurrection of the Witnesses occur synchronically with the second and third Vials. The relative position of these events during the final 2½ months is shown in the accompanying diagram.

The similarity between these seven *last* plagues, and the plagues inflicted by Moses upon the Egyptians, is so striking as effectually to remove all objections against the possibility of their literal accomplishment. The first plague will afflict Napoleon's worshippers with *noisome and grievous sores*, which they will continue to suffer from even during the fifth Vial, (ver. 11.) The next plague will cause the vast volume of water which is contained within the bed of the ocean to become like the coagulated and congealed blood of a dead man, and every creature within the sea, from the smallest animalculæ to the greatest monsters of the deep, will instantaneously cease to live. It is noticeable that at this very same time *the moon becomes as blood* under the sixth seal. The rivers and fountains of water will next be turned into blood for several days, so that those who *have shed the blood of saints and prophets* will in just retribution have given to them blood to drink: *for they are worthy's*) and thus the Righteous Judge, who once turned water into wine to minister to the enjoyment of his disciples, will show that he can equally turn water into blood to augment the sufferings of his foes. After this, the sun, which a few days previously was *black as sackcloth of hair*, will for about a fortnight shine with such fierce and angry glare as to *scorch men with fire and with great heat*. The miseries resulting from this fourth plague

Chronological order of the events of the final 2½ months or 75 days (1335-1260) which follow the Cotenant-week of 7 years, and also of the literal-day seven Vials, which commenced 2 days before the end of Anti-Christ's 1260 days, and continue over the last 77 days of the 1335 days. (Dan. xii. 12.)

1792	1259	Vial 1.	Napoleon's worshippers plagued with sores.		
1793	1260				Rev. vi. & vii.
1794	1261	Vial 2.	Sea becomes like blood.	During this first 3 days the witnesses becomes blood, lie dead, and there darkness prevails for a few is a great earth-quake, and the tenth part of the city falls & 7000 men are slain. Rev. xi.7, 13. The witnesses rise on the 1264th day.	Seal 6. The Moon & darkness prevails for a few hours about the 1261st day, the Sign of the Son of Man appears sometime between the 1261st and 1331st day. Matt. xxiv. 30; and the Son of Man himself about the 1331st day, Matt. xxiv.
1796	1263				
1798	1265	Vial 3.	Rivers and fountains become blood for about seven days. The Sun scorches men with great heat for about thirteen days. Darkness covers the throne of the Beast (Antichrist) for three days.		
1800	1267				
1802	1269				
1804	1271				
1806	1273	Vial 4.			
1808	1275				
1810	1277				
1812	1279				
1814	1281				
1816	1283	Vial 5.			
1818	1285				
1820	1287				
1822	1289				
1824	1291				
1826	1293				
1828	1295				
1830	1297				
1832	1299				
1834	1301				
1836	1303				
1838	1305		The river Euphrates is gradually dried up during the forty days from the 1290th, to the 1330th day to enable the Ten Tribes in Asia to march over it to Jerusalem; and simultaneously the three frog like spirits gather nearly all the armies of the world to Armageddon.		
1840	1307				
1842	1309	Vial 6.			The 144,000 Jews are mostly sealed during the 6th Vial.
1844	1311				
1846	1313				
1848	1315				
1850	1317				
1852	1319				
1854	1321				
1856	1323				
1858	1325				
1860	1327				
1862	1329				
1864	1331		SECOND TRANSLATION. III-day, Rv.xvi.15; xi.15 Third Woe—Battle of Armageddon. Christ descends and slays his foes.		Rev. vii. 9-17. Seal 7. Describ-ed in Rev. xix
1866	1333				
1869-72	1335				

(Left margin: These are inserted to compare the literal-day with the year-day fulfilment. First Month. Second Month. 15 Days.)

will probably be aggravated by the scarcity of water, as the effects of the previous Vial upon the rivers and fountains may not yet have passed away. There will next be—as regards the kingdom of Antichrist, which principally signifies Europe—a sudden transition from the scorching glare of the sun to total darkness, which will chiefly last for three days. These events will occupy the first month of the last 2½ months. The sixth Vial, causing the drying up of the literal Euphrates, that the Ten Tribes may march across it to Palestine, will then be poured out at the end of the 1290 days; (Dan. xii. 11,) and will last for about forty days, during which the armies of the world are gathered to the Battle of Armageddon. The Second Translation of living saints is at the end of the forty days, (ver. 15,) just before the seventh literal-day Vial,* which extends over the final four or five days, and none but the ungodly will be left upon the globe to endure the terrific judgments which will then be inflicted, for there will literally be a mighty and great earthquake, such as was not since men were upon the earth, causing the earth to shake from its centre to its circumference, and to reel to and fro like a drunken man. The territory of the great city, Babylon (Papal Christendom) will become divided into three parts, and throughout a considerable portion of it, including Rome, subterranean volcanic fires will burst forth, and their smoke will ascend up during the subsequent millennium as an unceasing memorial of God's vengeance, (Is. lxvi. 24.) So violent will be the earthquake that *the cities of the nations*, such as London, Liverpool, Dublin, Paris, Vienna, St. Petersburg, New-York, Bos-

* In the year-day fulfilment of the seventh Vial,-which lasts for four or five years, apparently from 1865–7 to 1872, the great and mighty earthquake signifies an unprecedented world-wide revolution: the division of the great city (Babylon) into three parts denotes the formation within Papal Christendom of three distinct parties of true Christians, Infidels, and Ultramontane Papists: the fall of the cities of the nations represents the dissolution of all the State Churches or hierarchies of the different nations, such as the Church of England, the Greek Church in Russia, etc.; the cup of wrath given to great Babylon refers to the spoliation of the Romish Church: the vanishing away of the islands and mountains emblematizes the overthrow of all ancient political institutions and governments: the great hail-storm, symbolises an invasion of the Roman Empire from the north.

ton, etc., *will fall*, and become heaps of shapeless ruins, scarcely one stone being left standing upon another. And the islands and mountains which were *moved out of their places* seventy days previously, by the *great earthquake* at the opening of the sixth Seal, will now, at this subsequent earthquake, altogether *flee away and not be found*. Simultaneously, hail-stones, *about the weight of a talent*, or hundred-weight, being in fact great blocks of ice, will fall upon men, and *the plague thereof* will be *exceeding great*. At the same time the Battle of Armageddon is fought, and Christ descending with his saints, *destroys them which destroy the earth*.

EVENT XIX. VISIBLE MANIFESTATION of Christ coming in the clouds of heaven, and Second Translation of living saints 5 days, before this Dispensation ends, and the Millennium begins. (Matt. xxiv. 31, Rev. xiv. 16.)

Rev. vii. 9: I beheld, and lo, a great multitude, which no man could number, of all nations, and kindreds, and people, and tongues, stood before the throne, and before the Lamb, clothed with white robes, and palms in their hands; and cried with a loud voice, saying, Salvation to our God which sitteth upon the throne, and unto the Lamb. And all the angels stood round about the throne, and about the elders and the four beasts, and fell before the throne on their faces, and worshipped God, saying, Amen: Blessing, and glory, and wisdom, and thanksgiving, and honor, and power, and might, be unto our God for ever and ever. Amen. And one of the elders answered, saying unto me, What are these which are arrayed in white robes? and whence came they? And I said unto him, Sir, thou knowest. And he said to me, These are they which came out of the great tribulation, and have washed their robes, and made them white in the blood of the Lamb. Therefore are they before the throne of God, and serve him day and night in his temple: and he that sitteth on the throne shall dwell among them. They shall hunger no more, neither thirst any more; neither shall the sun light on them, nor any heat. For the Lamb, which is in the midst of the throne, shall feed them, and shall lead them unto living fountains of waters: and God shall wipe away all tears from their eyes. (Lit-day.)*

* The year-day 6th Seal lasts for about 70 years from 1793-7 to 1866-7, and begins with the French Revolution, (Rev. vi. 12-17:) then an interval elapses for finishing the sealing of 144,000 wise virgins out of the various sects or branches of the Christian Church, (Rev. vii. 1-8,) and then these sealed ones, as well as the deceased saints, are caught up to meet Christ in the air, (ver. 9 to 17,) being thus a great multitude that will have come *from* (εκ, in the sense of escaping, as in Rev. iii. 10) the Great Tribulation, which follows during

VISIBLE MANIFESTATION OF CHRIST. 145

It appears that the raised saints and the Philadelphian *first-fruits*, (Rev. xiv. 4,) or 144,000 Wise Virgins, (or Manchild, Rev. xii. 5,) having been caught up into the air at the first stage in the Advent rather more than two years after the Covenant, will be judged while they remain in the pavilion-cloud for about 5 years, during the rest of the 7 years and 2¼ months: and they will then have awarded to them their future positions of honor in the Millennial Kingdom. At the end of about 5 years, when the process of adjudication is concluded, they will descend with Christ at their head upon Mt. Olivet at the Battle of Armageddon, and after slaying all rejectors of the Gospel, they will then begin to *reign on the earth*, and will thus stand on their respective lots or inheritances (κληρονομια) at the end of the 1335 days from the setting up of Antichrist's image in the Temple, according to the promise given to Daniel, (Dan. xii. 11, 13.) But just before this, the Second Translation takes place. As the First Translation is at the close of the year-day 6th Seal, 6th Vial, and 6th Trumpet, about 5 *years* before the End, so the Second Translation is at the close of the literal-day 6th Seal, 6th Vial, and 6th Trumpet, about 5 *days* before the End: and it will consist in the visible manifestation of Christ coming in the clouds and sending his angels to *gather together his elect from the four winds*, which is described in Matt. xxiv. 29-31, and Mark xiii. 24-27, as taking place very soon after the darkening of the sun, which immediately follows the 8¼ years' Great Tribulation, consequent upon the setting

the next five years. The literal-day 6th Seal lasts for about 70 days immediately after Antichrist's 8¼ years: it begins with darkness and an earthquake: 144,000 Jews are then sealed, and together with all the other saints are caught up in the Second Translation, and thus come *out of* (εκ) the Great Tribulation, having passed through it. The word εκ in this passage, like πολεμον and εις, (Rev. xvi. 14, 16,) has a slightly different meaning in the year-day from what it has in the literal-day fulfilment.
The following texts describe in the year-day fulfilment the Resurrection and First Translation, and in the literal-day fulfilment the Resurrection of Antichrist's martyrs and Second Translation: Rev. vii. 9-17; xi. 15-19; xvi. 15. This second stage in Christ's Advent is also exclusively referred to in Matt. xxiv. 30, 31; Mark xiii. 26, 27; Luke xxi. 27; Rev. xiv. 16; i. 7; Dan. vii. 13.

up of the abomination of Desolation. In neither of these two passages is the resurrection of the sleeping saints alluded to, for the reason that it will have occurred 5 years previously, at the First Translation, (1 Thess. iv.)

It is by no means certain that those who die a natural death during this 5 years, will have part in the First Resurrection by being raised up before the Millennium. With regard, however, to those who are martyred during the 5 years, and who refuse to worship Napoleon's image, it is expressly stated, in Rev xx. 4, 5, that when the saints constituting the Lamb's wife descend with Christ to the earth, (Rev. xix. 8, 14, 19,) and sit on thrones and have the judgment—that is, the government of the world given to them—then *the souls* (that is, the persons, Acts xxvii. 37) of Antichrist's martyrs will *live*, (that is, be raised up,) and will also reign ; and this will be the conclusion of the First Resurrection, which will have commenced with the First Translation, 5 years previously. There is some reason for supposing that those who die otherwise than by martyrdom during the quinquennial interval between the two Translations, will be included among *the rest of the dead* that *live not again* (that is, are not raised up) *until the thousand years are finished,* when there will be the Second Resurrection, (Rev. xx. 11–15,) comprising all who have died during the Millennium, as well as all who were not raised up at the First Resurrection. The Judgment before the great white throne which then ensues, evidently includes righteous as well as wicked persons, from the fact of the Book of Life being produced and opened, which would be unnecessary if only the wicked were present.

The living saints caught up in the Second Translation constitute the Laodicean *harvest*, (Rev. xvi. 15,) or the *great multitude*, (lit-day, Rev. vii.) and appear to amount to upward of from 25 to 50 millions persons. By the greatness of their past afflictions they will be thoroughly purified from all that lingering love of the world and that cold indifference to the hope of Christ's Advent which at present characterizes the majority even of truly pious people. Most of them will have witnessed, and, no doubt, have suffered from, the tremendous judgments of the literal-day Seals, Trumpets, and Vials. They will have seen the skies raining down blood, (Rev. viii. 7,) and the ocean and the streams of water changed into blood, and the moon becoming as blood, and the earth's bosom stained with the blood of millions of her slain. They will have beheld the sun at one time angrily emitting rays of burning heat, so as to scorch men with fire, and again mournfully hiding its face from the scene of terrestrial woe, and the whole heavens overspread with the blackness of darkness, as if the day of the world's funeral had arrived. They will have felt the earth shudder and quake as if horror-struck at the atrocities perpetrated by its inhabitants, and they will have seen pestilence, famine, and the sword covering its surface with myriads of unburied corpses. The description of the ancient martyrs will have become applicable to them, for they will have *had trial of cruel mockings and scourgings, yea, moreover, of bonds and imprisonment . . . being destitute, afflicted, tormented, wandering in deserts, and mountains, and dens, and caves of the earth,* (Heb. xi. 88.) Often will they have lamented that they did not earlier believe in and openly confess the imminence of Christ's Advent, so as to have been caught up in the First Translation. The prophecies of Revelation, which at present scarcely any one studies, will then be anxiously pored over by them, to ascertain how soon they will be delivered by the Second Translation. At last their suspense will be relieved by the appearance in the skies, some time during the first 6 literal-day Vials, of the Sign of the Son of Man, which (whether or not a gigantic cross emblazoned upon the concave of the firmament) will be some conspicuous and universally-visible object, at the sight of which the majority of mankind will mourn, but the saints will rejoice with exceeding great joy. Five days before the End, Christ himself will appear in the heavens, coming with *power and great glory.* All the elect, including the 144,000 sealed Jews, will be caught up to meet him, being the *great multitude* (οχλος πολυς) which come *out of the Great Tribulation,* (εκ της θλιψεως της μεγαλης, Rev. vii. 14.) After this, the literal-day 7th Seal will be opened and half an hour's silence follows, during which the newly-translated saints probably have their respective positions assigned to them.

The narrative of the Seals is then suspended at Rev. viii. 1, and recommences at Rev. xix., as the best expositors admit, for the intervening space is occupied with other visions of the Trumpets, Vials, etc. The whole of Rev. xix. is fulfilled exactly within the last five days. The half-hour's silence of Rev. viii. 1 is broken in Rev. xix. 1 by the *great multitude* in heaven (*much people*, οχλος πολυς, Rev. xix. 1, 6) praising God for his justice in taking vengeance on the harlot Papal Church, by destroying its chief seat, Rome, which becomes the scene of a perpetual volcanic fire 3 or 4 days before the Consummation, (lit-day, Rev. xviii., xvi. 19.) Amid their exclamations of joy there is heard for the first time the Hebrew word *Alleluia*, thereby showing, as commentators have often remarked, the presence among the *great multitude* of many Jews, who are, in fact, the recently-translated 144,000 sealed Jews. Their declaration that *the marriage of the Lamb is come, and his wife hath made herself ready*, appears to imply that the Lamb's marriage does not take place until that time, and consequently it is possible that they may form part of the Lamb's wife, although it might have seemed, from Matt. xxv. 10, that *the marriage* took place soon after the First Translation, and that the subjects of the Second Translation were excluded from it, and only admitted to the subsequent *marriage-supper*. This latter view is confirmed by the additional announcement: *Blessed are they which are called unto the marriage-supper of the Lamb*, which, (unless it refers to the Millennial saints,) when viewed in connection with the promise given to the Laodicean saints — that is, the saints on the earth between the two Translations, (Rev. iii. 14–22,) appears to indicate that the subjects of the Second Translation do not constitute part of the Bride, but are only admitted to the marriage-supper as wedding-guests, or friends of the Bridegroom, (John iii. 29,) and only sit down on Christ's throne, (Rev. iii. 21,) and not on the Father's throne, (Rev. xii. 5.) That there will be different companies of the redeemed in addition to the Bride or Lamb's wife, is indisputable, (Ps. xlv. 13, 14; Song Sol. vi. 8, 9,) as, for instance, the Millennial saints, who, after death will be taken up to heaven, must necessarily form a distinct body from those saints that constitute the Bride, who is married to the Divine Bridegroom just before the Millennium. It appears on the whole to be at least doubtful whether the Laodicean saints will form part of the Bride, and whether those of them who die otherwise than by martyrdom will be raised up until the post-millennial Second Resurrection; but these two points require fuller consideration than can here be allotted to them.

The Marriage of the Lamb, which is briefly mentioned in Rev. xix. 7, 8, is described at greater length in the subsequent vision of the New Jerusalem from Rev. xxi. 2 to xxii. 15, which is not the sequel and continuation of the vision of Rev. xix., xx., and xxi. 1, but is a distinct and retrogressive vision, and refers to the same period of time as Rev. xix. 7, 8. The New Jerusalem, which is no mere emblem, but is a visible and literal city, 1500 miles square, and constructed of the solid and substantial material of *pure gold like unto clear glass*, descends from the highest heavens down to the pavilion-cloud in the air, where the raised and translated saints have remained for about 5 years: and their immediate entrance into that city and investment with possession of the mansions that are there provided for them, principally constitutes the ceremony of the Lamb's marriage. For as at the marriage of an earthly monarch, his bride is publicly in the sight of his subjects, raised to the same exalted rank as himself, to sit upon his throne, to enter into his palace, to receive through life the title of Queen, and to exercise conjointly with her royal consort supreme power over the kingdom, so at the marriage of the King of kings, the saints constituting his Bride will openly, in the presence of the angels and archangels and principalities and powers in heavenly places, receive the lofty titles of *Kings and Priests unto God*, and they will be formally admitted to take their seat by his side upon the throne and to enter into his Palace, (Ps. xlv.,) the New Jerusalem, the Capital and Metropolis of the Universe, and thenceforth, as joint-heirs with him, will exercise royal authority and dominion over all things, both which are in heaven and which are on earth. Thus on almost the same day that the False Harlot Church of Rome sinks into irreversible perdition, and has its chief city, Rome, rendered the scene of an unquenchable volcanic conflagration, the Faithful Bride, the true Church, is married to the Lamb, and enters upon possession of the Holy City, *whose builder and maker is God.* This will be the Heavenly Home of the glorified saints, from which they will continually wing their way upon visits to the earth and other parts of the Universe.*

EVENT XX. THIRD WOE, during the final 3½ days consisting principally in the transformation of the territory adjoining Rome into a perpetual lake of fire, (Rev. xix. 3,) and the destruction of Napoleon and the Pope and five-sixths of their vast armies at the Battle of Armageddon, when Christ will descend on the earth and slay all incorrigible rejectors of the Gospel. (Isaiah xxxiv., lxvi., Ezek. xxxix., Zech. xiv., Rev. xi. 15, xvi. 17, xix.)

"And I saw heaven opened, and behold, a white horse, and he that sat on him was called Faithful and True, and in righteousness he doth judge and make war. . . And the armies which were in heaven followed him upon white horses, clothed in fine linen, white and clean. . . And I saw the Beast and the kings of the earth and their armies gathered together to make war against him that sat on the horse and against his army. And the Beast was taken and with him the False Prophet. . . These both were cast alive into a lake of fire burning with brimstone. And the remnant were slain with the sword of him that sat upon the horse."—Rev. xix.

The third year-day Woe, or 3½ years' War of Armageddon† consists in the series of conflicts that take place in

---

* Although the descent of the New Jerusalem into the air near the earth (partially constituting the Lamb's marriage) does not seem to occur earlier, yet the saints raised and caught up at the first Translation may perhaps enter into it previous to this period.

† During the 40 years of the year-day 6th Vial from 1826 to 1866-7, preparations are made for the nations being gathered to the 3½ *years'* WAR of Armageddon, which takes place during the year-day 7th Vial: the word πολεμον signifying *war*, and the word εις *towards*, (Rev. xvi. 14, 16.) During the subsequent 40 *days* of the literal-day 6th Vial here is another gathering of the nations to the 3½ *days'* BATTLE of Armageddon, which occurs during the literal-day 7th Vial: the word πολεμον signifying *battle*, and εις *into*. The double sense of εις is noticed by Elliott as occurring in Rev. xii. 6, 14. The year-day 7th Trumpet and 7th Vial begin about a year before the 3½ years third Woe, and so also the literal-day 7th Trumpet and Vial begin about a day before the 3½ days' third Woe.

the vicinity of Palestine during the year-day 7th Trumpet and Vial, and which will almost have subsided by the end of Antichrist's 3½ years. But the third literal-day Woe, or 3½ days' Battle of Armageddon, is a subsequent contest during the literal-day 7th Trumpet and Vial, to which, in a final paroxysm of rage and despair, Napoleon, filled with indignation against the Jews, as the supposed cause of the intolerable plagues of the literal-day Vials, will for the last time summon all his followers, saying: *Come, and let us cut them off from being a nation, that the name of Israel may be no more in remembrance*, (Ps. lxxxiii. 4.) As Pharaoh did but grow more hardened, after being visited with ten plagues, and pursued after the Israelites to overcome them, so Napoleon, after enduring five plagues, will only become confirmed in the determination to *destroy and utterly to make away* almost all the Jews. Although the ungodly will have been terror-stricken under the tremendous judgments of the first five vials, during the first month of the final 2½ months, yet as the next 40 days during the literal-day 6th Vial is an interval of respite, they will temporarily recover from their consternation; and their enmity against Christ's people will be stirred up afresh by the renewed activity of the unclean spirits of atheism and fanatical zealotry. Like a tumultuous torrent, they will rush from all parts of the earth to exterminate the Jews in Palestine, and that no element of success may be wanting, Napoleon himself, attended by his ten kings and his inseparable associate the False Prophet, will with great pomp accompany the expedition. At the close of the 40 days, just five days before the End, they will be found assembled in the Holy Land, in a place called in the Hebrew tongue Armageddon. At this very juncture the Second Translation takes place, (literal-day, Rev. xvi. 15.) Christ appears in the skies, coming with power and great glory, and the angels descend and take up into the clouds all the saints remaining on the earth, (Mark xiii. 27.) During the 5 days (the 1330th to the 1335th) that then elapse before the End, in the course of which the Marriage of the Lamb takes place in the clouds, the shining brightness of the glory of Christ's presence continues visible in the heavens, betokening his descent to be immediately at hand. This spectacle, so far from inducing

Antichrist to desist from his heaven-defying rebellion only hardens him in the resolve to contend with his utmost strength against the heavenly hosts which he perceives are about to come down to the earth. He no longer designs merely to extirpate the Jews, but now turns all his attention to opposing the celestial armies, whom he madly hopes to vanquish, determining to *fight neither with small or great, save only with the Divine King of Israel.* He will have become so infatuated from his unparalleled career of conquest as to say in his heart, *I will ascend into heaven: I will exalt my throne above the stars of God: I will ascend above the heights of the clouds: I will be like the Most High,* (Isaiah xiv. 13.) Having previously *made war with the saints,* and even with Elijah and the other Witness, *and overcome them,* he now thinks to *make war with the Lamb* with a like result. Forthwith he issues orders to his generals and captains to marshal their innumerable companies of cavalry and infantry and artillery in battle array. He will doubtless remind them of their past victories and of their hitherto indomitable courage and invincibility, and exhort them to fight against the supernatural foes that are approaching, with unfaltering valor and resolution. An interval of a day or two will follow, during which every preparation will be made by his hosts for engaging in the impending struggle; and then during the subsequent 3 or 4 days, consuming judgments will overwhelm them, by which five-sixths of their number will be slain. There will suddenly be a literal earthquake of unparalleled violence, and at the same time mutual hatred and discord will be disseminated throughout their ranks. *Every man's sword shall be against his brother*, and a scene of unexampled carnage will then be witnessed. The slaughter will be so great that it will afterward occupy the Jews seven months in burying the dead bodies, (Ezek. xxxix. 12;) and the bloodshed will be such that *the blood will come out of the wine-press, even unto the horses' bridles, by the space of a thousand and six hundred furlongs,* (Rev. xiv. 20.) This may refer to the length of Palestine, being about 1600 furlongs or 200 miles: but it principally seems to designate the square measure of the area in which the greatest destruction of life will occur, and which would thus be 25 square miles, each side being the length of 5 miles or 40 furlongs, which is the square root of 1600 furlongs. The sword will not be the only means by which the doomed five-sixths of this multitude will be slain; for great hailstones and fire and brimstone will be rained upon them, (Ezek. xxxviii.,) and an unprecedented plague will smite them. *Their flesh shall consume away while they stand upon their feet, and their eyes shall consume away in their holes, and their tongue shall consume away in their mouth. Every horse will be smitten with blindness and his rider with madness*, (Zech. xii. 4, xiv. 12.) During these final 2 or 3 days the descent of Christ with his glorified saints from the Heavenly Jerusalem to the earth takes place, and most probably it will occur on the 1335th day, 5 days after the Second Translation, since it also occurs on the 1335th year, 5 years after the First Translation. At the infliction of the first and second Woes the bottomless pit was opened, and supernatural locusts, and horsemen with red and blue and yellow breastplates, and mounted upon horses that seemed to breathe out fire and brimstone, appeared on the earth. But now at the infliction of this third Woe, heaven is opened and celestial horsemen, clothed in white linen and mounted upon white horses, descend from the skies, (Rev. xix.) They speedily consummate the work of vengeance upon Napoleon's armies, which has already been initiated. The Antichrist and the Roman Pontiff are at once captured, like wild beasts trapped in a pitfall, and are cast alive, without undergoing death, into the lake of fire, which appears, from Isaiah xxxiv., and lxvi. 24, and Rev. xix. 3, to be the region adjacent to Rome, which will at that time become the scene of a perpetual volcanic conflagration, and the sight of which will serve as a continual warning and restraint to the subsequent inhabitants of the earth. Thus will Napoleon and his ten kings *make war with the Lamb* and *against him that sits on the horse*, and *stand up against the Prince of Princes*, but *the Lamb shall overcome them* and *they shall be broken without hand*, (Rev. xvii. 14, xix. 19, Dan. viii. 25.) And thus the great Antitype of Pharoah, Senacherib, Nebuchadnezzar, Judas and Herod, after having reached (as implied by his number 666) the highest degree of human grandeur and perfection that is attainable apart from God, will finally *come to his end, and none shall help him* With him as its last Head, the Fourth Universal Monarchy or Roman Empire will pass away; and the Fifth Monarchy or Millennial Kingdom of the Lord Jesus will almost immediately commence.*

WHEN CHRIST THUS descends with his glorified saints upon Mt. Olivet, (Zech. xiv. 4, Acts i. 11,) at the end of 7 years and 2¼ months after Antichrist has been revealed, (2 Thess. ii. 3,) by his confirmation of the Jewish covenant, the MILLENNIUM of 1000 years (Rev. xx.) will almost immediately commence. Its leading features and the changes which it will introduce may be noticed under four heads. (1.) As regards the PHYSICAL CONDITION of the earth. It is important to remember that the earth will not be completely burnt up or depopulated at the Second Advent. The *day of the Lord*, in which the general conflagration is to occur, (2 Peter iii. 10,) is not a day of 24 hours, but is explained in 2 Peter iii. 8 to be a period of 1000 years, and is in fact the same period as the Millennium. The conflagration will take place partially at the beginning of the 1000 years, (Rev. xviii., Is. lxvi. 15, Ezek. xxxix. 6, 2 Thess. i. 8,) and more completely at the end of the 1000 years, (Rev. xx. 9, xxi. 1,) when there will be no more sea. Thus also the New Heavens and New Earth seem to commence partially with the Millennium,

---

* The expressions "the End" or "the Consummation," are used to signify the End of this dispensation at Christ's descent at Armageddon, 7 years and 2¼ months after the date of the Jewish Covenant.—The seven literal-day Seals (Rev. vi., vii.) describe the successive conditions of the visible Church, with accompanying Providential dispensations, during the 5 years 1 month and 5 days between the First Translation and Christ's Descent (See Diagrams II. and VIII). Seal 1 depicts the Church full of a Revival spirit (the white horse) for 9¼ months. Seal 2 denotes the growing degeneracy of the Church (the red horse) during a period of universal warfare the next 7 months. Seal 3 represents the increased apostacy of the visible Church (black horse), during a time of dreadful famine the next 18 months. Seal 4 signifies the Church's utter corruption (pale horse) during dreadful wars, famines, and pestilences the next 12 months. Seal 5 denotes a period of respite for the next 12 months. Seal 6 describes the completion of the sealing of 144,000 Jews, during the next 2¼ months, ending with the Second Translation. Seal 7 depicts the marriage of the Lamb's wife (Rev. xix.) during the last 5 days.

(Is. lxv. 17, lxvi. 22,) but are not completely perfected until the end of the Millennium, when the sea, having given up its dead, altogether disappears, (Rev. xxi. 1.) After the Battle of Armageddon some of the less hardened sinners will be spared and converted, and will be sent as missionaries to the nations and to *the isles afar off that have not heard the fame nor seen the glory* of the Lord, (Is. lxvi. 19.) But although a *few men are left*, (Is. xxiv. 6,) yet a great many of the remaining *inhabitants of the earth are burned* at that time, for the Lord Jesus *will send a fire on them that dwell carelessly in the isles*, (or different continents of the earth,) (Ezek. xxxix. 6,) and will *execute judgment upon all* (Jude 15) *with flaming fire, taking vengeance on them that know not God*, (2 Thess. i. 8,) and *by fire and by his sword will plead with all flesh: and the slain of the Lord shall be many*, (Is. lxvi. 16.) After the incorrigible rejectors of the Gospel are cut off, the surviving population of the earth (probably a tenth or twentieth part of its present population) will quickly increase and multiply, and live in successive generations; births, deaths, and marriages continually taking place as at the present time. The glorified saints that were caught up to the heavens at the Resurrection and two Translations, will live in the Heavenly Jerusalem, and constantly descend and ascend between it and this earth, over which they will, visibly or invisibly, reign as Kings. The curse that has rested upon the animal, vegetable, and mineral creation ever since the fall of Adam will be to a great extent repealed. As soon as *all the people praise God, then shall the earth yield her increase*, (Ps. lxvii. 7.) The hitherto sterile soil will become extraordinarily fruitful, and will require very little labor in order to produce abundant crops, (Amos ix. 13, Joel iii. 18, Is. xxx. 23.) Weeds will almost cease to grow naturally upon it. *Instead of the thorn shall come up the fir tree, and instead of the brier shall come up the myrtle-tree*, (Is. lv. 13.) There will be important atmospheric, meteorological, and geological changes, by means of which waste, wildernesses, such as the Great Sahara, and frozen regions, like those of Siberia, will become clothed with fertility and beauty, for *the desert shall rejoice and blossom as the rose*, . . . *and the parched ground shall become a pool, and the thirsty land springs of water,* (Is. xxxv.) Entire exemption from sickness does not seem to be promised to the Gentile nations as to the Jews: but *the leaves of the tree of life in the New Jerusalem are for the healing of the nations,* (Rev xxii. 2,) and will apparently be brought down from th New Jerusalem to those upon earth who are sick. Al the blind, deaf, dumb, and lame that are spared a Christ's descent will be healed, (Is. xxxv. 5.) Venomous serpents will become quite harmless, and ferocious animals, such as the wolf, the leopard, the lion, and the bear, becoming graminivorous instead of carnivorous, will live peaceably with sheep and cattle, (Is. xi. 6, lx. 25,) and may, perhaps, be used as beasts of burden. Man's lifetime will, perhaps, be prolonged; the express promise of longevity appears, however, to be only given to the Jewish nation, (Is. lxv. 20.) These changes will necessarily cause an unparalleled increase of the earth's inhabitants,* so that they will become as numerous as the sand upon the seashore, (Rev. xx. 8.)

* It will be interesting to observe during the Millennium how the difficulties arising from the great increase of population will be provided against. In England, the population, which is now 330 persons to the square mile, has doubled itself in 50 years, from A.D. 1800 to 1850, and political economists consider that, if unchecked by wars, scarcity of food, etc., it would easily double itself every 25 years. At this rate the earth's inhabitants, if only 50 millions at the beginning of the Millennium, would become 204,800 millions in the 300th year, which would be about 3400 persons to every square mile of land, for only 60 out of the 200 million square miles of the earth's surface consist of land. This would perhaps be as great a population as the earth could well contain, and would require about three fourths of its soil to be under cultivation, and sufficiently fertile to yield on an average from each acre (the 640th part of a square mile) enough food for seven persons. (Even now, one acre has been known to yield, by spade cultivation, enough to support 20 persons.) There will doubtless be special Providential arrangements, which will prevent too great a multiplication of the human race. This estimate of about 200,000 millions as the possible maximum of the earth's population (being 150 times greater than its present population of 1300 millions) will make the unglorified inhabitants of the Millennial earth to be 500 times more numerous than the glorified saints of the First Resurrection (Rev. xx. 6) who will reign over them—that is, if these latter (exclusive of deceased infants) be approximately estimated to amount to about 400 millions. There would also thus be probably more people living on the earth at one time than

(2.) As respects the POLITICAL AND SOCIAL CONDITION of mankind. One Man will be King over the whole earth, even Jesus of Nazareth, the God-man; and his kingdom, like the four preceding universal kingdoms of Babylon, Persia, Greece, and Rome, will be a literal, visible, and earthly kingdom (Dan. ii., vii. 11, Zech. xiv. 9) over *all people, nations, and languages*, (Dan. vii. 14,) a phrase which exclusively denotes nations as they at present exist in the flesh, (Dan. iii. 4, iv. 1, vi. 25.) Although he will from time to time manifest himself personally in the terrestrial Jerusalem, the earth's metropolis and seat of government, yet his principal residence, together with his glorified saints, will be in the celestial Jerusalem, the metropolis of the Universe, a *city of pure gold like unto clear glass*, and 1500 miles in length, breadth, and height, (Rev. xxi. 16,) which comes down into the air so as to be visible to the nations of the earth, (Rev. xxi. 24,) but is nowhere stated to come on to the earth; indeed, it would be quite incongruous for a perfectly square structure to be poised upon a globe only four times greater (24,000 miles) in circumference. The glorified saints associated with Jesus, as subordinate Kings in the government of this world, (Rev. xx. 6, Luke xix. 17,) will constantly pass to and fro between the Heavenly City and this planet, thus realizing the prophetic vision of Jacob's ladder, (Gen. xxviii. 12, John i. 51.) It is a question whether they will reign visibly over the unglorified inhabitants of the earth, or invisibly, (occasionally, however, manifesting their presence,) like the angels which at present have mankind intrusted to their charge and ministry, (Heb. i. 14, ii. 5, Ps. xxxiv. 7,) and which wear the titles of the kingdoms of this world, (Dan. x. 13, 20.) It appears that the nations will retain their distinctive customs and languages, (unless Zeph. iii. 9 signifies that there will be only one language,) but will probably all have the same laws, currency, and standards of measurement, by which their mutual commercial dealings may be facilitated. The earth's inhabitants will engage in agricultural, mechanical, scientific, and mercantile occupations, and follow the legal, clerical, and literary professions, just as in these the whole sum of all the successive populations during the past 6000 years.

days.* But the military profession will be forgotten. Peace will prevail universally, (Is. ii. 4, Hos. ii. 18; Ps. xlvi. 9.) No standing armies or warlike navies will be maintained. Bayonets and rifled cannon will be regarded as the relics of a bygone age of darkness and barbarism. There will be no despotism, tyranny, or oppression. Cases of crime will be very rare. The whole earth will probably be covered with a network of railways and telegraphs, and the surface of the ocean unceasingly traversed by innumerable vessels, maintaining constant intercourse among all the communities of the globe. England and North-America, released from the dominancy of Antichrist, will doubtless occupy the foremost position, next to Israel, among the regenerated nations. The Millennial state of the earth is strikingly illustrated by the scene of Christ's Transfiguration, which was a miniature picture of it, and therefore a prophetic vision of *the Son of man coming in his kingdom*, (Matt. xvi. 28; 2 Peter i. 16.) The six days (Matt. xvii. 1) typified the 6000 years, after which the Millennium commences, and Peter, James, and John represented the unglorified inhabitants of the Millennial earth, over whom the glorified raised and translated saints, represented by Moses and Elias, will reign conjointly with Christ.

(3.) As regards the RELIGIOUS CONDITION of mankind. Instead of three fourths of the human race being in heathen darkness as at present, all persons will then be ac-

* Although the business of the world will be carried on during the Millennium in somewhat the same manner as at present, yet it is vain for persons to think of retaining their possessions during the coming Tribulation, (Is. xxiv.,) and it would be impious for them to make any preparations in expectation of surviving on the earth after the Second Advent and during the Millennium. All converted persons will shortly be removed from the earth in the two Translations, and a few of the unconverted who are left behind will be afterward spared and converted, and will constitute the earth's population when the Millennium begins. It is clearly the duty of those who are true Christians, and who are therefore sure to be caught up in one of the two Translations, to spend as much of their remaining time and property as they can in preaching the Gospel and circulating Bibles and religious books as widely as possible, before the approaching infidel persecution puts a stop to such efforts. The present momentous crisis justifies Christians in relinquishing secular occupations, if they can do so without serious inconvenience to themselves or society, and devoting themselves exclusively to striving to enlighten the multitudes that are perishing for lack of knowledge.

quainted with the doctrines of Christianity, for *the earth shall be full of the knowledge of the Lord as the waters cover the sea,* (Is. xi. 9, Heb. ii. 16,) and Christ *will have dominion also from sea to sea, and from the river unto the ends of the earth,* (Zech. ix. 10, Ps. lxxii. 8,) *for all nations shall come and worship before* him, (Rev. xv. 4, xi. 15, xx., Ps. lxxxvi. 9, lxvi., II. Dan. ii., vii.) Although men will be free from the deceiving influence of Satan, (Rev. xx. 3,) yet they will have the same naturally sinful hearts as now, and this will necessitate the continuance of the means of grace and the preaching of the Gospel, which, however, will be accompanied by a much greater outpouring of the Holy Spirit than in these days, (Is. xxxii. 15.) Open wickedness, such as drunkenness, Sabbath-breaking, gambling, lying, dishonesty, cruelty, impure conduct or conversation, will be promptly punished whenever it occurs, and almost entirely repressed; but there will still be some unregenerate persons among the nations, (Zech. xiv. 19.) Probably not more than ten millions out of the thirteen hundred millions now upon the earth are truly converted or born again, but then the proportion of the converted to the unconverted will perhaps be nearly the reverse of this, so that if the earth's population is only as large as it now is, (and it might and perhaps will be 150 times greater,) there will be more adult persons saved in one generation than in all the past 200 generations, (without referring to those that die in infancy.) There may also be a further addition to the Bible for the Millennial dispensation, just as there was an addition to it for the Christian dispensation.

(4.) As regards the JEWISH NATION. After the Battle of Armageddon, all the surviving Jews throughout the earth will be converted and restored to Palestine, being brought *as an offering unto the Lord out of all nations, upon horses, and in chariots, and in litters, and upon mules,* (Is. lxvi. 20, see also Is. xi., lx., Jer. iii., xxxi., xxxiii., Zech. viii. to xiv., Ezek. xxxiv. to xlviii., Rom. xl., etc.) It seems that the ships of the maritime power called Tarshish (England or the American States, or both) will likewise assist in this work, (Is. lx. 9,) (it appears that they will, perhaps, have also assisted in the partial restoration under Antichrist seven years previous ly, Is. xviii.) Only one third of the Jews that were living in Palestine at the commencement of Antichrist's persecution will be surviving when the Millennium begins, (Zech. xiii. 9,) and those of them who are in Jerusalem when Christ descends on Mt. Olivet *will look upon him whom they have pierced*, (Zech. xii. 10, Matt. xxiii. 39,) and will immediately repent and become converted through the outpouring of the Holy Spirit, as typified by the miraculous conversion of the Apostle Paul, (1 Tim. i. 16.) The Jews will then possess the land from the Nile to the Euphrates, which although promised to them, (Gen. xv. 18,) they have never yet obtained. Jerusalem will be the metropolis of the earth, and will be 18,000 *measures*, or 36 miles, in circumference, and 9 miles square, (Ezek. xlviii. 35,) each *measure* being 6 cubits, (Ezek. xl. 5,) and the cubit of the sanctuary being 21 inches. Within it (if not throughout all Palestine) there will never be any weeping or crying, (Is. lxv. 19,) and *the inhabitant shall not say I am sick*, (Is. xxxiii. 24,) for the very leaves of its trees will furnish an elixir vitæ and a medicinal panacea for human maladies, (Ezek. xlvii. 12.) All the Jews will be truly converted, (Is. liv. 13, lx. 21, Jer. xxxi. 34,) and will mostly live to the age of several centuries, being only children when a hundred years old, and rivalling in longevity the trees of the forest, (Is. lxv. 20, 22.) They will be the chief of the nations of the regenerated earth. The Holy Land will become like the garden of Eden, (Ezek. xxxvi. 35, Is. vii. 21, 22, xxx. 23,) and will be divided afresh among the twelve tribes, (Ezek. xlviii.,) who will be governed by the twelve apostles, (Luke xxii. 30.) Over Mt. Zion will be a pillar of cloud by day and a pillar of fire by night, (Is. iv. 5.) The Jewish Temple will be rebuilt according to the pattern given in the last nine chapters of Ezekiel, which also prescribe the order of the future sacrifices and other rites; for Israel, though Christianized, will still observe the peculiar ceremonies of Judaism, not as expiatory or prospectively as a shadow of things to come; but as eucharistic, and retrospectively as a sacramental commemoration of the past *offering of the body of Jesus Christ once for all*. All the nations (or at least large delegations from each nation) will make pilgrimages to

Jerusalem every year to keep the feast of Tabernacles, or else no rain will descend upon them, (Zech. xiv. 19,) and such an unprecedented amount of travelling clearly implies an extraordinary abundance at that time of facilities for locomotion, such as railways and steam-vessels. The Dead Sea will also be completely purified by a river that will be caused to flow into it from Jerusalem, (Ezek. xlvii. 8, 10.) There will most probably be a channel opened for the passage of vessels between the Mediterranean and the Red Sea, by which Jerusalem will be placed upon the highway of commerce between the Atlantic and the Indian Ocean.

The following description of the Millennium is extracted from Purdon's Last Vials. "When the First Resurrection has taken place and the destruction of Antichrist has been completed, we may inquire in what form and character shall the Kingdom of Christ be revealed to the world during the Millennial period, or how will it differ from all that went before or that shall follow?"

"The nature of the Millennial Kingdom appears to be this: 1st.—The Lord shall reign directly over the whole earth. 2d.—The saints shall reign with and under him. 3dly.—Jerusalem shall be rebuilt, and Israel restored. 4thly.—The whole world shall become converted. 5thly.—The earth shall become more fruitful, and the seasons shall be altered. 6thly.—The saints who share in the First Resurrection shall not live upon the earth, but in the Heavenly City.

"The Heavenly City will be suspended over the earth during the Millennial reign, and probably over the earthly Jerusalem, and will be a visible object throughout all the land of Israel. This supposition solves a difficulty which must occur with regard to the millennial CLIMATE. We all imagine that some great improvement must take place in the climate, productions, and fertility of the earth, during the reign of Christ—and all the prophecies seem to concur in foretelling this improvement. But the question is, by what miracle shall this change be produced? We reply, that the Heavenly City will become a source of light, and heat, and fertility to all the world, being 1500 miles square measurement, being filled and lit up by the glory of God, (Rev. xxi.,) and being suspended not far from the surface of the earth, it will fulfil the office of an additional *sun*, especially throughout the land of Israel, and will thus produce that physical renovation of the earth which the Prophets have foretold as the effect of the reign of Christ. (See Isaiah xxxv.) But this City is described in such peculiar language, that it seems impossible to understand by it anything but a literal place of residence, a really existing structure, whether it be a City or otherwise, and a place whose materials will be the most magnificent and costly that imagination can conceive. A place filled with the glory of God, inhabited by resurrection saints, and containing within its walls the throne of the Lord Jesus Christ, as King of Israel and of the world. Around the palace of the King of kings will be seen the palaces of all his saints, each of whom will be himself a king and a priest unto God, having 'washed his robes, and made them white in the blood of the Lamb. Therefore are they before the throne of God, and he that sitteth upon the throne shall dwell among them: they shall hunger no more, neither thirst any more, neither shall the sun light upon them, nor any heat, for the Lamb that is in the midst of the throne shall feed them, and shall lead them unto living fountains of water; and God shall wipe away all tears from their eyes.' Nor is this the whole: for along with the presence of God, and the possession of more than royal magnificence, they shall possess irresistible power—they shall reign with Christ over the nations of the earth, and shall rule the ungodly with a rod of iron. The empire of Satan shall be broken—the reign of radicalism shall be swept away—the boastings of infidel science shall be silenced in darkness, and all power, knowledge, dignity, and wealth shall be transferred from the man of the world to the man of God. The whole course of things shall be inverted; the worldly man shall serve where once he ruled, and the saint shall rule where once he was despised. And the nations upon earth, looking up every hour to the heavenly city, and gazing with wonder upon its ineffable beauty, shall exclaim with a different tone than that of formal repetition :

"'Thou art the King of glory, O Christ!
Make us to be numbered with thy Saints, in glory everlasting.'

"When once the Lord shall have returned to Mount Zion, he will bring down heaven along with him, upon the earth, and spread the life and motion of celestial things throughout all the recesses of the globe. He will restore the tribes of Israel to their renowned and sacred land—rebuild Jerusalem, as the capital of the world and the joy of the whole earth—raise the temple, from its ruins to more than its ancient splendor, and fill its sanctuary with the brightness of his own presence. All the nations of the globe shall be attracted by the fame of his august dominion. They shall tell it out among the heathen, that the Lord is king, and that he shall judge the people righteously: and this report shall bring up all nations to Jerusalem, and there they shall hear his name as a familiar thing; their ears shall be filled with the history of that wondrous government. They shall walk through the streets frequented by glorified spirits—sit down at hospitable boards, where the common conversation will be of the presence of God, and of the expected visits of his glory. They shall go forth, from day to day, to witness some act of divine power, and to look upon the face of some resurrection saint, or to converse with some man fresh from heaven; and shall look beyond the limits of the earth, and see above their heads the brightness of the Eternal City. Then, perhaps, at some unexpected moment, the presence of the Lord will be made visible from the sanctuary, and a proclamation shall be heard throughout Jerusalem: '*The Lord is in his holy temple; let all the earth keep silence before him.*' And at this proclamation, an awful stillness shall close in upon every heart: And pilgrims of every kindred, garb, and complexion shall ascend together to the sanctuary, to worship the Lord in the beauty of holiness. Thus the deepest spirituality shall be spread throughout the world, for the hopes and interests of mankind will be gathered around the throne of CHRIST; and the hearts of nations will be purified by the contemplation of this wondrous vision.

"Our Lord, returning in glory to the place of his former humiliation, and surrounded by his saints, freed from all the miseries of mortality, will point out to his attendants those scenes immortalized by his sufferings: 'In that garden I endured the wrath of God, in agony and blood:

sweat—I was betrayed by Judas—dragged before Pontius Pilate—deserted by all mankind. In that spot I stood before the Roman governor—was mocked, buffetted, and spit upon; along that street I carried the cross, surrounded by the scoffing multitude, and on that little hill I endured the agony of crucifixion and death. I recollect it all! and as a man, I rejoice that the dreadful hour has passed away for ever. But I remember my native country with pity, not with anger—I love the spot in which I won the crown of victory—and henceforth let it be consecrated for evermore as the one that is dearest to my heart—and here, where once I was lifted up upon the cross, I will display the brightness of my presence, and draw men unto me from every nation.' Such, we may suppose, will be the conversation at the 'marriage-supper of the Lamb,' and we may add: '*Blessed is the man who shall eat bread in the kingdom of God!*' And how great will be the surprise and disappointment of all those who now fully reckon upon an instant admission to the presence of the Lord whenever he may come, but who have never looked forward to his coming as an especial object of faith and hope. There is much reason to fear that when the Bridegroom comes they shall be numbered among the foolish virgins, and though admitted to his presence in the end, may be shut out from the first bloom and freshness of his kingdom, and left for a time to struggle upon earth.

"When our Lord sets up his kingdom, he will divide its provinces among its saints, and will make them literally rulers over the whole world. He will himself be the paramount sovereign; but as all his saints are said to be one with him, they must necessarily take part with him in his sovereignty. The world will be divided into departments in the council-chamber of heaven, and each saint, according to his works, will be advanced to a corresponding rank in this heavenly government, and will rule over five or ten cities—over a larger or a lesser province, (Luke xix. 17.) What extraordinary light is thrown by this means upon the promises of the book of Revelation! 'To him that overcometh, will I grant to sit with me in my throne. He that overcometh, and keepeth my words unto the end, to him will I give power over the nations, and he shall rule them with a rod of iron.'

"If then we admit the Reign of Christ—if we believe that the nations of the earth will be divided among the saints—that each of them shall have some province made subject to his care—that he shall live with Christ in the heavenly city, and come down in his immortal body, visible or invisible, to encourage the righteous—to restrain the wicked—to regulate the world—to bring all things in subjection to the obedience of Christ—to be the dispensers of God's judgments and of his favors to mankind—to administer an authority which can not be resisted, and to possess a dignity which can not be impaired;—if we believe that the meanest saint, who now labors for his bread, may reach to so high an elevation, then we shall understand the force and truth of those promises: '*He shall sit with me in my throne. I will give him power over the nations.*' And we shall comprehend the fitness of that new and lofty song, which was sung by the Redeemed, around the throne: '*Thou hast redeemed us to God by thy blood, out of every kindred, and tongue, and people, and nation, and hast made us unto our God kings and priests, and we shall reign on the earth.*' What a change would come over the Christian world, were such a truth as this honestly examined, and then honestly preached. The great man would sacrifice his power, rather than lose, by worldly ambition, a greater authority in the future earth; the rich man would forsake his avarice, that he might lay hold upon those unsearchable riches of Christ. The noble would disregard his coronet, that he might be the more prepared for the crown of righteousness, and that he might wear it even upon earth, and in the sight of men. The radiant beauty of high life, whose only ambition is to dazzle for a season, would remember that a few more years would lay her in the dust, and look forward to the pure and ever youthful radiance of the glorified saint. The natural feelings and expectations of mankind will then be forced into the right channel, not by hollow preaching, which the preacher's own life contradicts, but by an irresistible power, drawn from this eternal truth: 'That whatever the earth contains, that is most precious, shall be possessed by the saints, UPON THE EARTH.' "

WHEN THE THOUSAND YEARS of the Millennium are ended, the reign of the glorified saints over the Millennial earth terminates, and the Gentile nations being left to try the experiment of self-government, and being at the same time exposed to the temptations of Satan, who is then released from incarceration, speedily manifest the corruption of the natural heart by universally apostatising. It is evident that this last generation which apostatises will never have been, like the preceding generations, truly converted; for if once converted, it could scarcely be guilty of such daring rebellion. The Jews alone remaining faithful to God, will become especially exposed to the wrath of these rebellious nations, who will forthwith proceed in countless multitudes to assault Jerusalem, but fire will come down from heaven and devour them. This Battle of Gog and Magog, so-called because the Gog and Magog nations are specially prominent in it, (Rev. xx. 8,) is similar to, but quite distinct from, the Battle of Armageddon, which occurs a thousand years earlier, and in which the Gog and Magog nations also take part, (Ezek. xxxviii.) After this the Devil is cast, not into the bottomless pit from which he was previously loosed, but into the lake of fire and brimstone, where Antichrist and the False Prophet were cast before the Millennium, and *shall be tormented day and night for ever and ever*. About the same period the renovation of the earth by fire, (2 Peter iii. 10,) which partially took place about 1000 years previously, will now be completely finished; the sea disappearing, and the New Earth and New Heavens being perfected, (Rev. xxi. 1.) The great white throne is at the same time set up, and the wicked dead are raised to life and judged before it. This Second Resurrection probably includes also the deceased Millennial saints. The judgment of the wicked appears to be a long-continued and deliberate process, in which the actions of each one of them will be made known to the assembled universe, (Rev. xx. 11–15, Luke xii. 2.) If the earth's inhabitants during the past 6000 years (excluding deceased infants) amount to only 100,000 millions, and if even a 200th part of them have been saved, the entire number of the wicked, including the innumerable Millennial apostates, (Rev. xx. 8,) will perhaps not be less than 300,000 millions, and it would occupy 34 millions of years to judge this multitude one by one, if the judgment of each lasted only for an hour; and if each stood upon a square yard of ground, they would cover a space rather more than 300 miles in length and breadth. All who have failed to become truly born again or converted will be then cast into a lake of literal fire and brimstone, in the same bodies which they had in their lifetime, and which will be raised up from the dust and rendered indestructible; they are thenceforth tormented in hell-fire for ever and ever. (Matt. xxv. 41, Rev. xx., Mark ix. 43.)

After the Millennium the EVERLASTING REIGN is established, and although death will be abolished, there will yet perhaps be successive generations living afterward upon the New Earth, since the covenant with Abraham was for a thousand generations, (Ps. cv. 8, Deut. vii. 9, Gen. ix. 12,) and in 1000 years there can only have been 270 generations. Thus *of the increase of Christ's government there shall be no end*, (Is. ix. 7,) and his saints with him will reign over the whole universe *for ever and ever*, (Rev. xxii. 5.)

A SOLEMN INQUIRY may here be put to every reader of these pages: Have you obtained that change of heart which consists in being *born again* or *converted*, and without which you can not gain admission into heaven? (John iii. 8.) You may be moral, upright, and amiable in your conduct toward your fellow-men, but yet unless you become really converted, you will be cast into hell-fire. True conversion causes a person not only to abstain from drunkenness, profanity, gambling, reading newspapers or worldly books on Sunday, or otherwise breaking the Sabbath, frequenting theatres or ball-rooms, and other openly irreligious acts; but it also leads him to take a previously unexperienced delight in private, family, and social prayer, in attending religious services, distributing tracts, visiting the sick and afflicted, and instead of criminally wasting time in reading novels or romances, to engage as much as possible in meditating on the sacred truths of the Bible. Nor is it presumption for any one who is converted to proclaim that fact to others, and to express a confident assurance of being finally saved, (Phil. i. 6,) for so great is the change of conversion, that those who have experienced it can generally remember the time and the place where they received it; and possessing the witness of the Spirit, (Rom. viii. 16,) can testify that they know and are sure that their sins are all forgiven. Neither can they ever be lost; for, at the moment of conversion, all their sins, future as well as past, those that they have not yet committed as well as those that they have committed, are entirely blotted out. The means by which this change is obtained is by offering up to God, in the name of Jesus, the simple prayer of faith, such as: "O God! for the sake of Jesus, pardon my sins and give me a new heart, and bestow upon me the influence of thy Holy Spirit." The 51st and other Psalms contain most suitable prayers of this character. And such supplications should continually be offered up by the penitent, not only on the bended knee, but also continually, at all times, and in all places; for many a prayer is inwardly breathed by Christians even while engaged in their worldly occupations. Nor should the unconverted consider themselves out of danger, until they *feel* that their prayers are answered, and *know*, from a peculiar assurance imparted to them by the Holy Ghost, that they have become converted, and that all their sins are forgiven. In order to walk closely with God, it is most important always to begin the day with spending at least about twenty or thirty minutes in prayer and in reading and meditating on the Scriptures, for such devotional exercises constitute the very mainspring of the Christian's strength.* At the present time, when with the utmost charity we can not suppose more than a tenth part even in the most Protestant countries

---

* Valuable remarks upon the necessity and advantage of a deeper study of the Scriptures and of stronger faith in God's promises are given in the *Life of Trust* (Boston: Gould & Lincoln. $1.25,) being a reprint of the *Lord's Dealings with George Müller* (London: Nisbit,) a book which the reader is strongly recommended to obtain and peruse. It shows how, by the prayer of faith, Müller has received and expended in charitable objects donations to the amount of a million dollars, and is now maintaining and educating a thousand orphans at Bristol, England, without any means of support except the contributions of the benevolent.

to be truly religious, it behooves every one to examine themselves whether they are boldly confessing Christ before men, so as to bear the character of being avowedly pious and religious, or whether they are mere nominal Christians, living in practical forgetfulness of the statement: "If any man love the world, the love of the Father is not in him." (1 John ii. 15.) Especially should true Christians arouse themselves now that there is little more than four years remaining during which the present opportunities will exist for preaching the word and circulating Bibles and religious books, which will be of such unspeakable value to those who possess them during the subsequent 3½ years' infidel persecution. A pointed and definite testimony regarding the awful judgments that will shortly accompany Christ's Advent requires to be loudly proclaimed. To this end, persons holding these views should go from place to place, giving lectures on the subject, and also preaching in the open air in the streets, market-places, or public squares, for many will never attend in-door services. Much ridicule and even persecution will be directed against those who boldly and prominently bear this testimony; but to such the promise is given: "*Rejoice and be exceeding glad, for great is your reward in heaven: for so persecuted they the prophets which were before you.*" (Matthew v. 12.) It will require, on the part of some persons, as much courage to declare Louis Napoleon to be the personal Antichrist as it required of Luther to assert that the Pope was the Papal Antichrist; but the proclamation must be made, at all hazards, in order to warn men against furthering the extension of his power, or in any way submitting themselves to his authority or influence, since it will ultimately be exerted by him for the purpose of causing them to renounce Christianity and to commit the unpardonable sin of worshipping his image. (Rev. xiv. 9.)

This chapter* may be suitably concluded by quoting the subjoined extract from appeals to the unconverted to come to Jesus and to seek the salvation of their souls:

* Those who may derive light and instruction from the perusal of these pages, are requested in return to supplicate the Giver of every good and perfect gift to accompany with his blessing the statements of divine truth as set forth by this work and its writer.

"Why did Christ, a king in the midst of heaven's glory, become a babe in the midst of earth's misery? You say: 'To save sinners!' Why did he toil, and weep, and preach, and pray, and sorrow for months and years among the worst and most hard-hearted, with hardly any reward but that of contempt, hatred, and persecution? You say: 'To save sinners!' Why did he bow his head in wondrous submission when torn with the pains of deadly agony in Gethsemane? Why was he silent when led by blaspheming murderers to the place of insult, and crowned as the king of sorrows with shame, and thorns, and misery? You say: 'It was to save sinners!' Why did he yield his body to be smitten with the hand and rod, and torn with the lacerating scourge, and pierced with the nails and spear; oh! why? You say: 'It was to save sinners!' Oh! then, if the immortal Jesus has passed through valleys of deepest humiliation — through shades of darkest misery — through flames of hottest tribulation — and the black waters of death itself — oh! if he hath sighed, and wept, and prayed, and preached, and lived and labored and suffered, and died to save sinners — to save sinners, oh! tell me, will he cast them out when they come to him? when they come and say,

'Thy blood can make the vilest clean;
Oh! let that blood avail for me!'

will he say, 'Depart thou guilty sinner'? will he say, 'I will have nothing to do with thee'? Nay, God forbid; he will rather say: 'Welcome, O thou poor penitent! welcome to the cross, O thou returning sinner! welcome to thy Saviour and to life eternal.' Can you doubt any longer? If you do, your doubt makes out Christ to be worse than you yourself are. Would not you receive a poor, benighted wanderer, in danger of dying from cold and starvation? and do you think Jesus will refuse to admit you if you seek him in wretchedness and penitence? But the case is stronger still. You would not turn your weeping child away from your door to die of hunger; and will he turn you away from his door to perish in your sins when you repent and cry for mercy? Yea, the case is still stronger. If you commanded your prodigal child to return, and promised that all should be forgiven and forgotten, and by means of those commands, and invitations, and promises prevailed with the child, and when he believed you, and came home, refused to admit him, would you not be both false and cruel? And has not Jesus, O sinner! commanded you to come, and entreated you to come, and promised 'in no wise' to reject you; and do you think he will prove so false and cruel as to break his word and cast you out? Are all your doubts now cleared away? If there is a single dark doubt still hanging over your head, and casting its shadow into your heart, take this thought and be enlightened and relieved. Now mark well: Christ never yet cast out a single sinner truly seeking him. The young and the old, the poor and the rich, the ignorant and the educated, the outwardly good, the confessedly bad, scarlet sinners and black sinners, all persons of all ages, degrees, and nations, who have ever applied to him during the past nigh two thousand years, have been alike received with compassion and treated with mercy.

"Behold him seated yonder by the way-side; some women with their children try to press through the crowd and come to him. "What do you want with him?" say the disciples; 'to bring your children to him? How foolish of you; take them away.' Christ overhears it, and straightway, with look and voice, rebukes them, and says aloud, 'Suffer little children to come unto me, and forbid them not;' and taking them in his arms, blesses them, keeping his promise: 'I will in no wise cast out.'

"Again, as he is walking along the road between Jericho and Jerusalem, with a crowd of people, a blind beggar, having found out who it is that passes, cries aloud: 'Jesus! thou Son of David, have mercy on me!' 'Hush!' say the people; 'hold your peace;' but he only crieth the louder, 'Jesus! thou Son of David, have mercy on me!' Then Christ hears, stops, and commands him to be brought, asks him what he wants, and when he answers, 'Lord, that I may receive my sight!' he touches only once his sightless eye-balls, and pours into them light and healing, keeping his promise: 'I will in no wise cast out.'

"Again, he is sitting at the table of Simon the Pharisee. A poor woman, who had been a dreadful sinner, comes behind him weeping, and stooping down, with the large, heavy tears that are falling faster than you can count from her eyes, washes his sacred feet, and then wipes them with her long locks of hair. Simon's eye is on him to see how he will act. Does he spurn the guilty woman, and crush with despair the heart already broken with sorrow? Ah! no, his soul melts with pity. 'Woman!' saith Jesus, 'thy sins are forgiven thee, go in peace!' keeping his promise: 'I will in no wise cast out.'

"Again, he is nailed to the cross of shame and glory. A wretched thief, hanging over the mouth of hell, turns to him his dying eyes; his white, furrowed face becomes stiffened with a look of intenseness of desire; his dry lips part and quiver. 'Lord!' he cries, 'remember me when thou comest into thy kingdom.' Did Christ answer, 'I can not hear you now—I am in pain; besides, it is too late—too late'? Oh! no, but he turned upon him a look in which love and sorrow shone together, and said, 'Verily, I say unto thee, to-day shalt thou be with me in paradise!' keeping his promise: 'I will in no wise cast out.'

"Come, then, O child of sin! in all thy weakness come to Jesus; he will take thee in his arms and bless thee, as he received such of old! Come, then, O sightless sinner! in all thy blindness come to Jesus; he will bid thee pray, and on thine eye-balls pour that light celestial which is 'marvellous' in power and glory everlasting! Come, then, O outcast sinner! in all thy misery come to Jesus; he will suffer thee to kneel beside him, and wash his feet with tears; and will pardon all thy guilt, and bid thee go in peace! And come, then, O dying sinner! in all thy hell-deservings come to Jesus; and he will hear thy groan of anguish, and answer thy prayer of penitence, and wash thy sins away, and carry thee to heaven! for, oh! he hath spoken of old, and hath kept in the past, and will keep till time shall be no more, this precious, ever precious promise: '*Him that cometh to me, I will in no wise cast out.*' (John vi. 37.)"

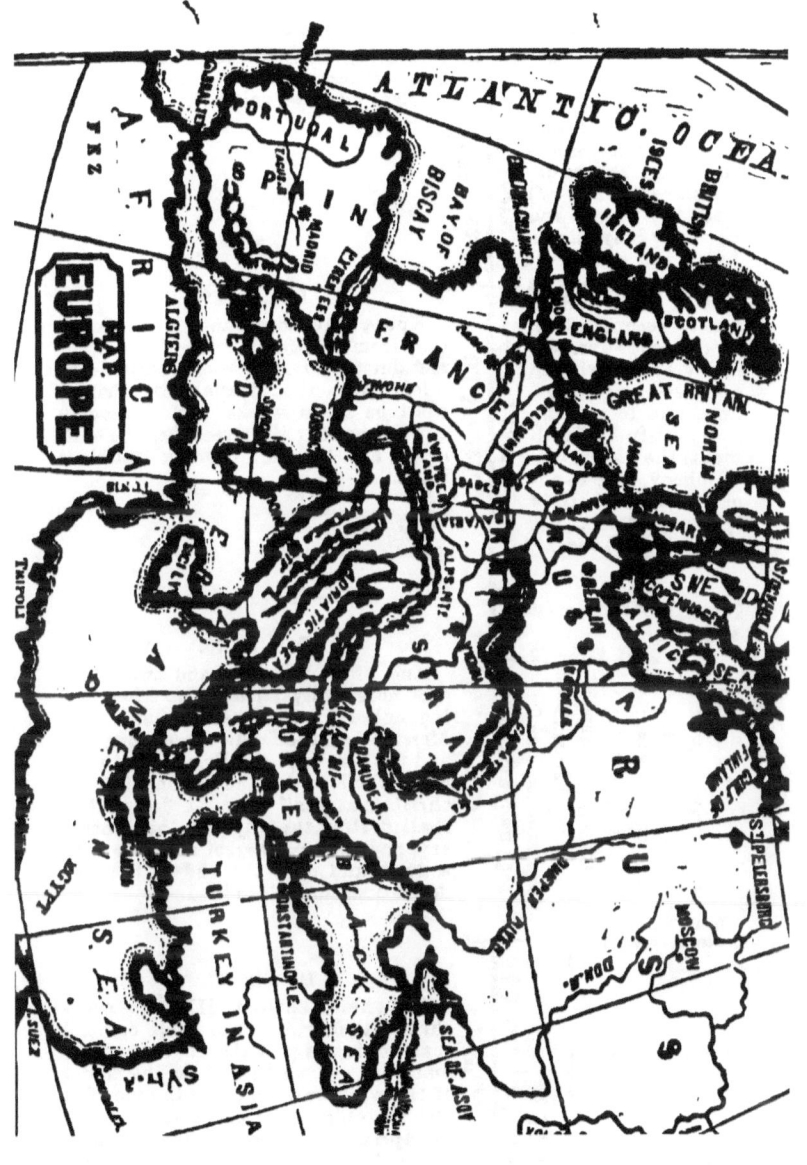

DIAGRAM 3.

FULFILMENT OF THE SEVENTY WEEKS
As subdivided into Three Parts of 7, 62, and 1 Week.

B. C. 457 or 455. — The going forth of the commandment to restore and build Jerusalem.— (Ezra vii., Nehemiah ii.)

Dan. ix. 24.
Seventy weeks (*shabua*, weeks of years— Gen. xxix. 27) are determined (or *cut off*) upon thy people and upon thy holy city, to finish the transgression, and to make an end of sins, and to make reconciliation for (or, cover over) iniquity, and to bring in everlasting righteousness, and to seal up (i. e., ratify by fulfilment) the vision and prophecy, and to anoint the Most Holy (place not person, i. e. the Holy of Holies).

49 Years. **7 Weeks.**

Dan. ix. 25.
Know, therefore, and understand, that from the going forth of the commandment to restore and to build Jerusalem, unto the Messiah the Prince, shall be seven weeks and threescore and two weeks; the street shall be built again, and the wall, even in troublous times.

434 Years. **62 Weeks.**

Messiah cut off in A. D. 29 or 33.
A. D. 27 or 29.

• nant with the Jews.
• his making a cove-
• that shall come by
• lation of the Prince
• siah, and the reve-
• cutting off of Mes-
• years between the
• of more than 1800
• ... Interval ...

Dan. ix. 26.
And after threescore and two weeks (not necessarily *immediately* after, but indefinitely, a short time after,) shall Messiah be cut off, but not for himself, and the people of the Prince that *shall come*, (the Romans, the nation of Antichrist that *shall come:* 1 Jn. ii. 18,) shall destroy the city and the sanctuary, and the end thereof shall be with a flood, and unto the end of the war desolations are determined.

Louis Napoleon makes the covenant.

His image set up in the temple.

He perishes at Christ's descent.

3½ Years | *3½ Years* *& 2½ Ms.* **1 Week.**

Dan. ix. 27.
And he (Napoleon III., the Antichrist "the Prince that shall come,") shall confirm a (not *the*) covenant with many for one week; and in the midst of the week he shall cause the sacrifice and the oblation to cease, and for the overspreading of abominations he shall make it desolate, even until the consummation, and that determined shall be poured upon the desolator.

CHAPTER III.

EVIDENCE FROM MORE THAN THIRTY EXPOSITORS SHOWING THAT DANIEL'S SEVENTIETH WEEK OF SEVEN YEARS WILL BE FULFILLED WITHIN ALMOST EXACTLY THE FINAL SEVEN YEARS OF THIS GENTILE DISPENSATION, AND WILL COMMENCE WITH A SEVEN YEARS' COVENANT BEING CONFIRMED BETWEEN THE PERSONAL ANTICHRIST AND THE JEWS. THEREFORE LOUIS NAPOLEON, IF HE IS THE PERSONAL ANTICHRIST, WILL CONFIRM A SEVEN YEARS' COVENANT WITH THE JEWS ABOUT SEVEN YEARS BEFORE THE END.

THE faith of professing Christians is about to be tested by a signal and extraordinary fulfilment of prophecy, which will be despised and rejected by those who are "fools, and slow of heart to believe all that the prophets have spoken," (Luke xxiv. 27,) but will be distinctly understood by the wise and watchful, so as to enable them to discover the date of Christ's approaching Advent. It was very generally believed by the early Christian Church, that Daniel's 70th week would be fulfilled at the time of the Second Advent, by the Antichrist being received by many of the Jews as their Messiah, and subsequently placing his image, "the abomination of desolation," in the rebuilt Jewish temple, which would thus be defiled during the latter half-week—the 3½ years of his tyranny. This view was very little advocated during the dark ages of papal corruption, but during the last half-century it has been extensively revived. It is thus expected that seven years before the End, Antichrist "will confirm a covenant with many of the Jews for one week of seven years, and in the midst of the week will cause the sacrifice to cease, even until the Consummation, (or End.)" As Louis Napoleon is clearly foreshown to be the Antichrist, and as the End appears, from the chronological prophecies, to be about or soon after 1872, therefore it now remains to be seen whether these interpretations will be proved to be true, by Napoleon making a seven-years' covenant with the Jews about or soon after 1864–5, Humanly speaking, there is no particular reason why Napoleon should ever make a covenant with the Jews, much less that it should be for exactly seven and not any other number of years; and also that, just about 9 or 10 months after the date of the covenant, the Jews should re-establish morning and evening sacrifices in some building then used by them as a temple. The little probability of such events so soon taking place, will, however, render their occurrence all the more remarkable.* but even then there will doubtless be unscrupulous and unprincipled individuals, including, perhaps, some persons of reputed piety, who, to obtain notoriety, or for the sake of gain, will labour, with plausible and specious arguments, to show that these events do not prove Christ's Advent to be near at hand. Or what will be almost as bad, some preachers, unwilling to encounter ridicule and opposition, shunning to declare the whole counsel of God, and being ashamed of these words of Jesus, (Acts xx. 27, Luke ix. 26,) will be content to maintain a shameful silence upon the subject.

But as an exterminating persecution will be carried on during the latter half of the seven years throughout all Christendom and many parts of Heathendom against those who will not worship Napoleon's image, or receive his mark, (Rev. xiii.) it is therefore necessary to warn persons at once that the commission of that act will be an unpardonable sin (Rev. xiv. 9) like that of blasphemy against the Holy Ghost. It will be too late to proclaim the warning when the persecution actually begins, for the voice of testimony will then be violently stifled. Now at the present time, and especially as soon as the covenant shall be made, believers in these prophecies should labour widely to diffuse these Second Advent and other Gospel truths, even thus expending all their property except what may be required to support them until the Ascension of the Wise

* In the author's "Coming Battle," published in 1860, Louis Napoleon was spoken of as certain to make the seven-years' Covenant with the Jews very soon. In this enlarged edition (1862) of the present work, Chapters I. III. and IV. are fundamentally the same as in the first edition, in June, 1861, in which the substance of Chapter II. was not inserted.

Virgins, two years and five or six weeks after the Covenant. Only those who practically evince their faith by acting thus, can reasonably expect to be caught up among the Wise Virgins.

THE IMPORTANT PROPHECY of seventy weeks, which are universally admitted to be seventy weeks, or *sevens* of years, that is, 490 years, is contained in Dan. ix. 24—27.

Seventy weeks are determined upon thy people and upon thy holy city, to finish the transgression, and to make an end of sins, and to make reconciliation for (or cover over) iniquity, and to bring in everlasting righteousness, and to seal up the vision and prophecy, and to anoint the Most Holy, (*in the Hebrew*, the Most Holy Place.) 25. Know therefore and understand, that from the going forth of the commandment to restore and to build Jerusalem unto the Messiah the Prince shall be seven weeks, and threescore and two weeks: the street shall be built again, and the wall, even in troublous times. 26. And after threescore and two weeks shall Messiah be cut off, but not for himself: and the people of the prince that shall come shall destroy the city and the sanctuary; and the end thereof shall be with a flood, and unto the end of the war desolations are determined. 27. And he shall confirm the covenant with many for one week: and in the midst of the week he shall cause the sacrifice and the oblation to cease, and for the overspreading of abominations, he shall make it desolate, even until the consummation, and that determined shall be poured upon the desolate.

The true explanation of this prophecy appears to be, that seventy weeks of years dated from the going forth of the decree in Artaxerxes' 7th year, were marked off as the period of God's dealings with the Jews while nationally gathered in their own city, and were to end with their complete redemption and deliverance, as described in verse 24. Had the Jews received the Messiah, when he officially came to them at the end of the 69 weeks by the Baptist's preaching and by his own public ministry, then apparently the 70th week would have followed continuously, and would have closed with the Son of David reigning over the house of Jacob for ever. But their rejection of Jesus caused the fulfilment of the 70th week to be postponed until they should be fully punished for that sin, and then the 70th week, after running its course, will end as originally intended, with the setting up of Messiah's temporal kingdom over Israel, and the bringing in of everlasting righteousness. Thus Israel's rejection of Christ has interposed between the 69th and 70th week, the long interval of the Gentile dispensation during which they are punished by their house being left unto them desolate.

This prediction must extend to the Second Advent, when the desolation of the Jews and of their holy city shall be finished, for it was given by Gabriel in answer to Daniel's prayer for the restoration of Israel to Palestine, and is intended to forewarn him of all their sufferings prior to their final deliverance. It could not, therefore, omit to mention their final and greatest persecution by the last Antichrist, which is the principal theme of Daniel and Revelation, (see also Ezek. xxxviii, Zech. xiv.) It was also declared to be an explanation of THE VISION, (verse 23) which could be none other than the last vision Daniel beheld in Dan. viii., which was expressly stated to relate to the *time of the end*, and to *the last end of the indignation* when *the transgressors are come to the full*, (Dan. viii. 17, 19, 23,) and which was not then understood, (verse 27,) and therefore received further explanation in Dan. ix.

That the 70th week is hitherto unfulfilled, clearly appears from reading, in their strictly consecutive order, the verses containing the prophecy.

VERSE 24. Seventy weeks are cut off, or measured out, as a period, which, with respect to the Jewish people and their city, Jerusalem, is to terminate with the finishing of the transgression, the making an end of sins, the bringing in of everlasting righteousness, &c., &c., and the anointing of the Holy Place (not the Holy Person.) All this cannot have been completely fulfilled with respect to Jerusalem and the Jews at the Crucifixion, for Jerusalem has ever since been desolate, and the sins of the Jews have been had in especial remembrance; but it will be fulfilled at the restoration and conversion of the Jews, after the Second Advent, when they "shall all be righteous," (Is. lx. 21,) and when the Holy Place in their rebuilt temple shall be anointed and consecrated for the perpetual worship of God.

VERSE 25. Seven and sixty-two weeks, altogether sixty-nine weeks, are explained to commence with the decree for restoring Jerusalem, which is generally understood to be

Ezra's* decree, in A. D. 457, in Artaxerxes' 7th year, and they are to reach "unto Messiah the Prince;" that is, unto his official presentation to Israel in A. D. 26, most probably by the preaching of John the Baptist. The ministry of the latter is believed to have lasted for 3½ years, and the subsequent ministry of Christ for a period of the same length. This seven years would fill up the interval from A. D. 26 to A. D. 33, if the latter date was the time of the Crucifixion. But if, as some think, the birth of Christ was four years before the Christian era, then his Crucifixion was in A. D. 29, and in that case, his official presentation to Israel in A. D. 26, would consist in the commencement of his public ministry, (Luke iii. 23.)

VERSE 26. After 69 weeks, Messiah was to be cut off, but not immediately after, because there must be some short interval between his official coming at the end of the 69 weeks, and his death. This latter event does not appear to have happened until about A. D. 29 or A. D. 33–4. After this, the Romans, *the people of* THE PRINCE THAT

* There were three commandments, or public decrees, as it appears, issued concerning the temple or city of Jerusalem. THE FIRST was given by Cyrus in 536 B. C., (Ez. i.,) but the erection of the temple, after being commenced, was discontinued until B. C. 519, the second year of Darius, who, in that year, issued the SECOND DECREE, (Ez. iv. 24,) and the temple was finished in his sixth year, (Ez. vi. 15.) But irregularities and abuses, in connection with the temple-worship, having afterwards crept in, a THIRD DECREE was given in B. C. 457, to Ezra, by Artaxerxes Longimanus, in his seventh year, (Ez. vii.) This decree, unlike the two former, related to the restoring of *the city*, as well as of *the temple*, for it commissioned Ezra "*to inquire concerning Judah and Jerusalem according to the law of thy God which is in thy hand*," (Ez. vii. 14,) and afterwards Ezra thanked God for having, "*extended mercy to us to set up the house of our God, and to repair the desolations thereof, and to give us a wall in Judah and Jerusalem*," (*the wall* built in troublous times, Dan ix. 25.) This decree is generally understood to be the commencement of the seventy weeks, (Dan. ix. 25.) Nehemiah's commission in the 20th year of Artaxerxes, seems to have been not a public decree or commandment, but only a private and personal commission, causing him to enforce and carry out more effectually the previous decree of Ezra, with whom he united his efforts. But whether the 69 weeks began with Ezra's or Nehemiah's commission, does not affect the 70th week, which is separated from them by more than 1800 years. Almost all writers, whatever chronology they adopt, allow the 69 weeks to end about A. D. 26–33.

SHALL COME, that is, of the future Antichrist, destroyed the city and the sanctuary of Jerusalem in A. D. 70. The construction of the language evidently requires "the Prince that shall come," to be the person who confirms the covenant in the next verse. He is also referred to in 1 John ii. 18, "Ye have heard that the Antichrist shall come." The phrase, "Ye have heard," implies, as in Matt. v. 38, "Ye have been told in Scripture." And this is obviously one of the passages which had informed the apostles that Antichrist (the Prince) "shall come."

VERSE 27. "And he shall confirm a (not the) covenant with many for one week (of years)." The person who shall confirm this covenant is evidently "the Prince that shall come," mentioned in the former verse, in apposition to Messiah the Prince, who had previously been cut off; the one being the future Antichrist, the false Messiah, and the other being the already crucified Christ, the true Messiah. Antichrist's Covenant with the Jews will be only for seven years, and even then not observed for more than half that time; but Christ's covenant with them will be an everlasting one, (Isa. lxi. 8.) The making of Antichrist's Covenant is mentioned abruptly as taking place some indefinite time after the cutting off of Messiah, spoken of in verse 26; and plainly cannot have yet occurred, because no "Prince of the Roman people," that is, no Head of the Roman Empire, has ever yet made a seven-years' Covenant with the Jews, and afterwards caused their restored sacrifices to cease, and placed his image, the abomination, in their temple. Moreover, it is shown in Rev. xiii. and xvii. that the Roman Prince, whose image, "the abomination," will be worshipped for 42 months, the last half of the 7 years, is the seventh-eighth, or last Head of the Roman Empire, that is, Louis Napoleon. And in Dan. xi. 21 to the end of Dan. xii. he is described as "a vile person," or wilful king, (see Chap. II., Event 4,) who, at the time of the End shall perish upon the glorious holy mountain of Palestine, and his previous Covenant with the Jews is mentioned no less than FIVE TIMES in Dan. xi. 22, 23, 28, 30, 32, (as held also by Tregelles, Strange, Kelsall, etc.) This Covenant is also mentioned in Isaiah xxviii. 18, xxxiii. 8, Psalm lv. 20.

No objection can reasonably be urged against interposing

nearly the whole of the Gentile Dispensation between the 69th and the 70th weeks,* for it has been justly said, that "Daniel's prophecies reach to the end of the world, and there is scarce a prophecy in the Old Testament concerning Christ which does not, in something or other, relate to his second coming." Examples of a sudden transition in the prophecies from Christ's first to his second coming, overlooking the long interval of the Gentile Dispensation, are not unfrequent. The sojourn of Christ in Capernaum is predicted in Isaiah ix. 1, 2, (compare Matt. iv. 14,) but the next three verses describe his final triumph over Antichrist at Armageddon. This last named occurrence is also spoken of in Zech. ix. 10, but the preceding verse mentions Christ's riding on an ass into Jerusalem; (compare Matt. xxi. 5,) although there is more than 1800 years between the two events. It might similarly appear from Micah v. 2, that the complete deliverance and restoration of Israel was to take place immediately after the birth of Christ in Bethlehem, (see Matt. ii. 5, John vii. 42.) So again in Jer. xxxi. 10—17, Joel ii. 28—32, Isaiah xi. 8, 4,

* While it has been almost universally admitted that the 7 and 62 weeks ended before the crucifixion of Christ, according to the plain statement, "After threescore and two weeks shall Messiah be cut off," yet many modern Commentators have glaringly erred respecting the remaining 70th week, by superficially concluding that it follows immediately after the 69 weeks. The strange discordance of their interpretations has sufficiently evinced the untenableness of this view. They have variously alleged that John the Baptist, or the Messiah, made a seven-years' Covenant with the Jews, although there is no evidence whatever in support of such a notion, and some have placed "the cutting off of the Messiah" in the midst, others at the end of the 70th week, though it is mentioned in verse 25 as occurring after the 69th and before the 70th week. Other Commentators, like Gill and Lloyd, have come a little nearer the truth by admitting that it is not "Messiah the Prince," but "the Prince that shall come," in verse 26, who is to confirm the Covenant for seven years, and taking the 69 weeks to end before the crucifixion, in A. D. 33, they place the 70th week from A. D. 63 to A. D. 70, when Jerusalem was destroyed by the armies of Titus, whom they suppose to be "the Prince that shall come." This arrangement is not quite so erroneous as the others, since it allows a break, or interval, between the 69th and 70th weeks, but it is untenable, inasmuch as Titus made no seven-years' Covenant with the Jews, nor can the sacrifice be shown to have ceased in A. D. 67, nor did Titus perish in A. D. 70.

lii. 13—15, xl. 3—5, and in Isaiah lxi. 1, 2, compared with Luke iv. 19, 20, prophecies relating to Christ's First Advent abruptly pass on, and merge into those referring to his Second Advent.

It is manifest that soon after Antichrist's covenant with the Jews the sacrifices will be renewed, because "in the midst of the week he shall cause the sacrifice and oblation to cease," and (as the Septuagint renders it) "in the temple shall be the abomination of desolation, even until THE CONSUMMATION, and that determined (namely, the plague of the vials) shall be poured upon the desolater." The word "abomination" in Greek constantly signifies "an idol." It is rendered, in 2 Chron. xv. 8, "the abominable idols," and used in the passage, "Chemosh the abomination of the Moabites." It here signifies Antichrist's image, that will stand in the temple from "the midst of the seven years" even until the End or Consummation, when Antichrist shall be destroyed at Christ's descent at Armageddon. The latter half of the seven years is plainly identical with the 3½ years which is mentioned in Dan. vii., xii., and Rev. xi., xii., xiii., as the period of Antichrist's persecution; but 30 and 45 additional days, altogether 75 days more, are given in Dan. xii. 11, 12, as the interval occupied with his subsequent overthrow by the literal-day outpouring of the vials. Thus there will be seven years and 2½ months (75 days) from the beginning of the 70th week at the date of the Covenant, until Antichrist's complete overthrow at Christ's descent upon Mount Olivet.

MORE THAN FIFTY EXPOSITORS are enumerated below who substantially interpret the 70th week in this manner. Among them are five Bishops of the early Church, whose distinct expression of this belief accords with the well-ascertained fact that the primitive Christians, some of whom had conversed with the Apostles themselves, (2 Thess. ii. 5,) almost universally entertained these views; the extracts from them are quoted in B. W. Newton's "Ten Kingdoms," and Maitland's "Apostolic School."

It may prevent repetition, to mention preliminarily, that futurist literal-day expositors, such as Burgh, Denny, Tregelles, Kelsall, B. W. Newton, Kelly, Molyneux, Scott Phillips, Guinness, etc., distinctly state that THE Antichrist *of* Man of Sin (2 Thess. ii.) is the same person as the eighth or last Head of the Beast, who is called in Revelation the Beast himself: also the same as "the little horn" of Dan. vii., and "the little horn or king of fierce countenance" of Dan. viii. and "the Prince that shall come" of Dan. ix. 26, 27, and the wilful king of Dan. xi. 36; and that he is not the Pope, but an individual man who shall perish at Christ's descent, about seven years after his covenant with the Jews. They likewise generally consider that the ten horn or toe kingdoms (Dan ii. 44, Rev. xvii. 12,) have not yet been completely formed within the whole territory of the Roman Empire; and that the abomination of desolation (Matt. xxiv., Mark xiii.) is the future image of Antichrist which will stand in the Jewish temple; and that the two witnesses (Rev. xi.) will be two real persons who will prophesy during the literal 1260 days or 3½ years of Antichrist's tyranny. They hold, moreover, that the 3½ years mentioned in Dan. vii. xii. and Rev. xi. xii. xiii. as *a time, times and a half*, or 42 *months*, etc. is the 3½ years of the Antichrist's future persecution, and is identical with the latter half of Daniel's 70th week of seven years, which commence with a seven-years' covenant being made between the Antichrist and the Jews. This does not conflict with the view that there has been a typical yearday fulfilment of that 3½ *times*, as 1260 years of Papal dominancy; and of the "little horns" of Dan. vii. and viii. as the Papal and Mahometan powers respectively.

In reading the works of literal-day expositors who interpret the 1260 days, 3½ times, and 42 months, to mean 1260 *literal days*, or 3½ years, and of yearday expositors who interpret the same periods to mean 1260 *years*, the prophetic student must not be stumbled at their sometimes mutually rejecting each other's views. Each system of interpretation is, however, equally correct, for there is a double fulfilment of most of the prophecies of Daniel and Revelation, primarily in years and secondly in days.

The certainty of England's submission to the Personal Antichrist because it was part of the original Roman Empire, is virtually admitted by Sir E. Denny, Purdon,*

---

* In the Last Vials for 1858, No. 6, (at G. J. Stevenson's, 54 Paternoster Row, London,) Purdon says, "As Britain is part of

Tregelles, B. W. Newton, Burgh, Kelsall, Taunton, and others, who fully acknowledge that all the old Roman Empire, Eastern as well as Western, including of course England, will undergo a final tenfold division, and fall completely under the power of the Antichrist, or Eighth Head, (Rev. xvii. 12.) About thirty out of the following fifty writers distinctly hold that Christ will translate the Wise Virgins to the heavens *before* the latter half-week or $3\frac{1}{2}$ years' Antichristian persecution : and twelve, including Purdon in 1852, Porter in 1856, Taunton in 1857, Scott Phillips in 1859, and the English author of "Armageddon" in 1858, have expressly shown Louis Napoleon to be the Antichrist who will make a seven-years' covenant with the Jews. The following are the extracts from the fifty writers referred to.

(1.) IRENÆUS, who was a Bishop in the primitive Church and a disciple of Polycarp, who was a companion of the Apostle John, wrote in A. D. 180 a work "against the heresies." He considered the worship of Antichrist and his image in the Jewish temple just before the Second Advent, to be the threatened abomination of desolation, and expected Daniel's 70th week to be fulfilled by Antichrist, of whom he says, "Putting away idols to persuade man that he is God, he will set up himself as a sole idol, combining in himself the manifold errors of all the idols. . . . He will sit in the temple of God, showing himself that he is God. In the temple at Jerusalem the adversary will sit, striving to show himself* to be the Christ: as also the Lord says, (Matt. xxiv. 15,) "When ye shall see the abomination of desolation, spoken of by Daniel the prophet, standing in the holy place, &c. . . . They shall believe, it says, in the False one, (the Man of Sin, 2 Thess. ii. 12,) that all may be condemned who believed

the Roman Empire we cannot discover the slightest hint in Scripture as to the probability of her escape from the tyranny of the Beast. . . Britain as part of the Roman Empire will, we believe, be subject to Antichrist," (whom he shows to be Napoleon III.)

* In these quotations the author of the present work has, for the assistance of the reader, occasionally inserted references to the chapters and verses of the texts spoken of, where such references were not in the original. For the sake of brevity in quoting from these thirty writers, much of what some of them advance on various points, is necessarily omitted.

not the truth, but had pleasure in unrighteousness. His coming John thus describes in the Apocalypse, (Rev. xiii:) The Beast, which I saw, was like unto a leopard, &c. And afterwards of his armour-bearer, whom he calls also the false prophet, (Rev. xix. 20,) He spake, it says, (Rev. xiii. 12,) like a dragon, and he exerciseth all the power of the first Beast before him, &c. This is said that all may know his miracles to be done not by divine power, but by magic art; and no wonder, if having demons and apostate spirits to help him, he through them performs miracles by which he deceives those that dwell on the earth. He will also command them to make an image to the Beast. (Cap. 28.)

"At the half of the hebdomad (or week) Daniel saith, (Dan. ix. 27,) the sacrifice and libation shall be taken away, and in the temple shall be the abomination of desolation and until the consummation of the time, a consummation shall be appointed upon the desolation—but the half of the hebdomad is three years and six months." (*Irenæus adver. Heres.* ch. 25.)

"And when this Antichrist shall have laid waste all things in the world, reigning three years and six months, and sitting in the temple of Jerusalem; then the Lord shall come from heaven in clouds, in the glory of the Father: and casting him and those that obey him into the lake of fire, will bring about to the just the times of the kingdom; that is, the rest, even the seventh day made holy. And he will restore to Abraham the promise of the inheritance; in which kingdom, saith the Lord, many shall come from the East and from the West, and shall sit down with Abraham, with Isaac, and with Jacob." (Cap. 30.)

(2.) HIPPOLYTUS, BISHOP OF OSTIA, (A. D. 220,) considered 69 of Daniel's 70 weeks to end with the first Coming of Christ, and that then, after the Gospel had been universally preached, Antichrist's abomination of desolation would be set up during the last half week of the 70th week, which would terminate with Christ's Second Advent upon the earth. The following are extracts from his works. "When the sixty-two weeks have been fulfilled, and Christ has come, and the Gospel has been preached in every place, and the times have run out, there will remain one week—

the last in which Enoch and Elias will come. And in the midst of that week there will appear the abomination of desolation, until Antichrist announces (or "even Antichrist who announces," as the Roman editor suggests,) desolation to the world. . . . And this the prophets Enoch and Elias will declare, saying, Believe not the coming enemy; for he is an adversary and destroyer, and son of perdition, he will deceive you and bring you -to ruin. But the sword shall smite them. . . . . And the dragon, it says, (Rev. xii.) beheld, and he persecuted the woman that brought forth the man-child. And there were given her the two wings of that great eagle, that she should flee to the desert, where she is nourished for a time, times and half a time, from the face of the serpent. These are the 1260 days, even the half-week during which the tyrant will rule, persecuting the Church as she flees from city to city. . . Blessed they who will then conquer the tyrant, they will take rank above former martyrs as more exalted and more glorious. With what praises and crowns will they not be adorned by Jesus Christ our King. . .

"The six thousand years must needs be fulfilled that the Sabbath may come—even the Rest, that holy day on which God rested from all his works. The Sabbath then is a type and image of the future kingdom of the saints when they shall reign with Christ after his coming down from heaven, as John declares in the Apocalypse. For a day of the Lord is as a thousand years.

JULIUS AFRICANUS (A. D. 220) was a cotemporary of Hippolytus, and is stated in the Rev. Dr. Burgh's "Second Advent Lectures," and by Jerome, to have considered the last half of Daniel's 70th week to be identical with the future Antichrist's 3½ years, but this statement being contradicted by others seems to be incorrect.

(3) THE CELEBRATED ORIGEN (A. D. 225) explained Dan. ix. 27 to be fulfilled by the future Antichrist, as will be seen from the last paragraph of the following extract from his works. "Through the assistance of his father, the devil, that wicked one will perform miracles, and signs, and wonders of a lie. For as wonders were wrought by magicians, through the help of those demons who seduced man into wickedness, so this man will receive from the devil himself power to do yet greater wonders to deceive

the human race. And concerning the so-called Antichrist, Paul speaks, teaching us, though with some reserve, the manner, the time, and the cause of his visiting the human race. And now, see if Paul has not spoken on this subject in a manner most grave, and not deserving even the slightest ridicule. 'We beseech you, brethren, by the coming of the Lord,' &c., 2 Thess. ii.

"To explain the whole of this is not our present business. But there is in Daniel a prophecy about this same Antichrist which cannot but excite the admiration of any one who will read it with common sense and candour. For there, in words truly divine and prophetic, are described the kingdoms that were to come, beginning from the time of Daniel, down to the destruction of the world. And this prophecy may be read of all men. Now see if Antichrist is not spoken of there also in these words: 'In the end of their kingdom, when their transgressions are filled up, there shall rise a king impudent of face, and understanding problems,' &c., (Dan. viii.)

"And that which I have already quoted from the words of Paul, that he will sit in the temple of God, showing himself that he is God—even this also is said by Daniel, and in this manner: 'In the temple shall be the abomination of desolations; and until the end of the time shall a consummation be given against the desolation,'" (quoting apparently from the Septuagint of Dan. ix. 27.)

(4.) VICTORINUS, BISHOP OF PETTAU, in Austria, and one of the Diocletian martyrs, wrote a Commentary on the Apocalypse about A. D. 290. He is stated, in Elliott's "Appendix on the History of Prophetical Interpretation," and in Maitland's "Apostles' School of Prophecy," (p. 202,) to have held the latter half of Daniel's 70th week to be identical with Antichrist's future 3½ years' persecution, and therefore all the 70th week to be yet unfulfilled. He says of this persecution, "The black horse (under the 3d seal, Rev. vi. 5,) means famine, for the Lord says, 'There shall be famine in divers places.' Now this saying properly extends to the time of Antichrist, when there will be a great famine, by which all men shall suffer. . . . . In the trumpets and vials there are described the execution wrought by the plagues sent upon the world, the madness of Antichrist himself, the blasphemy of the people, the variety of their plagues, the hope in the kingdom of the saints, the fall of the cities, and the fall of that great city, Babylon, that is Rome. . . . The Lord says in the Gospel, 'Then let them which be in Judea flee to the mountains,' that is, let as many as are gathered together in Judea, go to that place which is prepared for them, and be nourished there for three years and six months from the face of the Devil, (Rev. xii. 14, 15.) The water which the serpent casts out of his mouth, represents the army which he will send in pursuit of her; by the earth opening its mouth and swallowing the waters, is shown the vengeance that will be inflicted at the moment. . . .

"The False Prophet will cause a golden image to be set up to Antichrist in the temple of Jerusalem, and into this image the vagabond angel will enter, emitting voices and oracles. He will also cause both bond and free to receive a mark on their foreheads, or on their right hands, even the name, that none may buy or sell without it. Now Daniel had foretold this abomination and provocation, saying, 'He will set up his temple upon the glorious and holy mountain;' that is, he will then set up in Jerusalem an image, such as Nebuchadnezzar made. This the Lord explains, admonishing his churches against the last times and dangers, saying, 'When ye shall see the abomination spoken of by Daniel the prophet standing in the holy place,'" &c. (Matt. xxiv. 15, Dan. xi. 45.)

(5.) APOLLINARIUS, BISHOP OF LAODICEA, (A. D. 380,) as quoted by Jerome on Dan. ix., explained Daniel's 70th week to be awaiting its fulfilment at the end of this age in the time of Antichrist, whose 3½ years' persecution will synchronise with its latter half, and whose statue, then set up in the Jewish temple, will be the abomination of desolation. Maitland, Burgh, and B. W. Newton speak of him as entertaining this view.

(6.) PRIMASIUS, BISHOP OF THE CARTHAGENIAN PROVINCE, (A. D. 500,) who published a treatise on the Apocalypse, similarly considered Daniel's 70th week to be the last seven years of the Christian era, ending with Christ's descent to destroy Antichrist, whose 3½ years' universal reign would be the latter half of the 70th week, (as stated in Elliott's Appendix on the history of prophetic interpretation); this seems to have been the case also with other writers in the primitive Church, such as Barnabas, &c., whose works are not at hand to quote from.

(7.) THE REV. DR. BURGH, of the Church of England, published some able Lectures on the Second Advent, in Dublin in 1830–32, and also subsequently a very useful literal-day Exposition of the Revelation, both giving the same interpretation of Dan. ix. 27. In the former he says, "That Antichrist sets up 'the abomination of desolation' in Matt. xxiv. 16, I think further proved from the prophecies of Daniel, alluded to by the Lord Jesus. There are three passages in Daniel, where 'the abomination of desolation' is spoken of, and the first to which I would refer, is the continuous prophecy of chapters x. xi. and xii. In this context it is indeed twice mentioned, but it is very important to observe that the two notices, though rather far asunder, are one: the first foretelling '*the setting up,*' and the other, '*the duration*' of the abomination, (Dan. xi. 31, xii. 11.) The whole prophecy of these chapters, it will be observed, respects what should befall Daniel's people in the latter days, (Dan. x. 14.) . . . To proceed to the only other mention of 'the abomination of desolation' by this prophet, viz., that in connection with the prophecy of the seventy weeks, (Dan. ix. 24–27)—whatever difficulty there may be in forming a connected view of this prophecy, there is one thing about which I think there can be no doubt, viz., that it extends to the Second Advent of Christ, and includes *its* objects, as well as those of the First. For, independent of the words 'unto Messiah the PRINCE,' perhaps 'the determination upon Daniel's people and holy city'—'the finishing of transgression, making an end of sins and reconciliation for iniquity,' are expressions which in their application to the Jewish nation must be referred to another time than the First Advent, which was a day of vengeance to them, and the infliction of a judgment under which they still remain. The whole period is seventy weeks, (*i. e.* 'sevens,' or periods of seven years,) and this period is divided into parts of 62 and 7 and 1. The 'sixty-two,' we are informed, (verse 26,) reach to the First Coming and death of Christ. . . . There is yet one week to be accounted for, the last of the seventy, which we perceive is considered in the prophecy distinct from the 'sixty-two' and 'seven.' This last week it is with which our present subject has principally to do, and for its events we are referred to verses 26, 27. . . . 'The prince that shall come,' I take to be the last enemy of the Jewish people, the last invader of the holy city, 'the Antichrist.' His confirming the covenant with many for one *seven* (seven years,) I think is the same 'league' and 'deceitful working' and 'corruption by flattery' mentioned chap. xi. 23, 32, by which it would appear he will impose himself on many of the Jews and delude them, as the event proves, to their destruction. For half of the week (3½ years) he is true to this covenant; but he then breaks it, and for the last half, the remaining 3½ years, 'the time, times, and a half,' '42 months,' or '1260 days,' he causes the sacrifice and the oblation to cease, and for the overspreading of *abominations* he makes *desolate,*' or as the words evidently imply and another prophecy has expressed it, 'he places the abomination that maketh desolate.' That this last 'half-week' applies to the times of Antichrist I find to have been the opinion of the ancient fathers, as, for instance, *Irenæus, Julius Africanus, Hippolytus the martyr,* and *Apollinaris,* Bishops of Laodicea." (Pp. 140, 147, 152.)

Dr. Burgh, like other literal-day expositors, understands "the temple of God" in which the Man of Sin is to sit, (2 Thess. ii.,) to be the rebuilt temple at Jerusalem, in which the Jews will offer sacrifices soon after making the Covenant. He also considers that the final Antichristian apostasy will be far worse and more terrible than Popery; and that Antichrist's persecution and slaughter of the saints, who will not worship his image during the last half-week, or 3½ years, will prevail not merely in the Roman earth, but throughout all Christendom, until Christ's descent at Armageddon, (pp. 117, 181.) He says of Antichrist, (p. 89,) "No indecision of character or profession, no slackness of devotion or service, no merely nominal religion will be allowed; but his (Antichrist's) pretensions will be enforced by the alternative of Life or Death, and 'as many as will not worship him shall be killed.' In a word, he will realize his prophetic name of 'Antichrist'—denying Christ, by saying that he is the Christ, denying God, by saying he is the true God—owned by the unbelieving Jew as the Messiah, the Hope of Israel, and taking the wise of the Gentiles in their own craftiness, administering to their pride of reason, and desire for external evidence, 'deceiving them that dwell on the earth by means of the MIRACLES which he doeth,' (Rev. xiii.)

"That a monster of iniquity and blasphemy should accomplish the times of the Gentiles, and precede the establishment of Messiah's kingdom, was apprehended, more or less distinctly, even by the Jews of old, to whom the name 'Antichrist' (*i. e.* Anti-Messiah) was not unknown; but was fully acknowledged by the first believers in Christianity. Type and prophecy alike foreboded a last struggle with a WICKED ONE, the fulfiller and consummater of transgression, and thence also of Divine indignation—the rod of chastisement to 'the holy people,' and at the same time the scourge of the apostate nations. . . . The character of this enemy, moreover, as gathered from the prophecies, was, in general, that he should rival all his types and predecessors in tyranny, blasphemy, and oppression; that he should be supported by a confederacy of the nations, while his fury should be principally directed (as was that of all his precursors) against Israel; and that he should ultimately fall before Messiah standing up to avenge his people 'on the mountains and in the land of Israel,' and by means altogether superhuman. . . . 'The words of Bishop Horsley are well worthy of attention. 'The *Son of Perdition*, who is to rise out of an open, undisguised apostacy. That Son of Perdition, who shall be neither a Protestant nor a Papist; neither Christian, Jew, nor Heathen; who shall worship neither God, angel, nor saint; who will neither supplicate the Invisible Majesty of Heaven, nor fall down before an idol. He will magnify HIMSELF against everything that is called God, or is worshipped; and with a bold flight of impiety, soaring far above his precursors and types in the times of Paganism— the Sennacheribs, the Nebuchadnezzars, the Antiochuses, and the Heathen Emperors, *will claim divine honours to himself exclusively*, and consecrate an image of himself.' Bishop Horsley adds: 'I doubt not but this monster will be made an instrument of that pruning which the Vine (Isa. xviii. 5) must undergo,'" (pp. 54, 90.)

(8, and 9.) THE REV. EDWARD BICKERSTETH and Rev. T. Birks, Secretary of the Evangelical Alliance, unitedly wrote the chapter on Chronological Prophecies in Bickersteth's Guide to the Prophecies, published in 1839. The eminent piety, profound research into prophecy, and unsurpassed soundness of judgment of Bickersteth, give great weight to his views. They both distinctly affirmed their belief that the 2300 and 1335 years (Dan. viii. 14, xii. 12) would end about 1868, as the epoch of the Consummation, and that Christ would come to remove the Philadelphian saints, or Wise Virgins, before the last $3\frac{1}{2}$ years, from about 1864 to 1868; for they remarked upon Rev. xiii. 18, (p. 180,) "If taken as a date—in its rise from 533, 666 brings us to 1198-9, the time of Innocent III. From 1198-9, 666 brings us to 1864, just before Daniel's time of blessedness, leaving us only a period of half-a-week, mentioned in Dan. ix. 27, for the infidel persecution, from which the Philadelphian Church was saved, (Rev. iii. 10, xviii. 10;) but the Laodicean part left in it to be purified, and to be the last gathering of the Church to the marriage supper." By Jewish reckoning, 1864 ends about April or September 1865, and 1868 about April or September 1869. Moreover, 534 seems, rather than 533, to be the commencement of the Papal 1260 years' supremacy. Thus Bickersteth's and Birks' interpretation may be considered virtually to assign about 1865 for the translation of the Wise Virgins, and 1869-70 for the final Consummation, and therefore 1862-3 for the commencement of the 70th week, by the making of the covenant. Bickersteth, although a staunch year-day expositor, admitted that there would probably be an ultimate reduplicated literal fulfilment of many parts of Daniel and Revelation in connection with the last infidel Antichrist, who, as Birks shows from Dan. xi., will be worshipped, as God, in the rebuilt temple at Jerusalem. The following extract is from Bickersteth's Guide to the Prophecies, (7th edition,) by which it will be seen, that on the principle of a double fulfilment, they consider that two separate periods of 70 weeks are mentioned in Dan. ix. 24—27; first, in verse 24, a continuous, unbroken, complete ecclesiastical period of 70 weeks, or 490 years, from B. C. 457 to the Crucifixion, in A. D. 33; secondly, in verses 25, 26, 27, a subdivided trisected period of 70 weeks, the last week of which is the seven years of the infidel Antichrist's manifestation at the time of Christ's Second Advent at the Consummation.

"One of the most important chronological prophecies is that of the 70 weeks of Daniel. The interpretation which most satisfies the author's mind, from its simplicity, and following the order of the text, is this: the seventy weeks of verse 24 is a definite period of 490 years, ecclesiastically complete, from the decree of Artaxerxes given to Ezra 458, to the death and resurrection of our Lord in A. D. 33, which makes exactly 490 years. The period from which this era is to be reckoned is to be gathered from the vision (verse 23) of which it is the explanation. In that vision Daniel asks the question, (viii. 13, 14,) *How long shall be the vision concerning the daily sacrifice and the transgression of desolation, to give both the sanctuary and the host to be trodden under foot;* and he is answered, *Unto two thousand and three hundred days, then shall the sanctuary be cleansed.* The first renewing of the sacrifice, as we find, (Ezra vii. 12, 23,) was under the decree of Artaxerxes, 458 years before Christ. That decree was directly connected with the building of the temple, and the restoration of worship and the sacrifices. Of the whole period of 2300 years, *seventy weeks of years were determined*, נחתך or *cut off*, from the restoration of the daily sacrifice to the completing of the perfect sacrifice of Christ, when the spiritual temple was raised up, (John ii. 19, 21,) and the Most Holy was anointed. Heb. i. 9, ix. 24. We have here, then, the ecclesiastical period of seventy weeks, or 490 years, distinct and perfect.

"There is another period of seventy weeks, however, brought before us in verses 25, 26, and 27. As the seventy years' captivity had a double commencement, from the first captivity to the decree of Cyrus, and from the second captivity under Zedekiah to the decree of Darius, so this longer period of seventy weeks appears to have a double commencement. The second commencement is stated to be from the going forth of the commandment to restore and build Jerusalem. The date of Nehemiah's commission from Artaxerxes was 446. But it appears very clearly that the period mentioned by Daniel is to be reckoned in complete weeks, and not in parts of weeks; hence, as is the period of our Lord's burial, parts of time are reckoned for the whole. The commencement of a perfect week, therefore, in that course of weeks which had begun to run with Ezra's commission, must be taken, or the year 451. There are three periods, (1.) seven weeks, (2.) sixty-two weeks, (3.) one week. From 451 to A. D. 33 is just 483 years, or sixty-nine weeks. For seven weeks, or forty-nine of those years, constituting a jubilee, (a sacred measure of time,) there are predicted *troublous times*, as we may judge by the history of Nehemiah there really were, till the Jewish polity was settled. This seems to be one reason mentioned for the separation of the first seven weeks from the sixty-two; though it is probable there may be other reasons. Then follow the sixty-two weeks, which will reach to A. D. 33, when the Messiah was to be cut off, and (as it is in the margin) the Jews were to be no more his people. We have then, in verse 26, an indefinite period, the events of which are, the destruction of the city and temple by the Romans, and the Jewish desolation. This desolation was to last, as we learn by other prophecies, till the times of the Gentiles should be fulfilled. (Matt. xxiii. 38, Luke xxi. 24.)

"In verse 27 we have the additional week at the close of the times of the Gentiles, when the people of Israel are again taken into covenant, as pointed out Ezek. xx. 33, 38. This week is divided into two parts. The character of the first half-week seems to be set out (Isa. lxvi. 1, 3,) where the Jews are represented as, in a self-righteous spirit, rebuilding the temple and offering sacrifices; and the character of the second half, or *dividing of the week*, answers to Isaiah lxvi. 4—6, where they are represented as under the terror of the infidel Antichrist, who causes the sacrifice to cease; and at the close is the Consummation, in the destruction of that Antichrist, as set before us, Isa. x, 23. 25, 2 Thess. ii. 8.

(10.) Some "Lectures on the Hopes of the Church," delivered in Geneva, by J. Darby, were published in 1842. They advocate the futurist, or literal-day interpretation, and maintain Daniel's 70th week to be the final seven years of this dispensation, as held by the other writers here quoted. The same expositor considers the Rapture of the Wise Virgins to the heavens will undoubtedly precede the final 3½ years of Antichrist's persecution, or last half of the 70th week. He has also written some other works.

(11.) SIR EDWARD DENNY, BARONET, about 1845, published a valuable "Companion to the Chart of 70 Weeks," as an accompaniment to some large and ably executed chronological charts. He commences the sixty-nine weeks B. C. 457, and terminates them A. D. 26, seven years before the crucifixion, which he places in A. D. 33. The interval from A. D. 26 to A. D. 33, he considers to have been disallowed as the place for the 70th week, because of Israel's rejection of John the Baptist and the Messiah. The 70th week thus remains unfulfilled until toward the end of the Gentile dispensation. Sir E. Denny, as well as Tregelles, Kelsall, B. W. Newton, Strange, &c., maintain that the words in Dan. ix. 24, "to anoint the Most Holy" should be "to anoint the Holy of Holies," *i. e.*, the Holy Place, as is admitted by Lowth and other Hebrew scholars. He also looks for the Ascension of the Wise Virgins before Antichrist's 3½ years persecution. A condensed transcript of his work on the 70 weeks is here subjoined.

"This great septenary period is divided into three distinct parts,—SEVEN WEEKS—THREESCORE AND TWO WEEKS, and ONE WEEK, the first two of which follow in due continuous order, without interruption. Whereas between the last two, namely, the threescore and two weeks, and the one week, a long interval occurs; these last two being separated the one from the other by the whole period of Israel's dispersion.

"The period of sixty-nine weeks begins B. C. 457, and as to the point in history when it was to end, we find that sixty-nine weeks out of the seventy should elapse before the Messiah should be come; that is, I believe before whether they received him or not he should at least be offered to Israel. . And this occurred neither at the birth of the Lord, nor at the time when he himself came forth in ministry. No; but at the time when the voice in the wilderness, namely, John the Baptist, his messenger, the prophet of the Highest, proclaimed his approach. The history of Christ upon earth properly opens with the preaching of John, his forerunner. His coming to Israel is to be dated from thence; and hence the Lord, speaking of John, said, 'The law and the prophets were until John: from that time the kingdom of heaven is preached.' Besides which the Evangelist Mark speaks of the preaching of John as the beginning of the gospel of Jesus Christ, the Son of God, (Mark i.) Judging from all this then, I feel no hesitation in placing the end of this period, namely, the seven weeks and threescore and two weeks, just at the point where John the Baptist began to tell of Him who was coming, before he actually appeared on the scene. *And after (the) threescore and two weeks shall Messiah be cut off, but not for himself.* On hastily reading this passage, one would naturally suppose that the Lord was cut off at the close of this period. But in these words the preposition '*after,*' is indefinite. We do not read *immediately* after, as if at the end of the period exactly. It was at the termination of this period that John the Baptist appeared as the prophet—the Elias of his day—announcing the coming Messiah. Between the Messiah's announcement by John, and his death, an interval elapsed of seven years —or a week—divided into two equal parts—the first three years and a half being the time of John's mission—the next that of Jesus Christ himself.

"This *unnoticed week*, as I term it, of the Messiah's rejection is left an utter *blank* in the prophecy. For the Lord for the last time was giving Israel a trial, but they despised him and his testimony; and for this Israel was thenceforth rejected, and the name of reproach—the name of Loammi—was written upon them. The week of proffered blessing was, as it were, altogether *cancelled and blotted out.* The *one week* of this prophecy will come in at the end of the Christian Dispensation to *complete the full term of seventy weeks, and to supply the place of the* FORFEITED WEEK.

"The last week of Daniel thus detached from the rest, being the great crisis in the history of the world, previous to the setting up of the kingdom, the period of Israel's ripened apostacy, will be one of deep and awful interest, of unparalleled judgment: and between this and the forfeited week there will be a sort of moral *coincidence,* as well as of palpable *contrast:* inasmuch as one was the period when the true Messiah came forth and was rejected; the other will be a time when the false Messiah will rise and be received by the Jews as the hope of their nation.*

"*And the people of the prince that shall come shall destroy the city and the sanctuary, and the end thereof shall be with a flood.* Here the destruction of Jerusalem and the Temple by the armies of Rome under Titus, in the reign of Vespasian, follows next in historical, and at the same time in *moral* order, after the foregoing notice of the cutting off of Messiah, the sin of the Jews and their punishment being thus linked together. This occurred about the year A. D. 70. In this passage we should carefully mark the distinction between 'the *people* of the prince that shall come' and 'the prince' himself. 'The *people*,' that

---

* As throwing further light on this subject, and as proving that this is not a solitary instance of this sort of double fulfilment of prophecy, I next turn to consider the testimony of John and of Elias, the forerunner of Christ at his first and second appearance. Their's is, we shall find, exactly a parallel case; these prophets standing precisely as to their testimony in the same relation one to the other, that the two weeks above named do in the purpose of God.

In Malachi iv. we read, in connection with the Lord's second coming, as follows. "Behold I send you Elijah the prophet before the great and dreadful day of the Lord," which we need not say will yet be fulfilled. But in the meantime, when Christ at his first coming presented himself to his people, claiming their allegiance as the heir of the throne, he was preceded by one, who "in the spirit and power of Elias" "came to prepare the way of the Lord." Of him it was that the Lord said, "If ye will receive it this is Elias which was for to come."

It was all a contingency, it depended on this—had John been received, (his reception involving too that of him of whom he came to bear witness) he would have really proved what he ostensibly was, the harbinger of the kingdom—the very Elias and no other would have been needed to announce the coming glory of Christ, which would in that case even then have been revealed. But John and his testimony, as in the case of Jesus himself, have been alike set at naught; and hence the Elias originally foreknown in the counsels of God will come, and as Jesus declared of him after the slaughter of John by King Herod, Matt. xvii. 10, 11, shall restore all things, and be in the full sense of the word the prophet of the Highest. Yes, he will assuredly come: taking up the burden once uttered by John, he will really be what John ought to have been—the messenger of the covenant, the establishment of which will depend not on the will of the Jews, but on the power and grace of Jehovah himself. [*Sir E. Denny's Companion to the Chart of 70 Weeks.*]

is the *Roman Nation*, existed when the Lord was on earth, and was afterwards used, as we have seen, in chastising the Jews for their ill treatment of him. 'The prince that shall come,' on the other hand, is the *last head or king of this very same people:* the same as the little horn which Daniel beheld in his vision come forth out of the head of the great Roman Beast—who in the last day, when Israel shall have filled up their sin in owning him as their king—their promised Messiah, will be used as a scourge more fearful by far than Nebuchadnezzar or Titus, or any of those who like them have trodden Jerusalem down from the very beginning.

"*And unto the end of the war desolations are determined.* This passage refers to the present desolations of Zion, which began when the armies of Rome, under Titus, invaded, as we have seen, the holy city and temple, and which will continue to rage, in more or less violence, down to the time of the end, when the Seventy Weeks shall be accomplished, and Israel be owned again by the Lord.

"*And he shall confirm the covenant with many for* ONE WEEK. Here 'the prince that shall come'—the wilful king of Dan. xi. 36—is presented. His '*people,*' the Romans, many centuries before his birth, under the conduct of Titus, in the reign of Vespasian, had led the way in the work of destruction. But now he himself rises —he, the little horn in the fourth beast of Daniel, the great head and leader of Gentile apostacy, as well as the impious usurper of the power of David, here abruptly appears on the scene.

"Now, then, we have reached the last, or 'one week' of this prophecy, which, as I before said, will hereafter come in the place of the forfeited week of Messiah's rejection. And for this week this deceiver (for such he will be at the outset) will enter into a covenant with the deluded children of Israel. They slew Him who once came to them in the name of his Father, the true Hope of Israel; and in return for this they will now be left to themselves, so as to fall into the snare, and to receive another, who, coming to them in his own name, in the pride and blasphemous independence of man without God, will treat them, as we shall see, according to their treatment of Jesus, so that with the same measure they meted to him it shall be measured to them again. . . .

Satan is not yet chained as he will be; still, as the god and prince of this world, the spirit who works in the children of disobedience, he is never at rest. And when the evil of man has well-nigh reached its maturity, just before the second coming of Christ, he will at length meet with one who, so far as he is suffered to go, will carry Satan's plans into effect. One who, assuming to himself all the power and glory of the real Messiah, will draw to himself the admiration, the worship of all but the disciples of Christ; one whom Satan will clothe with all that is fitted to dazzle and captivate the natural mind, seeing that all the glory, the strength, the intelligence of our unrenewed nature, will centre in him, so as to exalt him, both in his own eyes and in the estimation of others. In him will be fully developed all the principles of evil which have ever lurked in the flesh since man fell. Human nature, in short, enslaved and debased by the enemy, will be shown forth in him.

"Such is the one who in the latter day will arise, and, as we read in the prophecy, will enter into a covenant for one week with the deluded nation of Israel, who will present himself to them, and be received as the expected Messiah; and then, in the end, be used as a means of chastising that nation, who slew the Lord when he came. And what wonder, if the whole Gentile world, as well as the children of Israel, that world which—urged on, it is true, by the Jews—nailed the Lord to the cross, should fall into the very same snare, and become their companions in evil? What wonder if, attracted and dazzled by the false glory and beauty of this mighty deceiver, with their ten kings at their head, they should give their power and their strength into his hands, and become tributary to him? The truth is, the whole world, both Jewish and Gentile united, will wonder after the Beast, will fall prostrate before him, and own him as King of kings and Lord of lords—names which we know belong only to Christ. Thus the week of this wilful one's empire will be the period of the world's ripened apostacy, when the unrestrained power of those three great agents of evil, the world, the flesh, and the devil, will be fully expressed, and will be seen linked in a daring attempt to cast the blessed God out of his own creation.

"*And in the midst of the week he shall cause the sacrifice and oblation to cease, and for the overspreading of abominations he shall make it desolate, even until the Consummation, and that determined shall be poured upon the desolate,* (desolator, see margin.)

"The Prince before named, having for the first three and a half years of his time, reigned in peace over the Jews, he now at the end of that time, that is, 'in the midst of the week,' as we here read, throws of the mask and discovers himself. He had acted as a deceiver at first, and now, having compassed his object, as in like instance has been always the case, he shows himself forth as a tyrant. He had set up at first, with a view to flatter his subjects, that species of worship which only would take with the Jews. But now this is all set aside, he causes the sacrifice and oblation to cease, and for the forty-two months, or three years and a half spoken of in Revelations and Daniel, namely, the latter half of the week, he opens his mouth in blasphemies against the God of heaven, while he at the same time oppresses his people.

"These according to the Lord's word, will be 'the days of vengeance,' when God, through the means of this false one, 'the enemy and the avenger,' as he is termed in the 8th Psalm, will punish his people. This will be 'the time of Jacob's trouble,' Jer. xxx. 7, 'the great tribulation,' so fearfully shown in Matt. xxiv. and in Rev. xiii., when the the holy city shall be trodden under foot, the abomination of desolation set up, and the image of the Beast, namely, that of the desolator himself, shall stand in the holy place, as the object of worship, and when all shall be slain, who will dare to refuse to worship the idol?

"There will be a sort of moral connection—a *similarity*, and at the same time a *contrast*—between the week of this wilful one's reign, and the cancelled week of Messiah's rejection. This is evident, if we compare them in the following manner:—John the Baptist came forth preaching, and then went out, we read, Jerusalem and all the region round about Jordan, confessing their sins. Their repentance was, however, false and deceitful, as was soon shown by their murder of him, in whose light they had for a season rejoiced. Afterwards, when Christ himself came, he was met by the open enmity of Israel, and at last put to death upon the cross. Now here was *deceit* in their treatment of John, and *violence* with regard to the Lord, which two sins will be visited upon them at last, through Antichrist, the bloody and deceitful man, as he is termed in Scripture, who will begin his reign with beguiling, and end it with oppressing his victims. And this, observe, will continue for the space of 42 months, or three years and a half, corresponding exactly with the time that the Lord walked a stranger and pilgrim through the land, enduring the hatred and scorn of those whom he came to deliver and bless.

"At length he whom we here read of as being used as a rod in the hands of the Lord, will be in his turn judged. This great wilful one having been suffered to go to the full length of his native iniquity, and displayed the evil of the flesh in all its enormity, will now at length come to his end, and none shall help him. At the battle of Armageddon, so fearfully described in the book of Revelations, (chapter xix.) the powers of the earth, with this great Apostate King at their head, are seen in personal conflict with Christ. And there his impious career is cut short—there Antichrist falls with all his confederates, both Jewish and Gentile. Thus then we reach the close of our period—the end of Antichrist's week—the last week of the seventy—the point when the Lord, who through their sin in rejecting his Son has been estranged from his people for ages, will show himself faithful to his ancient covenant with Abraham, and returning again to the scene of his former presence on earth, will be known once again as the God of Jeshurun, the rock of his people.

"Thus we have traced the history of the Jews to the Second Coming of Christ at the end of the Seventy Weeks. And what have we seen? Evil, nothing but evil, on the part of the creature: grace, wonderful grace, on the other hand, on the part of the Lord. That which appears to be especially sweet and profitable in these meditations on this 9th chapter of Daniel, is the application of the very same truth to ourselves, as individuals, which belongs to the Jews, as a nation. How often alas! do we find that we have but little heart for the blessing which the Lord graciously lays at our feet, just as Israel had at the first coming of Christ, the consequence of which is, that like Israel at present; we get awhile into deadness, darkness, and distance from God; and in the end, like the Jews in the latter-day under Antichrist, plunged into a sea of trouble and sorrow; all the result of our folly and sin in not walking in happy child-like obedience to God. Blessed however to know that such is not to be the end of the path either of the saint in this dispensation (however perverse in his ways) or of Israel hereafter, but that full blessing is reserved by the Lord for both one and the other."

(12.) DR. S. P. TREGELLES, LL.D., of Plymouth, an eminent Greek scholar, wrote "Remarks on Daniel" about the year 1846, giving the futurist interpretation of that Book, like Sir E. Denny, Kelsall, Strange, B. W. Newton, &c. He shows in a chapter on the Roman Empire and its divisions, that its entire territory, Eastern as well as Western, including England, will be formed into ten kingdoms, and become subject to the future Antichrist. He also gives an excellent exposition of the future actings of Antichrist as described in Daniel xi. 21–45. With respect to the Seventy Weeks, he considers the first sixty-nine of them to commence about B. C. 454 or 455, and consequently to end in A. D. 28 or 29, which he believes to be the year of our Lord's crucifixion, as he takes the date of the Nativity to be about four years before the common era. The last of the seventy weeks* he of course regards as yet to come at the end of this dispensation. The following extracts are from his work. (P. 106 to 113.)

"The seventy weeks when distributed into portions, will stand thus:

I. From the edict to the building of the wall, etc...... 49 years.
II. From the building to Messiah the Prince, and his cutting off............................ } 434 "
(Then an interval of unmarked length.)
III. The period of the covenant of 'the prince that shall come"... .... } 7 "

"The various things spoken of (in verse 24) 'to finish the transgression, to make an end of sins, to make recon-

---

* Dr. Tregelles justly rejects the idea that the translation of the Gentile Church from the earth will precede the 70th week as being Jewish time. He says, "Some have thought from the Church having become a constituted body upon the earth just at the end of the 69th week, that it was no longer found on earth when the interval is past, and the 70th begins. Nothing about the matter can be found from the vision, the Church not being mentioned in it." P. 116.

ciliation for iniquity, and to bring in everlasting righteousness,' are all I believe future. I do not regard any of them as referring strictly to the work of Christ upon the cross, (although we, as believers in Him, know that many of these things have a blessed application to us,) but it rather appears to me that they all belong to the time of Israel's blessing,—when the preciousness of the blood of Christ shall be applied to those 'who are spared of them': when 'thou shalt call me, my Father; and shalt not turn away from me.' (Jer. iii. 19.)

"VERSES 25 AND 26. The 483 years (the seven weeks and threescore and two weeks) from the issuing of the decree run on to 'Messiah the Prince':—it becomes then important to inquire to what part of our Lord's earthly path the reference is made. He was 'born King of the Jews'—but this appears to be something more than the mere title: now, the only time in which we find the Lord Jesus taking this title in the presence of Jerusalem, was six days before he suffered, when he came thither on the ass's colt:—He was then presented as King, and six days afterwards was put to death as the King of the Jews. I should regard the limit 'unto Messiah the Prince.' as reaching on to his having been thus presented to Jerusalem. It is worthy of remark, that the decree of Artaxerxes was issued in the month Nisan, the very month in which the passover was kept, and in which our Lord both rode into Jerusalem and was crucified. . . .

"The words which stand in our English version, 'but not for himself,' have often been taken as if they spoke of the vicarious character of our Saviour's suffering; this would however be, I believe, placing a most true and important doctrine upon an insufficient basis. I believe that the words simply imply, 'and there shall be nothing for him';—he will be rejected, and his earthly kingdom will be a thing on which he will not then enter.

"The series of years has run on unhinderedly from the issuing of the edict to the cutting off of Messiah;—but at this part of the vision, there are various events spoken of before the one remaining week comes into notice at all. 'And the city and the sanctuary shall the people destroy of a prince who shall come.' This refers, I have no doubt, to the destruction of Jerusalem by the Romans; as was also foretold by our Lord in Luke xxi., 'When ye see Jerusalem compassed about with armies, then know that the desolation thereof is nigh.' This destruction is here said to be wrought by a certain people; not by the prince who shall come, but by his people:—this refers us, I believe, to the Romans as the last holders of undivided Gentile power: they wrought the destruction long ages ago:—the prince who shall come is the last head of the Roman power, the person concerning whom Daniel had received so much previous instruction. It is most important to attend to the exact words of the passage; it is thus that we avoid the mistake of confounding the people and the prince who afterwards springs up.

"'And his end shall be in the overflowing': I suppose that this speaks of the end of the prince who shall come; in the expression 'the overflowing,' allusion seems to be made to some known event in prophecy; I suppose that it is the same overflowing as that which is alluded to in Isa. x. 22, and xxviii. 18. This would identify the time of this prince with the crisis of Israel's history:—this identification is (as we shall see) yet more decidedly brought out in the subsequent part of the vision. The interval up to 'the end,' is only characterized by war and desolations. . . .

"The vision gives us no intimation about the times of events which belong to the interval:—we only find at the cutting off of Messiah, one seven years is unaccomplished; this 'reserved week,' as some have aptly called it, belongs to the time of the prince who shall come.

"VERSE 27: '*And he* (the prince who shall come) *shall confirm a covenant with the many for one week.*' In 'Remarks on Dan. vii. and viii.,' I sought to show that the horn spoken of in the two chapters is identical, and here he again appears to come before us; in fact, the allusion seems to be made to known circumstances about him. He makes a covenant with the multitude; that of course means the multitude of Daniel's people;—they are leagued with him, and he with them. This takes place three years and a half before he causes sacrifice and oblation to cease;—hence it is clear that they go on as under his patronage for some time. This will, I believe, throw some light upon the two thousand three hundred days mentioned in chap. viii. 14. We find him there making a covenant for one seven years, then breaking it at the end of three years and a half; and the removal of sacrifice, etc., is so spoken of, as to connect it with the breaking of the covenant. This tends, I think, to show that one thing done in pursuance of this covenant had been the establishment of the temple worship. The period of two thousand three hundred days is a few months short of the whole term of the seven years,—enough being not included, it may be, to be allotted for those preparations which will be needful for the worship to be set up: then follows the time during which it is carried on under his auspices, and then follow three years and a half of distinct persecuting and blasphemous power.

"The character of this period of three years and a half is to be especially gathered from chap. vii., in which mention is made of 'a time, times, and a half,' and also from the forty and two months, 1260 days, etc., which are spoken of in the book of Revelation.

"The identity of the time, times, and a half, of chap. vii., with the last half week of this chapter, might almost be taken for granted:—the proof, however, is simple:—the horn in chap. vii., acts in blasphemy and persecution until the Lord Jesus and his people take the kingdom; the three years and a half run on to that point: here in this chapter, the whole period of seventy weeks issues in the absolute and established blessing of Israel, Daniel's people: —the week of this covenant is the last portion of the seventy weeks, and the half week after the sacrifice is taken away, is the latter portion of that week. Thus the period in chap. vii. and the concluding period before us run on to the same point;—they are also equal in duration; hence, they begin at the same time, and are altogether identical. If we would form a just estimate of the events of the last half week, we must gather it from chap. vii.:— here we have the same power in its local connection with Jerusalem.

"Dan. xii. 1. This time is one of trouble, such as has never been equalled:—our Lord, in Matt. xxiv., predicts a time of tribulation also unequalled, and that without the like ever having been before, or to be after. This, then, in Daniel, cannot be subsequent to that in Matt. xxiv., for our Lord's words would then be contradicted. Daniel's people are delivered at the time here spoken of, so that there is no place for the tribulation in Matthew as a subsequent thing;—hence it follows inevitably that the same period is spoken of in both places—the time of which it is said in Jer. xxx., 'It is the time of Jacob's trouble; but he shall be delivered out of it.' This tribulation is during the reign and blasphemy of the Antichrist, whose fearful power will be thus permitted of God. Past history will afford no parallel, and the energy of Satan will then have an unhindered character, which God at present does not permit, (p. 167.)

"His reign is a time of grievous and grinding oppression to Israel; his abominable idol (the image of the Beast, that the false prophet causes both to speak and breathe,) Rev. xiii., being set in the holy place, all who refuse to worship it are the objects of his wrath; death is the doom which their disobedience receives. But God preserves some in his own sovereign power, each one whose name has been written from before the foundation of the world in the Book of Life of the slain Lamb. This is proved by a remnant being spared, when the Lord Jesus comes with power of destroying judgment; for none can be spared who have joined in the Antichristian blasphemy: 'If any man worship the Beast and his image, and receive his mark in his forehead or in his hand, the same shall drink of the wine of the wrath of God,' etc., (Rev. xiv. 9, 10.) This remnant must not be confounded with those who have confessed Christ previous to his coming; they, as being an integral part of the Church of the first-born, will share his millennial reign in glorified bodies; this remnant, on the contrary, (however previously acted on by testimony,) will not know the Lord Jesus until they see him, and the Spirit of grace and supplications is poured out upon them, (p. 165.)

"These prophecies of Daniel, and the predictions of Christ in Matt. xxiv., will be used in the day of the setting of the abomination of desolation in the holy place. The Church ought therefore to know what these things are, in order to stand prepared, and not find these things taking her by surprise.

"There is a wide-spread incredulity at present as to Satanic agency and miraculous power—an incredulity which needs to be dispelled, because it leads many to be blind to their danger. The working of the 'mystery of iniquity'- commenced in the days of the apostles; it has gone on, including Popery and all other forms of corrupted and corrupting Christianity, and at length it will result in the manifestation of the 'man of sin,' who will arise accredited by Satanic miracles—'with all power, and signs, and lying wonders.' Surely this is not believed by many; and yet the Spirit of God here speaks of actual miracles, and no mere deceptions of men's senses. What some of these miracles are we read in Rev. xiii., where we are told of fire made to come down from heaven in the sight of men, and an image made to speak and breathe.

"If claims to miraculous power be made, let us take heed and hold fast the truth of God; it is nowhere told us in Scripture that God will give us any new revelation confirmed by miracles, but we are warned that Satan will thus introduce the Antichrist; and that *in this manner* men will be deceived. *No miracle can invalidate an antecedent fact.* The fact of redemption by the blood of the Son of God will remain as the sure ground-work of all Christian religion, even if ten thousand miracles were wrought to disprove it: this is a truth but little considered; and so little heed *will be paid* to it by men in general, that by miracles they will be misled, unless they have received the love of the truth of God into their hearts, by the operation of the Holy Ghost.

"To some it may seem a dark and discouraging prospect thus to contemplate what the issue will be of professing Christianity within the Roman earth; to see the corruption which goes on, as that which will at last increase so as to lead to full Antichristian apostasy—the rejection of God and of Christ. But, if it be different from the prospects which may have been imagined, we have only to ask whether this is not the truth of Scripture. If this be the case, then it is well for us to know it; for God never instructs us by holding out false expectations. Have not the Apostles Paul, (2 Tim. iii.,) John, (in speaking of 'many Antichrists' as the characteristic of 'the last time,') James, (v. 1—8,) Peter, (2 Epist. chap. iii.,) and Jude, all taught us that the concluding days of this Dispensation will be days of peculiar evil in the Church and in the world, up to the coming of the Lord, (p. 213, 214.)

"The Scripture presents a criterion and a safeguard to those who are watchful: 'If there arise among you a prophet, or a dreamer of dreams, and giveth thee a sign or a wonder, *and the sign or the wonder come to pass*, whereof he spake unto thee, saying, *Let us go after other gods*, which thou hast not known, and let us serve them; *thou shalt not hearken unto the words of that prophet*, or that dreamer of dreams: for *the Lord your God proveth you*, to know whether ye love the Lord your God with all your heart and with all your soul.' (Deut. xiii. 1—3.) Thus, if any miracle be wrought in confirmation of any contradiction of a truth previously revealed of God, then such miracle ought not to be received as though it accredited in any way the newly-introduced doctrine or opinion. The divine miracles of Scripture were in full accordance and harmony with every previous revelation, and their nature and character were distinctly opposed to Satanic power," (p. 24.)

(13.) HENRY KELSALL, M. D., R. N., wrote an admirable futurist literal-day treatise, in 1846, upon "Antichrist." Among many other remarks, he observes that the Chaldaic (a Gentile language) is used from Dan. ii. 4 to the end of Dan. vii., but the rest of Daniel is in Hebrew, implying that the prophecies of Dan. ii., iv., vii., relate more to the Gentile powers, and their connection with Antichrist, while those of Dan. viii., ix., xi., xii., refer chiefly to Antichrist's connection with the Jews and Jerusalem. He also notices that each of the four successive Empires of Babylon, Persia, Greece, and Rome, assumed its prophetic position of supremacy as soon as it fulfilled the three conditions of being a monarchy, and of having possession of Palestine, and of extending to the Mediterranean, "the Great Sea." He thus expresses his expectations as to the future:

"At first the Prince, Antichrist, makes a treaty or covenant with the Jews for one seven, or hebdomad, the last of the 70 weeks, (Dan. ix. 27,) but after making this seven years' covenant, he will break it in the midst, and cause the sacrifice and the oblation to cease, after which the period for the exercise of his open blasphemy exactly corresponds with the time times and a half of Dan. vii., at the commencement of which the abomination of desolation will be set up, and the worship of him and his image continue until the time of fulfilment. The abomination of desolation is probably the image endowed by Satan with the power of speech and breath or life. (Rev. xiii. 15.) . .

"That the Gentiles should worship the image of Antichrist is not difficult to conceive, seeing that idols, and crucifixes, etc., are even now adored by the nations of European Christendom. . . . Gentiles and apostate Jews will place the abomination that maketh desolate—fabricate the image and set it up. At this awful instant of time every one who 'understands' (Matt. xxiv. 15) will immediately quit Jerusalem. From this moment will commence that 'dreadful tribulation such as was not from the beginning of the world.' This will consist not only of the raging persecutions of Antichrist and the false prophet, but of the angry visitations of God which are now about to be poured out. This is the point of time when Antichrist breaks his covenant in the midst of seven years, and when the two witnesses (Rev. xi. 3) make their appearance in Jerusalem. Forty-two months are therefore left for the completion of these wonders. About the same time as the two witnesses, (probably Elias and Moses, p. 96,) there will appear in Jerusalem a false prophet, who will be empowered to perform astonishing miracles. He will cause an image of Antichrist to be set up in the sanctuary, which, by the agency of Satan, he will be enabled to endow with life and the power of speech. This image seems to be typified in Dan. iii. He will require every man to worship this image, and to receive a mark in his forehead, or on his right hand, as a token that he acknowledges Antichrist as God, and he will cause to be put to death all who refuse to receive the mark.

"*The Apostacy* (Atheism, and the self-exaltation of man) will probably, towards 'the end,' receive its great impulse from the progress of human learning (which Satan knows how to direct and to use for his own purposes.) Science daily now adds some new wonder to the knowledge which has been rapidly accumulating for the last sixty or seventy years; that short period only having advanced the Gentiles of Christendom further in every variety of science than the previous seventeen centuries. Should knowledge continue to progress in the same ratio for a similar period, to what must it eventually lead? The adoption of railroads throughout Europe, and of steam navigation to every quarter of the globe, will tend to bring the world to maturity. . . .

"The results of a more perfect acquaintance with the nature and powers of electricity are also perhaps incalculable. This comparatively recent discovery will eventually lead to important consequences; because it appears to be, or really is, the agent which God has appointed for the regulation both of organic and inorganic creation. When man finds that he can with certainty control and apply this wonderful power to the imitation of the ordinary, but hitherto mysterious operations of nature, the inevitable consequence will be the lifting up of his heart.

"The recent revival of Animal Magnetism is also worthy of notice; there can be no doubt that it is identical with the arts of sorcery practised in the early ages of the world. At present, only the elements of this long-lost art are understood. The phenomena already observed are sufficiently startling; but when greater perfection in Mesmerism shall be arrived at, it will probably be found capable of effecting all that sorcery ever performed. Witchcraft will be one of the characteristics of the latter days, and will co-exist with the idols of Antichrist, the Assyrian. Micah v. 8—15, prophesies of the vengeance which Christ, at his second coming, will execute upon the heathen; when the remnant of Jacob shall be among the Gentiles in the midst of many people; and when God will cut off witchcraft, and the Jews shall have no more soothsayers. Perfection of scientific knowledge will hurry on 'the times of the Gentiles' to the crisis."

This writer correctly states that precisely ten kingdoms (the ten toes and ten horns, Dan. ii. 44, Rev. xvii. 12,) will be formed out of the territory of which the Roman Empire consisted in the time of Trajan, including, of course, England; and will become completely subject to Antichrist. He says, (pp. 35, 102, 21, 22.)

"The quadruply divided Grecian was included territorially in the Roman earth: and when the final settlement of the latter into ten kingdoms takes place, the four ancient

Grecian kingdoms (Egypt, Syria, Greece, and Thrace, with Bithynia, &c.) will most likely be restored, and make four of the ten. . . . The ten Gentile kingdoms into which the whole Roman earth (*complete in the time of Trajan*) will be ultimately divided, and which are now developing themselves, will make their appearance so as to be distinctly recognised by those who take the light of prophecy as their guide. While the Jews, on Gentile sufferance, or under Gentile protection, are allowed to worship in their new Temple, and perform again all the ordinances of the Mosaic law, the maturing of the ten kingdoms will be effected. When these ten kingdoms are perfected, they will all become *nationally* apostate. . . .

"These, when they are formed, will be connected with 'the great sea;' England now has possessions there. Ireland was never brought within the limits of the Roman empire, and probably does not come within the scope of the prophecy. The present course of events in that island renders it possible that its separation from England may hereafter take place. Belgium was within the limits of the Roman earth; Holland was not; and lately (1832) they have been separated. The restoration of the kingdom of Greece within the last few years (1827,) is also worthy of observation. It seems as if the ten kingdoms were gradually developing themselves."

(14.) THE REV. C. MAITLAND, in his "Apostolic School of Prophetic Interpretation," (1849,) gives many valuable extracts from the Fathers of the primitive Church, and subsequent writers, showing that Antichrist was generally held to be an individual man, who would gain a universal empire, and be received by many Jews as their Messiah, and for 3½ years have himself and his image worshipped in the Jewish temple and throughout the earth, meanwhile being master of Rome and Jerusalem, and persecuting Christians to the death, but at last would be destroyed by Christ's personal descent at the Battle of Armageddon. He also believes, in common with some of the Fathers,[*]

---

[*] Some of these writers have been incorrectly stated to have thought that God would confirm the seven-years' Covenant with the Jews. But this cannot be the case, because they admit that Antichrist will cause the sacrifice to cease in the midst of the week, and therefore that Antichrist will previously have confirmed the

that 69 of the 70 weeks were fulfilled before our Saviour's crucifixion, but that the 70th week is future, its latter half coinciding with Antichrist's 3½ years, at about the close of which Christ will descend on this earth. He says, (p. 203.)

"The majority of the primitive writers make the latter half of the seventieth week identical with the three years and a half of Antichrist. In their favour may be urged:—

"First, the precise agreement of the time; the weeks being land weeks, or weeks of years.

"Secondly, The identity of the events assigned to each: for every thing said of the half-week is repeated in the prophecies relating to Antichrist. These things are, the the cessation of the daily sacrifice, the setting up of the abomination, the desolation thereby occasioned, the consummation of God's mystery, and the pouring out of the vials upon the Desolater.

"Thirdly, The events of the half-week are continued till the consummation: apparently the sounding of the seventh trumpet, when the mystery of God shall be finished."

The following graphic description from his work of Antichrist's future 3½ years' persecution possesses increased interest, now that we know Louis Napoleon to be this Antichrist.

"In that day of unequalled trouble, besides death, and perhaps bodily torment, there will be the torture of sickening doubt, withering and racking despair. The grounds of faith will be so obscured as to render argument hopeless: the counter-evidence apparently so overwhelming as to place all opposition in the light of wilful blindness. For that counter-evidence, as the Pagan long ago remarked with triumph, will appear to defy refutation: the only safety will lie in refusing to behold or to listen: 'If they say, Here is Christ, believe it not; if they say, He is in the desert, go not forth.' In former persecutions there has ever been an easy answer to the blasphemer; but now it will be a man's first difficulty to realize the faith for which he is called to suffer. Intellect, miracles, the course of Providence itself, all will appear to be ranged on

covenant, for these two acts are performed by one and the same person.

the side of the delusion: to doubt it will seem unbelief: to receive it, an act of required submission to the Giver of reason.

"The delusion, though of supernaturally rapid growth, will not be altogether the work of a moment. Many shall come, saying, I am Christ. There will be vague reports that a Christ is here, or a Christ there. Bede thinks that Antichrist himself will spread these rumours, in order to accustom men to the expectation of a new Messiah; but that at the beginning of the three years and a half he will say openly, I am Christ. For a time, several prophecies may seem to be in his favour; it will be a question (to him at least who has then to make his first acquaintance with their literal meaning) who it is that most truly builds again the ruined tabernacle of David; the Nazarene, whose coming was followed by the destruction of David's city; and by the departure of the sceptre from his tribe, or he who makes the holy city the seat of universal empire. And who is it that is set up as king upon the holy hill of Zion? The Nazarene, set up as a malefactor on the hill of Calvary, or he who, like a king, plants the tabernacles of his palace in the glorious holy mountain? In this way will be felt that sign of the latest days, 'perplexity.'

"Though the craftiness of Antichrist may at first lead him to employ these arguments, his pride will not long suffer him to appeal to the word of Another. He will hasten to set up himself above every god, and will open his mouth against the God of gods; even against his name, his tabernacle, and them that dwell in heaven. The style and character of his blasphemies we are not told: whether he will imitate the coarser forms of the French Atheists, or the more polished defiance of ancient Rome.

"Yet, in the absence of fuller particulars, two general expressions present themselves to our notice. The first—'He opened his mouth:' an idiom foreign to classical Greek, and used by the Evangelists in prefacing a set speech, such as the Sermon on the Mount. Of this character was the proclamation of Sennacherib, the closest parallel afforded by Holy Scripture: 'Whom hast thou reproached and blasphemed?' Even the Holy One of Israel.' And, secondly, 'There was given him a mouth.'

A phrase used elsewhere to express direct inspiration: 'I will give you a mouth and wisdom;' but seeming here to imply a peculiar Satanic gift of blasphemy, far exceeding in malignity the efforts of unassisted man. 'He shall speak marvellous things against the God of gods.' All this God shows to be mainly directed against himself; doubtless that, from the example of his own long-suffering, we also may learn patience.

"But how, taking up a position contrary to the instincts of human nature, will the imposter support his pretensions? 'He doeth great miracles.' Upon this passage the Church has evermore kept her finger; noticing with undisguised dismay, that the very words used to describe the Saviour's miracles are likewise applied to those of Antichrist. Some writers have proposed a qualification; but in vain; for St. Paul speaks of '*all* power, and signs, and lying wonders.' Even the word *lying*, on which they have built hopes, does not occur in the other passages; therefore we are forced to conclude, that even if unreal in essence, they will be proof against detection by human vision. The false prophet will call down fire from heaven, and will 'deceive those that dwell on the earth by the miracles which he hath power to do in the sight of the Beast.'

"At these miracles all the non-elect then living shall wonder, that is, they shall be deceived. The elect also would be deceived, but it is not possible, and for that reason alone they stand. The Church has long desired to know how near a doubt will be suffered to approach the mind, before it is repelled by the stern front of the eternal purpose. On this subject the first Gregory thought deeply; and, if it may be said without disparagement to his faith, his courage quailed at the prospect.

"While the elect behold with horror such signs and miracles wrought by the ministers of Antichrist, even they, though despising life, will feel a mist of uncertainty rising in their hearts. For as, through its miracles, the imposture flourishes, so in some degree does their steadfast vision grow dim. Therefore, by the influence of his lying wonders, a shadow of doubt will obscure the sight of the righteous; and, in the hearts of the elect, at the sight of the terrible miracles, a dark thought will gather form and substance."

"Compared with the history of our Saviour's life, faith

and unbelief will seem, in that day, to have changed sides. What it was blasphemy to say of the first, it will be soul-saving truth to think of the second: he truly "hath a devil, and is mad;" he lives and reigns "by the operation of Satan," for it is the Dragon that gives him that power, and seat, and great authority. For the heaven-sent messenger must be backed, not by miracles alone, but by every word of God. The same Scriptures that foretold good things of Christ have declared bad things of Antichrist. Seen by this light, his very miracles will resolve themselves into a fulfilment of prophecy; the supernatural wonders by which he will think to style himself God, will stamp him "Man of Sin;" for, if he did no miracles, he would not be the Antichrist of prophecy; if that prophet called down no fire from heaven, he would not be the false prophet of the Apocalypse.

"In Antichrist's persecution there is no death foretold but by decapitation, (Greek, the stroke of the axe, Apoc. xx. 4.) This state of things reminds us of the French revolution, in which two millions of persons perished by instant death. There will be a new and peculiar source of distress, a universal conflict in the heart of each country, each city, and each home. Without doors, the certainty of instant death; no refuge from the maddening anxiety, but at the fireside savage hatred and deadly revenge. The daughter is at variance with her mother; some word or or gesture betrays that their God is not the same God, and the executioner is called in to end the dispute. "Children shall rise up against their parents, and shall cause them to be put to death." In this desolation of hearth and home, one sanctuary, as it appears, shall be spared, for nothing is said of treachery between husband and wife. Nor need we attempt to supply the omission, since the worst is professedly revealed: "Behold, I have foretold you all things."

To the severity of that tribulation the prophets oppose its shortness. Its duration is reckoned in three ways: by God, by his Son, by the angels, and even by Satan, it is reckoned as short; but to the souls under the altar, and to the elect crying day and night, it will seem long. Therefore, as a common standard of reference, its actual length is given; and to suit the readers of all times, its duration is laid down in months, and in years, and in days. It will last for forty-two months, (Rev. xi. 2, 3, etc.)

It must be for some higher end than to gratify an idle wonder, that the limits of this trial have been so strictly defined. To know when things are at the worst, how much longer the worst will continue, is a consolation, which, till that day of rebuke and blasphemy, the believer cannot learn to estimate aright. For that knowledge, though it must preclude false hopes of an instant deliverance, will as certainly supply true hope, and banish utter despair. The tyranny, in proportion as by the lapse of time, it appears to be gaining stability, will thus be known to be most surely hastening to its fatal hour. The towers rise proudly, but their base is crumbling; the torrent foams madly, but its source is failing; "the ungodly is in great power, and flourishing like a green bay-tree;" but with equal truth shall it soon be added—"I went by, and lo, he was gone; I sought him, but his place could no more be found."

"Meanwhile, Israel's Keeper is neither slumbering nor sleeping. The earth is his, and the fulness thereof; though, for his own purposes, he has seemingly abandoned it to this ruinous tenant. And, first to provide for his own: the Church, which now in her worst troubles longs for the wings of a dove, will then, as Bede remarks, both need and receive the wings of a great eagle. Next, unveiling the secrets of his eternal purpose, God proceeds to show the world who are his, and who Satan's. This is done, perhaps invisibly, by the sealing angel; but beyond the possibility of mistake, by the plague of locusts. Before that plague is let loose each monarch marks his own: all will have either the sign of the Beast or the seal of the living God, (at least throughout the land of Judea, for none but Jews are sealed.) And, as the angel once passed by the blood-stained threshold, so will the locust, during those five months of woe, pass by the seal-bearing forehead.

"But the high office of witnessing for God in times so critical will not be left to the locusts only. 'I will give power to my two witnesses.' They shall prophesy, it says, twelve hundred and sixty days. It seems impossible to go far wrong in anticipating the substance of their discourse:

that, like their Master, they will begin at Moses and all the prophets, showing that, as he must needs suffer those things, and enter into glory, so Antichrist must needs achieve *these* things, and go into perdition; that while boasting himself supremely free, he is toiling slave-like to fulfil the Scriptures; that the duration of his power has been fixed to a day, and the letters of his name have been all numbered.

"The cry of the elect still goes up to heaven. The gale, charged with their sighs and unspeakable groanings, is further laden with the curses of the Antichristian herd. At heaven's gate both speak the same language, 'How long, O Lord?'

"But there is yet a triumph reserved for the powers of hell. The witnesses, though proof against human violence, fall before the infernal part of Antichrist's kingdom. Thus far it had seemed a drawn battle; miracles against miracles; fire breathed out, against fire called down from heaven. But now Satan is victorious at all points; the witnesses of truth have been slain; the foundations, it seems, are destroyed, and what shall the righteous do?

"The season for Divine interference has at length arrived. Till all else had failed, it was too early for the Son to quit the throne; but now earth, mastered by hell, has no helper, save in him who took other substance, and who, from the right hand of the Father, beholds the unequal struggle. 'For when,' asked one of old, 'when else should the true King come, but to dethrone a tyrant, to avenge his country, to restore a world? The alien Herod had usurped the Jewish sceptre, had subverted liberty and rule, had profaned the sanctuary, and had confounded the rites of worship; therefore, when things human were found failing, the Divine drew near to succour; the helper, denied in man, appeared in God himself. In like manner will Christ again come, to destroy Antichrist, to throw open Paradise, to strike off the fetters of a world, and, in the place of bondage, to establish eternal freedom.'

"Meanwhile the world prepares to take its fill of joy. There is now none to say to the fools, Deal not so madly; nor to the ungodly, Lift not up your horn. They send presents one to another: everywhere the word is, 'Peace and safety.' A bad omen, ror then sudden destruction is to come upon them.

"Immediately after the tribulation of those days shall the sun be darkened, and the moon shall not give her light, and the stars shall fall from heaven. Upon earth there is distress of nations with perplexity; a suspicion of the fatal truth strikes terror into the hearts of all. In that suspense of death-like syncope, a portentous sound adds horror to the gloom: 'The sea and the waves roaring.' Inanimate nature conceives a hope of the manifestation of the Sons of God; therefore the floods clap their hands, as if remembering the ancient saying, 'Let the sea make a noise, and all that therein is, for the Lord cometh to judge the earth.'

"But why this darkened hemisphere and these extinguished lights? The bright sign of the Son of Man is about to be displayed in heaven. By that sign all doubt is removed; the true Christ is none other than the Nazarene. He whom his enemies have seen for the last time, as he hung between two thieves, now reappears in glory amidst ten thousand saints.

"They shall look on Him whom they pierced. By the wound of their own inflicting, He condescends once more to be known. In that mark of the Roman spear, they read all that they dread to know; that their Judge is no new-comer, essaying for the first time, a reception among men, but a sojourner of old, who has already trodden their paths, and has carried away with him a token of their hate. But others, in that pierced side, will see mercy as well as judgment—the sin and the salvation, the rebellion and the pardon, the warfare and the triumph—all written with that iron pen in the Rock for ever.

"With supernatural firmness the impostor supports the blow: upon his heart, blasted by the operation of Satan, no dew of repentance may descend. In that hour he justifies the election of his master in his madness, defying heaven, and hastening to decide, at the sword's point, who is God of gods and Lord of lords. For this moment Satan has long been preparing; and at once the Dragon, the Beast, and the False Prophet beat to arms. (Rev. xvi. 13, 14.)

"All great battles receive a name: this is called 'the battle of that great day of God Almighty.' Of this encounter what prophet has not sung? At the thought of that conflict Habakkuk trembled; and Enoch, who dwelt beyond the flood, even he caught the din of that warfare, the thunder of those captains and their shouting. Then it was that, regarding neither the trackless distance nor the sounding flood between, he uttered the exulting cry, 'Behold the Lord cometh with ten thousand of his saints.'

"The kings of earth stand up, each at the head of his army. The rulers take counsel together, how they may break his bonds in sunder, and cast away his cords from them. At their matchless folly he that sitteth in the heavens shall laugh: the most merciful, that willeth not the death of a sinner, even he shall have them in derision. Like the disdainful warriors of old, he invites the fowls of heaven to feed upon their flesh. The white-robed army is now marshalled upon the heavenly plain.

"The fighting is soon ended. The Beast is taken alive, and translated to the lake of fire. And whither he goes, his disciples do not follow him now, but they shall follow him afterwards. For death and hell shall be cast into the lake of fire, and all who have worshipped the Beast and his image shall be tormented with him. Yet down that steep and flaming road the King of Pride goes not alone: the False Prophet, still his companion, shares with him the precedence in eternal fire. From that time it is said, as a synonym for the place of torment, 'Where the Beast and the False Prophet are.'

"And the remnant were slain with the sword of Him that sat upon the horse, and all fowls were filled with their flesh. 'And I saw the souls of them that were beheaded for the witness of Jesus, and for the word of God, and which had not worshipped the Beast, nor his image, neither had received his mark upon their foreheads, or in their hands, and they lived and reigned with Christ a thousand years.'"

(15.) PROSPECTS OF THE TEN KINGDOMS, published by B. W. Newton, in 1849, contains by far the ablest exposition extant upon the future division of the original Roman Empire into exactly ten kingdoms. The following remarks are also made upon the seventy weeks, in his consecutive explanation of the whole of Daniel.

"The seventy hebdomads of *years* mentioned in this

passage, Dan. ix. 24—27, are distributed into three divisions:

"The first consists of *seven* hebdomads, *i. e.* 49 years.
"The second of *sixty-two* hebdomads, *i. e.* 434 years.
"The third of *one* hebdomad, *i. e.* 7 years.

"The first of these divisions, viz., of 49 years, commenced when the commandment went forth to restore, and to build Jerusalem, and ends by the street being built again, and the wall in even troublous times.

"The second division, viz., of 434 years, commenced from this completion of the wall, and extends to the 'cutting off' of the Messiah. After threescore and two hebdomads, *i. e.* 434 years, shall Messiah be cut off.

"The third division, *i. e.* seven years, will commence when 'the Prince that shall come,' *i. e.* Antichrist, 'shall make a covenant with the multitude,' and ends by wrath being sent upon the Desolator, and blessing upon Jerusalem.

"The hebdomads, therefore, do not commence as soon as the prophecy was given to Daniel. It was given in the first year after the conquest of Babylon by Cyrus, *i. e.* B. C. 537: but it did not commence to be fulfilled, until B. C. 454 or 455.

"The 'seventy divided hebdomads,' are not concerned with any or every period in the history of Israel. They concern only periods in which God regards Israel as nationally gathered in their own city, and in which his hand is *directly* engaged in carrying forward his great plan of overthrowing the Gentile Oppressor, and of delivering his people. Consequently, the progress of the seventy hebdomads is stopped at the crucifixion: for then Jerusalem was virtually set aside, when the Lord Jesus, four days before his death said, 'your house is left unto you desolate.' The plans for its national blessing, and the destruction of its enemies, which till then, the hand of God had steadily carried forward, were suspended; and soon after, Jerusalem was utterly blotted out. The course of the hebdomads will not be resumed, until Israel, under a covenant formed with Antichrist, shall again assume a *national* existence in Jerusalem. Then again they will become in Jerusalem, the subjects of direct dealing from the hand of God, 'set to,' as he himself expresses it, to effect his own designs of final blessing. That blessing, however, is to be reached through judgment, and fiery indignation; that will consume the transgressors. Jerusalem is to be 'the furnace,' before it is the City of Peace. 'The Lord's fire is at Zion, and his furnace in Jerusalem.' (Ezek. xxii., etc.)

"I quote these texts in order to show how peculiarly the closing period of unbelieving Israel's existence in Jerusalem, is marked as one, in which the Divine hand begins again, in an especial manner, to act in Jerusalem, for the effectuation of its own purposes. The Great 'Desolator' is only an instrument, commissioned of God to effect this end: 'I will send him against an hypocritical nation, and against the people of my wrath will I give him a charge, to take the spoil and to take the prey, and to tread them down like the mire of the streets.' (Isa. x. 6.) The progression, therefore, of the hebdomads which was suspended at the crucifixion, has not been yet resumed.

"But as soon as Israel is again gathered back to Jerusalem for judgment, and nationally re-exist in their land and city, prophecy resumes its detail. The covenant made with Antichrist, that covenant of which it is said, 'your covenant with death shall be disannulled, and your agreement with hell shall not stand,' (Isaiah xxviii. 18,) will be a sign of their re-constitution as a nation, and then the hebdomads will again resume their course. To this period belong the concluding part of every vision of every prophet that speaks of judgment on Jerusalem. All the visions of the Revelation, from the sixth to the nineteenth chapter inclusive, belong to this period, especially to the latter half. The latter half of this last hebdomad, is 'the 1260 days,' or '42 months,' or 'time, times and a half time,' so often spoken of in Daniel and the Revelation.

"The hope that Israel cherishes of protection and rest under this covenant with Antichrist, will soon be dissipated. 'Wherefore hear the word of the Lord, ye scornful men, that rule this people that is in Jerusalem. Because ye have said, We have made a covenant with death, and with hell are at agreement, when the overflowing scourge shall pass through, it shall *not* come unto us: therefore . . . when the overflowing scourge shall pass through, then ye *shall* be trodden down by it.' They will think to escape desolation by making a covenant with the Desolator, but it shall not stand. They will soon have to say, 'he has put forth his hands towards such as be at peace with him, he hath broken his covenant.' At the half of the hebdomad he causes the sacrifice and oblation to cease; and the pinnacle of Israel's Temple becomes the pinnacle of an Idol—his own Idol. The wonderful history of this Idol is given with unusual minuteness of detail in the New Testament. He who commands it to be formed, will have power to give life unto it—that it should both speak, and cause that as many as would not worship it, should be killed. The Desolator, represented by this living Image, stands upon this pinnacle. The Temple of Israel becomes the place of his worship and of his power—and the world, throughout all the appointed sphere, bows before him, until the consummation—when that determined is to be poured upon the Desolator, (Rev. iii.)

"Here the vision of sorrow ends. Then comes the hour for everlasting righteousness to be brought in, and for the pinnacle of idolatry to be supplanted by the Holy of Holies, anointed for the worship and government of the Lord God of Israel. Then at last it will be said, 'Jehovah is in his Holy Temple, let all the earth keep silence before Him.'

"The present condition of the Jews—their wealth—their intellect—their energy—their readiness to gather around one, who should unite the greatness of Rome with the attractiveness of Greece, show too plainly, that they are fast ripening for the great transgression. In this state, they are to be re-gathered to Jerusalem, *there* to be the prey of the Last Great Destroyer—to be the victims of his delusions, and the partners of his plagues. 'Thus saith the Lord God; Because ye are all become dross, behold, therefore I will gather you into the midst of Jerusalem. As they gather silver, and brass, and iron, and lead, and tin, into the midst of the furnace, to blow the fire upon it, to melt it; so will I gather you in mine anger and in my fury, and I will leave you there, and melt you. Yes, I will gather you, and blow upon you in the fire of my wrath, and ye shall be melted in the midst thereof. As silver is melted in the midst of the furnace, so shall ye be melted in the midst thereof; and ye shall know that I the Lord have poured out my fury upon you.' (Ezekiel xxii. 19.) The words also of our Lord, respecting the final inhabitation of

Israel by the sevenfold power of Satan, will be remembered by those who have read the thirteenth of Matthew.

"The earliest period at which Antichrist brings himself into connection with the Jews, as a people in Jerusalem, is mentioned in the *ninth* chapter. He is there said to make a covenant with many, for seven years. This no doubt is the period, of which it is said, that 'by peace he shall destroy many.' But there is too much of the order, and ostensible worship of God, connected with Jerusalem, for him long to remain satisfied with the arrangements which for a time he will sanction there. The Jews, when they return to Jerusalem, will sooner or later rebuild their temple and re-institute their sacrifices: and although, such worship will be hateful to God, and 'he that killeth an ox will be as if he slew a man,' and 'he that offereth an oblation, as if he offered swine's blood:' yet, there will be enough that reminds of God in these things, to excite the enmity of him, who intends to 'exalt himself above all that is called God, or that is worshipped.' Antichrist will little care whether God does, or does not own the Temple, and accept the sacrifices. He will be the servant of Satan; and Satan knows, that these sacrifices, and that Temple, however prostituted and misused, stand before angels, and before men,—before God, and before Christ, as a memorial of truths, precious and everlasting; and therefore, he will desire to sweep such memorials utterly away. God, because of the transgression of his people, will not interfere to hinder. A host, *i. e.* power, will be given him against the daily sacrifice, and he will cause it to cease.

"But Judaism will not be the only object against which he will direct his fury. He will magnify himself against the Prince of Princes, *i. e.* Christ. He will not, indeed, be able to reach *Him*, for he is high above all heavens: but Christ's truth, and Christ's people, are yet within his grasp, and *them* he will persecute. 'He will cast down some of the host and of the stars to the ground, and stamp upon them.' The believing pepole of Christ are here denoted by one of their *prospective* titles. To the outward eye, they may be a feeble few, despised for their ways, and hated for their testimony; but in the estimate of God they are 'the Saints of the High Places'—'the host of the heavens'—'Stars'—that shall shine for ever and ever: for they will be recognised as reigning from Heavenly Places, in the bright radiancy of unearthly glory, as soon as the kingdom of the Son of Man is manifested. But during '*the time of the end*,' God will permit that 'the truth' should be cast down to the ground, and they will be cast down together with it."

Regarding the future ten kingdoms into which the Roman Empire is yet to become divided, and four of which will be the four Grecian horn-kingdoms, B. W. Newton made the following valuable remarks in 1849: and subsequent events have remarkably demonstrated their correctness.

"The first king of Grecia has arisen and has fallen; his four successors also have reigned; but they, too, have passed away, and their kingdoms have vanished, without the king of the fierce countenance having appeared, of whom it is declared, that he shall arise 'in the *latter* time of *their* kingdom.' (Dan. viii. 23.) Has then this prophecy been falsified?

"It has *not* been falsified. The eighth chapter throughout its whole course declares, that its burthen respects 'the time of the end, when the transgressors shall have come to the full;' and regards the four kingdoms of Alexander's successors, as *existent* at that closing hour. 'The latter time of their kingdom' agrees with the time 'when the transgressors shall have come to the full.' These four kingdoms, therefore, *must* be *revived*.

"We know from the preceding chapters, that the *whole* Roman Empire, and therefore, *that* part of it within which these kingdoms fall, is to be revived. We know also, that its Eastern as well as Western Branch, is to be divided. All, therefore, as to this, that we learn additionally from the eighth chapter is, that four of these divisions will be the kingdoms which passed from Alexander's successors into the hands of Rome; that is to say, Greece—Egypt—Syria—and the rest of the dominions of Turkey.

"A few years ago, perhaps, this would have been thought impossible. The maintenance of the integrity of the Turkish Empire, was made the object of such anxious effort on the part of the ruling kingdoms of the West, that nothing seemed more unlikely than its partition. Yet it has been in part dismembered; and Egypt and Greece, have already separate governments of their own. It is also a fact, that a similar separation of Syria has been in contemplation. Such a separation would be an almost necessary concomitant of the return of the Jews to Palestine; and as soon as that is accomplished, the four kingdoms will re-exist."

"There are three criteria, by which every interpretation regarding the ten kingdoms, must be rigorously tested:

"1st. The ten kingdoms represented by the ten toes of the image, are to be sought in the whole extent of the Roman Empire, *Eastern* as well as Western.

"2d. When once existent, they *continue till the end;* that is to say, until the stone smites them, grinds them to powder, and begins itself to fill the whole earth.

"3d. Their development must be a plain and recognised development, analogous to that of the Empires that have already been.

"No one doubts that Chaldea, Persia, Greece, and Rome, have existed and ruled as sovereign empires. The development of the ten last kingdoms must be no less decided. Such are the criteria. And seeing that no division of the Roman Empire answering to these conditions has ever taken place; it follows, that this part of the vision remains to be fulfilled."

"The changes, therefore, that may be expected in those nations which fall within the Roman Empire, may be classified under three heads:

"First, the introduction of popular monarchic principles into those countries which have not yet received them, (all ten toes being formed of clay and iron.)

"Secondly, an alteration in the present territorial divisions throughout the whole extent of the Roman Empire, so as to form ten kingdoms therein.

"Thirdly, the dissolution of governmental union between countries, one of which *did fall,* and the other of which did *not* fall within the Roman Empire.

"As regards the first of these, comparatively little remains to be accomplished. The countries in which popular-monarchic principles are not yet established, are Morocco—Egypt—Turkey—Luxembourgh—Rhenish Prussia on the west of the Rhine—Baden—Bavaria—Wirtemburg — Switzerland — Italy* — and Bessarabia. How the extension of the military power of France—or the commercial influence of England, and the return of the Jews to Palestine would effect or facilitate these changes, we can easily imagine. In Austria, the change was effected even without such influences.

"As respects the alteration of territorial arrangement, much more remains to be accomplished. The legs of the Image, corresponding with the division of the Roman Empire into Eastern and Western—would lead us to expect that five kingdoms will ultimately be found in the Eastern, and five in the Western part of the Roman dominions. The eighth chapter of Daniel places it beyond a doubt that Greece—Egypt—Syria, reaching to the Euphrates—and the rest of Turkey, both in Europe and Asia, will form four of the Eastern kingdoms. As these are the only four, out of the ten of which the Scripture speaks specifically, we cannot with certainty name any other kingdoms. But there seems little doubt, that France, Spain and England, will continue kingdoms to the end. We must, however, as to these specific points, wait the unfolding of events. The accomplishment of the final division will probably precede very little the closing hour of the dispensation.

"With respect to the third point, that is to say, the dissolution of unions at present subsisting between countries, one of which *did*, and the other did *not*, fall within the Roman Empire; there are two cases to be considered.

"First, there is the case in which a country *external* to the Roman Empire, *holds authority over* a country, that fell *within* the Roman Empire. Such was the relation of Holland to Belgium. It has been dissolved. We may expect to see a similar dissolution, in all cases where the German confederation exercises authority west of the Rhine, or south of the Danube. Baden, Wirtemburg, the chief part of Bavaria, and Rhenish Prussia, are the countries thus circumstanced.

* "The progress of liberal institutions in Austria, will no doubt equally affect Italy. I should expect Switzerland to be finally united either to France, or to Austria, and thereby to have her too democratic constitution modified. It may probably be divided according to its language: the French cantons connecting themselves with France."

"We may, therefore, expect their separation from Germany, and annexation to some of the countries that fall within the Roman Empire. We may also expect that Russia will resign Bessarabia, and that her influence will be supplanted in Moldavia and Wallachia; that is, if the full extent of the Roman Empire is to be taken, as it existed in the time of Trajan.

"But, secondly, there is a more difficult question, in cases where a country external to the Roman Empire, is *subjected to* a country within the Roman Empire. The countries thus circumstanced, are, Ireland, in its relation to England,—the central part of Hungary, which lies between the Danube on the West and the Vallum Romanum on the East,—also Bohemia and all German Austria North of the Danube, and the colonies of England, France, Spain, and Portugal.

"This question cannot perhaps be answered with the same confidence as the preceding; but I think there can be little doubt, that the union between such countries will be dissolved; if not fully, yet to the extent of distinct and independent legislatures being granted, as indeed, is already done, in the leading colonies of England. The importance of such separate legislation, may not, perhaps be fully apprehended now; but when the hour arrives for a decree to go forth, enforcing the worship of Antichrist, and the rejection of Christ and of God: the value of a separate legislature will be more distinctly felt."*

"Whether, therefore, we take the actual territorial division by Valentinian and Valens—or follow the more satisfactory guidance of Greek civilization, as determining the extent of the Eastern and Western branches of the Roman Empire; in either case, we may, I believe, safely take the boundary, which now separates Austria from Turkey, as the European line of demarcation. In Africa, I feel little doubt, that the districts of Cyrene and Carthage (Tunis) in which civilization was so early established by the Greeks and Phœnicians, will form the frontier countries of the Eastern division. This will establish the boundary of the Turkish Empire, as the limit in Africa also, between

---

* "The separation of Hanover from England may be regarded as an example."

the East and the West. It would give Tunis, Tripoli, Barca, and Egypt, to the Eastern division, and would make Algeria the first province of the Western. Tunis, which answers to the ancient Carthaginia, would, in connection with Tripoli and Barca, (ancient Cyrenaica) form one of the five divisions of the Eastern part of the Roman Empire. When we consider the eighth chapter, we shall see that we can with much certainty affirm, that (the other) four, out of the five, are formed by Egypt, Greece, Syria, and the remaining part of Turkey."

"We can scarcely form a more accurate notion of what the extent of the Eastern branch of the Roman Empire was, and is to be, than by marking the limits of the Turkish dominions, before Greece and Egypt were separated therefrom."

(16.) AN EMINENT EXPOSITOR, R. A. Purdon, a clergyman of the Church of England, has published in London a prophetical pamphlet of 16 pages every month since 1845, under the title of the "Last Vials." Although it may be thought that his zeal in rebuking the vices and follies of the present day is at times carried too far, and invests him more with the sternness of Elijah than the gentleness of St. John, yet it cannot be denied that he possesses great ability and genius in the interpretation of prophecy, and frequently striking eloquence of expression. He was almost the first to proclaim distinctly and emphatically that Louis Napoleon is the person who shall be manifested as THE Antichrist. This he spoke of in December, 1849, and in subsequent numbers of the Last Vials, and has continually foreshown from Scripture the universal spiritual and political dominion which Louis Napoleon is to acquire throughout the world. He has long held that the year-day and literal-day systems of interpretation are equally correct, but that the future literal-day fulfilment is the principal and most important one; also that Napoleon the Antichrist will make a seven-years' covenant with the Jews (Dan. ix. 27) seven years before the End, the latter half of which period will be the 3½ years' Great Tribulation: and that the first translation of exactly 144,000 living saints, or Wise Virgins, at Christ's coming in the air, will *precede* that 3½ years, and the second translation of living saints at Christ's descent on the earth, will *follow* the 8½ years; a description of this by him is extracted in the author's "Coming Battle." He also holds that soon after the covenant the Jews will re-commence their sacrifices in Jerusalem, which, however, Napoleon will abolish in the midst of the 7 years. The following extracts are from "The Last Vials" for 1852.

"When the Last Antichrist has attained to a certain degree of power we shall then—or perhaps before that—hear of a grand movement of the Jewish people toward the land of Israel. The Jews, wishing to strengthen their position in their own land, will look abroad for some powerful alliance, and finding the Antichristian king in supreme power, they will enter into a league with HIM for a period of seven years. (See Dan. ix. 27.) Encouraged by his patronage and alliance, they will next proceed to rebuild or complete the temple of Jerusalem. In the meantime the Jews will continue day by day to flock to Palestine, still under the auspices of the Antichristian king, and still confident as to the continuation of his friendship. But after the first three years and a half, a change will occur in the relations of the two parties towards each other. Antichrist having by this time arrived at the highest pitch of blasphemy and extravagance, will begin to claim divine honours for himself; and finding that 'all the world wonders after the Beast,' he will demand of the Jews to permit the erection of his image or statue in the holiest place of their temple, and also the recognition of his divinity. But the Jews, or at least many of them, will resist this claim to the utmost. However willing they may be to adopt him as their Messiah, they will not be prepared to accept him as their *god*, or to admit his image to their temple. From that moment hostilities will break out between Antichrist and the Jews. The Infidel King will succeed in setting up his image, by main force, in the newly-finished temple. And this will be the exact fulfilment of our Lord's prophecy, (Matt. xxiv.,) "When ye shall see the abomination of desolation standing where it ought not, then let those that are in Judea flee to the mountains." From the time in which the rupture takes place between Antichrist and the Jews, the 1260 (literal) days of Rev. xiii. will probably be reckoned. Beginning in the second half of the seven years' league, and continuing to the end of the seven years, and to the fall of the apostate king. . . .

"There can no longer be a doubt but that some terrible lesson is preparing for the nations of Europe, and that *the Empire of Napoleon is about to be revived.* We do not speak of the title of *Emperor*—that can be foreseen even by a London newspaper; but *the actual Empire* of Napoleon, in its *full territorial extent.* Louis Napoleon has already laid the foundation of his power with a depth and solidity that are truly superhuman. . . . In 1815 Napoleon I. fell, and not only was his empire broken up, but his name and family were annihilated in France. Napoleon was extinguished for ever! His nephew has arisen, and struck this record out of the book of Europe. He has taken up the line of empire exactly where the Allies broke it off. The interval is henceforth to be a blank. Napoleon is to be again as if he had never ceased to be. His name, his Empire, his ideas, his principles, his very eagles, are all to be revived. The interregnum of 35 years is to be 'even as a dream when one awaketh.' . . . But perhaps it may be said that we are travelling too fast, for that not a particle of the empire has yet (in May, 1852,) been revived. We believe *that the revival of the Empire is as certain as if it had already been effected:* that it is *predestined,* and that the whole creation could not prevent it. Louis Napoleon, we believe, will regain, year after year, all the provinces of the fallen Empire from north to south; and will add to them (what Napoleon I. never could do) the Turkish provinces in the East. He has already begun a *subterranean* work destined to undermine both Italy and Belgium. This work he will carry on until the time for open action has arrived; and then he will advance by military occupation or by right of conquest. He will not cease until he has regained all that Napoleon lost, and will add to the Empire what Napoleon was unable to acquire—the provinces of Asiatic Turkey. He will take up the destiny of Napoleon just where it was broken off at the siege of Acre, and will carry it out to its final consummation. . . .

"The eighth head is 'of the seven,' and as we believe that Napoleon I. was the seventh head, it appears that from his family the eighth head will take its rise. As it is not to be supposed that Louis Napoleon will now be superseded by one of his own relatives, we still adhere, not only to the family, but to the individual, especially as his name alone contains the number of the Beast. . . . The 'deadly wound' (Rev. xiii.) of the seventh head was received when Napoleon I was defeated in battle and sent to die at St. Helena; the healing of the deadly wound will be fully accomplished when his representative and nephew has assumed the dominion of the Empire of Napoleon. And then indeed 'all the world shall wonder,' (Rev. xvii.) That this Empire will be revived again, we have no doubt whatever. *And it seems equally certain that Louis Napoleon is the man destined to revive it.* . . . . . So subtle and profound has been his policy hitherto, that we may suspect that he will hardly imitate the violence of his predecessor. He may not undertake the conquest of the Western Empire by force of arms. He may invade the East—he may regain the Rhenish frontier by military force; but in general, it seems likely that he will proceed by subtlety and persuasion; by acting on the fears, the hopes, and the selfishness of the surrounding nations; and thus he will form that great confederacy represented in prophecy (Rev. xvii.) by the ten horns of the Beast. He himself being the Imperial Head, the ten kings of the Roman Empire will be his vassals and lieutenants. There may perhaps be no display of violence, and yet the eighth head and ten horns will very soon appear upon the Beast. The Beast, it should be remembered, has a *double* signification, representing the Antichristian Roman Empire itself, and also the last Antichrist, as the ruler of the empire. . . . . . The eighth head of the Beast will be worshipped as God, (Rev. xiii.) Such is the APPROACHING APOSTASY. . . . .

There are two circumstances that seem also worthy of being noticed. One is, the contemptuous designation so frequently applied to Louis Napoleon, "The Nephew of his Uncle." But this designation exactly corresponds to the prophetic description of the eighth head—"He is of the seven." For the Uncle being the seventh, and the Nephew being the eighth, we have a connection between the two exactly similar to the scriptural designation, "He is of the seven," (Rev. xvii.) Again, as the Latin name of Louis (Ludovicus) contains the famous number of the Beast, 666, it is remarkable that the word *Ludovicus* has just been forced upon the public notice by the religious formularies of the Papal Church in the public prayer, *Domine salvum fac Ludovicum Napoleonem*. . . .

"The whole French nation is the body, and Louis Napoleon is the MIND. An infinite number of railroads extend themselves from Paris, as a centre, throughout the whole territory of France and to all its seaports. These are the MUSCLES of the frame. The electric telegraph, terminating at Paris, conveys every sensation of the Great Capital throughout all its dependencies. The telegraphs are the NERVES. All are gathered together and centred in Paris. In the centre of the Capital there is ONE MAN of the most perfect individuality of character; bold, unscrupulous, and remorseless; thinking for himself in the darkest recesses of his heart; impenetrable to all; inflexible, deliberate, and yet rapid; a perfect specimen of unity and force. This man is the MIND. He has collected all the powers of the state in his own person; he has but to speak the word and the thing is done. . . . The body of the Great Image (the territories of the Chaldæan, Persian, Grecian, and Roman Empire, Dan. ii.) seems now to be in the course of re-construction, and the Head itself seems already to be prepared and in full activity. It has not yet assumed its prophetic form, because the whole Image is not yet completed. It may continue incomplete for several years to come, but we see decisive evidence of its progress and its formation. We see the scattered members dispersed, but we see them slowly drawing into one. We see the ruling HEAD increasing daily into gigantic proportions, and we see that head possessed of an indomitable will, and a complete unity of purpose. Can we doubt that the reconstruction of the Image of Nebuchadnezzar is at hand?"

(17.) THE REV. JAMES KELLY has published at Nisbet's, London, (1850) very valuable "Lectures on Prophecy," and also, "The Apocalypse Interpreted," giving, in many respects, an excellent futurist literal-day exposition of the seals, trumpets, and vials, which (although they have had a past year-day fulfilment) he rightly considers will be fulfilled literally during the period of rather more than $3\frac{1}{2}$ years, between Christ's coming in the air *for* his saints, and his subsequent descent *with* those saints.

In his expository remarks upon Revelation vi. and

xiii. 5, *And power was given unto him to continue forty and two months,* he says, "Such is to be the duration of the Antichrist's open tyranny and persecution, after having with his hosts captured Jerusalem, (Rev. xi., Dan. vii. 25.) As already observed, this period also runs parallel with that of the prophesying of the two witnesses; and appears to be the latter half of Daniel's week or hebdomad, (Dan. ix. 27,) during which for some provocation or other, having broken his covenant with the deluded Jews, he throws off the mask, and becomes their ruthless oppressor. At the expiration of this assigned time, we may conclude that the seven vials of retributive wrath are poured out upon him and his confederates, to be succeeded by the epiphany or manifestation of the Divine presence, in order to his destruction, (2 Thess. ii. 8.) . . . In that much canvassed prophecy, (Dan. ix. 27,) in which seventy weeks or *hebdomads* of years are spoken of as being to issue in the long promised blessedness of the Jewish people, in their own land, under Messiah, it would appear that seven of the number—49 years, and sixty-two—434 years, have already elapsed, bringing us up to the time of our blessed Lord's rejection by his own people, when he came to them as 'a minister of the circumcision, for the truth of God, to confirm the promises made unto the Fathers.' (Rom. xv. 8.) With this event, in like manner, as in all the prophecies which celebrate the advent and kingdom of Messiah, a pause in the fulfilment of the Divine purpose towards the Jews and the nations, has ensued, which at length, terminating in the removal of the *intercept* of this dispensation, the remaining week or hebdomad of the prophet will begin to run its course. What will then succeed is also recited by Daniel,—namely, the career of the Antichrist, under the denomination of 'the Prince that shall come' And here, as in the Apocalypse, a division of the seven years occurs: 'he shall confirm the covenant with many for one week, (one *hebdomad* of years:) *'and in the midst of the week* he shall cause the sacrifice and the oblation to cease,' (verse 27.)

This writer holds that a literal image of Antichrist will be worshipped, and a literal mark on the forehead or hand received by his worshippers, and says, regarding the verse, Rev. xiii. 8, *All that dwell upon the earth shall worship him.*

"As the preceding verse, (ver. 7, *Power was given him over all kindreds and tongues and nations,*) ascribes to the Antichrist a universal lordship over 'all kindreds and tongues and nations,' it is reasonable to interpret similarly this universality of worship which is to be rendered to him. All mankind 'whose names are not written in the book of life' will do him homage; though, of course, the inhabitants of the land (Palestine) may be especially included, as being the scene of the tyrant's most blasphemous usurpation—sitting in the temple of God, and showing himself as God," (2 Thess. ii. 4.)

(18.) WILLIAM KELLY speaks of Dan. ix. 27 in his able work on Revelation; and, also, in "The Prospect" in 1849 he said (after noticing that the coming of Christ to remove the wise virgins will precede Antichrist's 3½ years,) "The prophecy of Daniel had already revealed the leading features of the interval during which 'the prince that shall come' plays his terrible *role*. 'And he shall confirm a covenant' (see margin and compare Is. xxviii. 15) 'with the many' (*i. e.* of Daniel's people, the Jews,) for one week: and in the midst of the week he shall cause the sacrifice and the oblation to cease, and for the overspreading of abominations he shall make it desolate, even until the consummation, and that determined, shall be poured upon the desolate.'

"That this prince (Dan. ix. 27,) is not 'the Messiah the prince' is manifest, not only from this, that the former is described as one 'that shall come,' after the latter has already come and been cut off, as is plain from verse twenty-six, but also from the certainty that 'the prince that shall come' is the prince of the Roman people: *his* people 'shall destroy the city and the sanctuary.' We know who destroyed Jerusalem and the temple—the people of this future prince. The latter part of the twenty-sixth verse does not continue the thread of the history, further than the general expressions 'and the end thereof shall be with a flood, and unto the end of the war desolations are determined.' In the last verse we are transported to the epoch of 'the prince that shall come,' and his actings during the last week of the age. This period is shown to be broken into two parts, during the former of which, according to covenant, Jewish worship is resumed, but 'in the midst of the week he shall cause the sacrifice and the oblation to cease.' If chap. vii. be consulted, it will be seen that there is a certain little horn rising after the ten horns of the fourth Roman beast, before whom three of the first horns fell—'that horn that had eyes and a mouth, that spake very great things, whose look was more stout than his fellows.' (verse 20.) 'And he shall speak *great* words against the Most High, and shall wear out the saints of the Most High, (or of the high places,) and think to change times and laws: and they shall be given into his hand, until a time and times and the dividing of time.' (verse 25.) Is it not evident that in chap. vii. is a horn or king whose blasphemous pride brings judgment upon the beast, or Roman empire, and whose interference with times and laws, that is with Jewish ceremonial order, continues for three years and a half? and that for the same space of time, or the last half week, 'the prince that shall come,' the Roman prince of chap. ix., overthrows this ceremonial worship?"

(19.) THE LIGHT OF PROPHECY is an able futurist literal-day exposition, by T. Lumisden Strange, (1852.) He commences the 70 weeks in B. C. 450, thus terminating the first 69 of them in A. D. 33, at the Crucifixion, and referring the last week to the Second Advent. Among various remarks upon Dan. ix. 24–27, he says,

"The period was divided into three portions. The two first portions, we know, have been fulfilled . . . leaving one hebdomad more, or a period of seven years, to be accounted for. The operations with which the 70 hebdomads were to terminate, namely, the finishing the transgression, the making an end of sins and the making reconciliation for iniquity, have been thought to have been fulfilled at the death of Jesus; but that this was not the case is evident, for he was to be cut off at the 69th hebdomad, while these crowning results were not to be realized till after the 70th. It would seem to have been overlooked that the sacrifice of Jesus makes no end of sins, nor reconciliation for iniquity, unless faith in that sacrifice be accorded. God having set him 'forth to be a propitiation' only '*through faith* in his blood,' (Rom. iii. 25,) and that the mere act of shedding that blood, of itself, could not effect any of the required ends. The sacrifice then was to be offered up at the 69th hebdomad, and the fruits thereof realised at the 70th.

"It becomes us to know in respect of whom these fruits were to be realized. Clearly it must be answered, in respect of the Jews. The 70 hebdomads apply to them, and to no other nation on earth. It is not, of course, meant to be said that the sacrifice of Jesus extended no further than for them, but simply that, as it is here adverted to, and as regards the setting forth of these hebdomads, the Jewish nation are alone in question.

"This has been specifically intimated. 'Seventy weeks,' it was told Daniel, 'are determined upon *thy* people, and upon *thy* holy city, to finish the transgression, and to make an end of sin, and to make reconciliation for iniquity.' The people and the city of Daniel are exclusively the subjects vindicated; and no other nation, or place, than the Jews and the city of Jerusalem, are here treated of. Furthermore, the anointing of the holiest of holies, which could only exist in the Jewish temple, and which formed one of the features of the work to be wrought on the termination of these hebdomads, also fixes the whole upon the Jews.

"The Messiah then was to be cut off at the close of the 69th hebdomad, and, according to the tenor of prophecy, at the lapse of the 70th, or at the expiration of just seven years more, 'the iniquity of Israel' was to be 'sought for,' and there was to be 'none,' and the 'sins of Judah,' and they were 'not to be found,' (Jer. i. 20,) and everlasting righteousness was to be their portion. We see the nation, however, even now, when not seven, but more than eighteen hundred years have passed by, still in their sins, unable to accept the means of reconciliation provided for them, and 'concluded all in unbelief.'

"The operation of the prophecy must then have been suspended, and this is just the case. . . . The conditions necessary to the prophecy in the existence of the distinctive people and the holy city, ceased at the expiration of the 69th hebdomad, and the long unmeasured dispensation of the Gentiles has been introduced, and the 70th hebdomad has still to be looked for.

"And he (the said 'prince that shall come') shall confirm a (margin) covenant with many for one week: and in the midst of the week he shall cause the sacrifice and the oblation to cease,' (proving thus that these had been maintained during the former part of the week,) 'and upon the battlements shall be the idols of the desolater,' (margin, the image apparently of his own person,) 'even until the consummation, and that determined shall be poured upon, the desolater,' (margin.)

"The desolater who is to be destroyed at the time of the end, can, of course, be none other than the Antichrist, and he then, as the construction of the language so evidently necessitates, must be the prince adverted to as having to come. The Antichrist, as his name denotes, is to present himself as the antagonist of Jesus, taking up the place that he should hold, and hence the title under which he is here brought before us is the rival one of 'the prince,' shown just before to belong to Jesus."

This expositor shows the coming of Christ "in the air," for his saints to precede Antichrist's 3½ years' tyranny, after which Christ descends on the earth. Antichrist's actings, as set forth in Dan. xi. 21–45, are also ably described in his work.

(20.) THE REV. CAPEL MOLYNEUX, an eminent minister of the Church of England, in his discourses delivered in Lock Chapel, in London, in 1852, and published, as "Israel's Future," says, (chap. ii. and iii.,) "The whole seventy weeks of Daniel are divided into three periods, *seven weeks, threescore and two weeks,* and *one week.* The *seven weeks* and *threescore and two weeks* are connected together in themselves and the events which they embrace. Not so the *one week*: a long and indefinite interval is represented as elapsing between the close of *the threescore and two weeks* and the commencement of this *one week.* . . . This *last week* is quite separate and distinct in itself and its events, from the preceding sixty-nine: it is cut off from them, and a long interval elapses between them. This week closes the prophecy, and with it, also, the history of the present age. It is the end of this dispensation; and so far, therefore, it exactly agrees in time with the restoration of Israel; for this, also, is to be at the end of this dispensation, (p. 50.)

"The Man of Sin will make a covenant with Israel, which stands for three and a half years, but at the close of that time he will work deceitfully, break the covenant, and become their deadly enemy. At this time—the time when he breaks the covenant—he will set himself up in the temple of God at Jerusalem, showing himself that he is God, arrogating the very perfections, attributes, and glory of God, and claiming universal homage and adoration. He will then commence a system of persecution against Israel, and all in the world who refuse to acknowledge his pretensions, unprecedented in the history of man, which terminates at last in what is called 'Jacob's trouble,' or 'the great tribulation.' About this time, and while these persecutions are raging, two other remarkable individuals will appear, denominated 'the Witnesses;' they will be just what their name imports—*witnesses;* but witnesses for God and his cause against Antichrist and his cause. They will finish their testimony and accomplish their work in three and a half years; and, having so done, will be overcome by Antichrist and put to death; they will lie dead for three and a half days, and then will rise up on their feet, and ascend up in a cloud to heaven. About the same time, or immediately afterwards, there will be a gathering of all nations, under Antichrist their head, (for the nations will cleave to him though Israel reject him,) against Israel and Jerusalem, in order to the siege of the city, the accomplishment of the battle of Armageddon, and the events of the great day of God Almighty. At the close of this battle the Saviour, the Lord Jesus Christ, will personally appear in power and great glory, to overwhelm with utter destruction Antichrist and his host, and take to Himself the kingdoms of this world for ever and ever," (p. 67.)

This expositor considers that Elias will be one of the Witnesses, and Moses, Enoch, or St. John, the other. He also holds that, in the course of the first 3½ years, the Jewish temple will be reconstructed, and within it sacrifices offered, which Antichrist will abolish in the midst of the week of seven years. The subject of the first translation of the Man-child, or *first fruits* of 144,000 wise virgins, (Rev. xii., xiv.,) *before* the 3½ years' persecution, is not investigated in his exposition. The nature of the persecution he thus defines, (p. 66, 135,) "The Man of Sin will be a literal man, an individual human being, energized by Satan, and possessed; therefore, of supernatural powers;

and urging therewith marvellous pretensions; he will be accompanied by another individual, *the false prophet*, (Rev. xix. 20,) and this false prophet will cause an image to be made to the Man of Sin, which image will be made to speak, and almost universally worshipped.... The Beast 'has power over all kindreds and tongues and nations,' and all who refuse to worship his image and bow down to him, he causes to be put to death, (Rev. xiii. 7, 15.) And, doubtless, the number who suffer will be great; and, doubtless, also, that number, great as it may be, who do so suffer, and suffer for Christ's sake, shall be included among the number of the saved and glorified together with the Lord."

(21.) A MOST TALENTED AND MASTERLY exposition of Daniel and Revelation, in three octavo volumes, was published in 1857-8, at W. Macintosh's, London, by Mr. Beale, a Cambridge Master of Arts, under the title of *Armageddon; or, A Warning Voice from the last Battle-field of Nations.**
It is certainly the ablest and most complete modern work on Prophecy next to Elliott's which was Horæ Apocalypticæ, published in 1851, and though not characterized by quite so much discursive learning, is yet far superior to Elliott's exposition in the justness and accuracy of its interpretation. Both works, however, agree in the grand conclusion that the Advent of Christ and the final crisis will be within the period of 1865-70, after which the Millennial 1000 years will run their course. It fully expounds the year-day accomplishment of the prophecies with reference to the Papal Antichrist, and the Gentile Church; and their subsequent literal-day fulfilment in relation to the Personal Antichrist, Napoleon III. and the Jewish as well as the Gentile Church. Its views, which mostly agree with those of Bickersteth and Birks, are as follows—that the year-day seven seals represent the progressive stages of the Church Militant

---

* It was not spoken of in the first edition of the present work in June, 1861, because it had not then come to hand. Its high price of 2*l.* 10*s.*, or 12 dollars, must limit its circulation, which would be better promoted by publishing it at one-fifth of that price, in smaller volumes. It must not be confounded with a wild and rhapsodical effusion by Mr. Baldwin. of Cincinnati, (subsequently epitomized by a Mr. Pitt,) similarly entitled *Armageddon*, but which is more a work of imagination than prophetic exposition.

(It appears that Mr. Beale recently departed this life.)

during this dispensation from primitive purity to increasing apostacy, until its ultimate regeneration at Christ's Advent; that the year-day seven trumpets are parallel and synchronous with the seals, and denote the consecutive divine judgments inflicted on mankind during the same period; that the year-day seven vials, describe the final strokes of judgment from the French Revolution in 1790-4 to the Consummation in 1865-9; that the 1260, 1290, and 1335 years (Dan. xii.) begin with Justinian's grant of civil power to the Pope at the period 530-3, and thus the 1335 years end about 1865-9, as the period of the Second Advent and Resurrection; and that in the ultimate literal-day fulfilment, the 1260, 1290, and 1335 days commence in the midst of the Covenant-week of seven years, Daniel's 70th week; and are identical with Napoleon's 3½ years' Antichristian persecution, (Dan. xii. 1, Matt. xxiv. 21,) supplemented by the 75 days of his overthrow through the judgments of the literal-day seven vials.

The author of "Armageddon" also shows from the same arguments as are advanced in this work, and in the works of Faber, Frere, Vorner, Purdon, Jackson, etc., that Louis Napoleon is unquestionably the representative of the seventh-healed, (septimo-octave) or eighth Head of the Beast, (the Roman Empire,) and is therefore THE Antichrist, "who uniting in his own person all the powers of church and state, will strip the Roman Pontiff of all his temporal possessions, and degrade him into a secondary position as his special prime minister, and miracle-working False Prophet (Rev. xiii.) who shall cause all to be killed who refuse to receive the mark, and worship the image of his Imperial Master." (Chap. xi.) He further says of Daniel's 70 weeks, (chap. viii. p. 227, and xii. p. 77,) "We must look upon this 70th week as an insulated portion of the prophecy which is yet to receive its accomplishment under the last great enemy of Israel. . . . We have strong scriptural warrant for the application of the whole of this 70th week to the time of the end. David, in the 55th Psalm, passing on in the Spirit from his own personal enemies to the confederate armies of Antichrist assembled against Jerusalem in the last siege of the city, foretold in Zechariah xiv., says, "He has put forth his hands against such as be at peace with him: *he hath broken his covenant.*"

And Isaiah, foretelling in chap. xxxiii. 8, the consummating misery to fall upon the Jewish nation through the treacherous breaking of the covenant with them by Antichrist or the last Assyrian, to whom the action passes on in that chapter from the previous Assyrian invaders of the land, as it does in this prophecy from Titus to Antichrist, says, "The highways lie waste, the wayfaring man ceaseth; *he hath broken the covenant*, he hath despised the cities, he regardeth no man." . . .

"At the beginning of this week, said Daniel, shall he, that desolating Prince, come, who will enter into a covenant or treaty with many of the Jewish nation, but that in the *midst of the week* he will break that covenant, cause the accustomed sacrifices and oblations of the temple to cease, plant his idols on the battlements, and probably his own image in the Sanctuary, which we are told, (Rev. xiii.,) the False miracle-working Prophet will be permitted, through Satan's instrumentality, to endue with the power of speech to sentence all to death who will not fall down and worship this terrible antitype of the Golden Image of Nebuchadnezzar. All, however, it would seem, goes on smoothly between Antichrist and his followers throughout the earth during the first half of this last week of years. All are lost in admiration of the Beast, and it is not until the concluding half, or last 1260 days of it, that his tyrannic rule commences. And during these days it is, as we learn both from prophet and apostle, that those of the Church Militant, who shall be *left upon the earth* to encounter these fearful days, will be given into the hands of the Beast to be made war with and overcome. For, although many will, doubtless, like the faithful Albigenses and Waldenses of the historical fulfilment, flee for safety into the wilderness of Judea, and into the inaccessible retreats of the Gentile world, carrying "the everlasting Gospel in their hands to every nation and kindred and tongue and people," (Rev. xiv.,) yet will there be a great slaughter throughout Antichrist's dominions, of all who have neither the mark, nor the name, nor the number of the Beast. During these days, too, it is, that the two personal Witnesses will be empowered to deliver their testimony against the abominations of Antichrist, and the wickedness and unbelief of the Jewish nation. And these witnesses; who will they be?

"Enoch and Elias," says Tertullian, "were translated, their death was never known, for it was put off. But they are reserved for death: they will extinguish Antichrist with their blood." Testifying against the sorceries, abominations, and blasphemies of Antichrist, warning all, if they would avoid the wrath to come, not to receive the mark of the Beast in their forehead or in their hands, and to worship neither him nor his image, these two illustrious witnesses will ultimately, like their heavenly Master, seal their testimony with their blood. . . The Antichristian Beast of the bottomless pit, the Septimo-octave Head, shall be suffered to gratify his fierce revenge against them, and to slay them. Their dead bodies will lie for $3\frac{1}{2}$ days, (Rev. xi.,) exposed to the gaze and rejoicing of their murderers; but at the expiration of these days, they will again, to the terror of the beholders, stand upon their feet, and reascend in glory to those blessed mansions from which they had been sent back again to earth on this, their predicted, mission of mercy and salvation. . . It is during the remainder of the literal 1335 days that the last vials of God's wrath will probably be poured forth in all their terrible literality, ushering in the Millennium at their close. Blessed will that day be to the saints of the New Jerusalem, for then will they all visibly appear in glory before God and the Lamb, standing each of them with Daniel in their appointed lot."

The writer of "Armageddon" further considers, (chap. xii.,) that 1862 will most probably be the year when Louis Napoleon will make the seven years' covenant with the Jews. By Jewish reckoning, 1862 will not terminate until Nisan or Tisri, (about April or September,) in 1863; but whenever the covenant is made, there will be only 7 years and $2\frac{1}{4}$ months to the End or Consummation. He holds "the King of the South," (Dan. xi. 40,) to be the sovereign of Egypt, whom Napoleon, "the Wilful King," (ver. 36,) is to vanquish. He also views England as one of the doomed ten horn-kingdoms, (Rev. xvii. 12,) and says, (chapt. xxiii.,) "With the French army, the largest and best appointed of any in Europe, and its navy unceasingly increasing in all its branches to an unprecedented and overmastering power, what course is unhappily left us but submission to that 'Wilful King,' who, *to avenge the defeat of*

Waterloo, may at any time turn round upon and rend us?" He does not, however, give fully the chief argument which proves this view, and which is, that ALL the original Roman empire, (of which England was part,) MUST fall under the dominion of the seventh-eighth Head, or Antichrist, (Rev. xiii. 7, 8,) and at the same time be divided into exactly ten kingdoms, five in the Western, and five in Eastern division, (Dan. ii. 41, vii. 24. Rev. xvii. 12.)

It is correctly shown by this author that the ascension of the Man-child, (Rev. xii. 5,) in the year-day fulfilment, means the ascension of Christ personally in A. D. 33, about 500 *years* before the Papal Antichrist's 1260 *years*' persecution, (Rev. xii. 6, 14,) and that in the literal-day fulfilment it means the ascension of the Wise Virgins, the mystical Christ, before the Personal Antichrist's 1260 *days*' persecution. He omits, however, to state the necessary conclusion, namely, that the ascension of the 144,000 Wise Virgins must therefore occur about 500 *days*, (16. or 17 months,) before Napoleon's 1260 days' persecution, that is, the last half of the Covenant-week of seven years: and thus their ascension will be about two years and 5 or 6 weeks after the date of the Covenant, (see diagram 4,) as can be further proved by several other reasons. But he clearly shows that this first ascension or translation of 144,000 saints at Christ's coming in the air, will *precede* Napoleon's 3½ years' persecution, and the second translation of the remaining saints will be shortly *after* the 3½ years, when Christ descends and slays the unrepentant. Respecting this, he says, "It is, I think, manifest that the glorification of the 144,000 will not only precede that unparalleled Reign of Terror of Dan. xii. 1, of which the one in 1793 was but a fearful type, but precede also the glorification of the Great Multitude, (Rev. vii. 9,) since we learn from Rev. xii. 12–17, that before the last 'time times and half a time,' (3½ years,) of Antichrist begin, the Dragon will be cast down from the heavenly places to the earth and persecute, during that period, the remnant of the woman's seed left therein after the Man-child or First-fruits, the mystic Christ, the 144,000, (comprising the Wise Virgins,) shall have been caught up to God and to his throne. . . . And if the Queen of the 45th Psalm, and the Dove of the sixth of Canticles be the predicted representative of the

First-fruits, then the 'King's daughter attendant upon Queen, and *the Virgins her companions that follow her*, the threescore queens and fourscore concubines, *the Vir without number*, and daughters of the Church associa with the Dove will be identical with the palm-bearing n titude. Of these it is said that 'with gladness and rej ing shall they be brought unto the Queen: they shall e into the King's Palace,' (or the New Jerusalem,) Ps. x and that 'they saw, and blessed and praised the Do Song Sol. vi. 9. Thus, amidst the gladness and rejoi of the angelic hosts, and of the sealed ones, shall t king's daughters, and queens, and concubines, and vir without number, this palm-bearing multitude, that no can number, be brought out of this fiery tribulation deemed by the blood of the Lamb from the persecut of Satan and the power of Antichrist, and be joined ever to the Queen, the Dove, the First-fruits, in the cit the living God, blessing and praising them for their m trations during their 1260 days' sojourn in the wildern and God shall wipe away all tears from their eyes."

The same writer regards as erroneous the current that the Foolish Virgins, (Matt. xxv.,) are false-profes Christians. In common with Olshausen, Stier, D Alford, Dr. Seiss, etc., he considers that they are all Christians, but that the Wise Virgins are believers, the Foolish are unbelievers in the speedy second pers coming of the Bridegroom, and that the latter may saved either at death or at the second translation after th years' great tribulation. He says, "For some years the of 'the Bridegroom cometh,' has gone forth with a tinually increasing force. The wise virgins apparently the sincere believers in the event. . . . The united l which they give in the procession by means of the oi their well-trimmed lamps, that is, by their faith, is s bolical of that prophetic light which they will endeavou diffuse throughout a benighted world: of that public timony which, like Noah, that preacher of righteousn before the Deluge, they will render to the certainty of premillennial advent of the Bridegroom, and of the co quent near approach of the awful day of the Lamb's wr in which all the ungodly shall be drowned in a flood of as formerly by the flood of waters. The foolish virgins those who lacking faith in the literal coming of the Bridegroom, both as regards themselves and their influence with others, are without the oil of expectation wherewith to trim their lamps, and consequently without that light which would enable them to join in the wedding procession, or to assist in preparing their own people or the nations of the earth to meet the returning Saviour. Looking only for a providential, or a spiritual, or a postmillennial advent of the Bridegroom, they are seized with consternation at the unexpected cry, 'The Bridegroom cometh.' They seek aid from the wise, but are bidden to go and buy for themselves; that is, to search the Scriptures under the Holy Spirit's teaching, for that faith, that oil to trim their lamps, where alone it can be obtained. Whilst thus employed the Bridegroom comes, and the door is shut. At this they knock, seeking admittance with the agonising cry of 'Lord, Lord, open to us,' and are answered with the sad words, 'I know you not; words not denoting apparently, like the 'I never knew you,' or, 'depart from me, ye cursed,' of Matt. vii. 23, xxv. 41, eternal condemnation, but exclusion for a season from the marriage feast. This 'remnant of the woman's seed' are thus left without, to be brought, like the sons of Levi, through that fiery purification, the subsequent tribulation of the last (literal-day) 1260 days, which, it may be, will alone remove the veil from their hearts, open their eyes to the truth, and enlarge their faith to believe all that the prophets have spoken concerning the Bridegroom's promised premillennial return in glory to his widowed and waiting Church." (Chap. xiii.)

(32.) THE FIRST FRUITS is a useful prophetic treatise, by Alexander Porter, which was published in Philadelphia, United States, in 1856. It distinctly asserted that Louis Napoleon would be the future Antichrist, who should make the seven years' covenant with the Jews, seven years before the end. (Dan. ix. 27.) The following is an extract from it, (page 28.)

"'Behold, I will make thee know, or explain to thee, what shall be in the *last end* of the indignation; for *at the time appointed* the end shall be,' was the promise of Gabriel. (Dan. viii. 19.) He proceeds in Dan. ix. 26, to fulfil this promise. 'The people of the prince that shall come, (the Romans,) shall destroy the city and the sanctuary, (Jerusalem and the temple,) and the end thereof shall be with a flood, and unto the end of the war it shall be cut off by desolations,'—(*i e.* Jerusalem shall thenceforth remain trodden down of the Gentiles until *their times* (verse 27) shall be fully accomplished.) *Then he,* the Prince that shall come, (in the *last end* of the indignation,) shall confirm or make a covenant with many for one week of years, and in the midst or middle of the week, he shall cause the sacrifice and the oblation to cease, and for the overspreading of abomination he shall make it desolate *until the consummation,* when that determined shall be poured upon *the desolater.'* What is it that is determined upon this desolater? '*He* shall be *broken without hand.'* (Dan. viii. 25.)

"The person here named, 'The Prince,' I believe, is the present Emperor of France, LOUIS NAPOLEON, who possesses in a remarkable degree the characteristics of the king of fierce countenance, (who is to appear as the *head* of the ancient Roman empire,) '*when the transgressors are come to the full.'* (See Dan. viii. 23.) The expression, in this verse, 'of fierce countenance,' would be more truly rendered '*of obdurate countenance;* literally, *one whose firmness of features and complexion betray no emotion, and suffer no secret to be read—a man of imperturbable look.* The Jews will fill up their transgression by receiving him as their Messiah or deliverer—(as foretold by our Lord Jesus: 'If another shall come in his own name, *him ye will receive,'* John v. 45,)—and making a covenant with him for one week of years, he will confer upon them the privilege of restoring their sacrifices and worship at Jerusalem; but after three and a half years he will break his covenant with them, offer himself to them as the Messiah, and command them to worship him. At this point he will become the *Antichrist* of 2 Thess. ii. 8. 'Then shall that *wicked one* be revealed, whom the Lord shall consume with the spirit of his mouth, and shall destroy with the brightness of his coming.' Being filled with all the energy of Satan, he will have power to work with signs and lying wonders, and with all deceivableness of unrighteousness. 'All that dwell upon the earth shall worship him, whose names are not written in the book of life of the Lamb slain from the foundation of the world.' (Rev. xiii. 8.) 'Then shall be great tribulation, such as was not seen since the beginning of the world to this time; no, nor ever shall be. And except those days should be shortened, there should no flesh be saved.' (Matt. xxiv. 21.) The prophecies of Zechariah xii. and xiv.; Zeph. iii. 8th to 20th verses, and Joel ii., will, during his reign, be fulfilled. This will be the time of 'Jacob's trouble; but he shall be delivered out of it' by the appearing of the Lord Jesus and all his saints—in the clouds of heaven coming to Jerusalem. 'Then shall the Lord go forth and fight against those nations, (led on by THE Antichrist,) as when he fought in the day of battle.' 'And his feet shall stand in THAT DAY upon the Mount of Olives which is before Jerusalem on the east." (Zech. xiv . 3 to 5.) 'But HE (the king of impenetrable countenance,) shall be broken without hand.' 'He shall come to his end, and none shall help him.'

"This we believe to be the truth; and believing we rejoice in hope of the glory. Seeing the wonderful harmony of these prophecies, it seems that the hand of God has indeed guarded them, that the wise MAY understand according to the sure promise."

(23.) THE DAYS IN WHICH WE LIVE, is an excellent treatise on prophecy, by E. W. P. Taunton, (120 pages,) the first edition of which was published in Philadelphia, U. S., in 1857. He shows from much the same arguments as are adduced by Purdon, Faber, Rees, Frere, Phillips, &c., and at greater length in chapter I. of the present work, that Louis Napoleon is unquestionably the Eighth Head, who is to be developed as THE Antichrist, and make the seven years' covenant with the Jews; and during the last half of the seven years is to be worshipped as God in the Jewish temple, the sacrifices being abolished, and his image, 'the abomination,' being* set up there. He says,

* It is not surprising that a few writers should have imagined that some of the periods of 8½ years mentioned twice in Dan. vii. 25, xii. 7, and five times in Rev. xi. 2, 3, xii. 6, 14, xiii. 5, should signify the *first half* of the final week of 7 years, and others of these periods, its *last half*. It is a natural mistake for those to fall into, who do not understand how remarkably all the periods have had a precursory year-day simultaneous fulfilment within 1260 years, from A. D. 534 to 1794–95, and therefore they will all necessarily synchronise and run parallel in their future literal-day ful-

regarding the seventy weeks, "A time of trouble is fast coming, which will surpass anything of the kind that has ever preceded it. It is spoken of by the Prophet Daniel, (chap. xii. 1,) as 'a time of trouble such as never was, since there was a nation, even to that same time'; by our Lord, (Mat. xxiv. 21,) as a time of 'great tribulation, such as was not since the beginning of the world to this time, nor ever shall be.' These two scriptures must, of course, refer to the same period, as they both refer to the maximum of trouble.

"It will be seen by reference to Dan. ix. 24, that SEVENTY WEEKS were determined upon Daniel's people. The word 'determined,' signifies 'cut out,' or 'divided off,' that is, Daniel was informed that in coming time, seventy weeks were divided off, in order to accomplish a number of things relating to the Hebrew nation. The angel did not say that those seventy weeks would be consecutive, but only, that in coming time, seventy weeks belonged to the history of the Jewish nation. It is not needful for us to prove that this period means seventy weeks of years, or 490 years, or that it had its commencement 483 years before the Lord Jesus died on Calvary. Suffice it to say, that the 25th verse speaks of seven weeks, or 49 years, which commenced when Artaxerxes commanded that Jerusalem should be rebuilt, (Neh. ii. 8,) and terminated with the building of 'the street and of the wall.' Then follows a further period of sixty-two weeks, or 434 years, which terminated with the 'cutting off of the Messiah.' Lastly, we get the third period of one week, or seven years, which is still future, *because* the sin of Israel has not yet come to an end, and

filment within 1260 *days*, or the last half of the 70th week. Those literal-day expositors who shirk laborious investigation by blindly ignoring the year-day fulfilment, grope and stumble in the dark when they attempt to arrange the relative positions of the literal-day seals, trumpets, and vials, whereas this arrangement is discoverable in its minutest details, by deducing the literal-day from the year-day fulfilment, because the literal-day fulfilment of Dan. and Rev., within 2595 *days*, will be almost an exact fac-simile of their year-day fulfilment within 2595 *years*. (See diagram to chapter iv.) A few persons are mistakenly supposing that the wise virgins will be translated just before the seven years of the Covenant-week. Their translation, however, will be about FIVE YEARS before the end, (see chap. iv.)

the 'everlasting righteousness' of Israel has not yet been 'brought in,' both of which were to occur within the scope of these seventy weeks.

"Also, *because* the prophecy declares the abomination of desolation to be set up, when, in the middle of the week, the Antichrist compels a cessation of the daily sacrifice and of the oblation, (v. 27.)

"This event is also referred to in Dan. viii. 11, where the Antichrist is said to 'magnify himself even to the Prince of the Host, (the Messiah,) and to take away the daily sacrifice;' also, in the 13th verse of the same chapter, where one of the holy ones, in his inquiry as to its duration, connects the daily sacrifice with the abomination of desolation; also, in Dan. xi. 31. These three passages all refer to the same event, and to the same person.

"The Lord, in Matt. xxiv. 15, said, 'When ye therefore shall see the abomination spoken of by Daniel the prophet, standing in the holy place, (of the Temple,) flee! for then, (verse 21,) shall be great tribulation.' This tribulation we have already shown to be the same that Daniel refers to in chap. xii. 1. By the connection of all these scriptures, we establish beyond a doubt the futurity of the seventieth week.

"Then it follows, that if seven years still remain to be divided off to the Jewish nation, there must be an intervening space of time, a kind of interregnum or parenthesis, so to speak, between the termination of the sixty-ninth, and the commencement of the seventieth. This space is occupied with the gospel dispensation which is designed of God, 'to gather out of the gentiles, a people for his name.' When the Lord had concluded his last public address to the Jewish nation, he said, (Matt. xxiii. 38,) 'Behold! your house is left unto you desolate,' and this desolation they sealed upon themselves, when they cried out, 'His blood be upon us, and upon our children.' In consequence of this the natural Jewish 'branches were broken off because of unbelief,' and 'the wild Gentile branches grafted into their place,' (Rom. xi. 24,) and this was to continue 'until the fulness of the Gentiles be come in,' which also agrees with the words of Christ, (Luke xxi. 24,) 'Jerusalem shall be trodden down of the Gentiles, until the times of the Gentiles be fulfilled.' It is therefore evident that the gospel dispensation, or the heavenly calling of the Church, commenced where the earthly calling of the Jews broke off.

"We must here remark, that 'He' who confirms a (not the) covenant or agreement with many of the Jews for seven years, (Dan. ix. 27,) is the individual spoken of 'as the prince that shall come,' (yet to come.) The nation who destroyed the city was the Romans, therefore the expression 'the people of the prince, *the coming one*,' (literally,) connects *this coming prince* with the Roman empire, and proves that the man who will restore the Jewish people, and undertake to protect their worship for seven years, will be the Eighth Head of the Beast, or the Antichrist acknowledged as the prince of Israel. Under his guardianship they will repeople Palestine. Perhaps the day may not be far distant when Louis Napoleon will preside over a congress of European kings, and when he will assign pacific and political reasons for the expediency of the reoccupancy of the Holy Land by the Jewish nation. This might be brought forward as the most desirable method of tranquillizing this excited country. And if Napoleon III. wills it, what nation shall prevent it? Thus, he will accomplish one of the favourite projects of his uncle, who gathered together the chiefs of the Rabbins, at Paris, with that object in view; but, as God's time had not arrived, it came to nought. In this manner the seventieth week will probably begin, at least so we might expect from recent events."

This writer also correctly maintains that the whole Roman Empire, including England, France, Spain, Switzerland, Italy, Austria, Turkey, Egypt, Greece, and the North of Africa, will be formed into exactly ten kingdoms previous to the final 3½ years, (Rev. xvii. 12, 13,) and "will give their power and strength" to Louis Napoleon as king of their ten kings; and that Belgium will most probably be annexed to France. He likewise mentions some of the Scripture proofs that the coming of Christ "in the air" to raise the deceased saints, and to translate the Wise Virgins, will be some time *before* the 3½ years' Great Tribulation, and that there will be a second translation of living saints about *the end* of that 3½ years. He makes the following remarks upon the worship of Napoleon, the Antichrist, during the Tribulation, and of the actings of the Roman

Pontiff, who will cause him to be worshipped, (Rev. xix. 20.)

"The Pope, transformed into the False Prophet, will be the individual head of that astounding system of "Anthropotheism," or man-worship. As to the nature of the miracles that he will perform, by the power of Satan, they will equal any that may have been wrought by the power of God. He will, like Elijah, call down fire from heaven, he will impart life and articulation to the inanimate statue of the Antichrist, and he will command that all shall suffer the penalty of death, who will not bow down to this second Babylonian image. Of old, those who refused were cast into a burning fiery furnace; now they will be killed with the sword, or probably guillotined. But few, and they only the elect of God, chiefly the saints of Daniel's race, will refuse to bow down and worship. Men of the present day, confident in the boasted enlightenment of the age, are incredulous of such a statement, but we credit the Scriptures of truth, which declare that 'God will send them strong delusion, that they should believe a lie.' 2 Thess. ii. 11. Moreover, the Scripture clearly shows that the expectant in the Church of Christ will be translated before these events occur, and it is certain that a flood of demons will be cast down from the heavenlies into the earth, (Rev. xii. 7, 8, 9. Compare the Greek of Eph. vi. 12.) These things make it not difficult to believe in the possibility of strongly delusive signs and wonders, for how astonishing will be the effect produced upon the world at large, by the sudden transference of all those who are looking for the return of Christ, and by the actual presence of Satan and his hosts in the midst of the inhabitants of the earth and the sea, 'having great wrath, because he knoweth that he hath but a short time.' Religiously, politically, socially, and morally the world will be, under such circumstances, another chaos; infidelity, anarchy, injustice, and immorality, will reduce the earth to a condition not far removed from hell.

"We would here remark, that this counterfeit lamb-like power, (Rev. xiii. 11,) which is at present Popery, and other corrupt systems of the Christian faith, will so remain until within three and a half years of the close of the crisis, by which, we mean the manifestation of Christ in glory.

This is evident from the stated fact, that the persecution of the saints is to last that length of time. (See Dan. vii. 25, Rev. xiii. 5.) At the commencement of that three and a half years, it will become infidel, and this entire transformation of its system will probably be induced by the thorough disgust that the nations will exhibit for the Papacy, and this will cause the ten kings to 'hate the whore, and to make her desolate and naked, to eat her flesh and burn her with fire,' (Rev. xvii. 16.) They and their people will trample her polity under foot, and they will fall upon her wealth and fatness for a spoil. But, alas, it will be from bad to worse, from a religion professedly acknowledging God, to one in which God shall have *no place*, and man will lay claim to that worship due to Jehovah alone."

(24.) MAJOR SCOTT PHILLIPS, of London, wrote a work in 1859, called "Interpretations." He shows that most probably the earthquake that is to cleave the Mount of Olives asunder at the descent of Christ at the battle of Armageddon, (Zech. xiv. 3, 4,) will open a valley between the Mediterranean and the Dead Sea, and as the former is 1312 feet higher than the latter, the waters rushing downwards into the Dead Sea will cleanse it, and find an outlet by the ancient bed of the Jordan into the Gulf of Akabah, which constitutes part of the Red Sea. Jerusalem, the metropolis of the millennial earth, will thus stand upon the highway of vessels passing from Europe to Asia.

In regard to Antichrist, he says, (page 86,) "The papal system, under its successive popes, has been repeatedly proved by comparisons of history with Scripture to be the year-day Antichrist of 1260 years' endurance. Although the difficulty of proof has been increased by a literal individual Antichrist of 1260 days, being also to be manifested in extreme power and earthly glory immediately before Christ's coming to the earth. (2 Thess. ii.) But the last individual Antichrist, as well as the long-enduring Antichristian popedom, are now well conceived and recognised in the minds of faithful interpreters of prophecy."

After showing that Louis Napoleon is the seventh-revived or Eighth Head of the Beast or Roman Empire, and bears the number 666 in both his names, (Ludovicus and Ναπολέοντι,) and is to "destroy many by peace," (Dan. viii. 25,) he says, (page 91-95,) "Ever since 1847-48, the prospects of the Jews have tended more and more to their restoration; and it only remains that they should be restored to their own land by the agency of the Antichrist, who (Dan. ix. 27) shall confirm a covenant with them for a week of years, break it in the midst thereof, and himself be destroyed 1260 literal-days, or 3½ years afterwards, consumed by the brightness of our Lord's coming. . . . When from the troubled sea of the nations we behold the nephew of the great Napoleon upheaved by revolutionary passions —and when directly upon access to supreme power, he commences the strife about 'the holy places' at Jerusalem, we recognise an incipient connection between him and the Jews. . . . The king of fierce countenance and understanding dark sentences, (Dan. viii. 23,) that putter forth of riddles, who has, 'dethroned the sphinx,' has throughout the past seven years been spending an extra million annually on the increase of his war-steamers; he has cased ships in iron, invented screened gunboats, armed his boarders with six-barrelled revolvers, armed his immense armies with rifles, invented cannon of vastly increased powers, victualled his fortresses, especially completing the great menace to England, the fortress of Cherbourg. He has fortified Cevita Vecchia, filled Rome with troops, stimulated Sardinia to war: and all the while, though himself exercising vast bodies of men—50,000 at a time—he has repeated, L'Empire, c'est la paix—My Empire is an Empire of peace!" . . .

"Napoleon not daring to attack England directly, will, like the First Napoleon, turn his eye eastward. And he will make a covenant for seven years with the Jews, and restore them to Palestine. . . Breaking his covenant in the midst of the seven years, he will cause all who refuse to worship the Beast, or to receive his mark, or the number of his name, 666, in their right hands or on their foreheads, to be killed, (Rev. xiii.) thus commencing that most dreadful period, the last 3½ years, the literal 1260 days, during which the Devil gives to him 'his power and his seat and great authority.'—Immediately before this terrible period of 1260 days, if not at the commencement of the seven years, will take place the removal of the select people of God, of those who are watching and praying, and shall be accounted worthy to escape the sufferings which will come upon all the world, to try them that dwell upon the earth: and they shall ascend to meet Jesus Christ in the air, in order that at the close of the final period, be it seven years or 3½ years, they may return to judge the world, according to that which is written, 'the Lord my God shall come, and all the saints with thee,' (Zech. xiv.) and 'do ye not know that the saints shall judge the world,' for such honour have all his saints. (1 Cor. vi. 2, Ps. cxlix.) The wise virgins enter in unto the wedding feast, the foolish remain where they were. Then whoso will be saved during that great and terrible day of the Lord, must be saved yet so as by fire. Everywhere Antichrist has triumphed. He has lived to put down all opposition on the earth, (pp. 114, 120, 123.) . . . Subduing the territories once reigned over by Nebuchadnezzar, the four Empires foreshadowed by the 'great image,' (Dan. ii.) Antichrist will, as it were, reconstruct that image, work miracles by Satanic agency, speak great words against the Most High, wear out the saints of the Most High, and think to change times and seasons, and they shall be given into his hands until a time, times and half time, 1260 literal-days, or 3½ years, (Dan. vii.): at the close of which period, gathering his armies around Jerusalem, 'he shall come to his end, and none shall help him.' (P. 98.)

(25.) THE REV. H. G. GUINNESS, who is eminent for his evangelistic labours in Great Britain and America, published a prophetic pamphlet in 1861, (at Hamilton's, Philadelphia.) It consists principally of texts usefully arranged under different heads. He takes THE Antichrist, as held by futurist literal-day writers, to be a man who shall be the future *little horn, king of fierce countenance, wilful king,* and *healed,* or *eighth head of the beast,* who will confirm a seven years' covenant with the Jews, and during the latter 3½ of the 7 years will set up his idol, which is the abomination of desolation, (Mat. xxiv.) and be worshipped by all who dwell upon the earth. (Rev. xiii.) He says,

"With respect to the Jews, the word of God teaches that the children of Israel on account of their rejection and crucifixion of Christ, in unbelief, have been judicially blinded; their holy city and their temple destroyed; their house left to them desolate, thousands of their nation slain by the sword, and the rest scattered as outcasts among all nations; that Jerusalem shall be trodden down of the Gentiles, until 'the times of the Gentiles' shall be fulfilled; that Israel's judicial blindness shall last until the fulness of the Gentiles be come in; that they are still beloved for their fathers' sakes; that they shall yet be restored to their own land in unbelief; that having rejected Christ, they shall then receive the Antichrist; that by his means they shall be brought through unparalleled tribulation; that this 'great tribulation' shall be the climax of God's chastisement of them for their sins, and will result in the repentance of a faithful remnant of them; that there shall then come unto Zion the deliverer, and shall turn away ungodliness from Jacob; that Israel (the lost ten tribes,) shall be reunited to Judah; and that 'so all Israel shall be saved.'

"The prophet Daniel, speaking of the time of the end, and of Antichrist, says, 'He shall confirm a covenant with many for one week,' (of years, 7 years,) 'and in the midst of the week he shall cause the sacrifice and the oblation to cease, and upon the battlements shall be the idols' (or abomination) 'of the desolater, even until the consummation, and that determined shall be poured upon the desolater.' (Dan. ix. 27.) In allusion to this passage our Lord says, in Matthew, to his disciples, 'When ye therefore shall see the abomination of desolation spoken of by Daniel the prophet,' etc. (Matt. xxiv. 15–22; see Jer. xxx. 7; Dan. xii. 1; Zech. xiv. 1–3; Matt. xxiv. 15–21.

The arguments of the pamphlet in proof of Christ's Advent being *before* the Millennium conclude with the following exhortation.

"If, as the Scriptures prove, the last great Jewish trouble, 'the great tribulation,' will immediately *precede* the Jews' millennial blessedness; and if, as these Scriptures also show, the Lord will *personally come to deliver* the Jews from this their last and sorest affliction, and to turn away ungodliness from Jacob, *then the coming of the Lord Jesus will be premillennial.* Again: if, as these Scriptures prove, the world in the millennium will be filled with righteousness; and if, as these Scriptures also prove, the world will continue in its present unrighteousness until the second coming of Christ, *that coming must be before the millennium.* Again: if, as the Scriptures represent, the last head of the fourth (or Roman) Monarchy, that is Antichrist, is to perish before the millennium commences: and if, as these Scriptures also represent, that very Antichrist is to be destroyed at the second personal appearing of Christ, *his second personal appearance must be premillennial.*

"Again: if, as these Scriptures represent, no false professing apostate church will exist on earth in the millennium; and if, as these Scriptures also represent, the present false professing church will continue on earth until the second coming of Christ, and only perish at his coming, *that coming must be premillennial.* And lastly, if, as these Scriptures represent, the true Church of Christ will reign with him over the whole earth, in righteousness, blessedness, and visible glory, during the millennium; and if, as these Scriptures also represent, the true Church of Christ on earth will continue in an imperfect and persecuted state until the second coming of the Lord from heaven, *that second coming must be premillennial.* Do not close your eyes to these facts, dear brethren in the Lord. I solemnly assure you that these are but a few out of very many unanswerable arguments in proof of the premillennial coming of the Lord. 'Search the Scriptures' daily concerning these unspeakably important truths. And as the second coming of the Lord *is to be premillennial* (and there is not a single text in Scripture that states that it will not be so, while there are hundred of passages which prove that it will,) then make that coming the one great object of your hope, your daily desire, and hourly watching. Let it lead you, as it surely will if you yield to it, to separation from 'this present evil world,' whether it be the world professing or the world denying the religion of Jesus. Let it lead you to more true, earnest, and untiring effort for the everlasting welfare of all around you. Knowing the shortness of the time that remains for such labours, let it lead you to holiness of life, for 'every man that hath this hope in him, purifieth himself even as He is pure,' (1 John iii. 3.)

"A word to those who are unprepared for the Lord's coming. How fearful is your state! The appearing of Christ, which is the 'blessed hope' of saints, is a terror to you; for you know that he is to be 'revealed from heaven in flaming fire, taking vengeance on them that know not God, and obey not the gospel of our Lord Jesus Christ, who shall be punished with everlasting destruction from the presence of the Lord, and from the glory of his power.' O, were he to come this day, or even this week or month, what would you do? where would you appear? Poor, miserable sinner! He would come in love to millions, but not to you. He would come to break the chains of millions, but yours would be riveted for ever. He would come bringing marvellous light to the eyes of millions, but to you, the blackness of darkness for ever." He would come as the morning star, come as the altogether lovely, come as the hoped for, longed for, joy and rejoicing of all his saints, but to you only as the Almighty King and righteous Judge, the glorious and terrible God-man, Christ Jesus. O, man, woman, why die under 'the wrath of the Lamb'? Why perish under Christ's awful hand of judgment, when now, even now, his hand is outstretched to save you if you will come to him? He was made a curse for us! why reject the salvation, refuse the pardon, peace, eternal blessedness which his death puts within your reach, and thus come under the judgment of the wicked? Why should you compel his lips to curse you? why should you compel those lips which for long ages have spoken only grace to sinners, to utter the irrevocable sentence of your doom? Eternal destruction! The damnation of hell! O, perishing sinners, why will you die? You refuse mercy, you reject love, you despise compassion, you cast away salvation, and all for what? a few days of self-indulgence! an hour of false delight! a few moments of pleasurable sin! and for this you despise and reject the once crucified Jesus, with the everlasting salvation he offers, and to obtain this you cast yourself, with your eyes open, into hell! O, could my entreaties avail, I would beseech you by the name of the all holy God, our Maker and our Judge, not to trample on the agonies and blood and death of Jesus! not to close your eyes and turn away from his love, his grace so wonderful, from his outstretched arms, his solemn earnest invitations! O, come to him! Give up, poor sinner, give up! You have long enough rebelled. You have long enough been your own worst enemy. Now, have mercy on yourself! Refuse to commit suicide on your own soul. For the first time in your life, stop in your downward course. Stand still and refuse to go any further toward destruction. Turn, and look up to the blessed Saviour! Kneel down! Kneel at his feet! Yes, poor maniac, kneel down, maniac no longer, at the feet of Jesus! There is forgiveness there! Healing and peace are there! Righteousness and rest! And then to you, no longer the rebel, but now the pardoned, the accepted, Jesus will come as the star of morning, the morning of your everlasting joy! To you Jesus will come as the beloved, the beautiful, the altogether lovely! To you Jesus will come as the joy and glory of your soul, as the salvation of God, as your everlasting all! to you, even to you!"

(26.) THE LATTER DAYS OF JERUSALEM AND ROME is a lengthy and somewhat diffuse dissertation upon the prophecies of Daniel and Revelation, by Dominick McCausland, LL.D., Barrister at Law, published in 1859, at Bentley's, London.

It agrees with the other works here quoted, in regarding Daniel's 70th week as the last seven years of this dispensation, which are to be marked by unparalleled judgments, and by the persecution of Jews and Gentiles during the latter half-week by the personal Antichrist, or Man of Sin, who is then to arise. It is correct in the *general outline* of its views as to the visions of Daniel and Revelation describing the calamities that befall mankind within the final seven years, but its *particular applications* of the seals, trumpets, vials, and some other parts of the prophecies, are misty and indefinite, especially as to the chronological prophecies. It is written, however, in well-chosen language, and though not near so profound or accurate as Purdon's, Burgh's or Kelly's works, is yet, on the whole, a useful and timely production, containing many important elements of prophetic truth. Its writer justly considers "the abomination," mentioned in Dan. ix. 27, xi. 31, xii. 11, Matt. xxiv. 15, etc., to be the literal image of the future Antichrist, or Man of Sin, that will be placed in the Jewish Temple at the time of the Great Tribulation, (Matt. xxiv. 21,) during the latter half of the 70th week. He says, "This period of seventy weeks is, in the subsequent verses of the same chapter, divided by the angel into three parts,—the first consisting of seven weeks; the second, of sixty-two weeks, ending with the cutting off of the Messiah; and the third and last, of one week. These seventy weeks, denoting seventy weeks of years, or 490 years, commencing 'from the going forth of the commandment to restore and build Jerusalem,' began to run from the year 455 B.C.; and, therefore, the seven weeks, and sixty-two weeks, (sixty-nine weeks,) terminated A D. 29, which was the year of the Saviour's death, when, as appears from the twenty-sixth verse, the Jews are to be no longer his people, (margin.) The old dispensation was finished, and they became outcast. But, though they became thus outcast, and alien from the God of Abraham, and have so continued ever since; they are not to continue so for ever; for we are told in the next verse, (v. 27,) that 'he shall confirm the covenant with many *for one week*,' i. e. for the last remaining of the seventy weeks; and during that week, the abomination of desolation shall be set up in the restored temple, the sacrifice suspended, and the Jews subjected to the Antichristian persecution, or 'the great tribulation,' so often alluded to in Scripture. (P. 372.)

"This renewal of the covenant with the Jewish people in the latter days, is also spoken of in several other passages of Holy Writ. For instance, in the twentieth chapter of Ezekiel, when God is speaking of gathering the Jews out of the countries through which they are scattered, he says, 'I will cause you to pass under the rod, and I will bring you into the bond of the covenant,' (v. 37.)'

"Thus it appears that in the latter days of this dispensation, the Jews will be restored to their own land, their temple rebuilt, and their ceremonial worship re-established; while, at the same period, the Gentile nations, as such, shall have wholly thrown off their allegiance to God, and submitted themselves to the head of the revived Roman empire, the Antichrist, who shall not only deny Christ, but announce himself to be the Messiah, attesting his claims to divine honours by miracles and prodigies. (P. 376.)

"This creation of an image of the Antichrist, (Rev. xiii. 14,) is, we conceive, the setting up of 'the Abomination of desolation,' spoken of by Daniel the prophet, and referred to by our Saviour in his prophecy upon the Mount of Olives. It is clear, that by miraculous and diabolical agencies, the image shall be endued with life, for the purpose of luring the unfortunate Jews to turn from their expected Messiah to worship and submit themselves to the

'Destroyer of the Gentiles.' This will be the season of their last trial, denominated by the prophet Daniel, and by the Saviour, as 'the great tribulation, such as was not from the beginning of the world to this time, no, nor ever shall be.' And it is confirmed by the continuation of the Lord's prophecy,—'And except those days should be shortened, there should no flesh be saved; but for the elect's sake those days shall be shortened. Then, if any man shall say unto you, lo! here is Christ, or there; believe it not. For there shall arise *false Christs* and *false prophets*, and shall show *great signs and wonders;* insomuch, that if it were possible, they shall deceive the *very elect.*' Here there is a reference to the false Christs, (the Antichrist, or the first Beast,) and to false prophets, (the second Beast, which is afterwards styled 'the False Prophet,') and to their miraculous signs and wonders; and here, also, we find a reference to the 'very elect,' or those written in the Lamb's book, (v. 8,) who are to be the remnant that shall refuse to worship, or pay homage to the arch-impostor. (P. 382.)

"The ultimate triumph of Romanism and apostasy is inevitable; for the pages of prophecy reveal what daily experience and observation is confirming to the inquiring mind, that this unchanging system shall spread like a cloud over the face of the earth, and extinguish Gospel truth, before that it shall be itself extinguished. And when once the final triumph shall have commenced, the progress will be sure and rapid. As a system, it has, as we have seen, much to recommend it to unregenerate minds, which are influenced by events, and estimate the propriety of principles by results to the eye of sight, being wholly blind to that which is only discernible to the eye of faith. England has hitherto been hostile to Rome, and opposed a stubborn front to her aggressions even in the dark ages; and England may yet be permitted to continue to be a witness, defying her open hostility and withstanding her covert machinations.' But, if we have rightly interpreted these prophecies, the time will come when she too will be drawn into the vortex of apostasy and infidelity; when the people of God must enter into their secret chambers, and shut their doors about them for a little moment, until the indignation be past. (P. 509.)

"Christ appears, with his saints, to take vengeance of,

and to exterminate his foes, who at last appear in open rebellion, like Korah and his company, on the field of Armageddon, on the mountains of Israel. The Beast, and the Kings of the earth, (the Ten Kings,) with their armies, are vanquished. The Beast and his False Prophet are taken, and cast *alive* into the fire burning with brimstone, and the remnant are slain with the sword—they perish in the gainsaying of Core." (Jude 11.)

In the foregoing work* the following quotation is given from the year-day exposition of Daniel, by the Rev. T. Birks, Secretary of the Evangelical Alliance.

"It may be inferred from a careful comparison of several Scriptures, that at this time, (the Jewish Restoration,) the temple described in Ezekiel will have been built, and that *there this fierce and mighty king will seat himself as a sovereign, and claim to be the object of a divine adoration.*" And again—"The Papacy, directed by the Wilful King, in its last hours will fill up the measure of its apostasy, and gather to itself those partial features of Antichrist which are now to be seen in the Mahometan delusion, and its open rejection of the Son of God. At the same time a leader will arise, *the last personal head of the compound system of evil,* and the heathen Antiochus, the Pope, and the Turk, contribute to supply the features of this iniquity. The Wilful King, in this last stage of his power, and represented now by this leader, will gather in himself the predicted character of a King of the North, and then come down like a whirlwind on the land of Israel. Success for a time will attend his banners, so that, in the words of Habakkuk, 'he will gather to himself all nations, and heap unto himself all people.' *The faithful witnesses who protest against his idolatry and blasphemy, will be persecuted with great wrath, and hunted out for destruction.* The king of pride will *take Jerusalem, the holy city,* for his seat, where he will plant his standard, and probably claim divine honours from the subject nations; a worship to be paid, in

---

* Although it might seem from Ezek. xx. 37, quoted by this writer, that it will be *God* who will bring the Jews into the bond of the Covenant, yet this is not inconsistent with Antichrist making the covenant, for God will bring it to pass instrumentally through his agency.

his person, to the dignity of regenerate and glorified humanity, freed from the long delusion of past ages."

(27.) THE REV. W. MARRABLE, Prebendary of St. John's Episcopal Church, Dublin, published in 1858-9, a well-arranged prophetical pamphlet, entitled, "What the Lord saith concerning Israel and Jerusalem," and consisting of sixty-seven divisions, supported by innumerable passages of the word of God. It is briefly reviewed in the Quarterly Journal of Prophecy for July, 1859.

He maintains that the Gog of Ezekiel xxxviii. is identical with the Antichrist, or eighth head of the Beast—a view which is also upheld in the present work, (see page 100.) For, although Antichrist, the Eighth Head, is distinctly foretold in Rev. xix. 20, to be finally cast alive into a lake of fire, which would seem to conflict with the statement in Ezek. xxxix. 11, that in the valley of Hamon-gog "shall they bury Gog and all his multitude," yet this last-mentioned passage may merely mean, in a general sense, that Gog's hosts will be buried in that valley, and need not strictly imply that Gog himself will actually be interred in the soil of the earth, which, in fact, would seem irreconcilable with his being cast alive into a lake of fire, unless the word "buried" denotes the violent act of submerging and plunging Antichrist beneath the liquid sea of fiery lava, just as the phrase "buried with him in baptism," (Col. ii. 12,) signifies the submersion beneath the water of those who are baptized. But the expression, "Gog and all his multitude," may be a hendiadys for "all the multitude of Gog;" as in Rev. xii. 5, "God and his throne," is a hendiadys for "the throne of God." Antichrist, being certainly identical with "the wilful king" of Dan. xi., who is attended by the Ethiopians and Lybians, and finally perishes upon "the glorious holy mountain" of Palestine, clearly appears to be the same as Gog, who also is followed by the Ethiopians and Lybians, and at last perishes on "the mountains of Israel."

The Rev. W. Marrable further considers that the Antichrist, or Man of Sin, is to sit in the rebuilt Jewish temple, and that he is not the Pope, but an individual who will be Head of the revived Roman Empire, who is described in Dan. ix. 26, 27, as "the prince that shall come," and as the person "who shall confirm the covenant with many for one week," &c., after which there will be seven years to the Consummation—or End, as held by the other writers here quoted.

(28.) AN ISRAELITE, apparently possessing considerable acquaintance with the theological writings of the Jews, contributed some articles in 1861 to the Quarterly Journal of Prophecy, which is published at Nisbet's, in London. He intimated it to be the opinion of other Jews, beside himself, that Gog of Ezek. xxxviii: would be the last great oppressor of Israel, and was the person who at the latter end of this dispensation would fulfil Dan. ix. 27, "by confirming a covenant with many of the Jews for seven years," and at last, about the close of the seven years, would be destroyed at the coming of the Messiah.

His testimony is valuable, as showing that these passages in Ezek. xxxviii. and Dan. ix. 27, are not only applied by Christian, but also by Jewish commentators, to the final deception and persecution of Israel by the last great Head of Gentile power at the time of the future glorious Advent of the Lord Jesus.*

(29.) THE REV. DR. SEISS, the able and eloquent author of "Last Times," "The Day of the Lord," "Threatening Ruin," "Parable of the Ten Virgins," etc., and Minister of St. John's Lutheran Church, which is one of the largest in Philadelphia, United States, has recently given the same explanation, as these other writers, regarding the 70th week. He says, in a note appended to the second edition (1862) of his "Day of the Lord,"

"From Daniel ix. 27 it would seem that one week of years before 'the consummation,' Antichrist (supposed to be Louis Napoleon) will make a league with the Jews, pledging his protection and assistance in their return to Palestine, and the re-establishment of the temple services. It is thought by many that this covenant may be expected within a year or two. When it is made, it will constitute a very notable epoch, and will settle the point that we are then within seven years of the End."

Dr. Seiss also holds, that the 144,000 in Rev. xiv., re-

---

* His exposition not being at hand to quote from, the outline of his views is only given from memory, otherwise it would be stated at further length

presents the wise virgins, who are caught up in the first translation at Christ's coming "in the air" *before* Antichrist's 3½ years' persecution and he considers the great multitude in Rev. vii. 9, and "the harvest" in Rev. xiv. 15, 16, to denote the saints who are caught up in the second translation *after* that 3½ years. In his book, entitled "Parable of the Ten Virgins," (189 pages,) he clearly shows that the foolish virgins do not represent the ungodly, as is usually supposed, but denote true Christians who are in a backsliding state, devoid of real faith in the nearness of Christ's Advent; who, although left behind at the first translation, are not necessarily lost, but being in the main truly converted and godly persons, are eventually saved either at death or in the second translation, yet so as by fire, and after being in many cases exposed to the terrors of the Great Tribulation. All his published works having been composed as lectures, are written in an eloquent and popular style, which renders them most suitable and attractive treatises for beginners in the study of prophecy.*

(30.) ISRAEL'S ZUKUNFT, or "Israel's Future," is the name of a moderate-sized exposition of the prophecies relating to the Jews, which is published in German, by Ernst Bredt, at Leipzig. It is a German translation of an original French work, written by E. Guers, in 1856, and entitled, "Israel aux derniers jours de l'économie actuelle, ou Essai sur la restauration prochaine de ce peuple—par E. Guers, Paris, Grassart: Genève Emile, Beroud.) It is a futurist literal-day exposition, and explains Daniel's seventieth week to be the last seven years of this dispensation, and to

---

* These books can be had at the Lutheran Publication House, 42 North Ninth street, Philadelphia. "The Last Times" ($1,) contains about 190 pages, and treats of the Second Advent, Great Tribulation, Millennium, &c. It is almost the only popular elementary prophetic work that is easily obtainable in the United States. If republished in England, it would doubtless have a good circulation there. Dr. Cummings' recent prophetic works can be got at Rudd & Carleton's, New York; although very excellent, so far as they go, yet they do not touch upon many of the most important prophecies relating to the present momentous epoch. The Rev. Dr. Duffield's Second Advent Lectures, and Rev. Isaac Labagh's "Great Events of Unfulfilled Prophecy," are books admirably suited for general circulation. Shimeall's Bible Chronology (Barnes & Burr, New York,) is also a learned prophetic work.

commence with a seven years' covenant being made between the Antichrist and the Jews; the latter 3½ years of the seven years being the period of the Great Tribulation, closing with the personal descent of Christ at Armageddon. It is not known by the present writer whether or not its author perceives and states that Christ will come to take away some of the living saints, as is clearly shown in Scripture, *before* that 3½ years.

This book by E. Guers, being published both in French and German, and easily obtainable at Paris, Geneva, and Leipsic, is a most valuable work to give and to recommend for perusal to persons who only speak those languages, and may become a great blessing to such Europeans as read it, if it convinces them of the nearness of the Advent of the Lord Jesus Christ, and of the awful persecution that Christians will presently meet with from the Personage who will soon make the seven years' covenant with the Jews. Those who have French or German friends, should urge them to obtain and peruse it. It can, of course, be obtained in America or Great Britain, by ordering it through the usual bookselling agencies, from Paris or Leipsic.

(31.) TEMOIGNAGE is another futurist literal-day French exposition, which, from an extract given in the *Prospect*, seems to hold the same view as to Daniel's 70th week, for it speaks of the 3½ years' 'Great Tribulation mentioned in Dan. xii. 7, 11, as "the Great Tribulation of the last half-week," (evidently the last half of the 70th week,) after which the Lord descends in visible glory.

(32.) AN ANONYMOUS PAMPHLET called "The Difference between the Parousia and Epiphaneia," was published in London about 1859. It showed the distinction between these two Greek words, as they are used in texts referring to Christ's Advent—the first implying the presence of Christ "in the air," to raise the saints and to take away the Wise Virgins, *before* the final 3½ years' Tribulation, and the second denoting the manifestation of his presence at his descent on the earth *after* that 3½ years, which it further showed to be the latter half of Daniel's 70th week.

(33.) THE COMING BATTLE is a prophetic treatise by the author of the present work, in which the same views were presented. It was published in 1860, and some of the following remarks, written before the Secession of the Southern States, have already proved correct.

"The fifty million dollars that have been spent by England over the Chinese war had better have been reserved to relieve the poverty that will soon prevail among her operatives. For when the American Union is dissolved by the Secession of the Southern States, the exports of cotton are likely to be diminished by the outbreak of hostilities and servile insurrections. As this disruption may occur speedily,* perhaps even before 1861, England must soon feel the effects, in want of employment among the one-fifth of her population who are engaged in cotton manufactures. In the midst of the riots and disturbances that would necessarily arise, Napoleon might find a good opportunity to attempt an invasion of England. . . . It is probable that unforeseen political complications may arise, and events take such a turn, as to bring across the ocean, some of Napoleon's 600,000 French soldiers, and give them a foothold on American soil. The interference of France was sought and obtained in the last American War, and the precedent may be followed in the conflagration of intestine warfare which seems likely soon to rage with uncontrollable fury.

"The atheism which shall signalize the period of the Napoleonic Woe, will proceed to the assertion and establishment of the worship of man in the person of the French Emperor. The commencement of this, by the Jews receiving him as their Messiah, may be expected very speedily. This would not be inconsistent with the covenant on his part, to permit them to continue the observance of the Mosaic rites during the seven years. . . . The seven years to be mentioned in the agreement, will probably be the period for which Napoleon III. will engage to protect all Jews dwelling around Jerusalem, or to assist those who may wish to emigrate there, or to make free grants of lands to settlers. In the midst of the seven years, he will begin to tyrannize over them, setting up his image in their temple, and causing all to be slain who refuse to worship it. Liberty of commerce will also be granted to none but those who have imprinted on their forehead or right hand, the number 666, or one of the

---

* The Secession of the Southern States began in December, 1860.

words *Louis Napoleon*, or a certain mark which he will appoint. At the close of the three and a half years, during which this will continue, the Emperor will become indescribably exasperated with some acts of insubordination on their part, and will go forth at the head of a vast host, breathing out threatenings and slaughter, and resolved, in his fury, to destroy and utterly to make away many.

"Having concentrated his armed hosts upon Jerusalem, this modern Pharaoh will have already begun, in anticipation, to exult over the victory within his grasp; when suddenly, without a moment's premonition, a frightful tumult will arise from every quarter of his camp. A confusion more confounding than that of Babel will be heard on every side. The mutual hatreds and jealousies, that have been long fermenting among the various sections of his heterogeneous and ill-assorted host, will have burst forth in a tempest of irrepressible fury. 'Every man's sword will be against his brother.' Ezek. xxxviii. 21. European, Asian, African, German, Italian, Russian, all will be mingled in one chaotic, fierce, and sanguinary conflict of mutual slaughter. Simultaneously, great hailstones, and fire and brimstone, will be rained down upon the ill-fated combatants; and to accelerate their destruction, the earth will open her mouth, and engulph thousands, like Korah, Dathan, and Abiram, in the yawning chasm. In a shorter period than would be occupied by the recital, five-sixths' of these proud and heaven-defying warriors will have had their carcasses given as food to the fowls of the air, and to the beasts of the field. Meanwhile the Antichrist, who is gazing upon the scene with feelings akin to those experienced by the first Napoleon, at Waterloo, when the line of the Old Guard wavered and broke, is suddenly seized by the divine executioners of the 'judgment written,' and, together with the False Prophet, his intimate associate, is cast alive into the lake of fire."

*(34.) "THE MILLENIUM of the Doctrines of the Second Advent," by "Omicron," was published at Nisbet's, in London, in 1844. It stated that before the present dispensation terminates, the Roman Empire must revive, in its imperial form spoken of as "the beast that was, and is

* In this fourth edition, in 1862, fifty-seven instead of only thirty-three writers on the 70th week, are quoted, being twenty-seven more.

not, even he is the eighth, and is of the seven and goeth into perdition:" that this imperial power will kill the two witnesses, and have given to him a mouth speaking great things and blasphemies, and will continue forty and two months (or 3½ years) and make war with the saints and overcome them, and possess universal power over ALL kindreds, and tongues, and nations, and be worshipped by ALL that dwell upon the earth except those whose names are written in the Lamb's book of life: and will have a subordinate agent, the False Prophet or two-horned beast, who will deceive people by lying miracles and great wonders, and will cause as many as will not worship the image of the beast to be killed (see Rev. xi. xiii. xvii. throughout); but that, first of all, "this imperial power will make a covenant with the Jews, who will be partly restored to their own land in a state of unbelief, for a week or seven years: in the middle of the week he will break the covenant, put down their usual services, plant the abomination of desolation in the temple itself, and demand for himself the worship which belongs to God alone. Now will be fulfilled truly and literally the prophecy of the Man of Sin, or Wicked One (2 Thess. ii. 3–12). Such is the end of the present dispensation, as described in the book of God: and for this terrible end the professing Church is making ready with fearful rapidity."

(35.) THE REV. W. G. BARKER of the Church of England, wrote in the Quarterly Journal of Prophecy, in 1850, a short "Apology for Moderate Futurism," maintaining that both year-day and literal-day interpreters are in the main correct, on the principle that "what has been acted over by Popery in 1260 years, shall be acted over again by Infidelity in 1260 days, and close the scene of Satan's opposition to Christ by his strongest and most daring effort." He is also stated by Elliott to hold Daniel's 70th week to be the last seven years of this dispensation, in the same manner as W. Kelly, W. Trotter, etc., explain it.

(36.) ARTHUR REES, of Sunderland, in England, published a brief but striking treatise in 1852 called the "Death of Wellington and Resurrection of Napoleon," showing Louis Napoleon to be the future Antichrist or Eighth Head of the Beast, according to Rev. xvii. 10, 11, as demonstrated by Frere, Irving and others. He, moreover, referred to Dan. ix. 27, as to be fulfilled at the future restoration of the Jews by the Antichrist Napoleon. The most important part of his treatise will be found quoted in the Author's forthcoming fifth enlarged edition of the "Coming Battle."

(37.) JAMES HUNTER, in Plymouth, in 1854, wrote a pamphlet entitled "The Personal Coming and Reign of the Lord Jesus over the earth," which gives as good a futurist outline of the leading events attending Christ's Advent, as has probably ever been expressed within an equally small compass. He explains "the prince that shall come" who is depicted in Dan. ix. 26, 27 as making a seven-years covenant with the Jews, to be the future personal Antichrist or Man of Sin, to whom he also applies the description of the little horn, in Dan. vii. and viii. and of the vile person in Dan. xi. 21–45, and of the foolish shepherd in Zech. xi. He also holds that nearly all persons in the ten kingdoms that are to be formed out of the old Roman Empire, from England to the Euphrates, will worship this Antichrist for 3½ years according to Rev. xiii, and then the Man of Sin will be cast alive into the lake of fire at the Battle of Armageddon. The wise virgins, he believes, will be taken up to meet Jesus before the judgments fall on the earth.

(38.) THE AUTHOR of "Notes on Scripture," which were printed in the successive numbers of the Quarterly Journal of Prophecy* for several years following 1849, mentioned in Nos. 9 and 10, the passage in Dan. ix. 27, as referring to a covenant to be made by the personal Antichrist with the Jews, and then to be broken by him. He justly understands from Zech. xi. that Antichrist's right arm will be withered, and his right eye darkened, and from Rev. xiii. that his image will literally speak and breath. He also maintains that the 144,000 wise virgins in Rev. xiv. 1–5 will be translated before the Great Tribulation, which Antichrist's persecution will cause. In the course of his many excellent remarks he thus, in No. 27,

* The Rev. Dr. Horatius Bonar of Scotland is its editor. American readers would do well to obtain it from Nisbet's, London, and peruse its ably written articles.

meets the hackneyed objection that none can discover the time of Christ's Advent.

" The expression in Rev. i. 1, 'The revelation of Jesus Christ which God gave unto him to show to his servants things which must shortly come to pass,' implies that the revelation was a communication disclosed to Christ by the Father, and of which Christ had not been previously aware. The non-revealing of the day of the Lord to Jesus, while on earth, was part of his humiliation. 'Of that day and that hour knoweth no man; no, not the angels which are in heaven, *neither the Son*, but the Father' (Mark xiii. 32). After his resurrection, however, the Father appears to have made disclosures to him, and these we have in the Book of Revelation. How interesting and blessed must be the study of such a part of the Word!"

(39.) THE AUTHOR of a well-arranged "Syllabus of Fourteen Lectures," inserted in the twenty-seventh number of the Quarterly Journal of Prophecy, in 1855, explains the 70th week in Dan. ix. 27, as to be fulfilled by the future Antichrist at the epoch of the Second Advent, when the literal 3½ years in Rev. xiii. 5, Dan. vii. 25, will be accomplished by him. In giving the usual literal-day futurist views, this expositor considers *Apollyon*, in Rev. xi. 11, to be the name of the Antichrist, and the "abomination" in Matt. xxiv. 15, Mark xiii. 14, to be his speaking and breathing image that will be worshipped (Rev. xiii. 14, Hab. ii. 18); and also his acquisition of great treasures of gold and silver to be foretold in Dan. xi. 28, 38, 43, Ezek. xxviii. 4, 5, Hab. ii. 5–10.

This last mentioned feature in Antichrist's character seems, at the date of the fourth edition of the present work in 1863, to be already developing in Louis Napoleon, whose seizure of Mexico and therewith the Mexican silver mines is the prelude to his speedy possession of the gold mines in California, and before his career is ended, to the auriferous treasures of British Columbia and Australia.

(40.) THE AUTHOR of "The Church and the Kingdom," published in 1851, at Granvilles in Bristol, remarks that only the seven weeks and sixty-two weeks out of Daniel's seventy weeks were fulfilled before the cutting off of Christ, and that, therefore, "one week or seven years yet remains to be fulfilled," and that it will be accomplished at the period of the time of trouble of Dan. xii., "when the Church being already translated and in glory, and Satan cast down to the earth, events will thicken with a rapidity that has had no parallel in the history of the world—the short but fearful reign of Antichrist, the great tribulation, and to close the scene, the Lord Jesus personally appearing to crush his foes now made his footstool."

(41.) THE REV. F. G. MIDDLETON, of the Church of England, published a pamphlet in 1860, at Nisbets, in London, called "The Rapture of the Church," in which he maintained that the Advent of Christ to raise the deceased saints and translate the wise virgins (1 Thess. iv. 16) will precede the great tribulation. He also adverted to the 70th week in Dan. ix. 27, as awaiting its fulfilment at that final crisis.

(42.) W. C. BAYNES, of Montreal, Canada East, delivered in that city in 1859–60, very able futurist lectures on prophecy, some of which were afterwards published. He maintained that Antichrist will make a seven-years' covenant with the Jews about seven years before the Millenium, as stated in Dan. ix. 27, and that the Jewish sacrifices will be re-instituted in the restored temple soon afterwards, and that the wise virgins will be caught up before Antichrist's furious raging during the last half of the seven years. His general views are very like those of Denny, Tregelles, Trotter, etc.

(43.) A WRITER in the Advent Herald—a weekly prophetical journal in Boston, U. S. (to which the annual subscription is two dollars)—showed in some articles early in 1862, that Louis Napoleon is the embryo Antichrist, who will make a covenant for seven years with the Jews, seven years before the descent of Christ to destroy him (Dan. ix. 27), and will massacre Christians during the last half of the seven years according to Rev. xiii. 5. His other views were very similar to those of the writers above mentioned.

(44.) THE REV. G. BROOKMAN, of the Church of England, in London, Canada West, and formerly in India, has written and preached considerably upon the prophecies and firmly maintains, from Rev. xiii., xvii., that Napoleon III. is the incipient Antichrist, who will make a seven-years' league with the Jews, about seven years before his destruction at Christ's descent upon Mt. Olivet (Dan. ix. 27, Zech. xiv.); and that the first translation will precede the 3½ years Napoleonic infidel persecution. His views agree generally with Trotter's, Kelly's, Purdon's, etc.

(45.) H. P. SCHOLTE, in "The Israelite Indeed," published in New York, in Jan. 1862, speaks thus: "The signs of the times are portentous of great coming events The whole world is in commotion: and all the nations of the globe are in contact with each other. Science has conquered almost every obstacle of time and space: the pulsation of the heart at one place can be communicated in a moment to all the nations of the earth by telegraph: and an order emanated from a central power can be executed in a short space of time by steam motion. Religious indifference gains ground amongst Christians, Mahometans, and heathen. Every thing is prepared to bring about the last form of worldliness, which shall exist in the last or extreme part of the days of this world."

"In that last period God's promises to Israel shall be fulfilled. Then the broken chain of the seventy weeks of years will be resumed, and the last week will be accomplished. That last week will be full of trouble for the holy people; but the final issue will be for Jerusalem as well as for Daniel's people; 'to finish the transgression, and to make an end of sins, and to make reconciliation for iniquity, and to bring in everlasting righteousness, and to seal up the vision and prophecy, and to anoint the most holy,' Dan. ix. 27. The numbers in Daniel as well as in the Apocalypse have reference to that last year-week of Daniel when Israel will be again restored as a nation, and to the revelation of Antichrist against the middle of that week."

(46.) W. TROTTER, one of the best futurist literal-day interpreters, published in 1853–4 a series of "Plain Papers on Prophetic Subjects" at the Dublin Tract Repository, at 10 D'Oliver St., and at W. Macintosh's, London. In No. 15, upon "Israel in the approaching Crisis," he fully explains Dan. ix. 27 as to be hereafter accomplished by Antichrist, the eighth head of the Roman Empire, making a seven-years' alliance with the Jews, and in the midst of the seven years commencing his 3½ years' massacre of those who will not worship him, and at last perishing at

Christ's descent. He looks for the ascension of the wise virgins at some period prior to Antichrist's 3½ years persecution.

He says, "The seventy weeks were determined upon Daniel's 'people' and upon his 'holy city:' and whenever the seventieth week shall commence it will be Jerusalem and the Jews will be again in question before God. And he (that is, 'the prince that shall come') shall confirm a (see margin) covenant with many for one week: and in the midst of the week he shall cause the sacrifice and the oblation to cease, and for the overspreading of abominations, he shall make it desolate, even until the consummation, and that determined shall be poured upon the desolate.' Here we have the 'covenant with death,' and the 'agreement with hell' on the part of the Jewish rulers. Re-established in their land, under the protection of 'the prince that shall come,' the eighth, Satanic head of that people who long ago destroyed the city and the sanctuary, he will enter into an alliance with the Jews for seven years."

(47.) F. W. GRANT, in Canada West, wrote a brief prophetical publication in 1861-2, to show that the Advent of Christ will most probably occur within the next few years. He lectured in Toronto in 1861, upon Louis Napoleon being the future Antichrist or Eighth Head; he also explains Dan. ix. 27 to signify that a seven-years' agreement will be made about seven years before the Millenium, between many of the Jews and "the prince that shall come." He believes in a translation of saints before the Great Tribulation, and agrees in most points with the general futurist interpretation of Prophecy.

(48.) A. P. JOLLIFFE, an American prophetical writer, has held for some years past that Louis Napoleon is the coming Antichrist, who will make a seven-years' treaty with some of the Jews seven years before this dispensation ends; and that the prepared saints will be caught up at some period before his persecution of 3½ years rages during the last half-week, at which time the seals, trumpets and vials, etc., will be literally fulfilled.

(49.) J. FONDEY published some explanations of prophecy in the United States more than ten years ago, in which he justly maintained the 2300 days in Dan. viii. 14 to be, in its literal-day fulfilment, a future period beginning with the re-institution of the Jewish sacrifices at their return to Palestine, and ending with the descent of Christ on the earth. He has recently had printed a concise statement of his belief that Louis Napoleon will be the personal Antichrist, who will make a covenant with many Jews seven years before the consummation, and that the ready saints will be translated before Antichrist's 3½ years' massacre of Christians. His prophetical views agree in the main with those of the present work.

(50.) THE REV. D. BOSWORTH, in the United States, has for many years preached and written on Prophecy. He says of Dan. ix. 27, "The Jews are expecting a speedy return to their fatherland, there to enjoy all their former glory as a nation. In the leader then, whom they shall receive, may we not expect a fulfilment of Christ's prediction when reproving them for not receiving himself? 'I am come in my Father's name and ye receive me not; if another shall come in his own name, him ye will receive' (Jno. v. 43). We may expect then such a leader soon to appear, to make a covenant with the Jews for a prophetic week. In the midst of the week allying himself with others (perhaps spiritualists and Papists), he will break his covenant with the Jews, set his idols on the battlements of the temple, and perhaps himself in the temple of God; and after bringing untold miseries on the Jews, will perish at the earthquake tread of Christ upon Mt. Olivet," (Zech. xiv.)

(51.) DR. J. LITCH, editor of the Advent Herald,* in Boston, U. S., and author of several able prophetical treatises, believes, from Dan. ix. 27, that the personal Antichrist will confirm a seven-years' compact with some of the Jews, and that during the ensuing final years of this economy, there will be two translations of living saints at the two stages in Christ's Advent, with Antichrist's 3½ years' persecution intervening.

(52.) "THE PRESENT TESTIMONY," published at R.

---

* This valuable and evangelical newspaper was commenced twenty years ago, by the eminent and highly esteemed Second Advent minister, the Rev. J. V. Himes, who is about to publish a useful prophetical journal called "The Voice of the Prophets," at Buchanan, Michigan, U. S. He has long maintained the Advent of Christ to occur about 1867-8.

Groombridge's in London, contains various prophetical articles by the "Brethren," and in volumes v. and xii. in 1853 and 1861, gives expositions of Daniel and Revelation, in which Daniel's 70th week is explained to be the closing seven years before the Millenium.

(53.) THE REV. E. E. REINKE, of the Lutheran denomination, and one of the editors of an excellent little monthly periodical in Philadelphia, U. S.—the "Prophetic Times"—considers that Antichrist will fulfil Dan. ix. 27, and holds much the same views as Trotter, Kelly, Seiss, etc.

(54.) DR. WILLIAMSON, of Toronto, C. W., also has entertained substantially the same prophetical views as the writers just mentioned, for upwards of twenty years: and interprets Louis Napoleon to be the embryo Antichrist. He is about to issue a new work on prophecy.

(55.) J. L. HOPKINS, editor of a bi-monthly prophetical newspaper in San Francisco, California, U. S., called "The World's Crisis,"* similarly advocates these views in his journal.

(56.) THOMAS PARKER, of Newbery, Berkshire, England, published a work called "Visions and Prophecies of Daniel expounded," in London in 1646—two hundred years ago. He expected the Papal 1260 years to end somewhere near 1860, and he distinctly stated that Antichrist would fulfil Dan. ix. 27, by making a covenant with many Jews seven years before the Millennium, and carrying on his unparalleled persecution until his destruction.

(57.) O. STANLY, the esteemed author of various excellent religious and prophetical tracts at W. H. Broom's, Paternoster Row, regards England as certain to fall under Antichrist, by whom he also seems to expect Daniel's 70th week to be fulfilled.

THE FOREGOING SUMMARY of more than fifty testimonies as to the future fulfilment of Daniel's 70th week, (Dan. ix. 27,) by the Antichrist, (who has been shown in chapter I. to be Louis Napoleon,) should be carefully studied by every Christian who desires "to discern the signs of the times." The above quoted prophetic interpretations of

* As many copies of it are circulated gratuitously, and it is the only Second Advent journal in California, it is highly deserving of contributions and subscriptions, which will be thankfully received by its editor. The "Prophetic Times" is printed at Messrs C. Sherman & Son's, Philadelphia, U. S.

Purdon in 1849 and 1852, of Porter, in 1856, of Taunton in 1857, of the English author of "Armageddon," in 1857-8, and of Major Phillips in 1859, as to the certainty of Louis Napoleon becoming the Antichrist, and making the seven years' covenant with the Jews, will be of especial value as soon as this event shall have taken place. Meanwhile, the fact, that after that event there will only be two years and from four to six weeks before those of us who are the Wise Virgins will be caught up to be with Christ, should exert a most quickening and purifying influence upon our minds. As a practical application of the subject of the Second Advent, the following extracts from a valuable prophetic work, (Seiss's Parable of the Ten Virgins,) may here be introduced.

"Nor is it difficult to ascertain what are those works to which we must devote ourselves with a view to be ready for the Lord's coming. Having given ourselves unreservedly to Christ, we must try continually to be more and more like him, mortifying the desires of the flesh, employing diligently the means of improvement in sacred wisdom and grace, subjecting ourselves cheerfully to the rules of heavenly discipline, occupying our stations with industry, patience, and fidelity, endeavouring to be useful to the Church and to our fellow-men, and, by constant prayer and circumspection, seeking to abound in love, joy, peace, long-suffering, gentleness, goodness, faith, meekness, temperance, and charity, which are the proper fruits of a living union with the Saviour. When temptations arise, we must fight them, and resist, though it should cost us many an earthly loss, or even life itself. When a field of usefulness presents, and Providence calls us to occupy it, we must promptly enter it, as by God's own appointment, never tiring, and never relinquishing, as long as we have strength to labour or work to do. We are not to forsake our places in the world and turn pilgrims and anchorites, nor yet to seize upon offices in which God has not placed us, but to be faithful in our appointed stations, according to the graces severally dealt to us,—prophesying, ministering, teaching, exhorting, giving, ruling, showing mercy, and serving, with all godliness and honesty; abhorring that which is evil; cleaving to that which is good; not slothful in business; fervent in spirit; rejoicing in hope; patient in tribulation; continuing instant in prayer; distributing to the necessity of saints; given to hospitality; blessing them that persecute; rejoicing with them that do rejoice; weeping with them that weep; condescending to men of low estate; providing things honourable in the sight of all men, (Rom. xii. 6–17,) and all as under the immediate eye of Him to whom we shall presently have to account for the way in which we have fulfilled our trusts.

"This is the path to the honours of heaven. They can be reached by no other road. And he only who is found walking in this way, is prepared to meet his Lord, or can be said to fill out the great requirement in the command to 'watch.'

"It would seem as if heaven had no gifts of honour and glory higher than those which are to be distributed among the saints and made the everlasting possession of the faithful followers of the Lamb of God. I am amazed and confounded when I attempt to survey the transcendent altitudes of exaltation and power to which the poor sinful children of men are to be advanced by redeeming grace. We sometimes say to ourselves amid our many and daily provocations, and trials, and temptations, and failures, and discouragements, *Ah, it is a hard thing to be a Christian!* And it is even so. The evil with which we have to contend is so powerful, our own strength is so feeble, the opportunities, inducements, and incentives to wrong are so many, the burdens of a devoted life is so heavy to our poor depraved nature, that it is a hard thing to be a Christian. It requires incessant toil, and self-denial, and watchfulness, and prayer; and even then we seem to retrograde rather than progress. But when we consider what the Saviour has done for us, and think how that for these crosses come crowns; for these sufferings, thrones; for these toils, kingdoms; for these struggles, judgeships and princedoms in the high Empire of God, we have abundant reason to rejoice and give thanks in the midst of all the hardship, that we have been called on any conditions to enter upon the campaign for such transcendent honours.

"But there is quite as much in this to humble us as to exalt and rejoice. What a thing of weakness and infirmity is man! Look at him; survey his case; realize the utter vanity and wretchedness which appertain to such a being;

and then bring forward the fact, that of such as these God has chosen the people who are to judge the world, and to judge angels; to share in the grand administrations of the glorious Christ in renewing the world; to sit with the only-begotten Son of God in the exercise of dominion to which angels shall be in subjection, and to reign in immortal regency in the high princedoms to which the ransomed myriads of the new world's exalted population shall bow in cheerful and happy obedience,—and see whether there be not reason for us to blush and hide our faces, and to humble ourselves in the very dust, at the mere thought of being promoted to such astounding dignities! O my God, what is man, that thou art thus mindful of him?—or the son of man, that thou dost so exalt him?

And hence there is also much in this subject to enhance our appreciation of the dignity and value of a Christian life. It connects empire with our lowly discipleship, and sublime royalty with our penitence and prayers. Piety may subject us for a little while to the scorn and sneers of men, but it will presently introduce us into the fraternal esteem of angels, and secure for us recognition among eternal principalities. Even for the life which now is, it has its profit over all losses. And should we have to give up every thing which this world values, in Christ there still is ample compensation. The first disciples forsook all, and from fishermen and tax-gatherers they became patriarchs of the New dispensation,—pastors, and prophets, and princes upon apostolic thrones, and leaders of a vaster and sublimer host than monarch ever marshalled. In place of the friends and homes they left, they were made the beloved centres of another household, which gave them sons and daughters, brethren and sisters, in all lands, full of loving sympathy and undying affection. For the little estates which they relinquished, all things became theirs, and rich men laid their money at their feet, and streams of generous liberality broke into life whithersoever they went, furnishing them abundance for all their wants. And, with all the wrongs and persecutions to which their their new profession subjected them, there was an accompanying reward, rich and glorious, in the teachings and experiences of the gospel which it gave them. Even when the powers of evil pressed heaviest upon them, their souls still fed on hidden joys, and thrilled with liberty and peace, of which no adversity could deprive them. And never, unto this day, has any one forsaken aught at the call of Jesus, but he has found a recompense even *in this life*. Moses relinquishes the court and riches and dominion of Egypt for the promises of God; and from Jethro's sheepfold he rises to be the humiliator of Pharaoh, the liberator of enslaved Israel, and the prince of prophets, legislators, and historians. Daniel deliberately forfeits his life for the sake of communion with his Maker; and the hand of miracle interposes for his safety, and lifts him to the highest honour and authority in the gift of great Babylon's lofty king. Rosa Madiai persists in the devout reading of her Bible, in the face of imprisonment and chains; and instantly her humble name is heralded over the earth, and millions of hearts are touched, and flow with tenderest sympathy to cheer her in her dungeon and to enroll her among the modest heroines of the faith. The recompense may not always come in a form so marked, or in a degree so ample; but it will come, for it is the pledge of manifold Wisdom and almighty Love to attemper to each obedient child a reward and consolation even now for all the sacrifices exacted. But high over all such gains as these are honours to which all our attainments here are but the feeble indexes. To these are to be added thrones and dominions in eternal glory. Every thorough Christian is not only a child of God, and linked to him in indestructible communion and peace, but a rightful heir to enduring kingship. His very Christianity transmutes him into a being of wondrous dignity. When we look upon him, we behold a royal personage,—a being anointed of God to wield the sceptre of immortal empire,—a man who is presently to be invested with potencies to which even angels shall bow,—a future dispenser of administrations from which the great and holy interests of 'the world to come' are to take complexion, and the eternal ages to be shaped and conditioned. As yet, he dwells in flesh, amid weaknesses, necessities, and straits; but his name is in the books of heaven, and God hath decreed concerning him that he shall receive power and riches and glorious rulership, and reign for ever and ever. Great, wonderful man! beside whom the great ones of earth, at whose names the nations tremble, are but ciphers and mimic men! The very earth beneath his steps is being consecrated by reason of the exaltations to which he is called and predestined!

"From this subject may we, then, also learn to prize the preciousness of our Redeemer's cross. By that bloody instrument of eternal compassion it is that these dignities are put within our reach. Without that, instead of rising to take rank among the eternal principalities, we should all have been degraded and ever-sinking vassals,—the thralls of sin and hell's disgusting tyranny, the doomed and helpless victims of unholy domination. Had there been no Jesus to die for us on Calvary, there had been no world of peace and glory for man, no thrones there to be occupied. It is by his cross and passion that all these honours come. It is by his mysterious encounter with death and hell in their own dark domain that these princedoms have been won and rendered attainable to sinful men. And it is only through the victory which he completed by his resurrection from the tomb, that such kings shall reign, and such princes decree justice. For many reasons, the cross is a precious token. It is the everlasting monument to the perfections and glory of God. It tells of his eternal power and Godhead equally with the mighty products of his creating hand. It bespeaks a power of a higher sort than that which called the worlds into being. It preaches of an unswerving justice in a language more awful than the thunders that roll and bellow in the prison-house of the lost. And it proclaims a goodness, wisdom, and love, vast as a sea without a bottom or a shore. It is also the symbol of an agency, which all the universe beside could not furnish, by which Satan's dominion is broken from the enslaved souls of men, their sins blotted out, and they made to share once more the light and liberty of the sons of God. But, beyond and above all this, it is the enduring memento of a victory which has gained for us the privileges of eternal empire,—of a purchase by which we become 'kings and priests unto God,' to share the throne of the 'Heir of all things,' and to sit with him in immortal regency, as he is seated with the Father on the central throne of heaven. Oh, dear and blessed cross, that has been the instrument of such wondrous good to man!

"But above all should this subject serve to render us

heavenly-minded, and to deliver us from the frivolities of worldliness and the entanglements of an unsteady faith. If we are to be kings, we ought to conduct ourselves with reference to the positions of exaltation and authority which we expect to occupy. If we have been anointed to share in the sublime adjudications of the world to come, we should exhibit a corresponding bearing, and study, labour, and pray to be filled with that spirit of truthfulness, wisdom, justice, and harmony with the mind of God, which alone can qualify us for duties so responsible and sublime. People who expect to be judges dare not spend their years of preparation in idleness, or waste their time upon perishing and useless trifles. They must be diligent in their search into the principles of right and truth. They must be earnest in bringing themselves under a proper discipline to be able calmly to hear and weigh causes and to decide them righteously. They need wisdom, and training, and culture, which can only be obtained by long, faithful, and laborious application. And how much more is it needful to be instructed, trained, and exercised in righteousness, to be fitted to participate in those sublime administrations for which the saints are destined! Let us, then, go away from the contemplation of this subject, resolved to work and pray and study as we never hitherto have done. Let us show by our way of using this world that we do really regard it as the mere temporary scene of preparation for judgeships and kinghoods in the world to come. Let us deal with its poor honours and possessions, not as things in which to locate our affections, or to seek our portion, but as the mere perishable scaffoldings by which to mount up to far sublimer dignities, which are to endure forever. And as there are eternal princedoms placed with our reach, let us ever press forward to them, and see to it, above all things, that we do not 'let them slip.'

"And unto Him that loved us, and washed us from our sins in his own blood, and has engaged to make us kings and priests unto God, even the Father, to Him be glory and dominion, for ever and ever. Amen.

DIAGRAM 4.

Year-day Fulfilment of Dan. & Rev. during the last 2595 years (2520+75) Dan. iv, 28 ; xii, 12, from B. C. 724 to A. D. 1872. The date of each event is put in parentheses, and its distance from the beginning of the 2595 years is given.	Literal-day Fulfilment of Dan. & Rev. during the last 2595 days (2520+75), Dan. ix, 27; xii, 12, commencing with the date of the Covenant between Louis Napoleon and the Jews. The distance of each event from the beginning of the 2595 days is given.
FIRST TIME — 1 to 30, 60, 90, 120, 150, 180, 210, 240, 270, 300, 330, 360 — The 2520 years or "seven times" (Dan. iv, 23) began primarily B. C. 723–6. Their latter half synchronizes with the Papal Antichrist's 1260 years, or 3½ times of temporal supremacy. The 2300 years (Dan. viii, 14) began with the renewal of the Jewish sacrifices, partially B. C. 456–7, in the 270th year, and fully B. C. 431–2, in the 295th year.	**FIRST YEAR** — 1 to 30, 60, 90, 120, 150, 180, 210, 240, 270, 300, 330, 360 — The 2590 days or seven years of the Covenant-week (Dan. ix, 27) begin here; their latter half synchronizes with the Papal Antichrist's (Louis Napoleon's) 1260 days, or 3½ years of universal supremacy. The 2300 days (Dan. viii, 14) begin with the renewal of the Jewish sacrifices, partially about the 270th, and fully on the 295th day.
SECOND TIME — 390, 420, 450, 480, 510, 540, 570, 600, 630, 660, 690, 720	**SECOND YEAR** — 390, 420, 450, 480, 510, 540, 570, 600, 630, 660, 690, 720
THIRD TIME — 750, 780, 810, 840, 870, 900, 930, 960, 990, 1020, 1050, 1080 — The Manchild caught up (Rev. xii, 5). Seal 1. Primitive Zeal of Church (33 to 87¾), 159th to 1050th year. Ascension of Christ, A. D. 29 or 30-4, between the 764th & 799th year. Trump. 1 (290 to 395), 876th to 1091st year. Dragon cast down (324), 1050th year. Seal 2 (324 to 534), 1050th to 1260th year.	**THIRD YEAR** — 750, 780, 810, 840, 870, 900, 930, 960, 990, 1020, 1050, 1080 — The Manchild caught up (Rev. xii, 5). Seal 1, Church full of a Revival Spirit, 764th to 1050th day. Ascension of the Virgin, about or between the 764th and 795th day. Trumpet 1, Hail, 876th to 1091st day. Dragon cast down, 1050th day. Seal 2, War, 1050th to 1260th day
FOURTH TIME — 1110, 1140, 1170, 1200, 1230, 1260, 1290, 1335, 1380, 1410, 14 — Trump. 2 (395 to 412), 1091st to 1138th year. Wings given th Woman (379), 1105th year. Trump. 3 (412 to 476), 1138th to 1202d yr. Trumpet 4 (476), 1202d year. Pope supreme over 10 kingdoms. Seal 3 (533 to 1073), Spiritual Famine by Trumpet 5 (608 to 936), 1335th to 1662d year — First Woe of Mahomedan Incursions, 1362d to 1662d year.	**FOURTH YEAR** — 1110, 1140, 1170, 1200, 1230, 1260, 1290, 1335, 1380, 1410, 1440 — Trumpet 2, 1091st to 1138th day. Wings given to Woman, 1105th day. Trumpet 3, 1138th to 1202d day. Trumpet 4, partial darkness, 1202d day. Napoleon supreme over 10 kingdoms. Seal 3, Famine, 1260th to 1799th day. Trumpet 5, 1335th to 1662d day. First Woe of Literal Locusts, 1362d to 1662d day.
FIFTH TIME — 1470, 1500, 1530, 1560, 1590, 1620, 1650, 1680, 1710, 1740, 1770, 1800 — Trumpet 6, Second Woe of Seal 4 (1073), Turkish Invasions (1063 to 1438) Spiritual 1444), 1789th to Desolation of Church, 1799th to 2164th year.	**FIFTH YEAR** — 1470, 1500, 1530, 1560, 1590, 1620, 1650, 1680, 1710, 1740, 1770, 1800 — Trumpet 6, Second Woe of Seal 4, War, Pestilence & Famine, 1799th to 2164th day. Asiatic Armies Invading Roman Empire, 1789th to 2370th day.
SIXTH TIME — 1830, 1860, 1890, 1920, 1950, 1980, 2010, 2040, 2070, 2100, 2130, 2160	**SIXTH YEAR** — 1830, 1860, 1890, 1920, 1950, 1980, 2010, 2040, 2070, 2100, 2130, 2160
SEVENTH TIME — 2190, 2220, 2250, 2280, 2310, 2340, 2370, 2400, 2430, 2460, 2490, 2520 — Seal 5 (1438 to 1794), Season of Delay before Final Judgment, 2164th to 2520th year. Great Revival of Religion, commencing at Reformation in 1517—2245th year.	**SEVENTH YEAR** — 2190, 2220, 2250, 2280, 2310, 2340, 2370, 2400, 2430, 2460, 2490, 2520 — Seal 5, Season of Delay, 2164th to 2520th day. Great Revival of Religion (Rev. x), commencing about 2245th day.
75 yr. — 2550, 2580, 2595 — Seal 6 (1794), 2520th to 2590th yr. Seal 7, Trump. 7, Vial 7 (1866-7 to 1871-2), 2590th to 2595th year.	2550, 2580, 2595 — 75 days — Seal 6, 2520th to 2590th day. Seal 7, Trumpet 7, Vial 7, 2590th to 2595th day.

1260 years of the Papal Antichrist's Dominancy, of the Church's Persecution and of the Two Testaments' Sackcloth Testimony, Rev. xi, xii, etc.

1335 years, ending with the Standing of the Saints in their Inheritances (1872).

1260 days of the Personal Antichrist's Dominancy, of the Church's Persecution, and of the Two Witnesses' Prophesying, Rev. xi, xiii.

1335 days, ending with the Standing of the Saints in their Inheritances, Dan. xii.

CHAPTER IV.

TEN REASONS, PROVING THAT THE ADVENT OF CHRIST "IN THE AIR" TO RAISE THE DECEASED SAINTS, AND TO TRANSLATE THE WISE VIRGINS, WILL PRECEDE THE FINAL 3½ YEARS' GREAT TRIBULATION, OR NAPOLEONIC PERSECUTION, AND WILL BE ABOUT FIVE YEARS BEFORE THE END OF THIS DISPENSATION.

WHENEVER Louis Napoleon shall have confirmed the seven years' Covenant with the Jews, the point will then be settled, that, from the date of that event, there will only be seven years and two and a half months to elapse before the glorious descent of Christ upon the earth at the battle of Armageddon to slay the impenitent, and introduce the millennium.

It might, then, at first sight be thought that the resurrection and translation of the saints, which is to take place at Christ's Advent, would not occur sooner than the termination of this same period of seven years and 2½ months, since we are told that it is not until "the Lord himself descends from heaven," that the dead in Christ shall rise first, and we which are alive and remain shall be caught up together with them in the clouds, to meet the Lord in the air, and so shall ever be with the Lord, (1 Thess. iv. 16.) It would, however, be an error thus to suppose the resurrection and rapture of the saints to occur at so distant a period after the date of the Covenant; inasmuch as they are clearly declared in the prophecies to take place rather more than two years after the Covenant.

The Advent of Christ is shown to occupy about five years in its accomplishment, and to be effected in two stages. He first comes from the highest heavens into the air, and then the raised and translated saints are immediately caught up to meet him, (1 Thess. iv. 17:) and, consequently, the hosts of Satan, the Prince of the power of the air, are cast down from the air into the earth, and proceed, (after an interval,) to carry on, through the agency of Napoleon, the Antichrist, the final 3½ years' persecution against the unready Christians who have been left behind upon this globe, (Rev. xii.) Meanwhile, Christ, with his raised and translated saints, remains invisibly in the air, in the pavilion-cloud, until AFTER that 3½ years' Tribulation, (Matt. xxiv. 29, 30,) and then suddenly displays the Sign of the Son of Man in the heavens, and openly reveals his bright glory and majesty to the astonished inhabitants of the world below. At this point, he sends forth his angels to gather to him, in the air, all the saints that are found on the earth, including the surviving foolish virgins, and those who have been converted since the First Translation; and he then "rains a horrible tempest of fire and brimstone" upon Antichrist's hosts and all the ungodly, "purging out the rebels," but sparing and converting some of the least hardened, especially among the Jews and Heathen, (Is. lxvi.) This spared remnant constitutes the holy seed, or nucleus of the population of the earth during the subsequent millennium, and with their descendants will compose "the nations of them that are saved," (Rev. xxi. 24,) who will be governed during the 1000 years by Christ and his glorified, raised, and translated saints, these latter living principally in the heavenly Jerusalem, and visiting the earth daily in order to exercise rule over the successive generations of its mortal, unglorified inhabitants.

Upward of thirty-five prophetical treatises or writers may be mentioned,* that have of late years distinctly up-

* The following are the names of upwards of thirty-five prophetic treatises or authors which have been, (it is believed accurately,) ascertained to state that the Advent of Christ in the air to raise the deceased saints, and translate the wise virgins, will be several years before his descent on the earth, or will at least precede the 3½ years' Great Tribulation. The dates of the respective publications are enclosed in parentheses. Dissertations on the Prophecies, by Rev. Dr. Duffield, (1842); Hopes of the Church, by J. Darby, (1842); Millennial Tidings, by H. Livermore, (1843); Second Advent Lectures, by Rev. E. Winthrop, (1843); Rev. W. Pym, (1843); Time of the End, by W. Trenwith, (1845); Companion to Stream of Time, by Sir E. Denny, (1845); Apocalypse Interpreted, by Rev. J. Kelly, (1849); The Prospect, (1849); Things to Come, by Rev. C. Bowen, (1849); Plain Papers, by Captain Trotter, (1850); Light of Prophecy, by Judge Strange, (1852); Chronology of the Scriptures, (1854); The World's Crisis, by Rev. J. G. Zippel, (1854); First Fruits, by Alexander Porter, (1856); The Parousia

held and stated the general view, that the Advent of Christ to receive up into the air the raised and translated saints, would undoubtedly be several years before his visible descent on the earth to destroy the Antichrist at the battle of Armageddon, and would precede the Great Tribulation, (which is to last 3½ years.)

It is of the utmost importance that this view should be fully inculcated and understood, or else persons will be lulled into a dangerous state of unwatchfulness, and thrown off their guard in waiting for the Advent of Christ, by supposing that there is no prospect of his coming until after the Great Tribulation and Antichristian persecution have run their course.

It cannot be objected that there would thus be two Advents of Christ,—one at the beginning, and the other at the end of the period of about five years,—for the simple fact is, that the one sole act of Christ's Second Advent will occupy in all its circumstances and arrangements about five years from its incipient commencement to its final conclusion. And THE FIRST RESURRECTION, which consists principally of the resurrection of all the deceased saints at Christ's coming in the air at the beginning of the five years' interval, also includes the subsequent resurrection of the Witnesses, (Rev. xi. 11,) and of those who are martyred by Napoleon, the Antichrist, during that interval; these latter being expressly mentioned in Rev. xx. 4, because otherwise it might have seemed uncertain whether they

and Epiphaneia, (1858); Rapture of the Saints, by Lord Congleton, (1859); Interpretations, by Major Scott Phillips, (1859); Judgment of the Righteous, by Rev. Dr. Newton, Rector of the Epiphany, Philadelphia, (1862.) The rest of the writers or works mentioned in this list, expressly maintain not only that there will be the Resurrection and Translation of Saints BEFORE the Great Tribulation, (of 3½ years,) but also a second Translation of Saints about the end of that 3½ years, (Matt. xxiv. 29–31.) The Apocalypse, by W. Cuninghame, (1832); Commentary, by a Clergyman of the Church of England, (Dublin, 1835); Guide to the Prophecies, by Rev. E. Bickersteth, and T. Birks, (1844); The Translation, by Rev. J. Hooper, (1847); The Retrospect, (1847); Last Vials, by R. A. Purdon, (1852); Days we Live in, by E. W. P. Taunton, (1857); Armageddon, (published in London, 1858); Coming Events, (1858); A. P. Joliffe. (1861); J. Litch, (1861); "Parable of the Ten Virgins," and "Last Times," by Rev. Dr. Seiss, (1861); The Coming Battle, (1860.)

would be raised up at all before the Millennium. Although
Christ's coming "into the air" will be like the lightning,
(Matt. xxiv. 27,) and, therefore, probably accompanied by
a momentary brilliant glare throughout the whole heavens,
yet, with this exception, he will remain with his ascended
saints in the air, altogether unseen by the inhabitants of
the earth, until the end of the interval of about five years,
when he will descend in visible power and glory upon
Mount Olivet, (Zech. xiv. 4.) The statement that his Advent in the air will be accompanied with "the voice of the
archangel and the trump of God," (1 Thess. iv. 16,) seems
to imply that there will also be some loud mysterious noise
heard at the instant of its commencement.

It is much to be lamented that many pious Christians
altogether neglect the careful study of these prophecies,
and seek to justify such conduct by referring to the text,
"Of that day and that hour knoweth no man; no, not the
angels which are in heaven, neither the Son, but the Father," (Mark xiii. 32.) But these words being spoken
in the present tense, are not necessarily true of any period
subsequent to their utterance, when the knowledge, which
was then hidden, might be revealed by further prophecies.
Moreover, they can only hold good and continue in force
as long as the Divine Son himself does not know the day
or hour, which certainly cannot be the case at the present
period. It is not surprising, that such unthinking persons
as swearers, and drunkards, and other utterly irreligious
characters, should constantly cast this text in the teeth of
those who warn them that the Advent of Christ is certain to
take place during the next several years. But it is, indeed,
very deplorable that any ministers, or reflecting Christians,
should be guilty of the same gross perversion of that text;
for the least consideration would show, that Christ having
subsequently ascended to heaven, and received a fresh revelation from the Father, who alone knew the day and hour,
has now imparted to us knowledge which previously was
withheld.

Sixty years after the words of that text were spoken,
Christ delivered to St. John, in Patmos, further prophecies,
entitled, "The Revelation of Jesus Christ, which God gave
unto him, to show unto his servants things which must
shortly come to pass . . . and the things which shall be

hereafter . . . Blessed is he that readeth, and they that hear the words of this prophecy," (Rev. i. 1, 3, 19.) Here, then, is a disclosure of that which was before known only to the Father; and, in truth, the Book of Revelation, in its year-day and literal-day fulfilments, is a most wonderfully compendious map or chart, foretelling the history of the Church and the world from the First to the Second Advent of Christ. The marvellously skilful adjustment of its entire structure, its simple, and yet sublime imagery, its unrivalled blending of minuteness of detail with comprehensiveness of outline, and the amazing exactitude of the accomplishment of its predictions, signally stamp it as a master-piece of Divine wisdom, an emanation from the Divine mind, and a superhuman composition, altogether beyond the capacity of any mortal intellect to produce. Most criminal and reprehensible is the conduct of those who assume the responsible office of stewards of the Gospel mysteries, and yet never attempt to explain these prophetic visions to their hearers, and instead of earnestly urging them to explore the field of prophecy, which is flowing with the milk and honey of spiritual delights, untruly represent it as barren, unprofitable, and dangerous. God says of the Revelation, "Blessed is he that readeth the words of this prophecy:" "Here is wisdom, let him that hath understanding count the number of the Beast," (666) (Rev. i. 3, xiii. 18.) But the modern fashionable religious world, deeply tainted with semi-infidelity, cries out, "Here is folly! An enthusiast is he who deeply studies Daniel and Revelation, or affixes any definite interpretation to the prophetic numbers."

Expositors who distinctly assert that Louis Napoleon will be the Antichrist, and that Christ will come at the period 1866-71, may be often accused of presumption; but, in fact, those who so accuse them are, in reality, themselves guilty of presumption, because they condemn that which they cannot disprove, and which they are too slothful to investigate, and too ignorant to understand. So far from the period of Christ's Advent being unrevealed, the Scriptures distinctly state, as in the following texts, that it shall be discovered at the time of the end, from the prophecies and signs of the times. "The words are closed up and sealed *until the time of the end* . . . and none of the wicked shall understand, but the wise shall understand," Dan xii., *(the time of the end* is evidently nearly identical with the final seven years.) "Surely the Lord God will do nothing, but he revealeth his secret unto his servants the prophets," (Amos iii. 7.) "We have also a more sure word of prophecy, whereunto ye do well that ye take heed as unto a light that shineth in a dark place," (2 Peter i. 19.) "But ye, brethren, are not in darkness, that that day should overtake you unawares as a thief," (1 Thess. v. 4.) "Learn a parable of the fig tree; when the branch is yet tender, and putteth forth leaves, ye know that summer is nigh. So likewise ye, when ye see all these things, know that it is near, even at the doors," (Matt. xxiv. 32.) "If the good man of the house had known in what watch the thief would have come, he would have watched, and would not have suffered his house to be broken up," (Matt. xxiv. 43.) "If, therefore, thou shalt not watch, I will come on thee as a thief, and thou shalt not know what hour I will come upon thee," (Rev. iii. 3.)

These texts plainly imply the impossibility of watching for the Saviour's return unless we possess some knowledge as to the circumstances and time when it is to be anticipated. For watching does not consist in living in a vague, indefinite expectation of a given event happening at any time, but it imports the careful survey and attentive examination of occurrences as they transpire, so as to discover from the signs precursory to that event, when it is going to occur. It might also reasonably be concluded that, as the date of great events, such as the Exodus, the Deluge, the End of the 70 years' Jewish captivity, and the First Advent of Christ, &c., were all pre-intimated, so the date of the momentous event of Christ's Second Advent would be foretold. The predicted parallelism and correspondency between Noah's day and the Second Advent, also indicates that, as the Deluge was foretold to be at the end of 120 years, and then afterwards even the day was revealed, so almost the exact period of the Second Advent will be disclosed toward the end. Although, if in literal accordance with the text before mentioned, the day or hour may be unrevealed, yet it is clear that at least the week or fortnight in which Christ will come to remove the Wise Virgins, will be about two years and from four to six weeks after the date of the Covenant. For, as the year-day Man-child, (Christ,) was caught up about 500 years before the Papal Antichrist's 1260 years began, so the literal-day Man-child, (the Wise Virgins,) will be caught up about 500 *days* before the Personal Antichrist's 1260 *days*, or last half week, begins, (Rev. xii.,) as shown in diagram 4, and in the seventh of the subjoined ten divisions of this chapter. And Christ's coming is further shown to be about five years before the End, because it occurs at the beginning of the year-day 7th seal, 7th trumpet, and 7th vial, all of which commence about five years before the consummation, or close of this Dispensation.

The truth is, that the Apocalyptic Revelation given by God the Father to St. John, in Patmos, in A. D. 96, reveals "the times and seasons which the Father has put in his own power," and which "it was not for" the disciples sixty years previously to know, (Acts i. 7.) It is an exact chronological map of the Church's history between the first and second Advents of Christ, and the period of Christ's second coming is described on that map almost just as accurately as the latitude and longitude of London or New York is marked on a reliable geographical chart. There is NOT A SINGLE TEXT in the Bible that implies that the week or month of Christ's Advent will not be discovered beforehand. On the contrary, it is distinctly stated, that "the words shall be unsealed at the time of the end, and none of the wicked shall understand, but the wise shall understand," (Dan. xii. 10.) It is little short of blasphemy for persons to turn men away from endeavouring to find out from Daniel and Revelation the time of Christ's Advent, by asserting that the Bible declares that no one shall know the time, when, in reality, the Bible contains no such declaration at all. Even if the oft-quoted texts about "the day and hour," in Matt. xxiv. xxv., applied immediately to our own times, they could not fairly or reasonably imply that the week or month should not be known, for the word "day" being coupled with the word "hour," plainly shows that a literal day is meant. But in fact, it is just as unreasonable to say that the Saviour's words "of that day and hour knoweth no man . . not even the Son," (Mark xiii. 32,) apply to these days, or now hold good, as to say that his words "I thirst," (John xix. 20,) are actually true at the present time. It should be particularly noticed, that NOT ONE of these texts about "not knowing the time, or the day, or hour," are in the future tense; the obvious purpose of them being only to keep Christians in the early ages unacquainted with the predetermined length of time that was to elapse before Christ's Advent, and, therefore, expecting it as possible even in their own lifetime.

IT MAY BE WELL to mention here, that among the numerous proofs that Christ's personal coming will be premillennial, or BEFORE the Millennium of 1000 years, there are six arguments in particular, that are specially conclusive.

First. The matter is decisively settled by the FIRST RESURRECTION being foreshown, in Rev. xx., to occur before the 1000 years, in order that the glorified saints in their raised bodies may reign with Christ over the mortal, unglorified generations of mankind, who will live on the earth during those 1000 years. In Rev. xix. a description is given of the Marriage of the Lamb, which the Parable of the Virgins alone would show to be the Union of Christ to his raised and translated saints at his Second Advent. After the marriage ceremony, Christ and his saints descend in great majesty to the earth and destroy Antichrist's hosts. Then, in the next chapter, Rev. xx. 4, they are represented as having ascended their thrones to govern the spared nations of the earth during the 1000 years, and the revelator specially observes among them "*the souls*," (or *the persons*, consisting both of body and spirit, as in Acts xxvii. 37,) of those who were martyred by the Personal Antichrist, and who now "lived, (ιζησαν,)* and reigned

* "If, in a passage where two resurrections are mentioned, where certain ψυχαι εζησαν at the first, and the rest of the νεκροι εζησαν only at the end of a specified period after that first,—if, in such a passage the first resurrection may be understood to mean spiritual rising with Christ, while the second means literal rising from the grave,—then there is an end of all significance in language, and Scripture is wiped out as a definite testimony to anything. If the first resurrection is spiritual, then so is the second, which, I suppose, none will be hardy enough to maintain; but if the second is literal, then so is the first, which, in common with the whole primitive Church, and many of the best modern expositors, I do maintain and receive as an article of faith and hope."—*Dean Alford's Greek Testament*, Rev. xx.

with Christ a thousand years. But the rest of the dead lived, (εζησαν,) not until the thousand years were finished. This is the first Resurrection." It being undeniable that the word "lived" means "were raised up," it follows that this text alone, proves that some of the dead will be raised up before the 1000 years, involving, of course, Christ's premillennial Advent to effect their Resurrection.

Secondly. The final Battle of Armageddon, which consists principally in an exterminating assault, conducted by Antichrist's hosts against the Jews, is expressly stated to be accompanied by Christ's "coming as a thief," (Rev. xvi. 15, 16,) by his coming from heaven with the armies of his glorified saints, (Rev. xix. 8, 14,) by his "coming with fire and with his chariots, like a whirlwind, (Is. lxvi. 15,) by his descent with his saints to the earth, so that "HIS FEET SHALL STAND upon the Mount of Olives," (Zech. xiv. 4,) and by the manifestation of his *presence*, (Ezek. xxxviii. 20, this Hebrew word for *presence* invariably means an actual personal presence, as in Gen. iii. 8, Num. xx. 6, 1 Kings xii. 2, Is. lxiv. 3.) That "this Battle of that great day of God Almighty" at Armageddon takes place just before the Millennium is almost universally admitted, and is abundantly evident from the context of the above passages, and many parallel texts. All those passages distinctly show that Christ will then come personally, and not merely providentially.

Thirdly. In 2 Thess. ii., the Man of Sin, or the Antichrist, (1 John ii. 22,) is predicted by St. Paul to be destroyed by *the brightness of Christ's coming*, (τη επιφανια της παρουσιας,) by the appearing of his presence, which must mean Christ's personal coming; for, in *every* instance in which either of these two Greek words are used in the New Testament, they invariably denote actual personal presence, as shown elsewhere in this chapter. That Antichrist's destruction will be antecedent to the Millennium, is admitted by all standard expositors; for, of course, in a time of universal righteousness there can be no Antichrist, nor any mystery of iniquity, which, as St. Paul implies, was to continue to work from his own day until it issued in the revelation of the Man of Sin. The same prediction is also given in Dan. vii., where Antichrist, or the Little Horn, is foreshown to perish, together with the Roman Empire, at the visible Advent of the Son of Man, whose millennial kingdom is then established over the nations of this earth.

Fourthly. The Great Tribulation, and time of trouble and distress of nations, such as never has been, or shall be, obviously precedes the Millennium, for it is emphatically defined to be at the close of *the times of the Gentiles,* or present Gentile dispensation, just before Jerusalem shall cease to be trodden under foot, (Luke xxi. 24–27,) and also just prior to the time of Millennial blessedness, (Dan. xii. 12, 13,) and as soon as "the Gospel is preached for a witness to all nations," which is already the case, (Matt. xxiv. 14, Mark xiii. 10,) and likewise at the time of the Personal Antichrist's cruel oppression of the Jews, and persecution of Christians for 3½ years, (Dan. vii. xii., Rev. xi. xii. xiv.,) which issues in the Battle of Armageddon.* But this great tribulation, or time of trouble, is again distinctly stated to be the time of the resurrection, (Dan. xii. 1, 2,) which necessarily involves Christ's Advent, and also to be accompanied by Christ's "coming in a cloud with power and great glory, and sending forth his angels to gather in his elect," (Matt. xxiv. 29–31, Mark xiii. 24–27, Luke xxi. 27,) and to be at the time of the seventh, or resurrection, trumpet, (Rev. xi. 15–19.) By this line of argument, therefore, Christ's personal return is demonstrated to precede the Millennium.

Fifthly. The Scriptures foreshow that the earth will be increasingly wicked until the Second Advent of Christ, but will be universally righteous during the Millennium, which must, therefore, necessarily be subsequent to that Advent.

The Apostles spoke of the period in which they were living as *the last time,* (1 John ii. 8,) *these last days,* (Heb. i. 2,) *these last times,* (1 Peter i. 20,) and they predicted those last days, or times, to be characterized by continuously increasing wickedness until the coming of Christ; "Now the Spirit speaketh expressly, that in the *latter*

---

* The Battle of Armageddon, (Rev. xvi. 14, 16, xix.,) in which Gog, of the land of Magog, (Ezek. xxxviii.,) is the great Commander-in-chief, and which is *before* the Millennium, is wholly distinct from the battle of Gog and Magog, (Rev. xx.,) which is at the end of the Millennium, and in which the descendants of the premillennial Gog and Magog nations are specially prominent.

times some shall depart from the faith, giving heed to seducing spirits, and doctrines of devils, speaking lies in hypocrisy," etc., (1 Tim. iv. 1–3.) "This know also, that in the *last days* perilous times shall come, for men shall be lovers of their own selves: covetous, boasters, proud, blasphemous, disobedient to parents, unthankful, unholy, without natural affection, truce-breakers, false accusers, incontinent, fierce, despisers of those that are good, traitors, heady, high-minded, lovers of pleasure more than lovers of God; having a form of godliness but denying the power thereof," (2 Tim. iii. 1–5.)

These scenes of oppression, selfishness, and every sort of wickedness, are plainly implied by St. James, (chap. v. 1, 8,) to be endured until the Advent of Christ, "Go to, now ye rich men, weep and howl for the miseries that shall come upon you . . your gold and silver are cankered, and the rust of them shall be a witness against you, and shall eat your flesh as it were fire . . Behold the hire of the labourers who have reaped down your fields, which is of you kept back by fraud, crieth; and the cries of them which have reaped are entered into the ears of the Lord of Sabaoth . . Be patient, therefore, brethren, unto THE COMING OF THE LORD, for the coming of the Lord draweth nigh." St. Jude similarly predicts the growing wickedness of the ungodly from his own time until their destruction, by the coming of the Lord with his saints, as foretold by Enoch. The same intimation respecting the augmented prevalence of corruption until Christ's Advent, is conveyed in the parables of the Nobleman, the Sower, the Tares, and the Net, and in our Lord's prophetic discourses, (Matt. xxiv.,*

---

* Many of the standard expositors consider the word "generation" to mean "the Jewish race, or nation," in the passage, "This generation shall not pass till all these things be fulfilled," (Matt. xxiv. 34,) and in that sense it is fulfilled by the continued existence of the Jews even at the present day. Another explanation of this text is, that Christ here alludes to the first part of the two-fold question put to him, "When shall *these things* (the destruction of Jerusalem) be; and what shall be the sign of thy coming, and of the end of the world." He sums up his prophetic discourse by saying, "Verily I say unto you, this generation shall not pass till all *these things* (the destruction of Jerusalem) be fulfilled . . . But of *that day* and hour (the coming of Christ) knoweth no man, not even the Son," &c.

Mark xiii., Luke xxi.,) and also in the year-day prophetic septenaries of the seals, trumpets, and vials, which describe a progressive infliction of woes and plagues upon the increasingly apostate world, until the complete uprooting of apostacy at the Advent of Christ. Again, in Rom. viii. 23, the whole creation is stated to be groaning and travailing in pain, waiting for the *redemption of the body*, that is, the resurrection of the body at Christ's coming. This could not be the case if the Millennium intervened before the resurrection. And, in Rom. xi., the national blindness of Israel, which must end before the Millennium, terminates with the Deliverer coming out of Zion, that is, with the Return of Christ. It should be remembered, that many texts show, that in the midst of the latter-day climax of iniquity, there will be, nevertheless, great religious revivals, and outpourings of the Holy Spirit, (see page 145.)

Sixthly. The Scriptures declare that the Lord Jesus shall have a future, visible, earthly, temporal kingdom, over the nations, while existing as now, in their mortal, unglorified state, and that he shall reign over them as literally as David reigned over the kingdom of Israel. This must necessarily precede the final general judgment and conflagration of the earth, which occurs at the end of the Millennium, (Rev. xx. 11;) and it is foretold to commence at the destruction of the Roman empire, at the beginning of the Millennium,* (Dan. vii. 27; Rev. v. 10, xi. 15, xx. 6.)

The utter overthrow and demolition of the Roman empire,

---

* It is certain that the whole company of saints represented by the terms, the Church, or Bride, or Lamb's wife, is quite complete at Christ's Advent, and admits of no subsequent accessions after its marriage to Christ has taken place at the commencement of his temporal reign over the millennial earth. (Rev. xix 7.; Matt. xxv. 10.) This "Church of the first-born," (Heb. xii. 23,) is distinguished by special union with Christ and peculiar prerogatives and dignities far above those which belong to "after-born" saints, as for instance, the saints who will be born and die on the earth during the Millennium, and who will compose a distinct company of the redeemed. These again will be distinct from companies of saints that may be redeemed by the blood of Jesus in other ages, or in other worlds. There will be many varying degrees of glory in heaven: "one star differeth from another star in glory. (1 Cor. xv. 41.) "There may be, (says Bickersteth) and doubtless are, a thousand stages and varieties of union with Christ, distinguishable from the glory of the Church of the First-born."

the last of the four great Gentile empires, (the Babylonian, Medo-Persian, Grecian, and Roman,) is foreshown to occur at "the coming of the Son of Man with the clouds of heaven," (Dan. vii. 13, 14, ii. 44,) to whom there is then given a kingdom and dominion that *all people, nations, and languages*, should serve him. (Dan. vii. 14.)

This fifth universal monarchy must be homogeneous with, and of the same kind as, the four monarchies which preceded it, and cannot be a mere spiritual kingdom, but must, like them, be a visible, temporal, monarchical government, and it is to be exercised over *all people, nations, and languages*—a phrase which distinctively means people living on the earth in the flesh, in mortal, unglorified bodies, just as they existed in Daniel's time. (Compare Dan. iii. 4, 7, 29, iv. 1, v. 19, vi, 25.) Moreover, it was declared (Luke i. 32; Ps. cxxxii. 11,) that Jesus shall sit upon the throne of David—an expression similar to "the throne of the Cæsars," "the throne of the Bourbons," etc., and which implies that Christ will, like king David, visibly and literally reign over the kingdom of Israel. This expectation was, and now is universally established by the Jews, who justly understand in a literal sense the numerous promises of their future restoration to Palestine and earthly prosperity under the temporal reign of their promised Messiah. (See Isaiah ii., iv., xi., xxxv., xlix., lx.–lxvi.; Ezek. xxxvi–xlviii.; Jer. xxx., etc.) Christ himself distinctly encouraged them in this expectation, but intimated that the period was distant and undivulged, and would not arrive until the close of the times of the Gentiles, that is, the end of the four Gentile monarchies. (Luke xxi. 24, xix. 12–27; Acts i. 6.) This Messianic kingdom is prophesied of in the parables concerning the kingdom of heaven, and is prayed for in the petition, "Thy kingdom come." The heavens only receive and retain Christ until the "restitution of all things," or "regeneration, when the Son of Man shall sit on the throne of his glory, and the twelve apostles shall eat and drink at his table in his kingdom, and sit on twelve thrones judging the twelve tribes of Israel." (Acts iii. 21; Matt. xix. 27; Luke xxii. 30.) The Jews erred, not in expecting this temporal kingdom, but in failing to perceive that the Messiah must first suffer and be rejected. Many modern Christians err, by refusing to believe in the future temporal kingdom and reign of Christ, and only regarding him as a crucified and interceding Messiah.*

THE DIAGRAM PREFIXED to this chapter, shows the period of the Ascension of the literal-day Manchild or Wise Virgins, to be two years, and from four to six weeks after the date of the Covenant. This is demonstrated by deducing from the year-day fulfilment of Daniel and Revelation during 2595 YEARS, from 722-4 B. C to 1871 A. D., what their future literal-day fulfilment will be during 2595 DAYS, that is, seven years and 2½ months, from the date of Antichrist's approaching seven-year's covenant with the Jews, until his destruction at Christ's descent at Armageddon.

The 2595 YEARS is composed of two parts: firstly, of the seven times or 2520 years, (Dan. iv. 23; Lev. xxvi. 28,) which is double the 3½ times or 1260 years, (Dan. vii., xii.; Rev. xi., xii., xiii.,) and which was to be the length of the dominant oppressing power of the four Gentile Monarchies, to which supremacy has been temporarily transferred from the Jews; secondly, of an additional 75 years, which is the excess of 1335 years beyond the 1260 years or 3½ times— the latter half of the 2520 years or seven times—(Dan. xii. 7-12,) and which is the final interval of the completion of the destruction of the Gentile powers. The 2595 DAYS similarly consist of two parts: firstly, of the seven years of Daniel's 70th week, (Dan. ix. 27,) which is double the literal-day 3½ times or 1260 years, (Dan. vii., xii.; Rev.

* The expression, "the kingdom of God," "the kingdom of heaven," is used in more senses than one, and sometimes denotes the spiritual reign of God in the hearts of true Christians: "Except a man be born again, he cannot see the kingdom of God." (John iii. 3.) Its meaning in each passage must be decided by the context. The spiritual kingdom "cometh not with observation." Christ also said, "My kingdom is not of (α from) this world; if my kingdom were from this world, then would my servants fight that I should not be delivered to the Jews; but now is my kingdom not from hence." (John xviii. 36.) This kingdom is heavenly in its origin, in its support, and in its end: not established by the military violence or revolutions of this world, but by the supernatural interposition, from heaven, of God himself. "Koppe on the Thessalonians" is a book treating fully upon the different senses in which the word "the kingdom of heaven" is used.

xi., xii., xiii.,) and which reaches from the date of Antichrist's Jewish Covenant to the end of his dominant oppressing power; secondly, of an additional 75 days, which is the excess of 1335 days beyond 1260 days or $3\frac{1}{2}$ times—the latter half of the 2520 days or seven years—(Dan. xii. 7-12,) and which is the final interval of the completion of his destruction.

In prophetical calculations, fractional parts of a year are counted according to Jewish reckoning, as if the year contained only 360 days or twelve months of 60 days each; (compare Rev. xi. 2, 3, xii. 6, 14; Gen. vii. 11, viii. 8, 4,) but still its actual length is always reckoned as equal to that of an ordinary year—the period occupied by the revolution of the earth round the sun, and which in reality is 365 days. The expression, "a time, times, and half time," signifies "one year, two years, and half a year," that is, 1260 days, whether year-day or literal-day.

Among the following ten Scripture proofs of the Ante-Tribulation translation, the seventh is the most important, as it is the principal prophecy which shows the Advent of Christ to remove the Wise Virgins, to be two years, and from four to six weeks after the date of Antichrist's Jewish Covenant. The first six of the ten proofs show that translation to be at least *before* the $3\frac{1}{2}$ years' Great Tribulation, and the last three proofs demonstrate it to be within a few weeks of five years before the End.

I. Two DISTINCT TRANSLATIONS or removals of living saints from the earth at Christ's coming, are plainly described in literal-day, Rev. xiv.; the first being an earlier and smaller ingathering than the second, and consisting of 144,000 persons, called the FIRST-FRUITS, (ver. 4,) who are caught up *before* the fall of Babylon, and Antichrist's subsequent $3\frac{1}{2}$ years' persecution; the second being composed of all the saints found on the earth *after* Antichrist's $3\frac{1}{2}$ years' persecution, and who are called the HARVEST. (Rev. xiv. 15, vii. 9.)

In literal-day, Rev. xiv., 144,000 persons are exhibited in heaven, standing with the Lamb upon the celestial Mount Sion, which appears from Heb. xii. 22, to be the same as the heavenly Jerusalem. Their description shows them to be the Wise Virgins who have been caught up to meet Christ "in the air," and who have now got the name of God written upon them, according to the promise given in Rev. iii. 12, where they are prophetically termed the Philadelphian Church. They are here denominated the FIRST-FRUITS, and are thus obviously implied to be an earlier ingathering of saints from the earth, preliminary to a later ingathering spoken of in the latter part of the chapter as the HARVEST, (ver. 15,) which is clearly the same gathering in of the elect that accompanies Christ's coming in power and great glory, in Matt. xxiv. 31. As the first-fruits and harvest must necessarily both be of the same sort or kind, each, therefore, consisting of living saints, it would thence appear that the saints, who are alive at Christ's Advent, will be removed to the heavens in two companies, that of the first-fruits being earlier in time, although smaller in number than that of the harvest.

After Rev. xiv. has opened with this representation of the 144,000 Wise Virgins, or FIRST-FRUITS, having been translated to the heavens, then three angels successively proclaim three Gospel messages throughout the earth, warning mankind that the HOUR of God's judgment is come, (the 3½ years' hour, Rev. iii. 10, xvii. 12, xviii. 10,) and that Babylon, or the church of Rome, is fallen, and that whoever worships the Beast, (Napoleon, the Antichrist,) or his image, or receives his mark, shall be tormented for ever and ever. These messages will not be proclaimed until after the Wise Virgins are taken from the earth, and will be introductory to the 8½ years' universal worship of Antichrist, which is evidently described in the significant language of the next two verses, (12 and 13,) *Here is the patience of the saints; here are they that keep the commandments of God and the faith of Jesus.* These are the very words which are used in Rev. xii. 17, xiii. 10, in the descriptions of Antichrist's 3½ years persecution, and they are here obviously inserted as a note of time to show that this is the precise period in the narrative of Rev. xiv. for that 3½ years' persecution to intervene. This is further shown by the accompanying statement, *Blessed are the dead that die in the Lord from henceforth,*—words palpably intimating this to be a time of violent persecution, when death is preferable to life in the case of the righteous, (compare Isaiah lvii. 1;) and also intimating that the first stage in the Advent of Christ and resurrection of the righteous, or first resurrection, has already brought to the departed saints that special blessedness which is to be their peculiar prerogative, as stated in Rev. xx. 6: (the second stage in the first resurrection is *after* the 3½ years, Rev. xv. 2, xx. 4.)

After the semi-septennial interval of Napoleon, the Antichrist's 3½ years' persecution, has run its course, as indicated in verses 12 and 13; then, in the three next verses, the Son of Man is exhibited sitting upon a white cloud with a sickle in his hand, with which he reaps the HARVEST of the earth. This is unmistakeably the second translation, or ingathering of living saints from the earth AFTER the 3½ years' Great Tribulation, (Matt. xxiv. 15–29,) when all nations behold Christ visibly coming in the clouds with great glory; and it is the same event which is represented in literal-day, Rev. vii. 9–17, where a *great multitude* who have passed through, and come *out of* (ex) THE Great Tribulation, are beheld with Christ on the pavilion-cloud in the heavens, having manifestly been caught up at the close of the Tribulation. These second translation-saints are an indefinitely large, *unnumbered*, and almost entirely *unsealed* company, but the first translation-saints are represented as a comparatively small and definitely *numbered*, and individually *sealed* company of 144,000.

As soon as the HARVEST of the second translation saints is removed from the earth, (verse 16,) then the following verses describe the treading of the wine-press of God's wrath; in other words, the destruction of Antichrist and his hosts at the battle of Armageddon, as set forth in Rev. xix, and in the literal-day seventh vial, and seventh trumpet. Thus the fourteenth of Revelation contains a concise and graphic outline of the events of the five years' interval between the first and second translations.

As a harvest is at least from one to three hundred times greater than its first fruits, and as the FIRST FRUITS, or first-translation company of saints consists of exactly 144,000 persons, therefore the HARVEST, or second-translation company of saints, must necessarily consist of upwards of from fifteen to fifty million persons. They are intimated by their description in Rev. vii. 9, xiv. 6, and Luke xiv. 23, to be principally those that shall be comverted among heathen nations, and most of them will be converted during the five years between the two translations.

It should be observed that the righteous dead who are raised up at the first stage in Christ's coming are entirely distinct from the 144,000 who are then translated, because none of the sealed 144,000 will ever have undergone death. In the literal-day fulfilment of the seals during the final 1840 days; (or about 5 years,) the 144,000 mentioned in Rev. vii., consist entirely of Jews, who are preserved and caught up in the second translation *after* the 3½ years' Great Tribulation. Thus, there are two separate companies of 144,000 translated saints,—the one in Rev. xiv., consisting chiefly of Gentiles caught up in the first translation, and the other in Rev. vii., being composed exclusively of Jews caught up in the second translation.

In view of the approaching unparalleled conversions among the Jews and heathens, what a motive is furnished to Christians to sow broadcast in heathen countries the seed of the Gospel, and to circulate widely copies of the Word of God in various languages before the growing power of Antichrist, and the increasing revolutions, completely arrest, as they speedily will, all such evangelistic efforts. The certainty that an unparalleled blessing is about to crown all such efforts should be an additional inducement to persons "to lay up treasure in heaven" by enlarged liberality toward Missionary Societies. It is far better for Christians now to give away the greater part of their property in charity, than presently to have it violently taken from them, as will inevitably be the case during the coming Great Tribulation.

II. THE GENERAL DESCRIPTIONS of Christ's Second Advent intimate that he comes to remove the Wise Virgins at a time of comparative peace and prosperity, (Luke xvii. 28, etc.,) and then comes, after a short interval of awful tribulation, to gather up the remnant of saints, and to destroy Antichrist and the unrepentant, (Rev. xii. 17, Matt. xxiv. 29, etc.)

The following passages speak of the Second Advent as occurring at a period of general quietude and prosperity:

THE GREAT TRIBULATION.

Matt. xxiv. 37. But as the days of Noe were, so shall also the coming (παρουσια) of the Son of Man be. 38. For as in the days that were before the flood, they were eating and drinking, marrying and giving in marriage, until the day that Noe entered into the ark. 39. And knew not until the flood came and took them all away, so shall also the coming (παρουσια) of the Son of Man be, 40. Then shall two be in the field; the one shall be taken and the other left, etc.

Luke xvii. 28. Likewise also as it was in the days of Lot, they did eat, they drank, they bought, they sold, they planted, they builded; 29. But the same day that Lot went out of Sodom, it rained fire and brimstone from heaven and destroyed them all: 30. Even thus shall it be in the day when the Son of Man is revealed, αποκαλυπτεται, (i. e. *to the Wise Virgins that look for him and by whom alone he will then be seen*, οφθησεται, Heb. ix. 28) . . . 34. I tell you that in that night two men shall be in one bed, the one shall be taken and the other shall be left, etc.

Luke xxi. 35. For as a snare shall it come on all them that dwell on the face of the whole earth.

1 Thess. v. 2, 3. The day of the Lord so cometh as a thief in the night. 3. For when they shall say, Peace and safety, then sudden destruction cometh upon them, as travail upon a woman with child, and they shall not escape.

Another class of texts represent the Second Advent as taking place at a time of great affliction and calamity.

Dan. xii. 1, 2. And at that time, (*the time of the end*, Dan. xi. 40,) shall Michael stand up, the great prince which standeth for the children of thy people: and there shall be a TIME OF TROUBLE, such as never was since there was a nation even to that same time; and at that time thy people shall be delivered, every one that shall be found written in the book. And many of them that sleep in the dust of the earth shall awake, etc. (This resurrection is necessarily at the Second Advent.)

Matt. xxiv. 15–31, (and similarly in Mark xiii. 14–27.) When ye, therefore, shall see the abomination of desolation, etc. . . . woe unto them that are with child, and to them that give suck in those days . . . for then shall be GREAT TRIBULATION, such as was not since the beginning of the world to this time, no, nor ever shall be. And except those days should be shortened, there should NO FLESH BE SAVED, but for the elect's sake those days shall be shortened. Then if any man shall say unto you, Lo, here is Christ, or there, believe it not, for there shall arise false Christs, and false prophets . . . Immediately AFTER the tribulation of those days shall the sun be darkened, and the moon shall not give her light, and the stars shall fall from heaven, and the powers of the heavens shall be shaken. And then shall appear the sign of the Son of Man in the heavens, and then shall all the tribes of the earth mourn, and they shall see the Son of Man coming in the clouds of heaven with power and great glory. And he shall send his angels with a great sound of a trumpet, and they shall gather together his elect from the four winds. (This is the second translation at the second stage in Christ's Advent, *after* the 8¼ years' tribulation.)

Luke xxi. 25-27. And there shall be signs in the sun, and in the moon, and in the stars; and upon the earth distress of nations, with perplexity; the sea and the waves roaring; Men's heart's failing them for fear, and for looking after those things which are coming on the earth: for the powers of heaven shall be shaken. And then shall they see the Son of Man coming in a cloud, with power and great glory.

Rev. xvi. 17—21. And the seventh angel poured out his vial into the air; and there came a great voice out of the temple of heaven, from the throne, saying, It is done. And there were voices, and thunders, and lightnings; and there was a great earthquake, such as was not since men were upon the earth, so mighty an earthquake, *and* so great. And the great city was divided into three parts, and the cities of the nations fell: and great Babylon came in remembrance before God, to give unto her the cup of the wine of the fierceness of his wrath. And every island fled away, and the mountains were not found. And there fell upon men a great hail out of heaven, *every stone the weight of a talent*: and men blasphemed God because of the plague of the hail; for the plague thereof was exceeding great. (*The year-day fulfilment of this 7th vial with its terrific judgments clearly lasts for 4 or 5 years before the End of this dispensation.*)

Zech. xiv. 1—4. Behold, the day of the Lord cometh, and thy spoil shall be divided in the midst of thee. For I will gather all nations against Jerusalem to battle; and the city shall be taken, and the houses rifled, and the women ravished; and half of the city shall go forth into captivity, and the residue of the people shall not be cut off from the city. Then shall the Lord go forth, and fight against those nations, as when he fought in the day of battle. And his feet shall stand in that day upon the Mount of Olives.

The Old Testament prophecies also abound with intimations, (Isaiah ii. 12, xiii. 6, xiv. 17, xxiv. etc.,) that the DAY OF THE LORD, that is, the epoch when the Lord comes to judge the world, will be ushered in with scenes of appalling desolation. These scenes are further described in detail in the literal-day fulfilment of the seals, trumpets, and vials, in Revelation, during the final five years.

It is evident, then, that the two classes of texts abovementioned give two very different descriptions of the earth's condition at Christ's Second Advent, and, therefore, refer to two different stages in his Advent; for it is obvious that mankind cannot be said to be *eating and drinking*, that is, luxuriously indulging in banquetings and revellings, while there are dreadful famines and pestilences, (Rev. vi. 6, 8, xi. 6,) and "the curse hath devoured the earth, and they that dwell therein are desolate: therefore the inhabitants of the earth are burned, and few men left," (Is. xxiv.) Nor can they be *planting and building* while the earth is rocking to and fro with an earthquake so mighty and so great, as was not since men existed, and the cities of the nations are falling, and every island and mountain are being moved out of their places, (Rev. vi. 12, xvi. 18.) Nor is it likely that they will be *marrying and giving in marriage*, and entertaining each other at wedding feasts, while hail and fire, mingled with blood, is being rained upon them, and the tormenting stings of scorpion locusts are driving them to seek for death without being able to find it, and the third part of them is being killed during a year and a month, (literal-day, Rev. viii. ix.;) this being the time, also, when marriage, in common with all other Christian rites, will be almost entirely abolished during the Infidel Antichrist's 3½ years' universal supremacy, and slaughter of the saints. Moreover, it is not credible that the tribes of the earth will be crying *Peace and safety*, while peace is taken from the earth, (Rev. vi. 4,) and all nations are gathered to Jerusalem to battle, (Zech. xiv. 1, Rev. xvi. 14,) and they are mourning because of the signs of Christ's coming, and their hearts are failing them for fear, and they are blaspheming because of the plagues of the literal-day seals, and trumpets, and vials. Nor can people generally be said to be *buying and selling* at a time, of which it is declared, "Behold the Lord maketh the earth empty, and maketh it waste, and turneth it upside down, and scattereth abroad the inhabitants thereof. And it shall be as with *the buyer* so with *the seller* . . . the land shall be utterly emptied and spoiled," etc., (Isaiah xxiv.) In short, the desolate and woeful condition of this earth during the 3½ years' tribulation preceding Christ's descent upon it, will not in the least resemble the peaceful and prosperous state of the antedeluvian world, and of Sodom before their sudden destruction.'

A careful comparison of the two classes of texts, which are cited above, shows, then, that there are two distinct acts, or crises, or stages in Christ's Advent. First. He comes "into the air," (1 Thess. v. 16,) to raise the sleeping saints, and take the Wise Virgins, while the world is wrapped in the slumber of apathy and carnal security, profusely indulging, as in Noah's day, in all the pleasures and enjoyments of this life. Secondly. AFTER a time of unexampled trouble has run its course, during which, the general conviction that Christ has come, or is coming, will lead multitudes, in their bewilderment, to rush from unbelief into the opposite extreme of credulity, and eagerly follow after false Christs, who will arise and work great miracles, the Sign of the Son of Man will suddenly appear in the skies, and he will descend on the earth and slay all the unrepentant.

III. Two DIFFERENT Greek words, παρουσια and επιφανια, are used in Scripture to describe the Second coming of Christ,—the one signifying only his actual personal presence transferred to the vicinity of this earth, the other denoting the subsequent appearing or open manifestation of that presence. There are thus two distinct stages in his Advent.

A careful comparison of the passages in which these two words are employed to describe the Second coming of Christ, shows that the παρουσια, (parousia,) or presence of Christ, is spoken of with reference to the first stage of his Advent, when he comes "into the air," (1 Thess. iv. 16, 17,) with the spirits of his deceased saints, and reunites them to their raised bodies, and when the world is as prosperous as in Noah's day; but the επιφανια, (epiphaneia,) or visible appearing of Christ, is the term used in reference to the second stage of his Advent, when every eye will see him descending in glory, after the subsequent 3½ years' Great Tribulation, to destroy Antichrist by the *appearing of his presence*, (επιφανια της παρουσιας, 2 Thess. ii. 8,) which, until then, will be veiled in the clouds from the sight of the world at large.

The following are the only twenty-four places in the New Testament in which the word παρουσια, (the presence or coming,) is used, and in the first sixteen of them, it refers to the second Advent of Christ.

Matt. xxiv. 3. What shall be the sign *of thy coming*, τι το σημειον της σης παρουσιας.

CHRIST'S COMING PRECEDES HIS APPEARING. 805

Matt. xxiv. 27. As the lightning—so shall the *coming* (ἡ παρουσία) of the Son of man be.

Matt. xxiv. 37. As the days of Noah—so shall also the *coming* (ἡ παρουσία) of the Son of man be.

Matt. xxiv. 39. Till the flood came—so shall also the *coming* (ἡ παρουσία) of the Son of man be.

1 Cor. xv. 23. They that are Christ's *at his coming* (ἐν τῇ παρουσίᾳ.)

1 Thess. ii. 19. What is our hope, or joy, or crown of rejoicing? Are not even ye in the presence of our Lord Jesus Christ *at his coming* (ἐν τῇ αὐτοῦ παρουσίᾳ.)

1 Thess. iii. 13. To the end he may establish your hearts unblameable in holiness before God, even our Father, at *the coming* (ἐν τῇ παρουσίᾳ) of our Lord Jesus Christ with all his saints.

1 Thess. iv. 15. We which are alive, and remain *unto the coming* (εἰς τὴν παρουσίαν) of the Lord shall not prevent (be before) them which are asleep.

1 Thess. v. 23. And I pray God your whole soul and body be preserved blameless *unto the coming* (ἐν τῇ παρουσίᾳ) of our Lord Jesus Christ.

2 Thess. ii. 1. Now we beseech you, brethren, by (concerning) *the coming* of our Lord Jesus Christ, (ὑπὲρ τῆς παρουσίας,) and by our gathering unto him, that ye be not shaken in mind.

2 Thess. ii. 8. Shall destroy with the brightness *of his coming*, (τῆς παρουσίας.)

James v. 7. Be patient, therefore, brethren, unto *the coming* of the Lord, (ἕως τῆς παρουσίας τοῦ Κυρίου.)

James v. 8. Be ye also patient; stablish your hearts; for *the coming* of the Lord draweth nigh, (ἡ παρουσία τοῦ Κυρίου ἤγγικε.)

2 Peter iii. 4. Where is the promise of his coming? (τῆς παρουσίας αὐτοῦ.)

1 John ii. 28. And now, little children, abide in him; that when he shall appear we may have confidence, and not be ashamed before him *at his coming*, (ἐν τῇ παρουσίᾳ αὐτοῦ.)

1 Cor. xvi. 17. I am glad of the *coming* (ἐπὶ τῇ παρουσίᾳ) of Stephanas.

2 Cor. vii. 6. God—comforted us by the *coming* (ἐν τῇ παρουσίᾳ) of Titus.

2 Cor. vii. 7. And not by his *coming* only, etc., (ἐν τῇ παρουσίᾳ.)

2 Cor. x. 10. But his (Paul's) *bodily presence* (ἡ δὲ παρουσία τοῦ σώματος) is weak.

Phil. i. 26. That your rejoicing may be more abundant in Christ Jesus for me by my *coming* (διὰ τῆς ἐμῆς παρουσίας) to you again.

Phil. ii. 12. Wherefore, my beloved, as ye have always obeyed, not as in my *presence* only (ἐν τῇ παρουσίᾳ μου) but now much more in my absence.

2 Thess. ii. 9. Even him (the Man of Sin) whose *coming* (οὗ ἡ παρουσία) is after the working of Satan.

2 Peter iii. 12. Looking for and hasting unto the *coming* (τὴν παρουσίαν) of the day of God.

2 Peter i. 16. For we have not followed cunningly devised fables when we made known to you the power and *coming* of our Lord Jesus Christ, (τη παρυσιαν,) but were eye-witnesses of his majesty.

The word επιφανεια, translated *appearing*, or *brightness*, occurs only in the under-mentioned six passages in the New Testament, and in the first five of them refers to Christ's Second Advent.

2 Thess. ii. 8. 'And then shall that Wicked be revealed whom the Lord shall consume with the spirit of his mouth, and destroy with *the brightness of his coming*, (επιφανεια της παρυσιας αυτυ.)

Titus ii. 13. Looking for that blessed hope, and the glorious *appearing* (επιφανειαν της δοξης) of the Great God, even our Saviour Jesus Christ.

1 Tim. vi. 14. That thou keep this commandment without spot, unrebukable, until the *appearing* (μεχρι της επιφανειας) of our Lord Jesus Christ.

2 Tim. vi. 1. I charge thee, therefore, before God, and the Lord Jesus Christ, who shall judge the quick and the dead at his *appearing* (κατα την επιφανειαν) and his kingdom. (His millennial kingdom is here plainly implied to be subsequent to his appearing.)

2 Tim. iv. 8. Henceforth there is laid up for me a crown of righteousness, which the Lord the righteous Judge shall give me at that day, and not to me only, but unto all them also who love his *appearing* (την επιφανειαν αυτυ.)

2 Tim. i. 10. But is now made manifest by the *appearing* (δια της επιφανειας) of our Saviour Jesus Christ. (This refers to the first Advent of Christ.)

In the foregoing texts Christians in general are bidden especially to look for and love the *epiphaneia* of Christ, because it alone, and not the *parousia*, will be an object of sight; and the consummated blessedness of the world will not be brought in at the *parousia*, but at the subsequent *epiphaneia*. Moreover, the *epiphaneia* of Christ will be manifested to the Wise Virgins at His *parousia*, although not to mankind generally until a later period.

The fact that these two Greek words *invariably* denote the bodily personal presence of the individuals to whom they relate, is one of the strongest arguments against the postmillenial delusive theory, according to which they are interpreted to mean a mere spiritual or providential coming. It is also similarly apparent that the Man of Sin must be an individual person, and not a mere system, since his *parousia* is spoken of in 2 Thess. ii. 8.

IV. A DISTINCT PROMISE is given in Luke xxi. 36, and Rev. iii. 10, that those who faithfully watch for Christ's

Advent shall be kept altogether OUT OF *the hour of temptation*, that is, the 3½ years' Great Tribulation.

Our Lord having described in Luke xxi., the wars, pestilences, famines, fearful signs in the heavens, and the desolation of Judea by invading armies, which was fulfilled, typically, at the destruction of Jerusalem, but which will take place antetypically during the 4 or 5 years *time of trouble* preceding His descent upon Mount Olivet, then says, (ver. 28, 36,) "When these things BEGIN TO COME TO PASS, then look up, and lift up your heads for your redemption draweth nigh. . . . Watch ye therefore and pray always, that ye may be accounted to escape all these things that shall come to pass, and to stand before (εμπροσθεν) the Son of man," (i. e., to stand accepted as objects of His complacent approbation, as the Greek expression denotes—compare also Jude 24, Rev. vii. 9.) This passage clearly shows that at the very beginning of *these things that shall come to pass*, namely, the 4 or 5 years' final tribulation, all expectant believers in Christ's speedy advent, who have watched the signs of the times and prayed for deliverance, shall *escape* (εκφυγη) the tribulation by being caught up to the heavens to stand in the presence of the Son of man.

The same truth is stated in Rev. iii. 10, in the Epistle to the Philadelphian Church, which represents Christians who really believe in the nearness of Christ's Advent; for the seven epistles have long been considered to be prophetic delineations (1) of the leading features of Christ's Church during seven successive periods in this dispensation, and (2) probably of seven different classes of Christians existent at Christ's coming. The Philadelphian condition of the Christian church commenced at the French Revolution in 1793, for since that era the Church has been strikingly characterized by a continually increasing expectation of Christ's speedy advent, as evinced by the rise of numerous speakers and writers on the subject. To Philadelphian Christians who really cherish this expectation, it is promised, "Because thou hast kept the word of my patience, (the injunction to watch patiently for my advent) I also will keep thee from (εκ, out of) *the hour of temptation that shall come upon all the world* to try them that dwell upon the earth." This *hour of temptation* has certainly never yet come upon *all the world;* and it is manifestly identical with the Wild-Beast's *hour* of supremacy over the ten kings, (Rev. xvii. 10,) and the *hour* of Babylon's judgment, (Rev. xiv. 7, xviii. 10, 17, 19,) in other words, with the final 3½ years' great tribulation or infidel persecution. The word *hour* in the year-day fulfilment of Revelation, invariably means 3½ years, as is shown by the 3½ years in Rev. xi. 11, being called *the same hour* in Rev. xi. 13.

The Philadelphian Christians who really *love* and *look for* Christ's appearing, (2 Tim. ii. 8, Heb. ix. 28,) will be altogether kept *out of* this 3½ years hour of temptation, by sudden and simultaneous translation from the earth to the heavens. The Laodicean Christians, many of whom will be pious, but unwatchful and unbelieving in regard to the Second Advent, will be left behind to experience the terrors of *the hour of temptation*, and if they survive, will be translated at its termination, just before the Lord descends in visible glory at Armageddon, (Matt. xxiv. 29—31.) They are pictured as being *unclothed, and the shame of their nakedness appearing:* and under the year-day sixth vial, Rev. xvi. 15, it was threatened to him who would not watch for Christ's coming, that he should *walk naked and they should see his shame.* The remarkable correspondence between the phraseology of these two passages, plainly shows that the Laodiceans have been left in a naked and shameful condition, because they failed to watch for the Lord's coming, while the Philadelphians have been taken away from the approaching woe. Gracious promises are nevertheless held out to the Laodiceans, in case of their repentance, and it is believed that these promises will be savingly appropriated by millions, during the interval of about five years between the two translations.

V. In the Parables of the Ten Virgins and of the Marriage Supper, and in the Narrative of the Wise and Evil Servants, the Wise Virgins and Wise Servants are an earlier ingathering, and the Foolish Virgins and Evil Servants are a later ingathering, to the Marriage Supper of the Lamb. (Matt. xxv.; Luke xiv. 22, xii. 42; Matt. xxiv. 45.)

The word *Then*, with which Matt. xxv. begins, shows that the Church is not likened to Ten Virgins, until the period of Christ's Advent, which had been spoken of in

Matt. xxiv.; at first the foolish as well as wise virgins went forth to meet the Bridegroom, but while he tarried, they all slumbered, and remained asleep until the sounding of the midnight cry. This cry, (verse 6,) at which ALL the virgins will arise from their previous slumber, has not yet been fully raised; but probably when the covenant between Napoleon and the Jews is confirmed, attention will be directed far more generally to these prophecies, so that nearly all pious people will give some sort of heed to them. The wise virgins are those who have before-time obtained some of the oil of prophetic knowledge and of belief in the nearness of Christ's Advent, but who have relapsed into a state of unwatchfulness, until they are aroused by the midnight cry, and acquire a renewed belief in the proximity of Christ's coming, so as to be caught up at his Advent in the air before the 3½ years' tribulation. The foolish virgins are not unconverted nominal professors, but really converted, regenerate believers, and, as such, sure to be eventually saved; for a person who is once truly born again or converted, always remains so, and, however great a backslider, is certain to be ultimately saved. (Phil. i. 6; John x. 28.) Their lamps had once been lighted with the flame of genuine piety, although now almost *going out* through unwatchfulness; they were also *virgins* betrothed to the Bridegroom, notwithstanding their being foolish; and they arose and went out to meet their Lord,—an act which can never be ascribed to the unconverted. They represent, in truth, the numerous class of pious persons who do not believe in the speedy advent of Christ, and who will be beginning too late to investigate the subject, when He suddenly comes.

It should be noticed that it is not said to the foolish virgins, "Depart from me," but only, "I know you not," which denial of them is virtually implied in the very act of leaving them behind. Nor are they thus addressed by Christ in his character, as a Father, Redeemer, or Judge. It is only as a BRIDEGROOM (Matt. xxv. 1, 5, 6, 10,) that He "knows them not," because they lack the spirit of the Bride. But they afterwards obtain the oil of prophetic knowledge and of belief in Christ's speedy advent, and though left behind at the ante-tribulation first translation are yet, if surviving, caught up in the second translation, about five years later.

Rudolph Stier, Olshausen, and Dean Alford, in their Commentaries, and Dr. Seiss, of Philadelphia, in his exposition of this Parable, severally interpret the foolish virgins to be lukewarm, but yet in the main, real Christians, that may finally be saved.

Similarly, the wise and evil servants described in Luke xii. 42, Matt. xxiv. 45–51, are equally true *servants* of Christ, but the evil servants are in a backsliding state, thinking inwardly that the Second Advent is many years distant, and uniting with the wicked in persecuting those who proclaim the immediateness of the Second Advent. They will, therefore, be cut *off* (marginal reading) and *appointed their portion with the hypocrites* during the $3\frac{1}{2}$ years' great tribulation, where *there shall be weeping and gnashing of teeth;* but being totally distinct from the hypocrites, in whose company they are shut out from the first translation, they will ultimately be saved.

The parable of the Marriage Supper (Luke xiv. 22, 23,) clearly represents the two translations or ingatherings to the Marriage Supper of the Lamb (Matt. xxv. 10; Rev. xix. 7;) the second company of guests, which is much more numerous than the first, and which comprises a worse and more neglected class of society, evidently representing the Second-translation saints—the harvest of Rev. xiv. 15, and great multitude of Rev. vii. 9. The ingathering of the saints to Christ is also referred to in Matt. xxiv. 28, and Luke xvii. 37,—" Wheresoever the carcass (or body) is, there will the eagles be gathered together," for the Wise Virgins will mount up with wings as eagles, (Is. xl. 31,) to meet Christ at his coming in the air.

VI. THE ULTIMATE LITERAL-DAY fulfilment of the prophetic visions of Revelation obviously lasts for rather more than $3\frac{1}{2}$ years, (Rev. xi. 2, 3, etc.,) and is shown by the scenery of Rev. v., not to begin until after Christ has come and taken up the raised and translated saints to the heavens.

At the commencement of the Apocalyptic visions, St. John saw a door opened in heaven, and heard a voice as of a trumpet saying to him, "Come up hither," and immediately he was caught up to heaven, and beheld twenty-four elders sitting around the throne, with crowns on their heads, and crying out simultaneously with the four living creatures, "Thou hast redeemed us to God, by thy blood, out of every kindred and tongue and people and nation." A book sealed with seven seals, was at the same time delivered to the Lamb, who forthwith proceeded to break the seals, and during the successive opening of them, within a period of rather more than 3½ years, certain events took place as recorded in Rev. vi., vii., viii. 1, and xix., until at last after the seventh seal, the Lamb's marriage occurs, and then He descends with all his saints to destroy Antichrist and reign upon the earth.

In these scenes St. John is a symbolic or representative man, as in Rev. x. 8—11, and his ascension into the door of heaven in response to the invitation, "Come up hither," represents the ascension of the Wise Virgins at the Second Advent. The twenty-four elders are the representatives of the raised and glorified saints, and the fact of their having CROWNS upon their heads, incontestably shows that the first stage in Christ's coming or appearing, must have taken place, for Paul and Peter expressly intimate that the saints will not receive their crowns until that period, (2 Tim. iv. 8; 1 Peter v. 4.) Moreover, the exclamation, "Thou hast redeemed us," manifestly implies that their bodies are now redeemed from death and ransomed from the grave (Hosea xiii. 14; Rom. viii. 23,) by the resurrection which occurs at the Second Advent. Nor can the opening of the seven-sealed book of life, containing the names of the redeemed, be reasonably understood to take place earlier than Christ's second coming, especially as this epoch is defined, in Dan. vii. 10, to be the time when the books shall be opened. Again, the mention of *men* being in heaven at this period, as well as on earth (verse 8,) manifestly indicates that the saints in heaven now completely repossess their former *humanity* as much as people on the earth, and that they are no longer disembodied, incorporeal spirits, but have re-assumed their bodies of flesh and bone which by this time have been raised up from the grave.

Thus the scenery and descriptions presented in Rev. v., unmistakably show that the saints are raised and translated to heaven at the first stage in Christ's Advent, (1 Thess. iv. 16, 17,) before the subsequent visions of the seals, trumpets, vials, etc., undergo their real literal-day fulfilment. But it is fully admitted that there has been a sort

of typical year-day fulfilment of parts of those visions by
way of rehearsal on a larger scale, although they are to be
hereafter more completely and minutely fulfilled on the
smaller literal-day scale.

The manifestation of Christ to the Wise Virgins, but not
to the world at large, at the first stage in his coming, is
further prefigured by His appearing personally to St. John
(Rev. i.) before showing him the judgments of the seals,
trumpets, etc., and also by his parallel appearing to Daniel
(Dan. x.) before showing him the vision of the final $3\frac{1}{2}$
years' Great Tribulation, which is the principal theme of
Dan. xi. and xii. Moreover, the statement that St. John
was then in the Spirit on the "Lord's day," or "day of the
Lord," may not merely signify that he had this vision on
the Sabbath, but may also have the further and deeper
meaning, that he was carried forward in contemplation by
the Holy Spirit, into the beginning of the period called the
Day of the Lord, or Day of Judgment, commencing with
the Advent of Christ and comprising the millennial thousand years, (2 Peter iii. 8, 10; Zech. xiv. 1, etc.) This
view, which is supported by some writers, would additionally show that the main fulfilment of Revelation does not
begin until the first stage of the Second Advent; and, in
this case, the epistles to the seven churches would prophetically apply to different denominations or classes of Christians existent at Christ's return.

The Resurrection, and consequently the Second Advent,
is also implied to be before the final $3\frac{1}{2}$ years' Tribulation
by the statement in Dan. xii. 1, that it will take place at
the same time when the unparalleled Time of Trouble commences, which is foreshown in verse 7 to continue in its
chief intensity during the final $3\frac{1}{2}$ times, or years, although
it will have begun a year or two earlier, as intimated in Dan.
xi. 40. The predicted parallelism between Noah's day and
the time of Christ's Advent, likewise implies that, as Noah
was buoyed up in safety in the ark upon the surface of the
waters, while beneath him destruction was overwhelming
mankind and all their works; so the Wise Virgins will
have mounted upwards into the clouds before the $3\frac{1}{2}$ years'
flood of pestilences, earthquakes, famines, and Napoleon's
persecution overwhelms those who are left behind. The
five months during which Noah's ark floated above the

earth until at last it rested on Mount Ararat, also seems to typify the five years during which the Wise Virgins will remain in the pavilion-cloud until they finally descend with Christ upon Mount Olivet, (Zech. xiv. 4.)

The personal manifestation of Christ to the Wise Virgins, and their removal to the Goshen of the pavilion-cloud, about five years before the End, and in the third year of the seven years of the Covenant-week, is also apparently prefigured by Joseph's discovery and manifestation of himself to his brethren, in the early part of the third year of the seven years' famine, (Gen. xlv. 6,) and their removal to Goshen, where their posterity subsequently escaped the Egyptian plagues,—the types of the future literal trumpet and vial plagues. The mysterious removal of Moses at the end of Israel's forty years in the wilderness, and five years before the dividing of the promised land, and the reign of the Judges, (Deut. ii. 14, xxxiv.; Josh. xiv. 7, 10,) is likewise a remarkable type of the removal of the Wise Virgins at the end of the forty years of the year-day sixth vial, and five years before Christ's descent, and the final dividing of the Holy Land among the Jews, (Ezek. xl.—xlviii.,) and the Millennial reign of the glorified saints as judges. Similarly, the translation of Enoch BEFORE the Deluge, prefigures the first, or ante-tribulation, translation; and the translation of Elijah AFTER he had passed through the 3½ years' famine, (1 Kings xvii., xviii.; 2 Kings ii.; James v. 17,) typifies the second translation of the saints surviving after the 3½ years' Great Tribulation.

VII. IN THE LITERAL-DAY FULFILMENT of Rev. xii., expectant believers in Christ's advent are represented under the figure of a Man-child, as being caught up into the heavens before the 3½ years' Great Tribulation and infidel persecution commences.

Rev. xii. 1. And there appeared a great wonder in heaven; a woman clothed with the sun, and the moon under her feet, and upon her head a crown of twelve stars. 2. And she, being with child, cried, travailing in birth, and pained to be delivered. 5. And she brought forth a MAN-CHILD, who was to rule all nations with a rod of iron: and her child was caught up unto God, and to his throne. 6. And the woman fled into the wilderness, where she hath a place prepared of God, that they should feed her there.

thousand two hundred and threescore days. 7. And there was war in heaven: Michael and his angels fought against the dragon; and the dragon fought and his angels. 8. And prevailed not; neither was their place found any more in heaven. 9. And the great dragon was cast out, that old serpent, called the Devil, and Satan, which deceiveth the whole world: he was cast out into the earth, and his angels were cast out with him. . . . 12. Therefore rejoice, ye heavens, and ye that dwell in them. Wo to the inhabiters of the earth, and of the sea! for the devil is come down unto you, having great wrath, because he knoweth that he hath but a short time. 13. And when the dragon saw that he was cast unto the earth, he persecuted the woman which brought forth the man-child. 14. And to the woman were given two wings of a great eagle, that she might fly into the wilderness, into her place, where she is nourished for a time, and times, and half a time, from the face of the serpent. . . . 17. And the dragon was wroth with the woman, and went to make war with the remnant of her seed, which keep the commandments of God, and have the testimony of Jesus Christ.

In this vision the woman represents the collective body of saints living on the earth at the time of the events here predicted. Her birth-pangs denote the emotions of anxiety and earnest longing kindled by the expectation of the occurrence, which is signified by the birth of the Man-child. The birth and ascension of the Man-child indicates the separation of a part of the collective body of saints from the whole, and the removal of this separated part from earth to heaven. The subsequent flight of the woman, (after an interval,) into the wilderness, and her persecution for 1260 days, denotes the oppression and cruel treatment of the remnant of the saints left on the earth, and their successors, in other words, the Church Militant, during the period signified by the 1260 days, or $3\frac{1}{2}$ times, which is, of course, one and the same period.

It being generally recognised by the most thoughtful and discriminating expositors, that the greater part of Daniel and Revelation undergo first a year-day figurative fulfilment, in which the prophetic days are fulfilled as years with reference to the Papal Antichrist, and ultimately a more literal-day fulfilment, in which those prophetic days are fulfilled as literal days with reference to the Personal Antichrist, it results that Rev. xii. has a twofold accomplishment. In the year-day fulfilment, the birth-pangs of the Woman symbolize the anxious expectation of the Messiah's appearing that was prevalent at the time of

THE YEAR-DAY MAN-CHILD REPRESENTS CHRIST. 315

the first Advent, and the Man-child signifies Christ, who ascended in his glorified body to God's throne in A. D. 29–33, and who is to rule all nations with a rod of iron, (Ps. ii. 9, Rev. xix. 15.)*

* The following are some of the reasons for understanding the catching up of the Man-child, (Rev. xii. 5,) in the year-day fulfilment, to signify, (as held by Bickersteth, Shimeall, Dean Woodhouse, and many other expositors,) the ascension of Christ in A. D. 29–33. 1. The Man-child being predicted hereafter to "rule all nations with a rod of iron," can only be Christ, or his saints, concerning whom alone this same prediction is made in Ps. ii. 9, Rev. xix. 15, ii. 27. 2. Satan, the Dragon, acting through and animating the seven-headed and ten-horned Roman Empire, did remarkably strive to devour the Man-child, or "holy child Jesus," as soon as he was born, by the agency of Herod, and afterwards of Pilate, rulers in that empire. Peter testified to this in Acts iv. 27. 3. The Man-child being caught up to God's throne, (which cannot mean the Roman throne,) can only be Christ, (Heb. i. 13, Rev. iii. 21,) or his saints; and no person or persons have ever yet caused a stir of general expectation, and then, after being persecuted, have ascended in their body to God's throne except Christ. But the Wise Virgins will also do this hereafter. 4. The Man-child is implied to be "the seed of the woman," because those who are left behind after his abreption, or ascension, are called the remnant of the woman's seed, (Rev. xii. 17;) and "the seed of the woman" can only mean the saints, or Christ, who is to bruise the serpent's head, (Gen. iii. 15,) that is, Louis Napoleon, the Eighth head of the Roman Empire, in which the Serpent, or Dragon, is embodied. 5. Only one vision is contained in Rev. xii., xiii., and xiv., which constitutes its different parts; and Christ is called in Rev. xiv. 14, "the Son of man," evidently in allusion to his being "the Man-child" in the former part of the vision in the year-day fulfilment. In the literal-day fulfilment, the 144,000 of Rev. xiv., are obviously identical with the Man child. 6. If "the third part," in Rev. xii., refers, in the year-day figurative fulfilment, to the tripartition of the Roman Empire in A. D. 818, which only lasted several years, then the reference must be anticipatory and prospective, just as in Rev. viii. 12, and ix. 15, it is retrospective; but its real and literal meaning seems to be that Satan has drawn a third part of the angels—the morning stars, (Job xxxviii. 7,) into rebellion against God. 7. The woman represents the Church Militant, whether Jewish or Gentile,—all the saints living on earth at any given time, and cannot be restricted to mean only the Jews or only the Gentiles. 8. No objection can be urged against the vision reverting or retrogressing to the time of Christ's first Advent; for St. John, who lived in that generation, was commanded, (Rev. i. 19.) "Write the things which thou hast seen." 9. The Man-child could not be any Roman Emperor, for the Roman Emperor being universally held to be the sixth head of the Beast, could never be the

The watching of Satan to devour the Man-child was strikingly fulfilled by his energizing Herod and Pilate, rulers in the Roman Empire, to destroy Christ, which, however, could not prevent Christ's resurrection and ascension. The casting down of Satan was typically fulfilled by the downfall of Paganism in A. D. 323. The flight of the Woman into the wilderness for 1260 days, was figuratively

Man-child whom that Beast persecuted. No argument can be founded on Constantine being called "the Son of the Church," or on Christianity being said to be "seated on the throne of the Roman world." The sixth head was the Roman Emperorship, whether Heathen or Papal, just as the Queen of England was still a queen, whether a Catholic like Mary, or a Protestant like Elizabeth. 10. As to the idea, that the woman's year-day travail represents 40 prophetic weeks, or 280 years, from A. D. 33 to 313, it must first be shown that the Gentile Church began in A. D. 33, and not in A. D. 29 or 37, as some assert; furthermore, Constantine did not overthrow the Pagan Emperor Licinius until A. D. 323; the notion, also, that God's throne, (Rev. xii. 5,) is the Roman throne, which is called in Rev. xiii. 2, the Devil's throne, or seat, is utterly untenable. 11. Even if Diocletian first introduced the diadem-shaped crown in 303, yet no chronological argument can be built on such fact; for, in the shadowy, imperfect year-day fulfilment, the diadems on the seven heads or ten horns, (Rev. xiii. 1.) can only mean crowns in general. 12. It is also impossible that the rapture of the year-day Man-child could be much after A. D. 88, or so late as A. D. 313, because then the rapture of the literal-day Man-child, or Wise Virgins, would correspondingly be so late in the literal-day fulfilment as to be only seven months before the Personal Antichrist's 1260 days' persecution commences, (see Diagram 4:) and seven months would not be a long enough interval, (see page 82,) for the proclamation of the three angel messages, (Rev. xiv. 6—11,) or for the first two literal-day seals. Moreover, the year-day first seal being universally held to have commenced about, or soon after, A. D. 33, the literal-day first seal must correspondingly begin about 16¾ months before Antichrist's 1260 days, (see Diagram 4,) and the literal-day Man-child, (tho Wise Virgins,) is certainly caught up to heaven at Christ's Advent before the seven seals of the Book of Life literally begin to be opened, (Rev. v. 1 to vi. 1,) for the books are not opened until Christ's Advent, (Dan. vii. 10.) Likewise, the year-day seventh vial, trumpet, and seal, clearly commence about five years before the End, with the Second Advent, which involves the ascension of the literal-day Man-child, or Wise Virgins, at that time. 13. The Man-child clearly represents some person or persons who are caught up to God's throne in heaven in their *bodies*, and cannot denote a company of disembodied spirits, as of the martys. It can then only signify Christ, and resurrected or translated saints.

accomplished by the retirement of real Christians into comparative obscurity within the sphere of the Papal Antichrist's dominancy during 1260 years (536–8 to 1796–8.) The additional interval of 75 years beyond the 1260, as given in Dan. xii. 12, has to elapse before the complete destruction of every Antichrist about 1872–73.

In the secondary literal-day accomplishment, the birth-throes of the Woman denote the anxiety and perturbation that will exist in the Church at large at the time of the Second Advent, in consequence of the great stir that will be excited by the expectation of the ascension of the Wise Virgins, who are represented in this fulfilment by the Man-child, and who will be caught up to God's throne, and afterwards rule all nations with a rod of iron, (Rev. ii. 27.) The lying in wait of Satan, especially as embodied in the seven-headed and ten-horned Roman Empire,* and his attempt to devour the Man-child, signifies the hostility and opposition that Satan will manifest and stir up against the Wise Virgins. The casting down of Satan represents his literal expulsion or dejection from the regions of the atmosphere, or "high places," where he now partly is, (Eph. vi. 12,) and his consequent confinement to the surface of this earth, for as soon as Christ and his saints have come into "the air," (1 Thess. iv. 17,) Satan's presence there will no longer be tolerated. The subsequent flight of the Woman into the wilderness, signifies the retirement of many of the foolish virgins, and other Christians, who are then converted, into unfrequented places, in order to escape the 1260 days' persecution during the Personal Antichrist's universal dominancy for 3¼ years, the latter half of the seven years, which commence with Antichrist's covenant with the Jews. There is a further period of 75 days to follow the 1260 days, just as 75 years follow the 1260 years, before Antichrist's destruction is completed by

---

* It is a question, whether, in the literal-day fulfilment, the CROWNED heads of the Roman Empire, energized by Satan, (Rev. xii. 3,) do not indicate that Louis Napoleon, as the existing head of the Roman Empire, will be crowned by the time of the ascension of the Man-child, or Wise Virgins. His being hitherto UN-CROWNED, is plainly prefigured by the discrowned heads of the Beast, which appears upholding the Romish Church, in Rev. xvii. 3, and which remarkably represents his present position.

Christ's descent upon Mount Olivet; and this 75 days is the excess of the 1335 days over the 1260 days, or 3½ times, (Dan. xii. 7-12.)

The literal-day fulfilment will be almost the exact counterpart or miniature fac-simile of the year-day fulfilment, and there will be the same relative and proportionate distance between the events in the one fulfilment as in the other. This is shown in diagram 4, where, for the sake of convenience, the position of the events is specified as reckoned from the commencement of each fulfilment. Thus, since, in the year-day fulfilment, the ascension of the Man-child, or Christ personal, occurred in A. D. 29, or 33-4, at a distance of from 509 to 502 *years* before the commencement of the 1260 *years* of the Papal Antichrist's persecuting power in A. D. 536-8; therefore, in the literal-day fulfilment, the ascension of the Man-child, or Christ mystical, (that is, the Wise Virgins,) will occur at a distance of from 509 to 502 *days* before the 1260 *days* of the Personal Antichrist's persecuting power, which commence in the midst of the seven-years' Covenant-week—that is to say, it will occur at a distance of from 751 to 758 days after the date of the Covenant.

In other words, as the ascension of Christ, the year-day Man-child, in A. D. 29-33,* was from 751 to 759 *years* after the beginning of the 2595 *years* of the year-day fulfilment, therefore, the ascension of the Wise Virgins, the literal-day Man-child, will be from 751 to 759 *days* after the beginning

---

* As respects the precise date of the Crucifixion and Ascension of our Divine Lord, (the year-day Man-child,) there seems to be an uncertainty to the extent of five *years:* some chronologers, such as Clinton, Ideler, Benson, Browne, etc., considering it to be probably in A. D. 29; others, such as Usher, Prideaux, Cunninghame, Bliss, etc., holding it to be in A. D. 33, which is, perhaps, the more generally received view. Although it appears evident that our blessed Saviour was crucified at about the age of 33, (Luke iii. 23,) yet it is a question whether he was not born B. C. 4, about four years prior to the Christian era. There will thus be a corresponding uncertainty, to the extent of about five *days*, as to the exact date of the future ascension of the literal-day Man-child, (the Wise Virgins.) From these, and other considerations, it appears to the author of this work that, although about *the fortnight* can be clearly pointed out, in which Christ will come to translate the Wise Virgins, yet, perhaps *the precise day* of that event is not ascertainable.

of the 2595 *days* of the literal-day fulfilment; and it should be remembered that the 2595 years, or 7 *times* and 75 years, (Dan. iv. 23, xii. 12,) extend from B.C. 722-4 to A.D. 1871-3; and the 2595 days, or 7 years and 75 days, (Dan. ix. 27, xii. 12,) extend from the date of Napoleon's Jewish seven-years' Covenant to the End of this dispensation.

This period of five days, from the 751st to the 758th day after the Covenant, is thus distinctly revealed in Prophecy to be the time at which the Wise Virgins will be caught up to heaven; and if, for the sake of those who might hesitate, from weakness of faith, to calculate the time very closely, a margin of three or four days be added to each side of this period, we then have *the fortnight* from the 748th to the 762d day after the Covenant—that is, two years and from four to six weeks after the Covenant, clearly designated as the period within which the ascension of the Wise Virgins at the Advent of Christ in the air, (1 Thess. iv. 16, 17,) will take place.

It is obvious that this twelfth chapter of Revelation constitutes a decisive proof that the Wise Virgins must be caught up before the 3½ years' Great Persecution; for since the Persecution is actually caused by their ascension into "the air," and by the ensuing downfall of Satan to the earth, therefore, as the cause must precede the effect, so their ascension must necessarily precede the 3½ years' persecution, which subsequently results from it.

VIII. THERE IS AN INGATHERING of the saints to heaven at Christ's Advent, at the beginning of the seventh year-day Seal, about five years before the End, and also at the beginning of the seventh literal-day Seal, about five days before the End. (Rev. vii. 9–17, viii. 1.)

By far the best arrangement hitherto given of the year-day fulfilment of Revelation, is that contained in a diagram in Bickersteth's Guide to the Prophecies, and which is more fully explained in Birk's "Mystery of Providence." It is printed on p. 274 of this work, with some slight additions and alterations, and it represents the year-day interpretation that is followed in this book. Although Bickersteth was not so brilliant and popular as some writers, yet his deep piety and great soundness of judgment, united with long and careful study of most of the principal works on prophecy, enabled him, in conjunction with Birks, to arrange what may be considered almost a final adjustment of the year-day fulfilment. His explanation of the Seals agreed fundamentally with that of Vitringa, Woodhouse, Cunninghame, Bayford, etc., and he specified the dates of all of them, except the seventh, which, however, he apparently considered to be about four or five years before the End; and he said, (page 242,) "The events begin afresh after the seventh Seal," thereby admitting the subsequent re-fulfilment of Revelation.

The Seals in their year-day accomplishment, extend from Christ's Ascension to his Return: the successive changes in the prophetic horse and its rider, (compare Zech. vi., x. 3; Ps. xlv. 3—5,) symbolizing the gradual deterioration and degeneracy of the Church Militant. The first Seal denotes the spiritual conquests of the Church Militant from A. D. 38 to 324; the second represents the discord of the Church from 324 to 534; the third signifies the spiritual famine of the Church from about 534 to 1073; the fourth denotes the spiritual desolation of the Church from about 1073 to 1438; the fifth signifies a fierce persecution, with a subsequent period of respite, from about 1438 to 1794.

The year-day sixth Seal lasts for about 70 years, from 1794-5 to 1867: it opens with a great earthquake, and darkness and terror, among the kings of the earth—emblematizing the French Revolution and its resulting commotions, from 1794-5 to 1815; then four angels are commanded to hold back the four winds of havoc and desolation until the 144,000 Wise Virgins are sealed out of the different branches of the Christian Church, typified by the tribes of Israel, (Rev. vii. 1-9:) this denotes that for the remaining 50 years, from 1815 to 1866, the impending Great Tribulation will be withheld; but as soon as the 144,000 are all sealed, they are caught up at Christ's coming in the air, together with the deceased saints that are then raised, (1 Thess. iv. 16, 17:) and this whole company of raised and translated saints is thereupon exhibited as a *great multitude* standing before the throne in heaven, and having come *from* (ἐκ, *away from*, in the sense of escaping beforehand, as in Rev. iii. 10,) THE Great Tribulation, or Napoleon's persecution, which is subsequently to ensue for 3½ years. The year-day seventh Seal is opened immediately after this

CHRIST COMES FIVE YEARS BEFORE THE END. 321

First Translation and Resurrection, (Rev viii, 1.) and almost synchronically with the year-day seventh Trumpet and seventh Vial.* The literal-day re-fulfilment of the trumpets, seals, etc., then instantly commences, and runs on during the remaining five years, parallel with the concluding part of the year-day fulfilment; and the mutual and relative positions of each of the seals, trumpets, and vials, in this re-fulfilment, will be precisely the same as in the year-day accomplishment, only in days, instead of years. This is shown in diagram 4, and in the notes on pages 144 and 154.

The literal-day sixth Seal will, of course, last for about 70 days: it will open with a literal great earthquake, and darkness and terror, among the kings of the earth, continuing for about 20 days: and then there will be a brief lull for the remaining 50 days, at the end of which the 144,000 literal Jews, whose sealing will, by that time, be finished, will be caught up with a numerous company of surviving Gentile saints—unitedly constituting the *great multitude* that stand before the throne in heaven, and that have come *out of* (*ǫ*, in the sense of having passed through and emerged from,) the previous 3½ years' Great Tribula-

* Thus, it is entirely during the year-day sixth seal, from 1792-4 to 1864-8, that the 144,000 Wise Virgins, or mystic Israelites, (Rev. vii.,) are sealed; and this is, also, the very same time during which the first six year-day vials are poured out, (see page 317.) A most remarkable pre-intimation of this obvious fact, namely, that the sealing of the 144,000 is, (at least in the year-day fulfilment,) to be effected during the first six vials, is afforded in Ezek. ix. In that prophecy, six men with slaughter-weapons, prefiguring the first six vial-angels, go forth to slay the apostate, and, meanwhile, another messenger seals, in their foreheads, those who shall be spared. Both parties perform and finish their work simultaneously, clearly showing that the sealing takes place during the judgments of the first six vial-angels, (and, perhaps, also, in the literal-day fulfilment during the judgments of the first six trumpet-angels.) When the sealing is finished, it is shown, (Ezek. ix. 11, x.,) that the coming of Christ takes place, and then the sealed number will be caught up to him in heaven, (Rev. xiv. 1–5,) at the beginning of the seventh vial, seventh trumpet, and seventh seal. Another proof that the year-day seventh seal begins about five years before the End, is, that its subject-matter consists chiefly in the literal-day refulfilment of the trumpets, which obviously commences between 4 and 5 years before the End, (see Diagram 4.)

tion, or Napoleonic persecution. The literal-day seventh Seal begins immediately after this Second Translation, simultaneously with the literal-day seventh trumpet and seventh vial, and continues during the final five days within which Antichrist and his hosts perish.

Thus, in the year-day fulfilment, the Great Multitude (Rev. vii. 9,) represents all the saints caught up at the Resurrection and first-fruits-translation at Christ's Advent "in the air," (1 Thess. iv. 16, 17; Rev. xiv. 4,) just before the five years of the year-day seventh seal, and *away from,* (ix) or *before* the Great Tribulation. But in the literal-day re-fulfilment, that same Great Multitude represents all the saints caught up in the second, or harvest-translation, *out of,* (ix,) or *after* the Great Tribulation, (Matt. xxiv. 29–31; Rev. xiv. 15,) and just before the five days of the literal-day seventh seal, and the descent of Christ on the earth.

IX. THERE IS AN INGATHERING to heaven of raised and translated saints at the beginning of the year-day seventh trumpet, about five years before the End, and again at the beginning of the literal-day seventh trumpet, five days before the End, constituting two stages in the First Resurrection, (Rev. xi. 15–19, x. 7, xx. 6; 1 Cor. xv. 51, 52.)

The oft-repeated untruth, that scarcely any agreement exists among various prophetic expositors, is sufficiently confuted by the fact that hundreds of interpreters since the Reformation have explained the fifth and sixth year-day trumpets to denote the rise of the Saracen and Turkish powers between the seventh and fifteenth centuries, causing the fall of Constantinople in 1453. Bickersteth mentions a hundred of them in the preface to his "Signs of the Times." As regards the precise fulfilment of all the trumpets, (Rev. viii., ix., x., xi.,) the first represents the hailstorm of Gothic incursions into the Roman Empire from about A. D. 250 to 365; the second denotes the fall of Rome under the barbarian assaults from 365 to 412; the third symbolizes the poisoning of the channels of religious instruction by the Nestorian and other heresies of the East, from 412 to 476; the fourth signifies the deposition of Augustulus by Odoacer in 476, and the consequent

AWFUL VIOLENCE OF NAPOLEON'S PERSECUTION. 823

eclipse of the regal power in the western part of the Empire; the fifth represents the rise of Mahomedanism about 606–9, and the resulting Saracen persecutions of Christians, (the first woe,) for twice five months, that is, twice 150 year-day days, from 636 to 936; the sixth denotes the rise and prevalence of the Turkish persecuting power, (the second woe,) for twice a year and month, that is, twice 390 year-day days, from 1063 to 1453, the date of Constantinople's fall, and thence to 1843–4. On March 21, 1844, the Turkish Sultan abolished the law by which any Mahomedan embracing Christianity was put to death, and thus Turkey ceased nationally to persecute Christians.

We are now living in the interval between the close in 1843–4 of the year-day sixth trumpet, or second woe, and the commencement, about 1866–7 of the year-day seventh trumpet, comprising the third woe of 1260 days; our present position being indicated by the words, "The second woe is past, and behold the third woe cometh quickly," (Rev. xi. 14.) The awful severity of this approaching year-day third woe can easily be inferred from the tremendous violence of the two preceding Saracen and Turkish woes; and as the second or Turkish woe was far more terrible than the first, or Saracen woe, so the future Napoleonic, or third woe, will be much more dreadful than the second woe. It will, of course, be homogeneous with, and analogous in character to, the preceding Saracen and Turkish woes, but far more universal in its influence, and grievous in its effect; and like them, it must be inflicted during the present Christian dispensation, and must consist in the rise and prevalence of some mighty persecuting power.

As the nature and duration of the appalling judgments of the first and second woes are particularly defined, so the nature and duration of the third woe is equally specified. It is described in the literal-day refulfilment of Rev. xii. and xiii., which constitutes the subject-matter of the year-day seventh trumpet. It is there shown to consist in Satan being cast out of the air into the earth, as soon as the Man-child, or Wise Virgins, are caught up into the clouds, and in his then being filled with unexampled fury, and entering into and mightily energizing Louis Napoleon, the seventh-healed Head of the Roman Empire, who straightway proceeds to make war with and overcome the saints for 42 months, or 1260 literal-days, during which time multitudes will be killed, who refuse to worship his image, which the Roman False Prophet, the two-horned Beast, will cause to be set up.

The 1260 days' duration of this third woe will be literal days, instead of, like the 300 days of the Saracen woe, or the 780 days of the Turkish woe, being year-days; for the reason, that, at the sounding of the seventh trumpet, the mystery is to cease, (Rev. x. 7,) involving the commencement of the literal refulfilment of the prophetic periods and visions. This was perceived by the Rev. J. Fletcher nearly a century ago; he said, "Antichrist's last raging, or that tribulation which will be so uncommon, shall last 1260 common days, and not prophetical ones, because for the elect's sake those days shall be shortened." It is also especially observable, that the periods of these three woes, namely, 300 days, (twice 150,) and 780 days, (twice 390,) and 1260 days, are in exact arithmetical progression, 780 being the point of bisection between 300 and 1260. It is obvious, from Rev. xii. and xiii., that the year-day third woe being identical with the 3½ years of Antichrist's great persecution, will commence in the midst of the final seven years of the Covenant-week, and, therefore, the year-day seventh trumpet, which introduces it, (just as the fifth and sixth trumpets introduced the first and second woes, Rev. viii. 13,) is thus shown to commence shortly before the final 3½ years. The seventh trumpet will, however, begin a little sooner than the third woe, just as the fifth trumpet began rather earlier than the first woe.

Another proof that the year-day seventh trumpet begins shortly before the final 3½ years, consists in the fact, that it unquestionably commences at almost the same instant as the year-day seventh seal and seventh vial, which clearly begin about five *years* before the End. The words, "*And there were voices, and thunderings, and lightnings, and an earthquake,*" (Rev. viii. 5, xi. 19, xvi. 18,) are manifestly placed at the beginning of the year-day seventh seal, seventh trumpet, and seventh vial, as a chronological landmark, or note of time, to indicate that they all three commence almost simultaneously.

It consequently results that, as the literal-day refulfilment of the trumpets will be a miniature fac-simile of their year-day fulfilment, (see pages 83, 127, 131, 274,) therefore, the literal-day seventh trumpet will begin five *days* before the End, simultaneously with the literal-day seventh seal and seventh vial.

But as it is declared in Rev. xi. 15–18, and 1 Cor. xv. 51, 52, that at the sounding of the seventh, or last trumpet,* there shall be a translation of living saints, and a resurrection, judgment, and rewarding of deceased saints, therefore there must be a translation and resurrection at the beginning of the year-day seventh trumpet about five *years* before the End, and again at the beginning of the literal-day seventh trumpet five *days* before the End; the resurrection in the latter case being the resurrection of the righteous who will be martyred by Antichrist, (Rev. xx. 4,) or who will die, during the five years' interval between these two translations. This twofold resurrection and translation constitutes two stages in the one event of the First Resurrection, (Rev. xx. 5, 6,) which comprises all the translations and resurrections of saints that occur in connection with Christ's second premillennial Advent.

X. THE COMING OF CHRIST, accompanied necessarily by a translation and resurrection of saints, takes place just before the year-day seventh vial, about five *years* previous to the End, and also just before the literal-day seventh vial, five *days* previous to the End,—constituting the two stages in the Second Advent, (Rev. xvi. 15–17.)

According to the agreement of all modern year-day interpreters of eminence, the year-day seven vials, (Rev. xvi.,) commenced at the French Revolution, in 1792–5.

---

* The late Dr. Smucker, after writing a postmillennial exposition, was finally led to believe in Christ's personal Advent *before* the Millennial 1000 years, chiefly by the consideration that, as the seven trumpets are universally held to precede the Millennium, and as the seventh trumpet is manifestly the last, or resurrection trumpet, at which the righteous *dead are to be judged*, (Rev. xi. 18, 1 Cor. xv. 51, 52,) therefore the Second Advent, which accompanies the resurrection, (1 Thess. iv. 16, 17,) must also necessarily precede the Millennium. The *mystery* of the resurrection of the righteous, (1 Cor. xv. 51, 52,) is expressly predicted, in Rev. x. 7, to be finished, or accomplished, when the seventh trumpet *begins* to sound.

The first vial denotes the outburst of infidelity and anarchy, in 1792-3, throughout France, and other parts of the Beast's territory; the second symbolizes the consequent bloodshed and carnage during the Reign of Terror, in 1793-5; the third represents the retributive judgments that fell, in 1795 to 1802, upon the Romish Ecclesiastical powers, which had so corrupted the channels of education; the fourth signifies the scorching despotism of Napoleon Bonaparte,—the imperial sun,—from 1802 to 1815, until he sunk beneath the political horizon at Waterloo; the fifth denotes the resulting darkness of mortification, chagrin, and disappointment that fell upon France, *the throne of the Beast,* especially during the three years of its occupation by the allies, from 1815 to 1818.

The sixth year-day vial causing the drying up of the Euphrates, represents the gradual wasting and ruin of the Turkish Empire during the 40 years, from 1826 to 1866-7, in order that "the way of the kings of the East," that is, the Jews, "might be prepared;" for the decay of the despotic power of the Turkish Sultan removes the chief obstacle to the return of the Jews to Palestine. The 40 years' continuance of this vial, until five years before the End, is clearly typified by the 40 years' sojourn of the Jews in the wilderness, until five years before the final dividing of the Promised Land, (Josh. xiv. 7, 10,) as shown in the appended foot note.* During the latter part of the vial, three frog-like, unclean spirits of Infidelity, or Spiritualism, and of Revolution, ending in Despotism, and of Papal Zealotry, are represented as going forth respectively from the Dragon, or Devil, and from the Beast, or Eighth Head of the Beast, that is, Louis Napoleon, and from the Roman Pontiff, in order "to gather the kings of the earth, and of the whole world to the battle of that great day of God Almighty . . . towards (εις,) a place called in the Hebrew tongue Armageddon, (Rev. xvi. 14;) and most energetically have these three spirits been working during the past

---

* The year-day sixth vial obviously commences at the end of the 1290 years, (Dan. xii. 11,) in 1826-7, and continues 40 years, as the period of the drying up of the Euphrates, according to the manifest type of Israel's 40 years in the wilderness, during which the Red Sea and Jordan were transitorily dried up. Therefore, the year-day seventh vial must evidently commence in 1866-7,

CHRIST'S ADVENT FIVE YEARS BEFORE THE END. 327

fifteen years to bring all nations into such a condition that they may presently be gathered under Napoleon the Antichrist, to the great conflict at Armageddon.

It is just at the end of the 40 years of the year-day sixth vial, (in 1867-8) that the abrupt and solemn announcement is made by Christ himself, "BEHOLD, I COME as a thief," distinctly intimating that his personal Advent

and occupy the remaining five years until the 1835th year, in 1872, (Dan. xii. 12, see event xviii. chap. ii.,) when Daniel will stand in his lot, or Millennial inheritance, on earth. This type may be clearly seen from the following comparison:

During 430 years, (Exod. xii. 41,) the Jewish Church sojourned in a strange land, and was also oppressed and downtrodden under the yoke of Egypt, until the plagues of boils, and of water being turned into blood, and of darkness, etc., were inflicted upon its oppressors: then in the wilderness it enjoyed respite from bondage for 40 years, during which the Red Sea and Jordan were temporarily dried up, and at the end of which Moses mysteriously disappeared, (Deut. xxxiv.:) then, during the next five years, (Num. xiv. 30, 33, Josh. xiv. 7, 10,) Jericho was overthrown, and wars and fightings continued until the dividing of the Promised Land, and allotment to the Jews of their inheritances, and the reign of the Judges, (Josh. xiv., Acts xiii. 18-20.)

During 1290 years, (thrice 430 years,) from 534-7 to 1824-7, the Gentile Church was oppressed and downtrodden under the yoke of Papal Babylon, (the great city, spiritually called Egypt, Rev. xi. 8, xvii.,) until from 1794-7 to 1824-7, the mystic first five vial plagues of boils, and of water being turned to blood, and of darkness, etc., (Rev. xvi.,) were inflicted upon its oppressors: then it enjoys 40 years' respite, and comparative liberty and peace during the sixth vial, from 1821-7 to 1864-7 while the mystic Euphrates, (the Turkish power,) is being dried up, and at the end of which the 144,000 Wise Virgins mysteriously disappear at Christ's coming. (Rev. xvi. 15, 1 Thess. iv. 16, 17:) and during the next five years, from 1866-7 to 1872, (which ends the 1835 years,) the mystic Jericho of Antichristian Apostacies is overthrown under the 7th vial, and wars and fightings continue until Christ's descent, and the allotment to the Jewish and Gentile saints of their inheritances, and the Millennial reign of the glorified saints as Judges, (Dan. xii. 12, 18, Rev. xx. Matt. xix. 28, Ezek. xl. to xlviii.)

There seems to be an oblique intimation that 1866-7 is the year when the number of the Beast, 666, will first be imprinted on the Antichristians, in the fact that 1866 is the product obtained by multiplying the first part of the sum $(600 + 66)$ by 3. This finds a precedent in the above-mentioned circumstance, that the first part of the sum $(430 + 45)$ multiplied by 3, produces $(1290 + 45.)$

occurs at this precise period, immediately before the seventh vial is poured out; for it is most important to observe that the vials, seals, and trumpets, are in their respective septenaries *strictly consecutive*, and do not overlap each other. Thus the seventh vial *cannot possibly* commence until the whole of the sixth vial is completely accomplished, and until Christ has personally come. It will then, however, be poured out "into the air," causing the ejection and downfall of Satan, "the Prince of the power of the air," from that region into the earth, and producing the 3½ years' Great Tribulation, or Napoleonic Woe, as described in literal-day Rev. xii. and xiii.*

This year-day seventh vial is necessarily shewn to occupy the final five years, not only because it must follow the year-day sixth vial, which occupies, as above-mentioned, exactly the 40 years preceding those final five years, but also because it consists principally in "a great earthquake, (or revolution,) such as was not since men were upon the earth, so mighty an earthquake, and so great," which is obviously identical with the 3½ years' "Time of Trouble, such as was not since there was a nation even unto that same time," (Dan. xii. 1, 7,) and "the Great Tribulation, such as was not from the beginning of the world," (Matt. xxiv. 21, Mark xiii. 19.)

Thus, the words, "Behold, I come," (Rev. xvi. 15,) denote in their year-day fulfilment, the first stage of Christ's Advent, at the beginning of the final five *years* of the year-day seventh vial: and in their literal-day fulfilment, the second stage of Christ's Advent, at the beginning of the final five *days* of the literal-day seventh vial. (Read carefully event, xviii. chap. ii.)

From the last three of these ten proofs of the two translations,† we arrive at the distinct conclusion, that

---

* The fact of the original arms of France being three frogs, is an additional intimation that the three *infidel, revolutionary*, and *fanatical* frog-like spirits of the sixth vial, emanate from that country, as their principal centre.

† These points might be explained more clearly by further diagrams, were it not for the additional expense which they occasion. Pictorial illustrations would also be a great improvement to some of the previous parts of this work. It is an evil sign of the times, that, while the press pours forth numerous productions on every conceivable topic, yet the sublime scenery and visions of Daniel

there are at Christ's Advent, two translations of saints, because the seventh seal, seventh trumpet, and seventh vial unquestionably commence with a translation of saints; and, as in their double fulfilment, they commence, first, about five years before the End, and, secondly, five days before the End, therefore, there must be a translation of saints, first, about five years before the End, and, secondly, about five days before the End. (See also foot notes pp. 79, 155.)

Nor is this view inconsonant or inharmonious with the statement, in 1 Thess. iv. 16, 17, that at Christ's Advent, "*the dead in Christ shall rise first: then we which are alive, and remain, shall be caught up together with them:*" for this general statement tacitly comprehends the two parts or stages of the entire act of Christ's Advent,—a detailed explanation of which would not then have been seasonable or appropriate. At the beginning of the five years of Christ's Advent, all the righteous that have died up to that time will be raised up, and then 144,000 living saints will be caught up with them; and about five years afterwards the rest of the living saints will be caught up, together with all other saints who have died, or been killed, during those five years, and whose resurrection will then take place, thus completing the two stages in the Advent.

THE UNQUESTIONABLE NEARNESS of the $3\frac{1}{2}$ years' Great Tribulation, and the occurrence of Christ's Advent in its two stages, about 1866–72, should be loudly proclaimed, for a twofold reason,—first, in order to arouse the ungodly, and, secondly, to quicken those who are truly converted.

First. As regards its tendency *to awaken the ungodly*, it is manifest that this proclamation is a special generation and dispensation truth, which serves to drive home, and give a sharper edge to, the more familiar Gospel testimony. Many irreligious persons will listen with calmness and indifference to the most pointed statements regarding the future punishment of the unconverted, because they view that event as remote, and know that the chances are very greatly in favour of their yet living many years upon the

and Revelation attract scarcely any attention, although they afford an ample field for the research of the historian, the pictorial skill of the painter, the descriptive powers of the poet, and the arithmetical calculations of the mathematician earth; but they instantly become alarmed and exasperated at the statement, that, by about 1868, the awful calamities will commence that are to accompany Christ's Advent. This being something that they can understand and realise, cuts so completely at the root of all their worldly hopes, as to excite their utmost dread and hostility. And, though hypocrites often assert, that as our life here is but a moment compared with eternity, and as death may possibly come at once, therefore it is immaterial whether Christ's Advent is or is not to take place about 1867-73; yet, it may be asked, why are they so exceedingly opposed to this view if it really is of so little importance? Does not their very opposition betray their unpreparedness, and show that there is a pungency and power in this doctrine eminently calculated to arouse and awaken the worldly-minded.

Just as it was the duty of Noah, Lot, Jonah, Jeremiah, Amos, etc., to warn people, not merely to prepare for death, but also to prepare for particular judgments that were coming at a particular time, so it is now the obvious duty of ministers to forewarn persons regarding the terrible visitations of Divine wrath which prophecy shows to be approaching. It cannot be doubted, but, that if a loud-sounding testimony were to go forth respecting the appalling calamities that will commence about 1868, not a few heedless persons would, like the Ninevites, be sobered and solemnized, and induced "to seek the Lord while he might be found, and call upon him while he is near." The sentinel who fails to inform his comrades of approaching danger, does not act more reprehensibly than those spiritual watchmen who fail to "give the trumpet a certain sound" in regard to the impending Great Tribulation, (Ezek. xxxiii. 2-6.) Especially ought the youthful to be thus warned; for, whereas the chances would ordinarily be a thousand to one in favour of their living 30 or 40 years longer, it is now certain that, by about 1872 at the farthest, nearly all of them will be either in heaven or in hell. But some persons, instead of regretting their ignorance in relation to prophecy, actually glory in that which is their shame, like a leper boasting of his sores, and complacently exclaim, "Well, for my part, I do not pretend to understand the seals, or vials, or trumpets, or heads and horns of the

Beast; and I consider such subjects unpractical and unprofitable;" in other words, they daringly deny the Divine statement, (which is mentioned in significant connection with the prediction of latter-day infidelity,) namely, that "ALL Scripture is given by inspiration of God, and is *profitable* for doctrine, for reproof, for correction, for instruction in righteousness, (2 Tim. iii. 16.) It would be well for congregations to act upon the suggestion of this text, by requesting their spiritual teachers to give them expositions of Daniel and Revelation. And it should be remembered that the duty of testifying to the immediate nearness of the Great Tribulation is not discharged by merely stating that it will come *some* day: for people will care very little about it unless they are distinctly informed that it is "nigh, even at the doors."

SECONDLY. This proclamation should be loudly raised in order *to quicken those who are converted*. It is painfully evident that the Church is asleep, and even most of the Wise as well as the Foolish Virgins are slumbering in regard to the definite proximity of Christ's Advent; and yet, as predicted in the epistle to the Laodiceans, (Rev. iii.,) they resolutely refuse to be convinced of their lukewarmness in relation to this great event. The general tenor of the utterances from pulpit, platform, and press, evinces scarcely any recognition of the awful momentousness of the crisis at which prophecy represents us to have arrived. The discovery, from Revelation, of the *time* of Christ's Second Advent, is usually considered to be impossible, and even if admitted to be practicable, is declared to be virtually unimportant, upon the ground, that if we are truly converted, and therefore ready for death, we are ready also for Christ's Advent. This is, however, a most dangerous and fatal error, for the Scriptures plainly show, that *readiness for death is not necessarily readiness for Christ's Advent*, and that many true believers in Christ, who are really *virgins* and *servants*, but in a foolish, backsliding state, (Matt. xxv. 8, xxiv. 48,) will be left behind with the hypocrites to undergo the 3½ years' Great Tribulation, where there will be weeping and gnashing of teeth; and they will constitute "the Woman and the the remnant of her seed" that are persecuted after the Ascension of the Man-child, or Wise Virgins, at the First Translation, (Rev. xii.)

The very fact of the number of the Wise Virgins being literally only 144,000, (Rev. xiv. 1–5,) while there cannot be less than several million converted persons now alive on the earth, shows that only a portion of the living saints will be caught up in the First Translation, although all the surviving living saints, without an exception, will be caught up in the Second Translation, five years subsequently, by which time they will have been led by their sufferings to long for and to love that personal Advent of Christ, which, in these days of prosperity and worldly ease, they contemplate with secret aversion. Christians should be explicitly warned that only those who watch, and patiently wait for, and look for and love Christ's personal appearing, (Luke xxi. 36, Rev. iii. 10, Heb. ix. 28, 2 Tim. iv. 8,) shall be caught up at his Second coming; and it is utterly vain for the most pious and spiritually-minded persons to expect to be caught up unless they believe that event, from the signs of the times, to be close at hand.

Reluctance to have their particular plans and expectations interfered with, and an inability to say, "Thy will be done," lies at the foundation of the antagonism of Christians who oppose these views. This may be seen in the case of many excellent ministers who are comfortably settled in a pastoral charge, with a happy family, an attached congregation, and an enviable sphere of usefulness around them, and who are well aware that every additional day that they spend in the work of labouring for the conversion of sinners, and the quickening of saints, will increase their reward, and the brightness of their crown hereafter, (Dan. xii.-3, 2 Cor. ix. 6, Luke xix. 12.) Most unwelcome to many such is the news, that in about three or four years' time the Great Tribulation and Persecution will abruptly break up all these arrangements, together with the whole work into which they have so heartily thrown themselves, of founding colleges, building churches, establishing schools, etc. Comparatively few, even among true Christians, have sufficient grace to become at once reconciled to a state of things which will entail upon them or their friends considerable suffering, and will administer a summary deathblow to all their earthly schemes, even though the glory of God should thus be promoted.

The Church requires, then, no less than the world, to be

quickened and enlightened by prophetic truth, and a most beneficial effect would thus be produced upon many of its members, if they were thereby more weaned from "setting their affections on things on the earth." The luxurious living and accumulation of wealth, in which multitudes of Christians indulge, is glaringly inconsistent with their religious profession. Our Lord has commanded us, "Love thy neighbour as thyself," "Love one another as I have loved you," "By this shall all men know that ye are my disciples, if ye have love one to another," (Matt. xxii. 39, John xv. 12, xiii. 85;) and the Gospel continually testifies, that those who possess the spirit of Christ will manifest toward their fellow-creatures loving-kindness and charity, which, indeed, are the only evidences of their being really converted: nor can the hope of salvation belong to any who are deficient in such qualifications, (Matt. xxv. 35, Luke x. 37, xii. 33, 1 Cor. xiii., etc.)* This Christ-like love

* Those who have any articles that they might, without serious inconvenience, give to the service of the Lord, cannot excuse themselves from doing so on the ground of the difficulty of converting them into money; for that difficulty is obviated by the fact, that both in England and America there are most valuable benevolent institutions which will thankfully receive, in aid of their objects, any articles whatever. In ENGLAND, George Müller, at 21 Paul Street, Kingsdown, Bristol, has sent to him, besides money, all kinds of wearing apparel, gold and silver plate, and trinkets, coins, rings, brooches, seals, pencil-cases, bracelets, necklaces, watches, chains, ear-rings, books, etc., to be sold in aid of his Orphan Asylums, which have been established, and carried on entirely by the prayer of faith, for 30 years, and which now contain more than 1000 orphans. His receipts are also applied partly to support Home and Foreign Missions, and the circulation of tracts, Bibles, etc. His Narrative, published in Boston, as the "Life of Trust," should be read by every one, and not merely once, but continually; for it is the most effectual book, next to the Bible, to stir up persons to more faith and prayer. In AMERICA, Miss Clement, at the Bethesda Home, Chestnut Hill, Philadelphia, Penn., U. S., conducts a similar institution for destitute children, containing between 50 and 100 inmates. (see its Annual Report, printed at Bryson's, No. 2 North Sixth Street, Philadelphia.) Both these Institutions are carried on in entire dependence upon God to send in supplies, without asking for means from a single human being. They make known their wants to God alone. All Christians should assist these, and other Home or Foreign missionary labours with their prayers.

The following instructive remarks are made by George Müller, is evidently not manifested by persons who remain possessed of riches, while not a few of their fellow-men are perishing for want of that which they selfishly refuse to bestow. Such conduct is expressly condemned in Scripture. "It is easier for a camel to go through the eye of a needle, than for a rich man to enter into the kingdom of God." "Lay not up for yourselves treasure on earth," (Matt. xix. 24, vi. 19.) "Sell that ye have and give alms," (Luke xii. 33.) "Whoso hath this world's good, and seeing his brother have need, and shutteth up his compassion from him, how dwelleth the love of God in him," (1 John iii. 17.) "He that hath pity upon the poor, lendeth unto

in his Narrative: "In order to have your prayers answered, you need to make your requests unto God on the ground of the merits and worthiness of the Lord Jesus. You must not depend upon your own worthiness and merits, but solely on the Lord Jesus, as the ground of acceptance before God, for your person, for your prayers, for your labours, and for every thing else. Do you really believe in Jesus? Do you verily depend upon him alone for the salvation of your soul? See to it well, that not the least degree of your own righteousness is presented unto God as a ground of acceptance. But then, if you believe in the Lord Jesus, it is further necessary, in order that your prayers may be answered, that the things which you ask God should be of such a kind, that God can give them to you, because they are for his honour and your real good. If the obtaining of your requests were not for your real good, or were not tending to the honour of God, you might pray for a long time without obtaining what you desire. The glory of God should be always before the children of God, in what they desire at his hands: and their own spiritual profit, being so intimately connected with the honour of God, should never be lost sight of in their petitions. But now, suppose we are believers in the Lord Jesus, and suppose we make our requests unto God, depending alone on the Lord Jesus as the ground of having them granted; suppose, also, that, so far as we are able honestly and uprightly to judge, the obtaining of our requests would be for our real spiritual good, and for the honour of God; we yet need, lastly, to *continue* in prayer until the blessing is granted unto us. It is not enough to begin to pray, nor to pray aright: nor is it enough to continue *for a time* to pray; but we must patiently, believingly continue in prayer until we obtain an answer; and, further, we have not only *to continue* in prayer unto the end, but we have also *to believe* that God does hear us, and will answer our prayers. Most frequently we fail *in not continuing* in prayer until the blessing is obtained, and *in not expecting* the blessing. As assuredly as in any individual these various points are found united together, so assuredly answers will be granted to his requests." (John xvi. 23.)

the Lord; and that which he hath given, will he pay him again," (Prov. xix. 17.) "Blessed is he that considereth the poor: the Lord will deliver him in time of trouble," (Ps. xli. 1.) "To do good and distribute, forget not; for with such sacrifices God is well pleased," (Heb. xiii. 16.) "Charge them who are rich in this world, that they be ready to give, and glad to distribute," (1 Tim. vi. 17.)

If a man, whose house was full of bread, should allow hundreds of persons to die of starvation at his very doors, he would justly be regarded as little better than a murderer; but equally guilty are those who have articles of luxury, or money, in their possession, more than is needful for the proper maintenance of themselves or their families, and who are thus avariciously hoarding up the means which might help to bring temporal or spiritual salvation to their fellow-men. There is a vast amount of temporal and religious destitution in every part of Christendom; many useful benevolent societies are most inadequately supported in their work of mercy; and in Heathendom a thousand million Pagans are sinking into hell-fire, and eternal damnation, from which they cannot escape without hearing and believing in the Gospel of Jesus Christ, (Rom. x. 13–17, Acts iv. 12.) Every penny which is given to evangelical missionary, or other religious societies, assists, under God's blessing, to save souls from hell; and, therefore, if spent by its possessor in buying luxuries, is most iniquitously wasted. Christians should remember that every thing of value that they retain in their possession, beyond what is absolutely necessary to their condition in life, is virtually bought with the PRICE OF BLOOD; for, if applied to purchase and circulate tracts and Bibles, it might be made the means of saving those who are in the broad road that leads to destruction. Needless expense, and costly display in houses, furniture, wearing apparel, pictures, showy equipages, jewelry, gold and silver plate, musical instruments, or other articles of luxury, constitute the most palpable evidence of the heartlessness and inhumanity of those who possess them; and such selfish persons, unless they become converted, will find themselves condemned very soon at the Day of Judgment, amid the execrations of the assembled universe, as guilty of the MURDER of their fellow-creatures, who have perished from need of that which the money spent in those useless luxuries might have purchased for them. Vain is it for such persons to think to justify their conduct by the maxims of the fashionable religious world, which are often as different from the maxims of the Gospel as darkness is from light.

Those who are willing to take up their cross and follow Jesus, (Matt. xvi. 24,) who, "though he was rich, yet for our sakes became poor," and who frequently had not where to lay his head, must be ready not only to deny themselves the enjoyments and luxuries of this life, but also to endure privations and persecutions even unto death, in order to benefit their fellow-creatures, (1 John iii. 16.) And all the reproach and ridicule to which the wealthy might be exposed, who, like the eminent Lady Huntingdon, or Lady Powerscourt, should give away the greater part of their property in promoting the religious welfare of mankind, would be nothing compared to the reproach and sufferings which Jesus has undergone on their behalf, in order to provide deliverance for them from hell-fire. It would be infinitely the best for such at once to withdraw themselves from all scenes of gaiety and fashion, and to become crucified and dead to the allurements of the world, as much as if they were buried in the grave, and to spend the brief residue of their life entirely in prayer, and reading the Bible and religious books, and visiting and ministering to the sick and the destitute, (James i. 27;) and then, within a very few years, to be translated to heaven to meet Christ, and receive a crown of glory that fadeth not away.

It is highly improbable that any rich persons will be caught up among the Wise Virgins, because, if they were to obtain real faith in the positive nearness of Christ's Advent, and the self-denying, devoted spirit, which that faith must engender, they would then cease to be rich; for they would be constrained, like the primitive disciples, (Acts iv.,) to contribute largely to disseminate the Gospel, and relieve the poor, and would only retain in their possession sufficient property to support themselves and their families during the brief period that remains. As a matter of course, those who *really* believe that their present mortal life will terminate a little more than two years after the Covenant, will assuredly not make any preparations to live here below beyond that period, and will expend nearly all their possessions in deeds of charity before that time. If they do not act thus, they will stand convicted of not really entertaining that belief, whatever they may affirm to the contrary. Some, who may find it convenient to profess this belief, and who yet are too covetous and fond of money to follow it out practically, will, perhaps, assert that such texts as, "Occupy till I come," (Luke xix. 13,) signify that they are to continue to act until Christ's Advent in just the same manner as they ever have done. It is evident, however, that those texts only imply that we are to be laborious, and not slothful in our Master's service until his Coming, and we must decide, according to the present circumstances of the case, what labours are most useful to be engaged in. Common sense teaches, that a man must be guilty of great inconsistency, or hypocrisy, who should say that he believed he would depart this life about 1865-8, and yet was acting as if he might live here beyond that date. And it would be useless for him to refrain from giving away his means, under the plea of providing for the unbelieving members of his family, who might be left behind at Christ's Advent before the Tribulation; for almost all the possessions in Christendom will then fall into the hands of Antichrist's followers.

But these Second Advent truths should be proclaimed, not only *to prepare the Wise Virgins for their translation*, and to *stimulate Christians to more self-denying efforts in Christ's cause*, but also to *caution them against mingling in the scenes of political excitement and warfare, that will, ere long, culminate in the establishment of the reign of Antichrist*. Nothing can be clearer, than that we are now living in the latter part of the 40 years of the sixth year-day vial, from 1826 to 1866-7, during which period the three unclean spirits, of Spiritualism, Revolution, and Jesuitism, (Rev. xvi. 14,) are depicted as actively leavening society in order, presently, *to gather the kings of the earth, and of the whole world*, to the great war of Armageddon, consisting in a revival of the Crusades, under the leadership of Napoleon, who will, by that time, be manifested as the Antichrist, (event xvi. chap. ii.) His universal supremacy will principally result from the other nations being weakened by internal revolutions and divisions, and, therefore, every thing that tends to increase such commotions, indirectly contributes to hasten the introduction of his disastrous despotism. On this account, Christians should carefully refrain from assisting in the slightest degree to stir up in the hearts of their fellow-men bad passions, such as those of anger and revenge, and should inculcate the greatest forbearance, and the most patient endurance of wrongs and insults, so as to postpone as long as possible the terrible outburst of wickedness and violence that is about to desolate the world. All political or ecclesiastical institutions—even those which may have greatly benefitted mankind,—must now begin to be broken up to prepare the way for 'Christ's Millennial kingdom, that will be established about 1872, and, therefore, it is useless for persons to sacrifice their lives, or their money, to maintain the perpetuity of that which is about to perish. No human efforts can prevent Napoleon, the Antichrist, inevitably gaining his predestined "power over all nations," (Rev. xiii. 7,) and "evil" must now increasingly "go forth from nation to nation, and the slain of the Lord shall be from one end of the earth even unto the other end of the earth; they shall not be lamented, neither gathered, nor buried; they shall be dung upon the ground," (Jer. xxv. 33,) and God will now "make a full end of all the nations," as regards their present constitution, (Jer. xlvi. 28.)

At no period has the wisdom of the principles of peace and non-resistance, as held by the Quakers, become more apparent than now. They justly consider that true Christians are "pilgrims and strangers" upon the earth, and citizens of a heavenly country, (Heb. xi. 13, 16,) and are, therefore, *neutrals* as regards the governments of this world, just as a Spaniard living in China would be neutral with regard to the two contending parties in that nation. And they maintain that in this Christian dispensation the followers of the meek and lowly Jesus should never engage either in offensive or defensive warfare. The Jews lived under a dispensation of *stern law*, and demanded an eye for an eye, and a tooth for a tooth, etc., but Christians live under a dispensation of *grace and mercy*. The distinction between the two dispensations is clearly drawn by our Lord, in Matt. v., where, after pronouncing blessings upon "the poor in spirit, the meek, the merciful, and the peacemakers," he says, "ye have heard that it hath been said, an eye for an eye, and a tooth for a tooth, *but I say unto you that ye* RESIST NOT EVIL; but whoever shall smite thee on the right cheek, turn to him the other also; and if any man will sue thee at the law and take away thy coat, let him have thy cloak also; and whosoever shall compel thee to go a mile, go with him twain . . . I say unto you, LOVE YOUR ENEMIES." Thus, the Christian dispensation opened with the delivery to Christians of a new code of regulations, which enjoined non-resistance and patient submission to injuries, without attempting even self-defence. It may safely be left to common-sense to decide whether stabbing, shooting, or killing an enemy is a manifestation toward him of the tender love which these precepts enjoin. An instructive commentary upon them is furnished in the fact, that the primitive Christians universally considered that the Scriptures forbade them to bear arms, as is shown in Jonathan Dymond's "Inquiry into the Accordancy of War with Christianity,"*—a book that treats of this subject with

* This able work, (158 pages, octavo,) is sold at cost price, for twenty cents, at the Friends' Depositories, in Philadelphia, (804 Arch Street,) and other cities, as well as various low-priced tracts on the same subject. The following extracts are from it:

"During a considerable period after the death of Christ, it is certain that his followers believed he had forbidden war; and that, in consequence of this belief, many of them refused to engage in it, whatever were the consequence, whether reproach, or imprisonment, or death. These facts are indisputable: 'It is as easie,' says a learned writer of the seventeenth century, 'to obscure the sun at mid-day, as to deny that the primitive Christians renounced all revenge and war.'

"Maximilian, as it is related in the Acts of Ruinart, was brought before the tribunal to be enrolled as a soldier. On the the proconsul's asking his name, Maximilian replied: 'I am a Christian, and cannot fight.' It was, however, ordered that he should be enrolled, but he refused to serve, still alleging *that he was a Christian*. He was immediately told that there was no alternative between bearing arms and being put to death. But his fidelity was not to be shaken: 'I cannot fight,' said he, 'if I die.' He continued steadfast to his principles, and was consigned to the executioner. The primitive Christians not only refused to be enlisted in the army, but when any embraced Christianity while already enlisted, they abandoned the profession at whatever cost. Marcellus was a centurion in the legion called Trajana. While holding his commission, he became a Christian; and believing, in common with his fellow-Christians, that war was no longer permitted to him, he logical cogency of argument, and striking eloquence of thought.

The mere circumstance of religious persons being found in the ranks of an army does not at all justify the waging of war; for even devout persons sometimes act in an inconsistent and unscriptural manner; and our sole guide must be the Word of God, which abundantly shews that Christians should be meek, peaceful, and non-resistant, manifesting the same grace and mercy toward their fellow-creatures as Jesus has exhibited toward them, and never even going to law, or entering into judgment with one another. (See Matt. v., vi. 12, xviii. 33, xxvi. 52; Rom. xii. 17–21, 1 Cor. xiii., 2 Cor. x. 3, 4, Jas. iii., iv.; Heb. xii. 14, Phil., ii. 3, Col. iii. 12, 14, 2 Tim. ii. 24, 1 Thess. v. 15, Gal. v. 14–26, etc.)

threw down his belt at the head of the legion, declaring that he had become a Christian, and that he would serve no longer. He was committed to prison; but he was still faithful to Christianity. 'It is not lawful,' said he, 'for a Christian to bear arms for any earthly consideration;' and he was, in consequence, put to death. Almost immediately afterward, Cassian, who was notary to the same legion, gave up his office. He steadfastly maintained the sentiments of Marcellus, and, like him, was consigned to the executioner. Martin, of whom so much is said by Sulpicius Severus, was bred to the profession of arms, which, on his acceptance of Christianity, he abandoned. To Julian, the Apostate, the only reason that we find he gave for his conduct was this:—'I am a Christian, and, therefore, I cannot fight.' The answer of Tarachus is in words nearly similar: 'Because I am a Christian, I have abandoned my profession of a soldier.' Clemens called Christians 'the followers of peace,' and expressly tells us that 'the followers of peace used none of the implements of war.' Lactantius said expressly, 'It can never be lawful for a righteous man to go to war.'" Jonathan Dymond adds, "The idea of two communities of Christians, separated, perhaps, by a creek, at the same moment begging their common Father to assist them in reciprocal destruction, is an idea of horror to which I know no parallel. '*Lord, assist us to slaughter our enemies.*' This is their petition. 'Father, forgive them; they know not what they do.' This is the petition of Christ. . . . War and Christianity are like the opposite ends of a balance, of which one is depressed by the elevation of the other. The more effectually we are animated to war, the more nearly we extinguish the dispositions of our religion."

An able pamphlet on this subject, "Duty of Christians in the present Crisis," (4 cts.,) by the Rev. H. G. Guinness, is sold at 112 North Tenth Street, Philadelphia, where also a deeply interesting, and exceedingly well-written prophetic work, "Signs of the Times," (75 cents,) by H. L. Hastings, may be purchased.

MORE PROPHETIC WORKS SHOULD BE PUBLISHED. 341

HAVING NOTICED three special reasons for making these Second Advent truths widely known, we may next observe that the three principal methods by which this may be accomplished are, (1.) The extensive circulation of prophetical publications. (2.) The delivery of lectures on prophecy, and, (3.) Open air preaching. FIRST. As regards *the extensive circulation of prophetical publications*, all ministers, and others, especially writers of any eminence, who believe in these views, should, if they possibly can, publish, at least a pamphlet, if not a larger book, definitely enunciating their belief, and by thus bearing a public testimony which may reach all parts of the world, they will become one of the undaunted "cloud of witnesses" who are now in various countries "contending earnestly for this faith which has been delivered to the saints."* A book will often be read by people if they are acquainted with its author, when otherwise they would pay no attention to it; and, therefore, any one who publishes a pamphlet on prophecy, even though it should only reiterate what is stated in this or other books, is likely to assist in disseminating

---

* A thousand copies of a duodecimo pamphlet, of twelve pages, may be printed and published for a cost of about twelve dollars, or 2¼ pounds sterling, either in America or England; and if only 250 of them were sold at five cents each, the expense of their publication would be thus defrayed. Writers should take care to give their pamphlets as expressive a title as possible. They might suitably insert in them some of the diagrams from this work, and they should not hesitate to repeat the same fundamental truths which other writers have stated. It is a mistake, to suppose that a book like the present is not suitable for Sabbath reading; no time can be more appropriate than Sunday for examining and discussing the prophecies regarding Christ and Antichrist; and this work virtually furnishes, in its different parts, a year-day and literal-day exposition of Daniel and Revelation.

A very useful and interesting monthly prophetical periodical, called the "Prophetic Times," is to begin to be issued in January, 1863, Its Editor's address is Post Office, Box 2245, Philadelphia, U. S. The Rev. Drs. Duffield, Seiss, Newton, etc., have consented to write articles in it. The subscription to it is to be ten cents for one number, or a dollar, in advance, for twelve numbers. All who desire to study prophetic truths should, if possible, become annual subscribers, and strenuously endeavour to persuade their acquaintances to do so likewise. English subscribers can obtain, by mail, two copies every month for a year, by remitting by letter half a sovereign to its publisher.

these views at least in their own neighbourhood. Moreover, thousands of low-priced pamphlets may often be sold where there would be scarcely any sale for larger and more expensive works. It is to be regretted that there is very little prophetical literature in general circulation in America. With the exception of Cumming's, Seiss's, Shimeall's, and Lord's works, most of the few prophetic treatises that have ever been published are either out of print, or not easily obtainable. There are incomparably more books on prophecy published in England; but the public testimony there seems otherwise to be very vague and feeble; for the silence of nearly all the periodicals and newspapers on the subject shows that it is not being at all prominently agitated. The American religious press is, with very few exceptions, characterized by a similar silence in reference to the prophecies. Great responsibility devolves upon the editors of the public journals and serials, to impart information to their readers in relation to the momentous events which are indicated in prophecy to be immediately coming on the earth.

The most earnest efforts should now be put forth to warn the inhabitants of those regions which are especially to be the scene of Antichrist's persecution, (event xii. ch. ii.,) that Louis Napoleon is the Antichrist, and that to worship his image, or receive his mark, will be an unpardonable sin, (event x. ch. ii.) This is foreshown to be the last Gospel message in this dispensation, (Rev. xiv. 9,) and should begin to be delivered at once before it can be prevented by Napoleon's increasing influence. Almost unexampled facilities exist in Germany for sending copies of a book, on sale to the booksellers in all the leading towns, through the agency of any large publishing house, and a work like the present one, if translated into German, might thus be widely circulated in that country. Similar treatises might even yet be circulated in France, by erasing from them all direct mention of Napoleon's name, and tracts on the subject might be sent through the Paris Post office to all the clergymen in France. The prefatory synopsis to the first, second, and fourth chapters of this book* would constitute

---

* Readers of this work who may be acquainted with any additional facts illustrative or confirmatory of the views here advanced, would confer a favour by communicating them to the author for future

very suitable matter for tracts, and any one is at liberty to republish part, or the whole of the contents of this work.

SECONDLY. There is urgent need for many ministers and laymen, who believe in these truths, to travel through different parts of America and Great Britain, delivering in each place several LECTURES ON PROPHECY. A part of every lecture should, of course, invariably consist of an address to the unconverted to repent of their sins, and to come to Jesus for salvation; for the omission of this would be a most serious defect, especially, as some persons will attend a lecture on Prophecy who scarcely ever go to the ordinary preaching of the Gospel. Experience shows that it is almost a waste of time to occupy people's attention in a public lecture with much description of the year-day fulfilment of the prophecies, (except, perhaps, of the year-day vials,) for it is too abstruse to be satisfactorily understood by others than those who possess considerable historical information. Repeated mention should be made in every lecture of the seven years' Covenant between Louis Napoleon and the Jews, as soon as it is confirmed, (Dan. ix. 27,) for it will be unapproachably the most decisive indication of the time of Christ's Advent, and will not, like the longer dates, require any deep thought to comprehend. The prophecies concerning the Jews, and the general signs of the times, and the rise and actings of the Antichrist, Napoleon III., and the 3½ years' Great Tribulation, or infidel persecution, and the two stages in Christ's Advent, and the First Resurrection, and the Millennium, are the most profitable points to be enlarged upon before a general

publication, directing them to him at R. Brinkerhoff's, 112 William Street, New York, U. S. He proposes, in a subsequent work, to narrate, in an appendix, some remarkable visions that spiritually-minded Christians have recently had concerning the approaching Advent of Christ, (Joel ii. 28,) and any further information on this head would be acceptable.

In view of the shortness of the remaining time during which the present facilities for diffusing information on this momentous subject will remain, the author of this book desires to send, gratuitously, as many copies as possible of this, and other prophetical works, to such ministers, theological students, etc., as would otherwise not be likely to have their attention specially directed to these truths. He will thankfully apply to this object any sums of money which persons, who recognise the importance of such efforts, may send him for that purpose.

audience.* Expositions of prophecy, in proportion as they approximate to the truth, must approximate to each other; and, therefore, lecturers should not be afraid of repeating almost the same arguments as are set forth in this and other books; for, in teaching the rudimentary elements of prophecy, as well as of any other branch of learning, there is very little scope for originality of thought or expression. Moreover, many who might attend a lecture, would not have the means or time to obtain and read carefully even a moderate sized treatise like the present. For this reason, an unspeakably important service would be rendered by any laymen, ministers, or even ladies, who were simply to give public readings of interesting selections from popular prophetic expositions, such as Dr. Sciss's†

* A prominent announcement of such lectures, should, if practicable, and where time permits, be given beforehand, by placards, and notices in the local journals, and the subject of the discourses should not be worded vaguely, but should be explicitly stated to relate to the Advent of Christ about 1866–72, and Louis Napoleon, the Antichrist. Lecturers should also, if possible, take care to have, as an invaluable means of diffusing prophetical knowledge, a supply of moderate-priced books and pamphlets on these topics, which could be sold at the door of the place of the lecture, or at the local booksellers. As lecturers cannot, of course, be reasonably expected themselves to bear the cost of advertising, travelling expenses, hire of lecture-room, &c., it will, therefore, generally prove to be a suitable plan to have a collection for that object taken up after the lecture, when such expenses are not otherwise defrayed. Any admission fee, unless it is very small, would at once diminish the audience. The use of a church to lecture in may be sometimes more easily obtained, if it is understood that there will be no collection; and there is generally likely to be a larger audience in a church than in a hall. Unless more general interest in prophecy is excited, an ordinary lecturer would find that, in many places in the United States, he could get scarcely any audience, unless he obtained access to some of the churches or their lecture-rooms; and, in these times, his receipts would, humanly speaking, not be likely to equal his expenses. But some believers who have, like Franke, George Müller, etc., strong enough faith in, and dependence upon God previdentially to supply all their needs, have travelled about in this manner, and found that sufficient means have been given to them without even taking up collections at their lectures, which, however, possess the recommendation of affording a more convenient opportunity for persons to contribute.

† Copies of his valuable work might be obtained in England, by ordering them through Messrs. Wertheim & Macintosh, Paternoster Row, London.

"Last Times," etc., embracing an accompanying Gospel exhortation to sinners. This is particularly needful in small towns, and villages, and rural districts, where the majority of the population would never otherwise obtain much information on these subjects. In every neighbourhood there are some Christian people who are, at least, able to read aloud intelligibly, and if they could not obtain any hall or church, they might gather some of their neighbours into their own house, or in the open-air, for this purpose. The same plan might be beneficially adopted, not only for reading prophetic expositions, but also popular revival sermons, such as those by Spurgeon, Guinness, McCheyne, Bonar, Cumming, Ryle, Caughey, etc. A solemn responsibility rests upon ministers, trustees, churchwardens, deacons, elders, and others who have the control over any places of worship, to act in as liberal and accommodating a manner as possible, in allowing the use of those places to Christian persons who may offer to deliver discourses on prophecy.* If they really have the generous, self-denying, loving spirit of Jesus, they will not care about the slight inconvenience or trouble which such permission might occasion. And they will be amply recompensed for their liberality by Jesus at his coming. The severest vengeance

* The popular prejudice against these truths operates powerfully to prevent their proclamation from the pulpit; but it would be much wiser for persons to give them a full hearing, than to refuse to listen to them, as is often the case. The writer of this work has personally, or by letter, offered to most of the ministers of the orthodox denominations in Boston, New York, and Philadelphia, to give, in their churches or lecture-rooms, without any reimbursement, discourses, showing the evidences for expecting the Great Tribulation and Return of Christ to occur very shortly. As the result, he obtained permission to give a discourse or two in about a dozen churches in Boston and New York, and in about twenty in Philadelphia, chiefly the Protestant Episcopal churches. As he is at present continuing to visit, and lecture in the principal cities in the United States and Canada, he takes this opportunity of again offering to any orthodox ministers and congregations, to give one or more discourses in their churches, if they signify to him their willingness to that effect, and if time and place be convenient.

In these times, every one should personally request the pastor of the congregation to which they belong to give them a series of expository lectures on Daniel and Revelation, instead of refusing "to give heed to this sure word of prophecy."

will, on the other hand, be then inflicted upon those who, with deplorable illiberality, refuse such permission where it can reasonably be granted; for, in refusing it to Christ's servants, they are guilty of nothing less than of refusing it to Christ himself, (Luke x. 10–16, Matt. xxv. 45.) In view of the terrific persecutions and woes that will commence about, or soon after 1866, and will break up all Protestant congregations, and destroy most of the Protestant churches, there ought rather to be meetings unceasingly held in such churches, and every effort put forth during the brief remaining period to persuade the unconverted to believe truly in Jesus and be saved. This is the work to which many Christians might much more profitably be now directing their energies, instead of labouring to found institutions which will just be established by the time of Christ's Advent, when they will no longer be wanted; or in busily discussing denominational questions which will just be settled by the time that denominational distinctions will all be swept away, like scaffolding before a hurricane.*

THIRDLY. This message of prophecy should be widely proclaimed by *open air, or street preaching;* for, being of such immediate importance, it should be carried to men wherever they can be found, instead of waiting until they may choose, of their accord, to come and hear it.

Any persons who can express themselves intelligibly in ordinary conversation, and who are really converted, or born again by the Holy Spirit, (John iii.,) are thoroughly competent to preach in the open air to all who will come to listen to them. They can do a great deal of good by simply reading aloud the Word of God, or some tract, or book, and making a few remarks upon it, or narrating their own spiritual experience. The most timid and feeble may soon obtain, by prayer, unexpected boldness for engaging in this work, and with a little practice, they will quickly throw off the first feelings of awkwardnesss and restraint, and be able to stand up in any place and begin to speak with complete calmness and indifference to the opinions of

* A well written year-day exposition of the past historical fulfilment of the seals, trumpets, and vials, is given in a work, "Providence the Key of Prophecy," (Seely's, London.)

such worms of the dust as their fellow-men. Every converted person is authorized to imitate the men, to whom Jesus said, "Go home to thy friends and tell them how great things the Lord hath done for thee, and hath had compassion on thee. And he departed, and began to publish in Decapolis how great things Jesus had done for him," (Mark v. 19.) The example of the early Christians at Jerusalem should also be followed; all of them are declared to have preached as well as the Apostles: for when, by persecutions, "they were all scattered abroad throughout the regions of Judea and Samaria, *except the Apostles*," then, "they that were scattered abroad went every where *preaching the word*," (Acts viii. 4.) Similarly, in the recent revival in the north of Ireland, some of the most effective preachers were newly converted mechanics, or labourers, or business men, or even girls and boys, whose only library was the Bible, and whose only instructor was the Holy Ghost.

The Scriptures expressly state, that during the next few years, and especially in the approaching two great seasons of religious revival, (ch. ii., events vi. and xvii.,) God will mightily work in the hearts of persons, particularly of young people, and even of those who are "babes and sucklings" physically, as well as mentally, (Ps. viii. 2, Joel ii. 28–32,) and will cause them to preach regarding the Second Advent, and to testify against Napoleon, the Antichrist, "the enemy and the avenger." The widest publicity should be given to such testimonies of the voice of God, speaking through children and others; and those who deride, or disregard, or try to silence them, will be guilty of the most awful blasphemy and wickedness, (Matt. xviii. 6, xxi. 15; Luke ix. 50.)

There is need of earnest prayer to God, that he would raise up numerous preachers, like the primitive disciples, (Luke x.,) to go throughout the country, trusting, if necessary, entirely to Providence for their temporal supplies, and preaching all day long in the most public places of the cities, towns, and villages, that men should repent of their sins, and call upon the name of the Lord, (Rom. x. 13,) who has died for them, and who is now coming to inflict terrible judgments upon this earth about 1866–72. As all converted persons are sure to be removed to the heavens in one or other of the two translations at that period, therefore they may just as well entirely devote the brief residue of their present life to thus preaching the Gospel; for it is certain that the highest honours and dignities will be bestowed, at Christ's coming, upon those who, in the spirit of John the Baptist, go forth as heralds of the Second Advent. Nor should any person suffer want of means to deter them from following this course; for, if they exercise firm trust in the Saviour's promises, "I will never leave thee, nor forsake thee," and "Lo, I am with you always," (Heb. xiii. 5, Matt. xxviii. 20,) he will not allow any sufferings to befall them, except what are needful for the trial of their faith. There would be no great difficulty in following this course, if hospitality was practised as much by Christians as the precepts of their faith enjoin; but the command, to "be given to hospitality," and to "be not forgetful to entertain strangers, (not merely friends or acquaintances,) for thereby some have entertained angels unawares, (Rom. xii. 13; Heb. xiii. 2,) is, in these days, entirely disregarded by many Christians, but yet they should remember that their heavenly reward will be in precise proportion to their zeal and liberality while on earth, (2 Cor. ix. 6, Luke xix. 12–27,) and that they will be recompensed for showing hospitality to the humblest disciple of Christ, just as if it were shown to Christ himself, (Matt. xxv. 40.) Pious persons should make a point of tendering their hospitality to preachers who transiently visit their neighbourhood for a few days, or a week or two, and should bear in mind that such guests require to be much alone, and undisturbed, for the purpose of secret prayer and meditation upon the Scriptures.

The most dreadful retribution will be inflicted, at the approaching Day of Judgment, upon all who, in the least degree, countenance the interposition of obstacles in the way of open air preaching. Magistrates, mayors, aldermen, policemen, and other official authorities, should remember that they will soon have to give a strict account to God of all their actions in relation to this matter. Any human laws which forbid street preaching in a city, stand in the most iniquitous antagonism to the law of God, which commands Christians to "go and preach the Gospel to every creature;" and street preachers who may be arrested, in consequence of such laws, are as much martyrs as missionaries who are imprisoned for the same cause in heathen lands. Religious persons should use their utmost efforts to have such prohibitory enactments repealed wherever they may hitherto have existed, and whether they are wholly or only partially prohibitory.* In order to preach the Gospel to every creature, it is not sufficient merely to build places of worship, and invite people into them, for only few comparatively will accept the invitation; but it is also necessary to follow the Saviour's example, who often preached,

---

* The best place for street preaching, is any spot like a recess, or corner, close to a stream of people passing and repassing, and where a score, or fifty, or more persons can stand together without much obstruction of the thoroughfare. If the preacher commences, and continues speaking, or reading a few verses of Scripture, then persons will gradually gather around him. It is not, by any means, necessary, in such impromptu preaching, to stand with the head uncovered. Any disturbance should be borne with very patiently; but, if it is unusually great, it is best to withdraw to some other street, or else discontinue and recommence when the crowd has dispersed. In some towns there will be more opposition to street preaching than in others, therefore, it is well to remember the text, "When they persecute you in this city, flee ye to another," (Matt. x. 23.) Street preaching is quite a different thing from open air preaching at Methodist camp-meetings, for the latter exposes a person to no opposition, or obloquy, like the former.

The writer of this book has preached out of doors, in the most public places, of about fifty American towns and cities, and has found that considerable difficulty and opposition, or else contemptuous indifference has often to be encountered, owing to the rarity of such an act, and the ungodly scorn with which it is regarded. He has recently preached in the open air nearly every day for about three months, in Astor Place and Jackson Square, in New York; and, also, almost daily, for several months; at various times, on Market Street, or in front of the State House on Chestnut Street, in Philadelphia. This last named spot is perhaps the most suitable for street preaching that can be found in America, as from twenty to fifty people may be collected round a speaker within a few minutes. A great amount of good might be done by always having preaching there every afternoon and evening. An audience can be gathered there from the passers-by all day long, but especially in the evenings, between six and ten. It is much to be regretted, that of late years, scarcely a minister or layman has been known to preach there, (with the above exception,) although thousands might thus be reached who never attend an evangelical place of worship.

not merely in synagogues, but likewise on the mountain side, the sea-shore, the steps of the Temple, and the public places in cities. It is an unspeakably injurious fallacy and delusion to suppose that any number of church buildings can render street preaching unnecessary.

It is estimated that not less than four or five hundred persons, chiefly among the laity, constantly preach in the open air in London. There is, thus, a great difference between England and America in this respect; for, in Canada and the United States, street preaching is, with very few exceptions, scarcely ever practised. In Boston, (200,000 population,) New York, (900,000,) and Philadelphia, (600,000,) four or five sermons are sometimes preached out of doors on the Sabbath, in the summer months, but on week-days such a thing is almost unknown; although, of course, several hundred persons might most usefully engage in that work every day in different parts of those cities, for one-half of their population is computed scarcely ever to enter an evangelical place of worship. Some ministers of eminence, in England, such as the Bishops of London and Oxford, who have personally taken part in this branch of Home Missionary labour, have thereby set an example which it is devoutly to be wished that more of the leading American ministers would follow.

It is difficult to understand how a preacher can be much filled with the love of Jesus, or a love for souls, if he can live in a populous city, and be content only to preach Sunday after Sunday to comparatively the same few persons, who are probably so surfeited with religious instruction as to become quite critical and fastidious, while thousands who never attend any evangelical place of worship are perishing in their sins around him. It must be admitted, that in the most moral cities, scarcely more than one person out of ten is a truly converted Christian; the remaining nine-tenths are under a greater condemnation than even the heathen, because they are more responsible, and sinning against greater light and privileges. The necessity for ministers to stand in the streets and highways to warn these practical rejectors of the Gospel to flee from the wrath to come is quite as urgent, (especially in view of the approaching terrible judgments,) as for foreign missionaries to stand in the streets of Madras or Pekin, to preach to the native heathen there, (Luke xiv. 21, Rev. xxii. 17.) The time which it is necessary to spend out of doors every day to inhale the fresh air for the preservation of health, may just as well be occupied in this manner as in any other."

Open air preachers should especially avail themselves of occasions when many persons are congregated together in the streets, on public holidays, or at fairs, markets, elections, races, exhibitions, and also at factories, and on wharves, and on ships and steamboats. And these prophetic truths should be honestly and fully proclaimed, although, in many cases, they will expose the preacher to considerable ridicule and scoffing, if not personal ill-treatment; and more so, than if he merely set forth the ordinary Gospel testimony, (2 Peter iii. 4.) Young men of piety had better spend the brief residue of their mortal life in thus "doing the work of an evangelist," (2 Tim. iv.,) instead of wasting their time in preparing, by academical studies, for a future career of usefulness, which they will never live long enough to enter upon.

At this momentous epoch, all Christians should, as they value the salvation of themselves and their families, carefully abstain from attending any places of worship, where such soul-ruining and unscriptural doctrines, as those of Universalism, Unitarianism, Romanism, or High-Church Tractarianism, are taught: or where there is more intellectual, or political, or cold and lifeless preaching. They should lay aside sectarian prejudices, and attend the ministry of any evangelical, spiritually-minded, orthodox preacher who has the courage to declare, that, those who die unconverted will be damned in the eternal fire of hell, (Matt. xxv. 41, Luke xvi. 26, Mark ix. 48, Rev. xiv. 10, xx. 15, etc.,) and who maintains the necessity of having the heart changed, and of being born again, or converted by the Holy Spirit in order to be saved, (Matt. xviii. 3, John iii. 3,)—at the same time setting forth the Lord Jesus in his work, his person, and his offices, as the God-man who has died in the room and the stead of all who repent of their iniquities, (Is. liii. 6, Tit. ii. 14,) and cordially trust in him for salvation, and openly confess him before men. But, in addition to constant attendance every Sabbath upon a faithful Gospel ministry, it is most important to spend an hour or two every day in reading the Bible, and praying to God, as well for ourselves as for others, that the unconverted may be led to love the Saviour, "who came into the world to save sinners," (1 Tim. i.,) and "to seek and to save that which was lost," (Luke xix. 10,) and who says, "Come unto me all ye that labour, and are heavy laden, and I will give you rest," (Matt. xi. 28;) for, "if we walk in the light, his blood cleanseth us from all sin," (1 John i. 7.)

Every one should, without further delay, diligently study the books of Daniel and Revelation, with such aid as prophetical lectures, discourses, and expositions can afford them, but, above all, with earnest prayer to God in the name of Jesus for the enlightenment of his Holy Spirit to "guide them into all truth, and to show them things to come," (John xvi. 13, 23,) and then they will speedily become convinced that the personal Second Coming of Christ to judgment is foreshown to occur about 1867-73, and that Louis Napoleon is the last Antichrist, who is to gain "power over all kindreds, and tongues, and nations," (Rev. xiii. 7,) and thus to be the Destined Monarch of the World.

NOTE.—The author is preparing for the press two other prophetic works, on "Wondrous Events at hand from 1865-6 to 1873, including reference to the future history and destiny of Louis Napoleon, England and America; and also on "Napoleon III., the Jews, the Pope, and the Millennium," which can be ordered from James S. Claxton, No. 606 Chestnut Street, Philadelphia, from whom the present work can be obtained, post paid, by remitting $1.00—its selling price. A liberal reduction for a large order. Twenty-five per cent. off to any one buying a dozen copies of James S. Claxton.

Any one may reprint or republish anywhere part or the whole of any books by the author of the present work, as the wide dissemination of these views is his chief object.

APPENDIX I.

The Six Thousand Years traced in the Bible from Adam to the Millenium in 1872-3.

Anno Mundi.	Before Christ.		
0	4128	(1) The Creation of Man to the close of the Deluge. (Gen. v. and viii. 13, 14.).......	1656
1656	2472	(2) The close of the Deluge to the birth of Terah. (Gen. xi. 10 to 24.)................	222
1878	2250	(3) Terah's birth to his son Abraham's removal to Canaan. (Acts vii. 6; Gen. xi. 32, xii. 1-5.)..	205
2083	2045	(4) Abraham's removal to the date of the Exodus. (Ex. xii. 40; Gal iii. 8, 17.)...............	430
2513	1615	(5) The Exodus to the Distribution of the Land. 1 yr. Num. x. 11 to xlii. 25, and 45 yrs. Josh. xiv.)....................................	46
2559	1569	(6) The Dividing of the Land to the end of Samuel's Judgeship. (Acts xiii. 20.).....	450
3009	1119	(7) Reigns of Saul, David, and Solomon (40 yrs. each.) (Acts. xiii. 21; 2 Sam. v. 4; 1 Kings xi. 42.).................................	120
3129	999	(8) End of Solomon's to the end of Jehoiachin's Reign. (1 Kings xi. 43, to 2 Kings xxv.) [Reckoning 11 years' interregnum from Amasiah to Azariah. 2 Kings xiv. 2, 23, xv. 1.]	393
3522	606	(9) The 70 years' captivity from Jehoichain's capture until Cyrus' 1st year. (2 Kings xxiv. 8 to 16; Ez. i.; Jer. xxv. 12.)......	70
3592	536	(10) Cyrus' 1st year to the midst of Artaxerxes Longimanus' 7th year (by the common chronology.)....................................	79
		[Cyrus' 7 years, Ahasuerus and Artaxerxes (Ez. iv. 6, 7) 8 years, Darius (Ez. vi. 1) 36 1-2 years, Xerxes 21 years, Artaxerxes Longimanus' 6 1-2 years.	
3671	457	(11) The midst of Artaxerxes Longimanus' 7th year to the birth of Christ. (Dan. ix. 24-26; Ez. vii.)............................... [Daniel's 70 weeks are generally held to begin about A.D. 457, in Artaxerxes' 7th year.	457
4128	0	Total, from the Creation of Adam to the birth of Christ.....................................	4128
		Add (for the period of the Christian dispensation)	1872
		Total, from the Creation of Adam to the Millenium..	6000

APPENDIX II.

The following are the titles of more than seventy expositions which show the End of the Christian Dispensation to be either about 1864, 1865, 1866, 1867, 1868, or 1869-75. There are also others, of which the author has not been able to obtain the exact titles. The date of the publication is placed first, and the year, which it designates as the End, is then enclosed in parentheses. Many other prophetic treatises have been published, which, however, fix no time; but the following treatises define a precise time, and all, except the Postmillennialists, expect the *personal* coming of Christ at the End of the Christian Dispensation, before the Millennium begins. IN GERMANY: in 1562, Chrytræus, (1866;) in 1575, Matthias Flacius, (1866.) IN ENGLAND: in 1794, J. Bicheno, "Signs of the Times," (1864;) in 1804, Rev. G. S. Faber, "Dissertation on the 1260 years," (1864-6;) in 1815, J. Frere, "Combined View of the Prophecies," (1867;) in 1820, Rev. J. Fletcher, "Letters to Wesley;" in 1820, J. Bayford, "Messiah's Kingdom," (1864;) in 1825, Rev. E. Cooper, "The Crisis," (1867;) in 1825, "Dialogues on Prophecy," (1867;) in 1827, "The Apocalypse," or "Apocalyptic Sketches," (1867;) in 1827, Rev. E. Irving, "Babylon Fore-doomed," (1867;) in 1828, Rev. Dr. Croly, "Apocalypse," (1868;) in 1828, The Honourable and Rev. Gerard Noel, "Prospects of the Christian Church," (1867;) in 1829, Rev. W. Pym, "Milleparianism," (1867;) in 1831, J. L. Jackson, "Millennial Church," (1868;) in 1831, G. H. Wood, "Believers' Guide," (1868;) in 1833, F. Sargent, "Advent of Messiah," (1868;) in 1836, B. D. Bogie, "The Crisis," (1867;) in 1836, Rev. E. Bickersteth, "Guide to the Prophecies," (1868;) in 1837, Cunninghame, "Exposition of the Apocalypse," (1867;) about 1840, Gisborne, and, also, Rev. T. Birks wrote, stating this view; in 1843, Rev. Dr. Keith, "Signs of the Times," (1867;) in 1844, Rev. E. Elliott, "Horæ Apocalypticæ," 4 vols. octavo, (1865-8;) in 1844, Rev. J. Scott, "Outlines of Prophecy," (1867;) in 1847, Rev. J. Hooper, "Signs of the Times," (1867;) in 1847, Rev. R. A. Purdon, "Last Vials," published monthly, (1864-70;) in 1847, "The Retrospect," (1867:) in 1848, Rev. Dr. Cumming, "Apocalyptic Sketches," (1865-8;) in 1852, J. Thomas, "The Coming Struggle," (1867;) in 1853, H. Verner, "Battle of the Nations," (1868;) in 1858, "Terminal Synchronism of Daniel's Two Periods," (1867;) in 1860, Rev. G. Potter, in a published Sermon, (1866;) in 1860,

Rev. Dr. Taylor, "Lecture before Reformation Society, (1866;) Rev. Mr. Galloway's "Exposition," (1868;) "Armageddon," (1869;) in 1859, Major Scott Phillips, "Interpretations," (1867-70;) Major Bolton, "The Revival," (1867-8;) in 1860, "The Consummation," (1865;) Thomas Stephens' "Exposition of Daniel, etc." (1864;) in 1861, W. Goble's "The Beast" (1866-9) in 1862, Robert Baxter's "Providence the Key of Prophecy," (1868) Among Postmillennialists: in 1848, Rev. Dr. Wylie, "The Seventh Vial," (1865;) in 1851, Rev. M. Whittemore, "The Seventh Head," (1866;) in 1848, "Popular Readings in Revelation," (1866-67.) IN AMERICA: in 1804, Rev. R. Farnham, "Prophetic Dissertations," (1864;) in 1842, Rev. Dr. Duffield, "Dissertations on the Prophecies," (1867;) in 1846, Rev. E. Davis, "Seven Thunders," (1866;) in 1853, Rev. L. Pise, "Tracts for the Times," (1866;) in 1856, G. W. Baum's "Sealed Prophecies Unsealed," (1866;) Rev. J. Seiss, "The Last Times," (1865-70;) in 1859, Rev. R. C. Shimeall, "Our Bible Chronology," (1868;) in 1860, Rev. J. V. Himes and A. Hale, "Voice of the Prophets," (1868;) in 1860, Rev. M. Baxter, "Coming Battle," and in June, 1861, "Louis Napoleon, destined, e'c.;" in 1861, Rev. Dr. S. H. Tyng, in the New York Protestant Churchman, of Nov. 9, 1861, speaks of "the year 1868 as the appointed period of the Lord's coming." In 1840, G. Truar, "The Second coming," (1864.) In 1861, "Exposition of Esdras," (1864.) Among Postmillennialists: in 1818, Rev. O. Hulburd, Middlebury, Vermont, "Sermons," (1866;) about 1840, Dr. Cogswell, "The Millennium," (1866;) Rev. Mr. Harkness, "Messiah's Kingdom," (1866.)

Also in 1786, M. H. Remusat, Canon of Marseilles Cathedral, "La proximite de la fin du monde" (1860; in 1807, Dr. T. Coke, "recent occurrences," (probably 1866); in 1844, Rev. C. Bowen, "Chronology of 6000 years" (1872) ; about 1855, Fynes Clinton, "Fasti Hellenici," (1862); about 1840, Rev. J. Usher (1867); in 1858, Rev. E. Nangle (probably 1866-75); in 1835, Rev. J. Fry, "Unfulfilled Prophecies" (probably 1872-8); about 1859, Rev. B. Saville (1868); in 1860, Dr. Wardle (1868); in 1862, "Coming of Christ" (1863) ; in 1863, J. Fondey (1870), and Rev. W. C. Thurman (1870-5).

www.ingramcontent.com/pod-product-compliance
Lightning Source LLC
Chambereburg PA
CBHW020310240426
43673CB00039B/757